Historic
SITES
OF SOUTH AFRICA

Historic SITES

OF SOUTH AFRICA

DEIRDRÉ RICHARDSON

PHOTOGRAPHIC CREDITS

COVER (ANTI-CLOCKWISE FROM TOP)
Durban City Hall with Cenotaph in foreground: © CLB/SIL
Houses of Parliament, Cape Town: © CLB/SIL
The Union Buildings, Pretoria: © Walter Knirr/SIL (repeated on spine and pages 2–3)
The first Governor's House, Robben Island: © Shaen Adey/SIL (repeated on page 1)

Struik Publishers (a division of New Holland Publishing (South Africa) (Pty) Ltd
Cornelis Struik House
80 McKenzie Street
Cape Town
8001

Copyright © in published edition 2001: Struik Publishers (Pty) Ltd
Copyright © in text 2001: Deirdré Richardson

First published in 2001

10 9 8 7 6 5 4 3 2 1

All rights reserved. No part of this publication may be reproduced, stored in a retrieval system, or transmitted, in any form or by any means, electronic, mechanical, photocopying, recording or otherwise, without the prior written permission of the copyright owner/s.

EDITORS: Joy Clack, Cecilia Barfield
CONCEPT DESIGNER: Petal Palmer
DTP: Beverley Dodd
COVER DESIGN: Beverley Dodd

Reproduction by Hirt & Carter Cape (Pty) Ltd
Printed and bound by CTP Book Printers

ISBN 1 86872 495 6

CONTENTS

Introduction and acknowledgements 6

CAPE

Eastern Cape 7

Northern Cape 46

Western Cape 67

Free State 167

Gauteng 190

KwaZulu-Natal 216

Mpumalanga 251

Northern Province 259

North West Province 263

Explanatory notes 272

INTRODUCTION

South Africa has a rich heritage, both natural and man made, to which numerous cultures have contributed. Because this heritage is valuable and non-renewable, each generation has a responsibility to act as its trustee and pass it on to future generations. Cultural and historical heritage is vital to our sense of identity, and its protection is in the interest of all South Africans.

All the sites in this publication were initially declared by the Historical Monuments Commission, and later by the National Monuments Council, which has recently become the South African Heritage Resources Agency (SAHRA).

Since my retirement from real estate, I have had the opportunity to indulge my hobby and interest in places of historical interest. As KwaZulu-Natal is my home, that was also my starting point, but over the years my interest has extended to all the provinces of South Africa. To all who use this book as a travel field guide, I wish you many happy days and hope you achieve as much enjoyment on your travels as I have on mine.

ACKNOWLEDGEMENTS

I wish to extend my appreciation to all those who so unconditionally gave me assistance. Unfortunately they are too numerous to mention by name, but they were originally the town clerks, librarians, museum staff and tourist information officers. Later I concentrated my efforts at the Natal Society Library and referred to the *Government Gazettes* covering a period of some 64 plus years! To the staff who over the months of research were most helpful and obliging, my sincere thanks. Ultimately this source of information was exhausted as numerous declarations contained no details or descriptions. I was faced with no alternative but to turn to SAHRA with the details at source, without whose help the compilation of this publication would never have reached fruition.

In the interests of maintaining the book at a practical, field guide size, yet including the majority of South Africa's declared historic sites, it is unfortunate that much detail has perforce been left out from some of the entries. In a few instances, it proved impossible to find any information at all on a particular site. Those sites have been omitted.

DEIRDRÉ RICHARDSON
KWAZULU-NATAL
2001

EASTERN CAPE

Until 1994 most of the region that now makes up the Eastern Cape was known as the Eastern Province. The Eastern Cape now incorporates the former Bantu homelands of the Ciskei and Transkei, including Pondoland. This region's history is synonymous with the 1820 British Settlers and the many frontier wars fought between the British and indigenous Xhosa tribes.

ABERDEEN

This small town was laid out on the farm Brakkefontein in 1855 as a Dutch Reformed Church settlement. It is named after Aberdeen in Scotland, the birthplace of the Reverend Andrew Murray. The town became a municipality in 1858.

MAGISTRATE'S COURT AND POST OFFICE
(GREY STREET)
These sandstone buildings with tiled roofs were built in 1898 in the Art Nouveau style.

ADELAIDE

Founded as a military post in 1834, the town was named after Queen Adelaide, wife of William IV of England. It attained municipal status in 1896.

HISTORIC OLD PARSONAGE
(QUEEN STREET)
This parsonage was erected in about 1860 for the Reverend GW Stegman. The double-storey building is predominantly in the Georgian style and has large adjacent outbuildings dating from the same period. A 'voorhuis' and Voortrekker room show early Cape furniture, while the outbuildings (laundry and dairy) feature yellowwood flooring, ceilings and beams. The parsonage presently serves as a museum, known as Our Heritage Museum.

ALEXANDRIA

This town was originally known as Olifantshoek, but was renamed in 1873 after Alexander Smith, a Scottish minister of the local Dutch Reformed Church. The town attained municipal status in 1940.

DIAS CROSS MEMORIAL (KWAAIHOEK)
The original remains of the cross erected at False Island by Bartholomeu Dias in 1488 are housed at the University of the Witwatersrand. A replica of the cross has been erected in the Alexandria Coast Reserve.

DUTCH REFORMED CHURCH
(VOORTREKKER ROAD)
This predominantly neoclassical building replaced the original little church. It was designed by architect William White-Cooper and inaugurated on 11 December 1896. In 1926 the church was enlarged and altered.

ALICE

Alice was named in 1847 by the Governor, Sir Peregrine Maitland, after Princess Alice, the second daughter of Queen Victoria. It attained municipal status in 1852.

DOMIRA HOUSE (LOVEDALE MISSION STATION)
Domira House was the residence of Charles Lennox Stretch, Diplomatic Agent to the Gaikas

(1836–1846). It also served as the headquarters of Sir Andries Stockenström during the Seventh Frontier War (1846–1847) and was fortified in 1847 by the Royal Engineers.

ALIWAL NORTH

Aliwal North was founded in 1849 and named by Sir Harry Smith, Governor of the Cape Colony (1847–1852), in commemoration of his decisive victory over the Sikhs under Runjeet Singh at Aliwal in India in January 1846. The town attained municipal status in 1882.

ANGLO-BOER WAR BLOCKHOUSES
(OFF BARKLY STREET AND VALK STREET)

These blockhouses played an important strategic part for the British forces during the Anglo-Boer War against the invading Republican commandos.

ROCK ENGRAVINGS (FARM KALKOEN KRAAL)

Cave 1, or the White Lady Cave, contains rare and important rock paintings that are often compared to those in the well-known Brandberg Cave, in Brandberg, Namibia.

SAUER BRIDGE (OVER THE KRAAI RIVER)

This sandstone bridge, with its four graceful arches, was opened on 23 September 1881 by the then Minister of Railways and Harbours, JW Sauer.

BALFOUR

FORT ARMSTRONG (FARM HERMANUSKRAAL)

These are the ruins of a stone fort, which was built in 1835 and named after Captain AB Armstrong, who had commanded a camp on this site before the construction of the fort. It was captured by rebel Hottentots in 1851, and recaptured by British troops under Lieutenant-Colonel Henry Somerset.

BARKLY EAST

Laid out in 1874 on the farm Rocky Park, the town was named after Sir Henry Barkly, Governor of the Cape from 1870–1877. It attained municipal status in 1881.

LOCH BRIDGE
(OVER KRAAI RIVER, FARM TYGERKRANTZ)

This is one of four similar sandstone bridges constructed in the north eastern Cape by the Cape Department of Public Works during the latter part of the nineteenth century. The site was selected by WM Grier, Chief Inspector of Works, and the bridge was designed by the District Inspector of Works in King William's Town, Joseph Newey. Construction began in November 1881 under the supervision of W Birnie as Clerk of Works, with a workforce that included 24 stonemasons from Cornwall in England. Built of dressed sandstone and comprising five elliptical arches, the 80.5m-long bridge was opened on 6 December 1893.

NAUDE'S NEK PASS (SITUATED BETWEEN BARKLY EAST AND MACLEAR)

Two brothers who farmed in the area, Stefaans and David Naudé, took it upon themselves to peg out a course, some distance to the south of Lehana's Pass, for the proposed road in 1896. Construction on the first half began in 1903 under the guidance of road engineer W Bain and was completed in 1905.

NEDERDUITSE GEREFORMEERDE KERK
(MOLTENO STREET)

Designed by architects Kallenbach & Reynolds of Johannesburg, and constructed by a Mr Mountjoy, the church's foundation stone was laid on 15 December 1906 and consecration took place on 14 December 1907. This church is a fine example of its period; the tower is mounted by a spire with pinnacles and gables, and is also decorated with balconies.

BATHURST

Founded in 1820, the town was named by Sir Rufane Donkin (1733–1821), Acting Governor of the Cape at the time (1820–1821), after Lord Bathurst, Secretary of State for the Colonies.

BAILEY'S BEACON AND 1820 TOPOSCOPE (TRAPPES VALLEY ROAD)
It was here that Colonel Jacob Cuyler's camp stood when he supervised the settlement of the 1820 Settlers on their allotments. The Governor, Sir Rufane Donkin, also pitched his camp here when he determined the site of the town of Bathurst. From here the beacon offers magnificent views, and the toposcope identifies the original 1820 British settlement.

BLEAK HOUSE (TRAPPES STREET)
This double-storey stone building is a typical Bathurst cottage of the 1820 period.

BRADSHAW'S MILL (SITUATED ON BATHURST RIVER)
This water-driven wool mill was built in 1821 by Samuel Bradshaw, an 1820 Settler and weaver from Gloucestershire. Brought from Wales to Port Elizabeth as a ship's ballast, it played an important role in the beginning of the wool industry in South Africa as it was the first wool mill to be built in the Eastern Province and probably the first in South Africa. The mill was in production until 1835 when it was set on fire by marauding Xhosa.

LOMBARD'S POST (DISTRICT)
Lombard's Post was originally granted to Pieter Lombard in 1790 as a loan farm. It served as a military fortification during the Fourth (1811–1812) and Sixth Frontier Wars (1834–1835). During the second half of the nineteenth century, the farm buildings were fortified by the then owner, Benjamin Keetman.

METHODIST CHURCH, CEMETERY AND RINGWALL (YORK ROAD)
This chapel was built by Samuel Bradshaw in 1832 and inaugurated by Reverend JW Shrewsbury. It served as a place of refuge for women and children during frontier conflicts such as the War of the Axe (1846–1847). The original thatch roof has been replaced.

OLD POWDER MAGAZINE (STAR FORT COMPLEX)
This historic powder magazine was erected in 1821 and carried a regular stock of approximately 273kg gunpowder, 7 000 ball cartridges and 60 rifles. It is an excellent example of early nineteenth century British architecture.

PIG AND WHISTLE HOTEL (KOWIE ROAD)
The original portion of the hotel was built and opened in 1821 by Thomas Hartley as the Bathurst Arms. The hotel holds one of the country's oldest liquor licences.

ST JOHN'S CHURCH (DONKIN STREET)
This fine church was built of stone from the Freestone Quarries, by the 1820 Settlers. The foundation stone was laid in May 1832. With the outbreak of the Sixth Xhosa War in December 1834, all building ceased and by January 1835, it had become a military post of the British forces. After the war, construction resumed and the church was opened on New Year's Day, in 1838. The church repeatedly served as a place of refuge and fortification during times of war, such as the War of the Axe, when it became a refuge for some 300 people.

BEDFORD

Founded in 1854 on a portion of the farm Maasstrom, the owner, Sir Andries Stockenström, named the town after the Duke of Bedford. It attained municipal status in 1856.

GLENTHORNE PRESBYTERIAN SETTLERS CHURCH AND CEMETERY (FARM GLENTHORNE)

Glenthorne was granted to John Pringle in 1824. He built this stone church in 1840 and it has been used as such ever since. Reverend John Forbes Cumming was the first minister and incumbent there until 1868.

BERLIN

Founded in 1857, the town was named after the German capital by German Settlers of the British-German Legion. A village management board was established in 1884.

MOSER COTTAGE AND RUDOLPH VON RONNOW HOUSE (DISTRICT)

Both these historic houses are typical of the homes of German Settlers who settled in the Eastern Province (Eastern Cape) in the 1850s.

BETHELSDORP

The town was originally established as a mission station in 1803 by JT van der Kemp on Theunis Botha's farm, Roodepas. The London Missionary Society named it after the Hebrew Baith-eel, meaning 'house of God'.

ALMS HOUSES (ALMS STREET)

These semidetached houses were erected in 1822 in the vernacular style to house the poor of Bethelsdorp. They form an essential part of the historic section of the town.

VAN DER KEMP CONGREGATIONAL MEMORIAL CHURCH (CHURCH STREET)

This church was erected in 1926 by Dr Johannes Theodorus van der Kemp, a Dutch medical doctor, who became a minister for the London Missionary Society and was sent to Graaff-Reinet. His good relationship with the burghers soon soured when he began preaching to the Khoisan and Xhosa people. He thought that these people had been robbed of their land and that they should be given equal rights with settlers in the Cape Colony.

BIZANA

Situated approximately 56km from Port Edward, the town became the seat of the Magistracy of East Pondoland in 1894. Originally part of the Transkei, the town has been incorporated into the Eastern Cape.

CRETACEOUS DEPOSIT (MZAMBA BEACH, BIZANA COAST FOREST RESERVE)

Cretaceous (chalk) deposits were formed in the last period of the Mesozoic era, between the Jurassic and Tertiary periods. Fossilised tree trunks and shells of invertebrates were discovered there by Captain Garden of the 54th Regiment, and described by WM Bailey in 1855.

BRAUNSCHWEIG

Named after Braunschweig in Germany, the town was laid out as a settlement in 1856 for the men of the British-German Legion.

LUTHERAN CHURCH BUILDING, THE PARSONAGE AND SCHOOL BUILDING

The Lutheran Church complex – consisting of the neogothic church building of 1904, the parsonage of 1860, and the school building of 1860 with its extension of 1904 – is closely associated with the arrival of the British-German Legion in 1857, and thereafter other German settlers in the 1850s.

BURGERSDORP

Established in 1847 on Gert Buytendach's farm Klipfontein, the town was possibly named in honour of the burgher commandos during the Seventh Frontier War of 1846–1847.

ANGLO-BOER WAR BLOCKHOUSE (FARM KLIPFONTEYN)
A stone structure built by the British during the Anglo-Boer War (1899–1902) and known locally as the 'Brandwag', this blockhouse is part of a line that extended from Queenstown to Burgersdorp and Bethulie.

CHRIST CHURCH (CHURCH STREET)
This church, with its neogothic features, dates from the 1860s. The chancel was built in 1902.

COETZEE HOUSE (51 PIET RETIEF STREET)
This typical Karoo-style cottage was erected shortly after the founding of Burgersdorp. It was originally the townhouse of the Coetzees of the farm Swartfontein.

DE BRUIN HOUSE (66 VAN DER WALT STREET)
This Karoo-style cottage was also erected shortly after the founding of Burgersdorp and was originally the townhouse of the De Bruin family of the farm Witkop.

DUTCH REFORMED CHURCH (COETZEE STREET)
Architecturally this stone church is a large neo-Romanesque building with a domed roof. The spire to the east of the building has a fish-scale roof. Gables to the side of the church have circular windows of varying sizes, filled with stained glass of abstract design. The cupola also has stained glass windows at its base. Arched doors and windows were used to further complement the Romanesque architectural style.

The interior of the church is dominated by a vast steel dome, around the base of which is a mezzanine level with an ornate moulded balcony. Apart from natural light through the coloured windows, three Art Nouveau light fittings provide further light. The unusual combination of the Romanesque style with Arts and Crafts windows and interior decorating, is unique. As such, this building is an exceptional example of eclectic architecture, which prevailed during the Edwardian period.

OLD GAOL (PIET RETIEF STREET)
This gaol was completed in 1861 and played an important role during the Anglo-Boer War (1899–1902) and the Rebellion of 1914.

OLD PARSONAGE OF THE REFORMED CHURCH (PIET RETIEF STREET)
This Victorian house dates from the middle of the nineteenth century. From 1868 it served as the parsonage for Professor Dirk Postma, founder of the Reformed Church in South Africa. Professor Jan Lion-Cachet also lived here from 1895.

TAAL MONUMENTS (BURGER SQUARE)
Because the original monument had been vandalised during the Anglo-Boer War, it was removed. It was found again in Kimberley in 1939 and returned to Burgersdorp, by which time a replacement had already been erected.

VICTORIA JUBILEE FOUNTAIN (BURGER SQUARE, CHURCH STREET)
The decorative cast-iron fountain was ordered from a catalogue of Walter MacFarlane's Saracen Foundry in Glasgow, Scotland. Erected by the inhabitants of Burgersdorp and District in commemoration of Queen Victoria's Diamond Jubilee (1897), it is set on an eight-sided pedestal with cast-iron pillars, and crowned with a canopy of filigree motifs.

CAPE ST FRANCIS

This town takes it name from the nearby Cape St Francis headland, which in turn took its name from St Francis Bay, named by Portuguese navigator Manuel Pestrello, who named it in honour of the patron saint of sailors.

SEAL POINT LIGHTHOUSE (SEAFRONT)
The Cape St Francis lighthouse is a cylindrical structure that stands on a rock foundation, and is one of the tallest lighthouses in South Africa. Building began in 1870 and was completed in 1878. Architecturally, the tower and original keepers' houses form a unique complex.

CATHCART
Originally the site of a military camp in 1850, the town was developed in 1856 and named after Sir George Cathcart (1794–1854), Governor of the Cape from 1852–1854. It attained municipal status in 1881.

FAÇADES OF CATHCART FRUITERERS AND ELLIOTTS BUILDINGS (MAIN STREET)
These buildings were erected in 1882 by two brothers, attorneys Henry and Humphrey Elliot. The Cathcart Fruiterers Building is a sandstone single-storey with a curved pediment and a verandah resting on iron pillars, while the Elliotts Building is a double-storey with a pedimented front gable.

FAÇADE OF PUBLIC LIBRARY (MAIN STREET)
With its neoclassical façade and entrance porch, this Public Library was initiated by a Mr Blackler. The building was inaugurated in 1885, but shortly afterwards the next owners, Bell & Company, altered its appearance.

FAÇADE OF STANDARD BANK BUILDING (MAIN STREET)
This double-storey has straight end gables and an arched front gable of sandstone. It was built by W Seiler and completed in February 1921.

FAÇADE OF TOWN HALL BUILDING (MAIN STREET)
The Town Hall is in the Art Nouveau style and was inaugurated on 9 November 1905.

HILTON METHODIST CHURCH COMPLEX (FARM HILTON)
Construction on the original church started in 1874 and the cornerstone was laid in February 1874 by Ann Miles, a descendant of the first owner of the farm Hilton. The parsonage was built during the ministry of G Weaver, who was appointed in 1880. Behind the original church there is a T-shaped building that served as a school at the time. It was erected during the ministry of Reverend T Spargo, appointed in 1893. The second church, in the neogothic idiom, was built in 1903. With its prominent steeple and adjoining avenue of trees it is reminiscent of a typical English village church.

HISTORIC 1853 MILESTONE (SITUATED ON FARM STONE RIDGE, DISTRICT)
Constructed of blocks of buff Beaufort sandstone, the milestone stands approximately 1.5m high on a square platform. It bears the following lettering: (north side) 'VR 1853 Queens Town 45 miles'; (south side) 'VR 1853 Kabousie Post 18 miles'; (east side) 'VR 1853 King William's Town 60 miles'; (west side) 'Eland's Post 39 miles, Whittlesea 31 miles'.

KENYA CORNER COTTAGES
This row of ten small Victorian houses dates from 1880 and was erected shortly after the completion of the railway line between Cathcart and Queenstown on 3 November 1879. The wood and galvanised-iron houses were erected to accommodate railway workers. During the early 1950s these houses were rented out to former Kenyans who had fled to South Africa to escape from the Mau Mau riots. The site has been known ever since as Kenya Corner.

SETTLER COTTAGE AND SETTLERS FORTIFICATION (FARM HILTON)
This Settler Cottage was erected in about 1853 by John Miles. From 1867 it was also used for

Methodist Church services. The nearby fortification dates from the same period and was erected as a defence centre for the owner and his neighbours.

CLARKSON

The town was established by Bishop HP Halbeck in 1839, and was named after Thomas Clarkson, who was instrumental in abolishing the slave trade.

MORAVIAN MISSION COMPLEX (CHURCH STREET)
This is the historic core of the Moravian Mission, which became a refuge for slaves freed in 1838. The complex was established on the farm Koksbosch in 1839, and includes the church, church bell, parsonage and mission store (previously the old mill), cemetery with surrounding wall and entrance gate, post office, registry office and memorial to Pastor Nauhaus. The church is a rectangular structure with a high thatch roof and the parsonage is T-shaped. The school was a complex of several thatched buildings, the oldest of which is probably the L-shaped section nearest the church. Unfortunately the school was severely damaged by fire in September 1993.

CLUMBER

CHAPEL GROUND WITH THE METHODIST COMPLEX (FARM CHURCH, TORRENS RIVER VALLEY)
On this site, the Nottingham party of British Settlers held a service of thanksgiving on their arrival in 1820, and built the first church in 1825. It was damaged during the Sixth Xhosa War of 1836. The second church, which replaced it in 1837, served as a defence station in 1846 during the Seventh Frontier War. The present church was opened in 1867. A school was founded in 1837 and served as a farm school until 1977. The graveyard dates from the 1820s.

CRADOCK

The town was established as a frontier outpost in 1813 on the farm Buffelskloof, and was named after Sir John Francis Cradock (1762–1839), Governor of the Cape from 1811–1814. It attained municipal status in 1840.

CAPE DUTCH HOUSE (38 BREE STREET)
Governor Van de Graaff sold this plot to J Cornelis in 1823 and it was resold in the same year to a Mr Van Jaarsveld. In March 1831, AH Helberg took transfer of the property, by which time a house had already been built. The house is Cape Dutch in style and has a simple concavo-convex front gable.

DUTCH REFORMED CHURCH (STOCKENSTRÖM STREET)
This church building is situated on the same site where the first Dutch Reformed church was built between 1821 and 1824. Construction work on the present church commenced in January 1864, and it was consecrated on 10 September 1868. The building is in the neoclassical style, with tall Doric pillars, and has a beautiful pulpit. It bears a remarkable resemblance to the Church of St Martin-in-the-Fields, London.

HISTORIC CONGREGATIONAL CHURCH (1 HIGH STREET)
This neogothic church was erected in 1853 by the Reverend Robert Barry Taylor, the then missionary in Cradock of the London Missionary Society. It is a replica of the Harpenden Chapel in England.

OLD DOORNFONTEIN FARMSTEAD AND OUTBUILDINGS (MOUNTAIN ZEBRA PARK)
The old farmstead opened in 1967 as a Cultural History Museum and comprises the farmstead, the coach house, a dairy, a water mill (still in

working order), kraals and stone walls. The farmstead is traditionally furnished, and its kitchen and pantry contain candle moulds and a sausage machine; the nursery has a baby carriage and toys, and there is a collection of clothes. There are also firearms dating from the nineteenth century, stone ornaments made by Boer prisoners of war during the Anglo-Boer War (1899–1902), and a stinkwood settee made in Cradock in 1815. The coach house contains a fully tented ox wagon, a Sandveld wagon and other vehicles.

OLD DUTCH REFORMED PARSONAGE AND OLD CART SHED (87 HIGH STREET)

This property was probably granted to the council of the local Dutch Reformed church early in the nineteenth century, although the building of the parsonage and cart shed only commenced in 1848. The parsonage, which was used as such until 1904, is mainly associated with the Reverend John Taylor, who served as minister in Cradock for several decades. With its long, straight walls and imposing gables, the parsonage is also of architectural importance and, together with the cart shed, forms an interesting complex. It now serves as the Great Fish River Museum.

OLIVE SCHREINER HOUSE (9 CROSS STREET)

Olive Schreiner (1855–1920) was the author of many books, most notably *The Story of an African Farm*. Her father came to South Africa in 1837 under the auspices of the London Missionary Society. Restored and now the Schreiner Museum, her nineteenth-century Karoo townhouse is one of the oldest dwellings still standing in Cradock.

OLIVE SCHREINER SARCOPHAGUS (BUFFELSKOP MOUNTAIN)

Olive Schreiner was originally buried at Maitland, Cape Town, but as a later date her remains were reinterred on the summit of Buffelskop. The ironstone sarcophagus was erected by J Mann and also contains the remains of her husband, SC Cronwright, their infant daughter, and her dog Nita.

VICTORIAN TOWNHOUSE (38 STOCKENSTRÖM STREET)

This townhouse, which dates from 1841 and was bought by a farmer, Petrus Jacobus Venter, in 1855, is still owned by the same family. It forms an integral part of the architectural characteristics of Stockenström Street, as well as the historic core of Cradock.

CUYLERVILLE

This town is named after Jacob Glen Cuyler (1775–1854). When the British Settlers of 1820 arrived aboard the ship Chapman, Cuyler, the landdrost of Uitenhage settled them in the district he named Albany.

ST MARY'S CHURCH AND SCHOOL BUILDING

Reverends William Boardman and George Porter, and Charles Bailie held services and ran a school in the original small building of 1825. It was rebuilt in 1831. In 1834 the Sixth Xhosa War broke out and the church was used as a laager but later abandoned. Colonel Henry Somerset laid the foundation stone of the present church on 17 June 1839, and it was inaugurated on 15 September 1840. In 1843 stone walls were built around the church to strengthen its defence.

DORDRECHT

Established in 1856 on the farm Boschrand, the town was named after Dordrecht in Holland after the historic Synod of Reformed Churches was held there in 1618–1619. The town attained municipal status in 1867.

DUTCH REFORMED CHURCH (90 GREY STREET)
This rectangular stone church building, with its elegant stone tower of 46.94m is one of the best examples of the Gothic-Revival building style. The corner stone was laid on 20 May 1882, and the building was officially inaugurated on 18 August 1883. The stone wall with iron trelliswork was added in 1929.

EAST LONDON

The city was first known as Port Rex, probably after John Rex, the second son of George Rex, founder of Knysna. It was developed in 1845 as a landing place for the troops during the War of the Axe (1846–1847). In 1848 it was annexed to the Cape Colony and renamed East London. It attained municipal status in 1873 and city status in 1914.

ANN BRYANT ART GALLERY (9 ST MARKS ROAD)
Although the Victorian neoclassical and Renaissance features of the façades are the main attraction, the building can, in its own right, be described as unique.

CANNONS SALVAGED FROM THE WRECK OF THE SHIP *NOSSA SENHORA DA ATALAIA DO PINHEIRO*
The following cannons were wrecked with the ship in July 1647 near the Great Fish River:
+ Bronze Bocarro Cannon
  (23 Rocklands Road, Beacon Bay)
+ Bronze Feyo Naval Cannon
  (3 Botha Road, Selbourne)
+ Bronze or Brass Naval Cannon
  (23 Rocklands Road, Beacon Bay)

CITY HALL (OXFORD STREET)
Construction on the hall began with the laying of its foundation stone on 20 February 1897 by the Mayor, David Rees. Designed by Edwin Page of East London, it was officially opened on 5 October 1899 by Mayor WC Jackson.

CUSTOMS AND EXCISE BUILDING
This double-storey, 15-bay eclectic Edwardian building was designed by the Public Works Department in 1902. It is dominated by a high clock tower with a square door and Ashlar surrounds, and has a balcony and verandah. To the rear there is a small triangular gable with the date 1904 inscribed.

FAÇADE OF CUTHBERTS BUILDING
(110 OXFORD STREET)
This imposing three-storey building, with its Flemish-Renaissance gables, was designed by the architects Parker & Forsyth of Cape Town. It was erected in 1901, under the supervision of J Pender West of the same firm, for WM Cuthbert. The fine cast-iron balustrading that tops the verandah roof is also noteworthy.

GATELY HOUSE (PARK GATES ROAD)
Completed in 1878, this house belonged to John Gately, a well-known local dealer and member of the municipality. The building, now a museum, contains a unique collection of Victorian furniture, which belonged to Gately.

HOOD POINT LIGHTHOUSE (WEST BANK)
Constructed in Birmingham in 1894 and shipped out and erected in 1895, this square, white-painted lighthouse has a 19m-high masonry tower and a range of 31 sea miles.

LOWER NEEDS CAMP (BETWEEN EAST LONDON AND KING WILLIAM'S TOWN)
Fossils of bryozoans (aquatic invertebrate of the phylum Bryozoa), *echinoids* (a class including sea urchins and sand dollars) and ostracods (a crustacean of the mainly freshwater subclass Ostracod) have been identified in the quarry.

OLD METHODIST CHAPEL (NCERA, KIDDS BEACH)
Built on land donated by Frederick R Goddard to the Wesleyan Methodist Church of South

Africa, the chapel was erected by farmers who settled in the area from about 1860 onwards. The property was purchased by the State in 1984 and transferred to the South African Development Trust.

OLD POWDER MAGAZINE (FORT GLAMORGAN)

Fort Glamorgan was built by Lieutenant Terrois of the Royal Engineers on the instruction of Sir Harry Smith at approximately the same time as (probably 1846), and a short distance from, Fort Buffalo. The powder magazine is situated on the west bank of the Buffalo River, overlooking the harbour.

Although the almost simultaneous construction of two forts seems illogical, a close study of the relevant correspondence reveals that Glamorgan was an addition to Fort Buffalo and comprised only a barracks, a small hospital and outbuildings.

OLD WEST BANK POST OFFICE (BANK STREET)

This property was granted to William Thomas Vandof in 1860, sold to others in 1865 and then sold to the Colonial Government on 16 July 1866. The following year a courthouse was erected and by 1888 it was used by the Department of Justice, and as a post office.

OLD WOOL EXCHANGE (50–52 CHURCH STREET)

The foundation stone was laid by Lulius Hofman on 30 October 1929 and the building was erected shortly after. Wool auctions were held here regularly until 30 June 1981, after which the Wool Exchange moved to Port Elizabeth. The building is currently occupied by Rhodes University.

PROVINCIAL BUILDING (64 TERMINUS STREET)

Formerly the old Standard Bank Building, this magnificent double-storey building, which is a fine example of neo-Renaissance revivalism, was erected in two stages. The original building was erected on Lot 11 in 1900, then extended onto Lot 12 in 1927. Predominantly situated on a corner site, the building forms an integral part of the architectural townscape of East London and is a landmark in the town.

PUBLIC LIBRARY
(CNR CAMBRIDGE AND ARGYLE STREETS)

This building, with its Victorian neoclassical and Renaissance features, forms an integral part of the historic and architectural core of East London.

QUEEN'S PARK (BEACONSFIELD ROAD)

The original part of Queen's Park was donated to the inhabitants of East London in about 1880 by John Gately for use as a public park. This park is of particular botanical interest.

REDHOUSE PRIMARY SCHOOL
(HUDSON AVENUE, VINCENT)

Built in 1907, Redhouse is a fine example of an early twentieth century Mediterranean-type mansion. It was acquired by Hans Hasso Malcomess in 1921 but eventually became the Redhouse Hotel. During this period it was offered to King George VI when he was invited to South Africa to recuperate from ill health. However, he died in 1952 prior to his proposed trip. The hotel closed and was converted into a convent by the Dominican Order of St Catherine of Siena. It was later purchased by the state and incorporated into Hudson Park Primary School.

FORT BEAUFORT

Named after Governor Lord Charles Somerset's father, the Duke of Beaufort, the town was laid out in 1837 around Fort Beaufort, a fort built in 1822 by Lieutenant-Colonel H Maurice Scott to keep a check on marauding Xhosa tribes. It attained municipal status in 1883.

MARTELLO TOWER (20 BELL STREET)
The circular tower was built in 1846 to replace the fort. Manned until 1869, it was built of dressed stone, and a small cannon on a revolving wooden platform was erected on top. This type of tower was considered best at the time for coastal defence.

OFFICERS' MESS (44 DURBAN STREET)
This historic officers' mess dates from about 1830, and is one of the oldest existing buildings in Fort Beaufort. It is closely linked with the history of the town, as well as the military history of the Eastern Cape. It became the Fort Beaufort Historical Museum in 1938.

OFFICERS' QUARTERS (20 BELL STREET)
The officers' quarters were built in 1849. Together with the neighbouring Martello Tower, they form a unique historic and architectural group, worthy of preservation.

OLD MILITARY HOSPITAL BUILDING
(FORT BEAUFORT HOSPITAL, BELL STREET)
This U-shaped hospital building, which was erected shortly before the Seventh Frontier War (1846–1847), was designed by Captain JE Walpole of the Royal Engineers. From the 1870s – when the British army vacated the premises – until 1950 it was used as a Magistrate's residence. At present the building serves as stores and lecture rooms for the Provincial Hospital Complex.

OLD WATER MILL (MILL BANK, DISTRICT)
Machinery, including the water wheel, for this mill was imported from Leeds, England. The first locally produced flour was available on 21 September 1859. According to newspaper reports of the time, the mill owner, Mr Ainslie, succeeded in his difficult undertaking of leading water from the Kat River, through several miles of furrow, to his mill. After a few years the wooden wheel had to be replaced by a cast-iron version but the old wooden pulleys and leather belts were still in use up until the closure of the mill in 1963.

POST RETIEF FORT (DISTRICT)
Post Retief was designed by Major CJ Selwyn and built in 1836 to protect the Winterberg district. The farm on which this fort is situated originally belonged to Voortrekker leader Piet Retief; sections of the walls of the Retief home are included in the fort. The buildings of the fort form an important historic and architectural group in the military history of South Africa.

ST JOHN'S CHURCH
(WINTERBURG, POST RETIEF, DISTRICT)
This small church is situated just north of Post Retief Fort. The cornerstone was laid on 25 November 1885 and the building was consecrated by Bishop Henry Cotteril of Grahamstown. Near the church is a cemetery, and a small one-roomed school.

VICTORIA BRIDGE (VICTORIA STREET)
This bridge carries the Queen's Road, once an important military road across the Kat River. It was designed by Major CJ Selwyn of the Royal Engineers, and built of dressed stone. The bridge was completed by 1844.

GLEN LYNDEN

This village is situated in the Baviaans River Valley. It was settled by a contingent of Scottish Settlers from the 1820 Settlers. It is presumed that the name Lynden related to their homeland.

TWO HISTORIC DUTCH REFORMED CHURCHES
BUILT IN 1828 AND 1874 (BEDFORD DISTRICT)
The older church, which dates from 1828, was erected by the Scottish party of the 1820 Settlers

originally as a Presbyterian church. Built of stone, initially with a thatched roof, it has an interesting T-shape. Together with the neighbouring church, erected in 1874 in neogothic style, they form an important architectural group.

GRAAFF-REINET

Founded in 1786, the town was named after Cornelis Jacob van de Graaff, Governor of the Cape from 1785–1791, and his wife Cornelia Reynet. It attained municipal status in 1845. Graaff-Reinet is the third oldest town of the former Cape Province and is known for its historic buildings, many of which date from the late eighteenth and early nineteenth centuries. Gert Maritz, Sarel Cilliers and Andries Pretorius, well-known leaders of the Great Trek, lived in or around Graaff-Reinet.

DEWDNEY HOUSE (38 CALEDON STREET)
This property was first granted in 1825 to John Ludwig Leeb, a land surveyor. Built around 1850, it served as the premises of the drapery business of the Dewdney brothers from 1881.

DROSTDYHOF AND HISTORIC SLAVE COTTAGES (STRETCH'S COURT)
These 13 slave cottages, built in the vernacular style, were erected by Captain Charles Lennox Stretch, an Irish immigrant, with the object of retaining his best workers after the emancipation of slaves in 1834. From 1965, Historical Homes of South Africa Limited bought the properties and restored the cottages situated on them with great care. They now serve as an annex to the nearby Drostdy Hotel.

DROSTDY HOTEL (28–30 CHURCH STREET)
Designed by Louis Michel Thibault and erected in 1804–1806, this building is built on an H-plan with eight gables. Until 1847, the hotel served as a Drostdy (the residency and office of a Landdrost, a judicial official of the Cape Colony between 1685 and 1828). Since 1876 it has been used almost continually as a hotel, and was recently fully restored.

DUTCH REFORMED CHURCH BUILDING AND CHURCH BELL (ADENDORP DISTRICT)
The original section of this building, which was erected in 1879, was a small church hall that also served as a school. In 1918, with the addition of two wings and a vestry, it was altered into a cruciform-style church. The church bell was installed in 1880 by the municipality.

FIRST CHURCH BUILDING (104 CHURCH STREET)
This building, with its Cape Dutch gables, was erected in 1792 and was the first church building of the Dutch Reformed congregation of Graaff-Reinet. Rebuilding and alterations took place in 1945.

GRAAFF-REINET CLUB HOUSE (3 CHURCH STREET)
The Graaff-Reinet Men's Club was started in 1875 and is believed to be the third oldest in the country. The property was transferred on 17 January 1881 to the Trustees of the Graaff-Reinet Club Company Limited, and in October 1926 to the Trustee of the Graaff-Reinet Club.

GRAAFF-REINET PHARMACY (24 CALEDON STREET)
The double-storey Georgian building, which was presumably erected in about 1870, was adapted in 1900 to be a pharmacy. This mid-Victorian pharmacy and its valuable antiques are of exceptional cultural-historic importance.

GROOTKERK (CHURCH STREET)
The towering Grootkerk was designed by Cape Town architect J Bisset, in Victorian-Gothic style as an imitation of Salisbury Cathedral, England. It was built in 1885 from local sandstone.

HISTORIC BUILDINGS (10 PARSONAGE STREET)
These Georgian buildings date from the first quarter of the nineteenth century and are excellent examples of the Karoo style of building.

HISTORIC HOUSES
The following buildings, with Georgian-Karoo and Victorian characteristics, date mainly from the nineteenth century. They form an integral part of the historic and architectural core of Graaff-Reinet.
BOURKE STREET (1, 2, 7, 24, 39, 41, 43, 45, 47, 54, 60, 62, 66): Victorian dwelling houses
BOURKE STREET (4, 46, 63): Karoo-style cottage/houses
BOURKE STREET (26, 58): Victorianised Cape Dutch dwellings
BOURKE STREET (100, 102, 104): Georgian-Karoo-style cottages
CALEDON STREET (53, 55, 57): Façades of the Trinity Methodist Church, Dudley Hall and Wesley Manse, together with the cast-iron fence around the buildings
CALEDON STREET (63): Late-Victorian/Edwardian dwelling house
CALEDON STREET (76, 83, 85, 86, 87, 88, 91, 98, 100, 102, 106): Karoo-style dwellings
CALEDON STREET (110, 118): Georgian-Karoo-style dwellings
CAROLINE STREET (17): Karoo-style cottage
CHURCH STREET (18): Old Library Building, known as the Reinet Museum
CHURCH STREET (32): Façade of Georgian building
CHURCH STREET (34): Façade of Victorian dwelling house
CHURCH STREET (61): Cape Dutch dwelling house
CHURCH STREET (81): Façade of Edwardian shop building, known as Adampie Building
CHURCH STREET (83): Karoo-style house
CHURCH SQUARE (4, 6, 8, 10, 12): Semidetached Karoo-style Georgian houses
CHURCH SQUARE (14, 18): Karoo-style Georgian houses
COLLEGE ROAD: Façade of the original Graaff-Reinet College for further Education
CRADOCK STREET (7, 15, 40, 65): Victorianised houses
CRADOCK STREET (23): Façade of Georgian-Karoo-style dwelling house
CRADOCK STREET (37, 44, 45, 47, 48, 58, 72, 73, 74, 75, 76, 83, 85, 100, 104, 117, 119, 124, 126, 128, 135, 136, 152, 155, 162, 164, 166, 176, 180): Karoo-style Georgian houses
CRADOCK STREET (80): Victorian house with central gable
CRADOCK STREET (84): Victorian double-winged dwelling
CRADOCK STREET (86, 92, 95, 96, 107, 109, 150): Victorian houses
CRADOCK STEET (87, 89, 91): Victorian-Cape Dutch dwelling house, together with garage and Karoo-style annex
CRADOCK STREET (138a, 138b): Semidetached Georgian-Karoo-style houses
CRADOCK STREET (140, 140a, 142, 156, 158): Façades of Karoo-style dwelling houses
CROSS STREET (4, 7): Karoo-style cottages with stepped parapet
DONKIN STREET (5, 93): Georgian-Karoo-style dwelling houses
DONKIN STREET (6): Victorian dwelling house
DONKIN STREET (10, 11, 13, 15, 16): Karoo-style houses
DONKIN STREET (24): Façade of Karoo-style cottage
DONKIN STREET (64): Victorianised Cape Dutch dwelling
DONKIN STREET (69, 71, 72, 75, 76): Karoo-style houses
DONKIN STREET (77): Four-bay Victorian cottage
DONKIN STREET (79): Karoo-style house with straight parapet
DONKIN STREET (89): Single-storey Georgian-Karoo-style cottage

MARKET SQUARE (14): Cape Dutch dwelling
MILNER STREET (1): Edwardian dwelling with verandah on both sides
MILNER STREET (3): Large Victorian winged dwelling with hipped roof and verandah
MULLER STREET (7a): Karoo-style dwelling with stepped parapet
MURRAY STREET (49): Georgian-Karoo-style dwelling house
NAPIER STREET (8, 12): Victorian dwellings
NORTH STREET (7, 10, 13, 18, 21, 22, 23): Karoo-style dwellings
NORTH STREET (19): Victorian saddle-roof dwelling house
NORTH STREET (24): Victorian five-bay saddle-roof house
NORTH STREET (28): Façade of Georgian house with Victorian elements
NORTH STREET (38): Victorian house with three-bay hipped roof
NORTH STREET (42): Karoo-style dwelling with stepped parapet
PARK STREET (4, 7, 39): Victorian three-bay saddle roofed houses
PARK STREET (6): Karoo-style dwelling with mouldings and stoep
PARK STREET (8, 9): Karoo-style dwellings
PARK STREET (18): Victorian five-bay saddle-roof dwelling
PARK STREET (19, 24, 26): Karoo-style dwellings with stepped parapets
PARLIAMENT STREET (6): Façade of Victorian dwelling house
PARLIAMENT STREET (8, 10): Two-bay attached Karoo-style cottages
PARLIAMENT STREET (16): Façade of Victorian cottage
PARLIAMENT STREET (18): Façade of flat-roofed cottage with Georgian elements
PARSONAGE STREET (2): Georgian dwelling house
PARSONAGE STREET (3): Victorian-Karoo-style three-bay, end-gable dwelling
PARSONAGE STREET (6, 8): Karoo-style cottages with stepped gables
PARSONAGE STREET (9): Four-bay house with saddle-roof and verandah
PARSONAGE STREET (12): Three-bay saddle-roof cottage with walled stoep
PARSONAGE STREET (14): Karoo-style cottage with pedimented parapet
PARSONAGE STREET (16): Karoo-style cottage with stepped parapet
PARSONAGE STREET (17): Victorianised Cape Dutch T-shaped house
PARSONAGE STREET (18): Victorian house with saddle roof
PARSONAGE STREET (20): Karoo-style house with straight parapets
PARSONAGE STREET (22): Karoo-style cottage with stepped parapet
PLASKET STREET (11, 32, 34)
QUEEN STREET (3): Façade of Karoo-style dwelling house
RABIE STREET (15)
ROTHMAN STREET (5): Victorian dwelling house
RHYNEVELD SQUARE (13): Karoo-style dwelling house
SOMERSET STREET (22, 25, 25a, 27, 27a, 38, 42, 44, 48, 55, 66, 67, 72, 79, 80, 83, 84, 87, 90, 90a, 94, 102, 104)
SOMERSET STREET (24, 26): Façade of Victorian dwelling house
SOMERSET STREET (73): Georgian dwelling house
STOCKENSTROOM STREET (10, 30, 32, 33, 34, 44, 45, 46, 48, 49, 60, 62, 63, 65, 72, 77, 79, 90)
Te WATER (1, 3)

HISTORIC OLD PRISON (MIDDLE TERRACE)
Built between 1859 and 1861, this excellent example of a nineteenth-century prison has remained virtually unaltered. The exterior and some interior walls are made of local stone, plastered with cement. During the Anglo-Boer War, rebels and Boer fighters were held prisoner here.

HISTORIC RIETVLEI HOMESTEAD AND COACH HOUSE (FARM RIETVLEI)
The Rietvlei homestead is a T-shaped Cape Dutch gable house, believed to have been built in approximately 1820. The wagon house possibly predates the homestead.

HYENA TRAP (FARM BLUEGUM HOUSE)
This corbelled hyena trap was built to catch predators. Corbelled or truss bracket buildings were usually built of brick or stone in which each course of stones projects a little further inwards than the previous, until the walls almost meet at the top. The trap is an important material link with the pioneering way of life in South Africa.

KROMM'S INN (3 PARLIAMENT STREET)
This single-storey symmetrical three-bay house with stepped parapet to the front and moulded cornice, is an excellent example of a flat-roofed building with a fretwork verandah.

NOOITGEDACHT CAPE DUTCH MANOR HOUSE (DISTRICT)
This farm was originally granted in 1818 to Pieter Johannes Naudé and Hendrik Petrus Janse van Rensburg as quitrent land (the rent payable by a freeholder or copy holder to his lord, releasing him from liability to perform services). The manor house, which dates from 1818, forms a unique Cape Dutch architectural group of considerable historic and architectural importance to the Eastern Cape.

OLD JEWISH CEMETERY
This property was granted to the Hebrew community of Graaff-Reinet on 9 January 1858, by Sir George Grey, then Governor of the Cape.

OLD MISSION CHURCH AND PARSONAGE (21 AND 23 PARSONAGE STREET)
The historic parsonage was erected before 1848, while the Mission Church was built at a later stage by the London Missionary Society. These two buildings form an architecturally important section of Parsonage Street.

OLD NEOGOTHIC CHURCH BUILDING (41–43 MIDDLE STREET)
This old church building now houses the Jan Rupert Centre.

OLD POWDER MAGAZINE (MAGAZINE HILL, NORTH OF GRAAFF-REINET)
This old powder magazine was built in 1831 by a firm of merchants to store gunpowder for blasting, as well as firearms for the protection of its workers. It was erected on freehold land granted to John Biddulph in 1834.

REINET HOUSE (MURRAY STREET)
A nineteenth-century Cape Dutch H-shaped house (presumably built in 1812), Reinet House was formerly a Dutch Reformed Church parsonage occupied by both Reverends Andrew and Charles Murray. Between them, father and son served Graaff-Reinet for more than 80 years. The house has been authentically restored and is home to a large vine, planted in 1870 by Charles Murray.

ST JAMES CHURCH (35 SOMERSET STREET)
In 1848 Bishop Robert Gray paid a visit to Graaff-Reinet, when a plan for an Anglican church was accepted. The building was consecrated on 29 October 1850 and now forms the nave of the present neogothic stone church with plastered and moulded window reveals. The earlier thatched roof was replaced with a corrugated iron roof in 1885. Arched windows are fitted with stained glass. The church has not been altered much internally and the exposed roof trusses and joinery in Oregon pine are still in good condition. This building is reputedly the oldest church building still in use in Graaff-Reinet.

TE WATER HOUSE (32 SOMERSET STREET)
This Victorianised single-storey H-plan Cape Dutch house, was built on a site originally granted to Andrew Stockenström on 9 September 1818. After changing hands a number of times, it was passed to Frans Karel te Water in 1854, a member of the Legislative Council and Mayor of Graaff-Reinet.

THE OLD RESIDENCY MUSEUM
(2 PARSONAGE STREET)
The Residency is a well-preserved model of an early nineteenth-century H-plan gable house, which, together with Reinet house, forms a unique architectural group.

TOWN HALL (CHURCH SQUARE)
Designed by FW and F Hesse, architects in the neo-Flemish style, the town hall's foundation stone was laid on 26 June 1902 by the Mayor, CA Nesser. It was to be called the Victoria Hall to commemorate the reign of Queen Victoria, and was officially opened on 5 September 1911.

URQUHART HOUSE
(CNR MURRAY AND SOMERSET STREETS)
The land on which Urquhart House is situated was granted to JG Pichel in 1806. The earliest record of a structure on this site is shown on Thompson's plan of 1823 and is assumed to be the present Urquhart House. The building was used as a hotel from about 1850. In 1912 the property was bought by prominent Graaff-Reinet businessman, Herbert Urquhart MBE, who served as the town's Mayor from 1915 to 1936. Now a museum, this fine Cape Dutch house, with its unusual gable and ground plan, was recently restored.

VALLEY OF DESOLATION (APPROXIMATELY 5KM SOUTHWEST OF GRAAFF-REINET)
Famous for basaltic columns rising 90–100m in height, the valley is an interesting geological occurrence. Its rocks belong to the Beaufort Series of the Karoo System, which in South African geology also comprises the Dwyka, Ecca and Stormberg Series. The Beaufort Series reaches a thickness of some 696m, and dates back some 160 to 180 million years.

GRAHAMSTOWN

In 1812, a military headquarters was established on the farm Rietfontein, around which Grahamstown developed. The town was named after Colonel John Graham, and was laid out in 1815. It became the main centre for the 1820 British Settlers and attained municipal status in 1862. It also obtained the status of bishopric in 1853.

CHAPEL HOUSE (8A, 9-11 BARTHOLOMEW STREET)
This Georgian double-storey building was erected in 1823 and is the oldest Baptist Church in South Africa. The foundation stone was laid on 6 January by William Miller, the 1820 Settler founder of the Baptist Church in South Africa. The church was consecrated on 7 September and used until 1843, when it was replaced by the church in Bathurst Street. It was converted soon after into three dwellings, but is now occupied as a single unit again, known as Chapel House.

CHAPEL OF ST MARY AND ALL THE ANGELS
(RHODES UNIVERSITY CAMPUS)
This Basilican chapel was built in 1915–1916. Its foundation stone was laid on 2 June 1915, and the chapel was consecrated by Bishop Phelps on 14 October 1916. The impressive altarpiece of the Madonna and Child above the altar was painted by Sister Margaret from 1924–1929.

COCK HOUSE (10 MARKET STREET)
The property is situated on land originally granted to Benjamin Norden in January 1826. Norden was an 1820 Settler who farmed near

Bathurst before he moved to Uitenhage and became involved in the ivory trade. At one stage the property was occupied by the Honourable William Cock, a member of the first Legislative Assembly. He came to the Cape as head of his own party of 1820 Settlers and was primarily responsible for the development of Port Alfred as a harbour.

DIVISIONAL COUNCIL BUILDING (94 HIGH STREET)
This three-storey building is built in two sections to a symmetrical plan. The first section dates from 1860–1862 and the second from the late 1860s. Its façade is of outstanding architectural merit and is unequalled by any other of this period in South Africa.

DOUBLE-STOREY FARMHOUSE (FARM HILTON)
This magnificent Georgian double-storey was erected in 1834 for AG Cumming by Richard Gush. The bow-fronted design is unique; only a few of its kind have remained unaltered.

DROSTDY GATEWAY (SOMERSET STREET)
This gateway was designed by Captain CJ Selwyn of the Royal Engineers, as the entrance to the military establishment. Together with its walls and flanking guardhouses, the gateway was completed in 1842.

DWELLING HOUSE (56 BEAUFORT STREET)
This double-storey house is the only known example in South Africa of the European-Chinese architectural style of the eighteenth and nineteenth centuries. Dating from the 1830s, it has two projection pavilions with bow-fronted ends, while the pagoda and handrail on the verandah are typically Chinese.

EASTERN STAR GALLERY
(4 ANGLO AFRICAN STREET)
The gallery takes its name from the *Eastern Star* newspaper established in Grahamstown in 1871. A restored 120-year-old Wharfdale printing press housed in the building is similar to the press used until 1887 to print the newspaper.

FAÇADE OF BEAUMONT AND RICE BUILDING
(112 HIGH STREET)
This building is a double-storey shop erected in 1881, the sandstone façade of which has remained unaltered. The building has a predominantly Georgian style with Victorian elements. It forms part of the exceptionally impressive street image of High Street, the oldest street in Grahamstown.

FAÇADE OF BUILDING (8 BARTHOLOMEU STREET)
This building forms part of the Artificers' Square. These structures were erected during the 1820s and early 1830s by artisans who arrived in Grahamstown after the immigration of the 1820 Settlers. It is one of a large group of similar buildings, of which the façades of most have been declared national monuments.

FAÇADE OF CHECKERS SUPERMARKET BUILDING
(42–44 HIGH STREET)
This property was originally allocated to Lieutenant John Bell in 1814. In 1817 it was bought by Piet Retief and from 1820 to 1824 it belonged to Captain Huntley. After a fire in 1906, the present façade was erected by Codgebrook, Muirhead & Gowrie, who formed a partnership and opened a shop well-known for materials and furniture. This double-storey building was generally known as the Muirhead & Gowrie Building. Its neo-Baroque decorations and Art Nouveau characteristics are worthy of mention.

FAÇADES OF DOUBLE-STOREY SEMIDETACHED
SHOP BUILDINGS (36, 46–48 HIGH STREET)
These two buildings form an integral part of the unique row of semidetached double-storey shops, of which the façades feature a combination of

free Renaissance, neoclassical and Georgian styles, blending to form a harmonious architectural feature in High Street. The latter comprises a collection of late nineteenth-century residential and commercial buildings.

FAÇADES OF DOUBLE-STOREY SHOP BUILDINGS
(32–34, 50, 54–56, 58–60 HIGH STREET)

These late nineteenth-century shops, with their neo-Renaissance façades, form an integral part of the architectural character of High Street and are an important element in the historic city centre of Grahamstown.

FAÇADES OF THE TRINITY CHURCH COMPLEX
(55, 57, 59 HILL STREET)

The Trinity Church, mainly neoclassical in style, was built by trustees and members of the Union Chapel, established on 8 August 1827. The cornerstone was laid on 13 April 1840 and the building was completed on 11 December 1842, coinciding with a name change from Union Chapel to Trinity Church. It was formally transferred to the presbytery on 19 April 1876. Erected in 1859, the neoclassically styled hall was originally a schoolhouse for the adjacent church. The Georgian double-storey cottage dates from the mid-nineteenth century.

FARMERFIELD METHODIST CHURCH
(FARM FARMERFIELD)

This neogothic Methodist Church was designed by the Reverend Thornley-Smith and was erected in 1844. It originally served a community established by the Reverend William Shaw as an experiment in social rehabilitation. The building is still used as a church and school for local farm labourers' children.

FORT BROWN (FARM HERMANUSKRAAL)

Originally built in 1817, the military post was converted into a fort in 1835 and garrisoned by the 72nd Highland Regiment until 1861.

FORT SELWYN (GUNFIRE HILL)

The fort, in the shape of an asymmetrical seven-pointed star, was completed in 1836 and named after Captain (later Major) Charles Jasper Selwyn, who commanded the Corps of Royal Engineers from 1835–1841. The fort was transferred to the Artillery in 1841 and served as its barracks until 1868, thereafter becoming a magazine and guardhouse until 1870. A museum was established in 1977.

GEORGIAN DOUBLE-STOREY BUILDING
(48–50 BATHURST STREET)

The first owner of this property was Dr Peter Campbell, an Irish 1820 Settler and member of John Bailie's party. He was Grahamstown's first registered independent medical practitioner.

GEORGIAN DOUBLE-STOREY DWELLING
(19, 21 WEST STREET)

This house dates from 1841 and is built from local sandstone. It is surmised that Benjamin Leech, an 1820 Settler and stonemason by profession, helped to build it for Robert Walker, as he was responsible for the erection of the adjacent double-storey. On 1 July 1852, the property was transferred to David Hume, a transport rider and later well-known hunter.

GOVERNOR'S KOP SIGNAL TOWER
(FARM GOVERNOR'S KOP)

Two lines of signal towers were established from here (one to Fort Beaufort and the other to Peddie), both built during 1843–1844. Intended as a means of communication with soldiers at forts along the Fish River, this method of communication proved unsuccessful on account of frequent misty conditions. The Governor's Kop Tower was in use for five years.

GROCOTT'S MAIL BUILDING (40 HIGH STREET)

Thomas Henry Grocott was the founder of *Grocott's Free Paper*, established on 7 May

1870 from these premises. The gable of this impressive building, with its Victorian and Flemish features, bears the date 1869–1906, while the present façade was added in 1906 after a devastating fire. The building, which forms an integral part of the architectural character of High Street and is an important link in the history of Grahamstown, still houses a printing and stationery operation.

HILL ORGAN (METHODIST COMMEMORATION CHURCH, HIGH STREET)

This chamber organ, made by William Hill of London between 1832 and 1837, measures three metres in height and two metres in width. It has a single manual of 58 notes, 12 pads, eight registers and one swell pedal, and must be blown manually.

The organ was imported by Major Henry Somerset as a present to his wife. She, in turn, donated it to the chapel in Fort England, at that time the headquarters of the Cape Corps, which Major Somerset had formerly commanded. From there it was transferred to its present location in 1914.

HISTORIC BAPTIST MOTHER CHURCH (BATHURST STREET)

The cornerstone of this historic church was laid on 5 October 1843 by Martin West, and the building was officially opened on 12 March 1849. The building, with its simple, classical façade, is the oldest church used by the Baptist Union in South Africa.

HISTORIC CORBELLED HUT (SPRING FARM, DISTRICT)

This corbelled hut is an excellent example of the ingenuity of the early pioneers in building a house with whatever material was available to them. The hut, therefore, represents an important link in the development of vernacular architecture in South Africa.

HISTORIC CORBELLED HUTS (FARM GLENFIELD, DISTRICT)

These two corbelled huts are also excellent examples of the vernacular architecture of the pioneers in the Karoo region during the nineteenth century.

HISTORIC PILLAR POST BOX (CNR WORCESTER AND SOMERSET STREETS)

Manufactured by Smith & Hawkes of Birmingham and erected in 1860, this is one of the oldest known British-manufactured flute-type post boxes in South Africa.

HISTORIC TROMPETTER'S DRIFT FORT AND FORTIFICATION RINGWALL (FARM KOODOO, DISTRICT)

The fortification was named after a Hottentot captain, Hans Trompetter, who had his kraal at this fort. It was built to protect the ford and to serve as a base for patrols operating in the thickly wooded vicinity.

HUNTLEY STREET SCHOOL (HUNTLEY STREET)

Built from local Witteberg quartzite in English Gothic-Revival style, it is generally accepted that this is the oldest Anglican school building in South Africa. The foundation stone was laid on 18 June 1844 by the wife of Colonel J Hare, Lieutenant-Governor of the Eastern Districts. This building was opened on 4 October 1849 and was intended to serve as a Sunday School for St George's Church, later to become Grahamstown Cathedral. It was also decided to use it as a day school and became St George's Cathedral Grammar School and continued as such until 1901. When St Andrew's College was established in 1852, the first classes were held here, as well as the first Synod of the Diocese in 1860. Later it became a government research laboratory, but by 1918 it was transferred to the Anglican Community of the Resurrection for educational purposes again.

JOHAN CARINUS ART CENTRE (KNOWN AS TRURO HOUSE) (48 BEAUFORT STREET)

The land on which this house is situated was originally granted to Charles Lennox Stretch on 15 June 1823. The original portion of Truro House, with its Georgian and Victorian elements, dates from the 1840s and was probably built by George Gilbert, who owned the property at the time. The bow window was added in the early 1850s by Richard Austen.

METHODIST COMMEMORATION CHURCH (SETTLERS MEMORIAL CHURCH) (HIGH STREET)

Built by Thomas F King in 1845 to celebrate the 25th anniversary of the arrival of the 1820 Settlers, the church contains many memorial windows to settler families. The foundation stone was laid by the wife of Reverend William Shaw on 10 April 1845.

OATLANDS HOUSE (10 CAROLINE CLOSE)

This manor house was built in 1823 for Colonel Henry Somerset. At the time it was the centre of the mainly military community of Grahamstown. After the Oatlands property was sold to Walter (later Sir Walter) Currie in 1852, it still remained the centre of local society.

OBSERVATORY MUSEUM (10 BATHURST STREET)

Originally a nineteenth-century jeweller's shop and family home, it was built by Henry Carter Galpin, who took a scientific interest in astronomy, geology and meteorology. This so-called observatory, or camera obscura, was erected in 1850 and has three turreted structures on the roof containing a big clock, telescope and various instruments with which to read time using the sun. The camera obscura allowed people an opportunity to view the surrounding landscape, reduced to miniature size. Images were projected onto the surface of a flat table by means of a system of lenses and mirrors.

OLD GAOL (HIGH STREET)

The construction of the old gaol commenced in 1813, shortly after the founding of Grahamstown in 1812. In 1814, one of the walls of the gaol served as a line for the surveying of the Main Street, and thus also as a basis for the layout of the whole town. The building was completed in 1818, but served as a school after 1824 and later as Grahamstown's first Public Library until 1863.

OLD GAOL (SOMERSET STREET)

The original portion of this building, with its predominantly Georgian elements, was designed by WO Jones and built in 1823–1824 by AB Dietz. The completed building was handed over to the government in April 1824 and served as a prison for about 150 years.

OLD MILITARY BUILDING COMPLEX (RHODES UNIVERSITY CAMPUS)

The complex includes the Old Drostdy Barracks, Old Drostdy Lodge, Old Military Hospital Buildings and the Old Royal Engineers Building. The hospital is of special significance in that the Cape Parliament had its session at Grahamstown in 1864. Shortly before the garrison vacated the building and it was prepared for the Legislative Assembly, the three wooden huts beside the hospital were used for the Legislative Council. After the opening of Shaw Hall on 28 April 1864, the members of the two houses moved into the hospital and the three huts, where they sat for three months dividing the Cape Colony into the Eastern and Western Provinces.

OLD PROVOST BUILDING (LUCAS AVENUE)

Built by the Royal Engineers during 1836–1838, and probably designed by Charles Selwyn, the building's ingenious design incorporates cells grouped around a semicircular courtyard that has a centrally situated dominating high tower.

Within the tower were the guard room and gaoler's quarters, with a view across the courtyard extending to the entrance and approach to the prison. The Provost served as a gaol for most of the nineteenth century.

OLD ST BARTHOLOMEW'S CHURCH SCHOOL BUILDING (BARTHOLOMEW STREET)

The school consists of a single hall with the same type of construction as the church hall.

OLD WESLEYAN CHURCH AND OLD SCHOOL HALL (FORT ENGLAND HOSPITAL)

These two buildings form an integrated portion of the historic Fort England Hospital complex erected in 1875 on the grounds of the former military installation of 1814, and it is the oldest asylum in South Africa. The cornerstone of the neogothic church was laid on 5 December 1860 and the building was inaugurated on 10 November 1861.

The building symbolises two pioneering services, which, for a period of over 120 years, served the garrison troops and later the mentally disturbed. The school hall's cornerstone was laid on 17 August 1895 by John E Wood Esq. The hall was initially used as a Sunday School and was later used for teaching purposes and activities of the asylum. After the Methodist properties were sold to the government, the hall was used first as a school and later as an occupational therapy centre.

ORIGINAL CITY HALL BUILDING, SETTLERS MEMORIAL TOWER (HIGH STREET)

The foundation stone of this building was laid on 28 August 1877 by His Excellency Sir Henry Bartle Frere, Governor and Commander-in-Chief of Her Majesty's Colony of the Cape of Good Hope. The foundation stone of the British Settlers Jubilee Memorial Tower (1820–1870), which was erected by public subscription, was laid by the Honourable Robert Godlonton on 23 May 1870. The latter also commemorates the heroic ride of Dick King from Port Natal to Grahamstown from 26 May to 4 June 1842, resulting in the relief of the British garrison at Durban.

ORIGINAL PORTION OF THE BOTANICAL GARDENS (GUNFIRE HILL)

The land on which these gardens were laid out was granted to the Albany Botanical Gardens in 1853 by the Governor of the Cape, Sir George Cathcart. These botanical gardens are the second oldest in South Africa and originally formed part of the Drostdy Estate. A cottage, which dates from the 1830s, on the grounds was erected in the romantic country style, known as Cottage Orné, with peaked Gothic windows and a Georgian chimney. The cottage is unique in the Eastern Cape.

PRIESTS HOUSE (87 BEAUFORT STREET)

This double-storey house with its Georgian and Romanesque features was built by Bishop Patric Moran in 1860 as a residence for the priests of St Patrick's Cathedral. Bishop Moran was succeeded by Reverend James David Richards, the resident priest. One of the windows of this building bears the latter's initials, which he engraved while involved in the testing of the Eureka diamond identified in 1867. The house is now the National English Literary Museum.

RAILWAY STATION BUILDING (HIGH STREET)

Including its courtyard, platform and an 'ERII' wall post box, this station building is the terminal of the Alicedale-Grahamstown railway, which was opened on 3 September 1879.

REMAINS OF SHAW CHAPEL (4–6 CHAPEL STREET)

The cornerstone of this tiny chapel, used for church services by Anglican, Methodist and Presbyterian congregations, was laid in 1821 by the well-known Methodist pioneer William Shaw. It was the first building erected for the Christian faith in Grahamstown and reflects the efforts of the Methodist Church to establish Christianity in the town.

ST BARTHOLOMEW'S CHURCH AND HALL
(CNR MARKET AND BARTHOLOMEW STREETS)
This nineteenth century stone church and hall form a special architectural unity.

SETTLER COTTAGE JOHN OATS
(2 CROSS STREET, ARTIFICERS SQUARE)
This Settler cottage was erected by the artisan John Oats during the 1820s on land granted to him by the government. The cottage forms part of a unique historic and architectural complex, associated with the British Settlers of 1820.

SETTLER COTTAGES (ARTIFICERS' SQUARE)
These cottages comprise John Bigg's Cottage (1 Cross Street); Edward Searle Cottages (3, 5 Cross Street: semi-detached); and Thomas Webster Cottages (7, 9 Cross Street). They were all transferred to their respective owners on 1 December 1827.

SETTLER COTTAGES (4, 6, 8, 10 CROSS STREET; 8A BARTHOLOMEW STREET; 1, 2 SHEBLON LANE, ARTIFICERS' SQUARE)
These Settler cottages are known as John Payne Cottage, Thomas Wells House, Samuel Bannin Cottage, Cecil John Wright Shop and Cottage, Samuel Jefferies Cottage and Charles Wood Cottage. They were erected by artisans during the 1820s on land granted to them by the government on the understanding that a house of burned brick or stone be erected within 18 months. Most of the properties were, however, only transferred to the owners in 1827. The cottages form a unique historic and architectural complex, closely associated with the British Settlers of 1820.

SHAW HALL (22 HIGH STREET)
Inaugurated on 16 December 1832 and known as Wesley Chapel, the hall was used as a church until the Methodist Commemoration church replaced it in 1850. It was renamed Shaw Hall after the missionary Reverend William Shaw. On 28 April 1864, the Cape Parliament was opened in this hall by Sir Philip Wodehouse.

SOLE MEMORIAL METHODIST CHURCH
(HIGH STREET)
This building was originally erected in 1838 as a school and was enlarged in 1842. It was named after John Henry Sole, who devoted most of his life to the advancement of the coloured community of Grahamstown.

TEMLETT HOUSE (53 BEAUFORT STREET)
This is a fine example of an early nineteenth-century Georgian dwelling in South Africa.

THE ORIGINAL OLD ST BARTHOLOMEW'S ALMS HOUSES (21–23 LAWRENCE STREET)
These comprise two semidetached facebrick cottages under a roof of original Welsh slate. A stone over the entrance bears the date 1869.

THE RETREAT (1 PRINCE ALFRED STREET)
This property was transferred to Piet Retief on 16 July 1821. It is presumed that he built the oldest section of this building, although the remaining portion of the double-storey house dates from the 1840s. Another prominent pioneer of the Eastern Cape, Major Charles Selwyn, owned the property from 1841–1848.

TRYALL SETTLER COTTAGE
(19 SOMERSET STREET)
The original portion of this sandstone Settler cottage was built in approximately 1824 and enlarged in 1850. The cottage was purchased by the Grahamstown Training College in 1920 for the purpose of staff accommodation.

HANKEY

The town was established as a mission station by the London Missionary Society in 1825, and named after its treasurer, William Alers Hankey. It was intended to settle Hottentot converts on irrigable land.

OLD IRRIGATION TUNNEL AND WATER FURROWS

The mission station's old irrigation tunnel as well as the water furrows are a notable engineering work of pioneer farmers, under the guidance of the Reverend William Philip. They were completed in 1844.

HERTZOG

Originally named Tamboekievlei, the town was renamed in 1837 after Willem Frederik Hertzog (1792–1847), Assistant Surveyor-General of the Cape Colony from 1828. Coloured people were settled there in 1829 by Andries Stockenström to assist in the protection of the eastern frontier of the Cape Colony.

DUTCH REFORMED MISSION CHURCH

The cornerstone of the Dutch Reformed mission church was laid on 4 June 1834, but was only completed at the beginning of 1845 due to devastation resulting from the Sixth Frontier War (1834–1835).

HOFMEYR

The town was originally named Maraisburg after Daniel Marais, who played a leading role in its establishment. To avoid confusion with the town in the Transvaal, in 1911 it was renamed Hofmeyer after 'Onze Jan' Jan Hendrik Hofmeyr, who lobbied for the acceptance of Dutch as an official language of South Africa. The town obtained municipal status in 1913.

OLD MAGISTRATE'S COURT AND POST OFFICE
(CNR VOORTREKKER AND MARKET STREETS)

An interesting combination of neoclassical and Victorian elements, this building was erected in 1907, incorporating the remains of the original town hall, which partly burnt down in the 1880s.

HUMANSDORP

Laid out on the farm Rheeboksfontein in 1849, the town originated as a church village. It was first named Human se Dorp after the owner of the farm, Matthys Human. It was administered by the Church Council until 1896 and attained municipal status in 1900.

KLASIES RIVER CAVES COMPLEX
(FARM GEELHOUTBOOM, FARM SANDPUNT, KLASIESRIVIERMOND)

The Klasies River Caves are the oldest sites of anatomically modern man to be found anywhere in the world. They contain what is probably the oldest evidence for the use of marine resources, as well as fossils of several mammal species, including extinct types.

JANSENVILLE

Laid out on the farm Vergenoegd in 1854, the town was named after General Jan Willem Janssens (1762–1838), the last Batavian Governor of the Cape. Jansenville attained municipal status in 1881.

DUTCH REFORMED CHURCH (23 MAIN STREET)

This neogothic church was designed by the architect KO Hager, although the plans were altered in 1882 by AH Reid, a Port Elizabeth architect. The foundation stone was laid on 16 August 1884 and the church was officially consecrated on 20 June 1885. The church is an important part of Jansenville's historic core and of Main Street's architectural character.

KARIEGA

This town presumably takes its name from the nearby Kariega River, a name of Hottentot origin.

BAPTIST CHURCH
The foundations and part of the walls of this church were built in 1834. It was to have been the first Baptist Church in South Africa outside of Grahamstown, but three successive Frontier Wars delayed its completion in 1854.

KING WILLIAM'S TOWN

The town was founded in 1835 on the site of a mission station established there in 1825. It became the headquarters of the Province of Queen Adelaide and later, in 1847, the capital city of British Kaffraria. The town was named after King William IV of England. It acquired borough (municipal) status in 1861.

BRITISH KAFFRARIAN SAVINGS BANK BUILDING (MACLEAN SQUARE)
Erected in 1908, this building portrays the architecture of the period 1900–1910 and lends character to Maclean Square.

BROWNLEE MISSION CONGREGATIONAL CHURCH (RESERVE ROAD)
This building was erected in 1860 by the Reverend John Brownlee, missionary and founder of King William's Town.

CITY HALL (MACLEAN STREET)
The foundation stone of this imposing stone building was laid in 1866, and the city hall was officially opened on 4 December 1867. During the Ninth Frontier War (1877–1878) it was used as a waiting room for the Civil Defence Force. After the Anglo-Boer War (1899–1902), large-scale alterations were made to the building, which was then reopened on 6 May 1904.

DALE COLLEGE PRIMARY SCHOOL BUILDINGS (ALBERT ROAD)
The cornerstone of this red brick building, designed by the well-known architect Sir Herbert Baker, was laid on 20 March 1907. The building was officially opened on 26 February 1908 by Dr Thomas Muir, Superintendent-General of Education. The Primary School, which previously formed part of Dale College, became autonomous in 1961 and was housed in this building.

DEEDS OFFICE BUILDING (CNR ALEXANDRA AND QUEENS ROADS)
This blue sandstone building, which served as the Deeds Office until 1933, forms an integral part of the architectural character of Alexandra Road, as well as the historic core of King William's Town.

FORT MURRAY (FORT MURRAY OUTSPAN)
The fort was established in 1848 on the Buffalo River and named after Captain AS Murray of the 72nd Highlanders.

GREY HOSPITAL (CNR EALES AND LONSDALE STREETS)
Grey Hospital was erected between 1856 and 1859 at the insistence of Sir George Grey, and intended mainly for the Bantu population of the former British Kaffraria. The hospital was designed by Edward Pilkington and opened on 11 June 1859. Architecturally, it is particularly imposing with its central bell tower, porch, and two double-storey wings.

HOLY TRINITY CHURCH (PRINCE ALFRED SQUARE)
The foundation stone of this church was laid on 16 January 1850 by Colonel G MacKinnon, assisted by Archdeacon N Merriman. The foundation and walls were constructed by soldiers from several regiments. At the outbreak of the Eighth Frontier War (1850–1853), the

building was eventually completed and opened in February 1856 by Bishop John Armstrong. It was officially consecrated by Bishop Henry Cotterill on 21 February 1861.

KAFFRARIAN MUSEUM
(CNR ALEXANDER AND ALBERT ROADS)
The site includes the Kaffrarian Museum Complex, comprising the museum and Daines Building (Old Public Library). The Kaffrarian Museum originated from the Natural History Society, which was founded in King William's Town in 1884. The original museum building, designed by Johannesburg architect PE Treeby and opened by Mrs James Weir on 5 October 1898, was extended in 1953 and linked to the Daines Building in 1974. The latter was originally built as a public library, thanks to the efforts of Thomas Daines, a pharmacist at Grey Hospital, and was designed by the architect S Stent and opened on 23 July 1877. Both buildings reflect classical and neogothic elements. The museum is also well known for its magnificent mammal collection, the largest of its kind in South Africa.

LONSDALE CHAMBERS (TAYLOR STREET)
A double-storey building, with predominantly neoclassical features, Lonsdale Chambers was designed and built in 1924 by the architects Cordreaux, Farrow & Stocks. The building was named after James Faunce Lonsdale, founder member and later Secretary of the British Kaffrarian Savings Bank.

OLD METHODIST MANSE (BERKLEY STREET)
This manse was built in approximately 1855. It is a simple, double-storey building with a corrugated-iron roof and a wooden balcony that stretches from one side of the front façade to the other. The manse and the neighbouring old Methodist Church together form an interesting architectural and historic group.

OLD MILITARY COMMISSARIAT STORE
(MILITARY RESERVE)
This L-shaped stone building was completed in 1849, shortly before the outbreak of the Eighth Frontier War (1850–1853). It was also used in times of peace, for example to store corn in 1857 during the so-called Xhosa Suicide.

OLD MILITARY HOSPITAL BUILDING, AND OLD
BLACKSMITH (FORMERLY OLD MILITARY RESERVE)
The original portion of the old Military Hospital stone building dates from 1848 and was enlarged in 1860. The old Blacksmith Shop was constructed before 1862.

OLD MISSION CHURCH AND OLD PARSONAGE
The historic parsonage was erected before 1848, while the Mission Church was built by the London Missionary Society in 1848.

OLD OFFICERS' HOUSE (5 HOOD STREET)
This mid-nineteenth-century double-storey house is closely associated with the military history of King William's Town, at a stage when the town was at the centre of a Frontier War. The neogothic windows and Victorian wooden balcony are particularly noteworthy.

OLD POST OFFICE AND MAGISTRATE'S COURT
(ALEXANDRA ROAD)
First occupied in 1877, the old post office and Magistrate's Court accommodated various government departments. It has an imposing clock tower with a memorial clock installed in memory of John Brownlee, first missionary and founder of King William's Town.

OLD POWDER MAGAZINE (MILITARY RESERVE)
This powder magazine is one of the largest and best preserved examples of its kind in South Africa. It was probably erected in two stages, between 1852 and 1860, and between 1864 and 1875.

OLD RAILWAY STATION BUILDING (ALEXANDRA ROAD)

This stone building was officially opened as a railway station on 1 May 1877. After the relocation of the station it was acquired in 1933 by the De Vos Malan Primary School and is now used as School Board offices. The old station is closely associated with the history of the extension of the railway line from East London to the north.

OLD RESIDENCY (QUEEN'S ROAD)

The historic residency was erected around 1846 and is situated on the spot where the London Missionary Society's Mission Station was built by John Brownlee after his arrival in 1826. This building is closely linked to the history of King William's Town and is regarded as one of the most important historic buildings in the Eastern Cape.

PRINCIPAL'S RESIDENCE OF THE EXCELSIOR SCHOOL (MILITARY RESERVE)

This U-shaped building was erected in 1849 as an officers' mess at a time when King William's Town formed the centre of the Frontier Wars, and accommodated a large garrison. The building was used in this capacity until 1884, after which it served *inter alia* as a dwelling for the Paymaster, the Inspector-General and the Military Chaplain.

PROTEA ASSURANCE COMPANY BUILDING (CNR ALEXANDER AND CATHCART ROADS)

This double-storey office building was the first headquarters of the Sun Life Insurance Company in South Africa. Designed by the architects Cordeaux & Walker of East London, it was built by a contractor, Mr Ireland. The foundation stone was laid on 7 November 1904 by Mrs AB Gordon, wife of the manager of the company in South Africa. This building was used by the Sun Insurance Company until it moved its head office to Johannesburg in 1953. The firm was renamed Protea Assurance in 1964, and in 1987 moved its head office to East London.

SOUTH AFRICAN MISSIONARY MUSEUM (BERKLEY STREET)

This historic old Methodist church was built in 1855 in neogothic style. It was later used by the local German Baptist congregation and now houses the South African Missionary Museum.

STEVEN BANTU BIKO HOUSE (698 NGXATO STREET, GINSBERG)

Born in King William's Town in 1946, Steven (Steve) Biko was expelled from Lovedale High School on account of his brother's political activities and arrest as a suspected Pogo member. Steven then continued his schooling at St Francis College at Marianhill in Natal, and later enrolled at the medical faculty of Natal University.

Banned as a black consciousness activist, he was placed in detention on a number of occasions in 1977 and was taken to Walmer Police Station in Port Elizabeth where he was held in custody without clothing, ostensibly to prevent him from hanging himself with his clothes. Biko died in Pretoria in September 1977 after 26 days in police detention.

SUTTON HOUSE (DALE COLLEGE, QUEEN'S ROAD)

The cornerstone of Sutton House was laid on 6 September 1877 by the Governor of the Cape Colony, Sir Henry Bartle Frere. The building was officially opened on 17 December 1878 and was named after the Reverend JG Sutton, headmaster of Dale College from 1890–1912.

SYNAGOGUE (BERKLEY STREET)

It is thought that this predominantly neogothic building dates from the 1850s and was used for several decades as a school by the

Wesleyan Methodist Church. In 1908 it was acquired for use as a synagogue and has functioned as such ever since. With two adjoining buildings, also originally built by the Wesleyan Methodist Church, it forms an impressive building complex.

UPPER NEEDS CAMP GEOLOGICAL RESERVE
Originally used for the exploitation of lime, the area now encompassed by the Upper Needs Camp Geological Reserve was discovered to include Tertiary limestone that contained fossil impressions of mammals, which had become dominant during this period.

VICTORIA DRILL HALL (QUEEN'S ROAD)
This Victorian building, with its neoclassical features, was designed by J Laughton and was named in honour of Queen Victoria to commemorate her 60th year of rule over the British Empire. The cornerstone was laid on 21 June 1897. Since its completion, the building has been in continuous use as a drill hall.

KIRKWOOD

Originally called Bayville in 1885, the town was re-established on the farm Gouvernmentswoning in 1913 and named after John Somers Kirkwood, who was instrumental in pioneering the development of local irrigation systems. Kirkwood attained municipal status in 1950.

THE LOOKOUT (SITUATED ON PART OF TREGANAN AND BUCK KRAAL)
Sir Percy Fitzpatrick (1862–1931), author of the much loved book, *Jock of the Bushveld*, built the original high, wooden lookout tower as a vantage point overlooking the Sundays River Valley after he purchased this land. The tower was later replaced with a brick platform and parapet. It is also the burial place of Fitzpatrick.

KOMGA

The town was laid out in 1877 on the site of the 1847 military camp. Its name, formerly spelt 'komgha', is a Hottentot word meaning 'brown clay'. The town attained municipal status in 1904.

OLD PUBLIC LIBRARY (12 ST JOHN'S STREET)
This library building, with its neogothic features, is one of the oldest buildings in the town. It was erected in 1892 to serve the inhabitants of the town that grew around the military base.

ST PAUL'S ANGLICAN CHURCH
The original part of this church was completed in 1866 and was used as a temporary fort during the Ninth Frontier War (1877–1878). The chancel was added in 1880, and the castellated tower early in the twentieth century.

LADY GREY

The town was founded in 1858 on the farm Waaihoek and was named after the wife of Sir George Grey (1812–1898), Governor of the Cape Colony from 1854 to 1859. It attained municipal status in 1893.

DUTCH REFORMED CHURCH (JOUBERT STREET)
Designed by the architect CH Smith and constructed by the building contractor CJ Orr, the church building is a neogothic sandstone structure. The foundation stone was laid by the Reverend JP Wolhuter on 27 April 1912.

MACLEAR

Founded as a military camp in 1876, the town was named after Sir Thomas Maclear (1794–1879), the Astronomer Royal at the Cape, who laid the foundation for a trigonometrical survey of the Cape Colony. Maclear attained municipal status in 1916.

SITE OF THE DINOSAUR FOOTPRINT FOSSILS
(FARM OAKLEIGH)

Trace fossils exposed here are dinosaurian footprints preserved in overbank sediments of the Molteno formation (Late Triassic Period, approximately 200 million years ago). Until this discovery, no traces of dinosaurs had been found from rocks below the overlying Elliot Formation. They therefore represent the earliest known evidence of dinosaurs in South Africa.

MIDDELBURG

Laid out on the farm Driefontein in 1852, the town was named Middelburg because it is equidistant from Graaff-Reinet, Cradock, Colesberg, Steynsburg and Richmond. The town attained municipal status in 1913.

DUTCH REFORMED CHURCH (MEINTJIES STREET)

This neogothic church building was erected in the years 1861–1862, soon after the Reformed Church was established in 1859. It is the oldest Reformed Church building in the Eastern Cape.

HAYSTEAD AND FORD BUILDING
(7 MARKET STREET)

This building was erected c.1910 during a boom in Middelburg, shortly after the Anglo-Boer War (1899–1902), when between 12 000 and 15 000 British soldiers were stationed here. A partnership between C Haystead and 'Jack' Ford formed around 1906. The building is one of the few local commercial sites from the period to have remained virtually intact.

KAREL THERON SCHOOL (VICTORIA STREET)

The foundation stone of the original section of this school was laid by Sir Walter Hely-Hutchinson, the then Governor of the Cape Colony, on 8 November 1907. This school opened its doors in November 1908. The original section consists of a facebrick building with a gabled entrance portico and a corrugated-iron roof, and is of a predominantly Georgian design.

OLD OFFICERS' MESS (HUIS KAROO)
AND PW VORSTER MUSEUM
(GROOTFONTEIN AGRICULTURAL COLLEGE)

The original Grootfontein homestead was built by Nicolaas van der Walt in 1827. A British garrison was stationed here from 1903 to 1909 after the Anglo-Boer War, numbering 7 000 cavalry and artillery, and 2 000 horses. The old officers' mess is a Victorian building comprising 20 rooms.

After the troops were gradually dismissed from 1908 onwards, the Union Government took over the farm in 1910. Grootfontein Agricultural School was opened in 1911 by FS Malan, the then Minister of Agriculture, and attained college status in 1952.

MKAMBATI

MKAMBATI PONDOLAND COCONUT PALMS
(MKAMBATI GAME RESERVE)

Discovered by Charles Ross in 1910, this is one of four palm species indigenous to South Africa. The *Jubaeopsis caffra* (consisting of a single species) only occurs in Pondoland. These palms grow to a height of about six metres, while the fruit is almost spherical and has no 'milk'.

MOLTENO

The town was laid out in 1874 and named after Sir John Charles Molteno (1814–1886), first Prime Minister of the Cape Colony (1871–1878). It was established because coal was discovered in the area; old coal mining sites can still be seen in the district. It attained municipal status in 1883.

OLD MAGISTRATE'S COURT BUILDING AND CLOCK TOWER (SMITH STREET)

This late Victorian sandstone building originally housed the post office until 1937. The clock and bell tower was erected in memory of Queen Victoria and was inaugurated on 10 September 1903 by the Governor of the Cape, Sir Walter Hely-Hutchinson. The tower received recognition countrywide when it was used by the chemist and photographer, A Lomax, as the registered trademark for his medicines.

PEARSTON

Laid out on the farm Rustenburg in 1859, the town was named after John Pears, Dutch Reformed minister at Somerset East and the first relieving minister of Pearston. Pearston attained municipal status in 1894.

CARL E FROELICH'S SHOP BUILDING (58 VOORTREKKER STREET)

This historic shop building, with its predominant Victorian features, was erected by CE Froëlich in 1894. It forms an integral part of the architectural character of Voortrekker Street, as well as the core of Pearston, and still displays old articles such as a typewriter, money drawer/register and spittle basins.

OLD DROSTDY BUILDING, INCLUSIVE OF THE OLD WATER MILL AND DAM (RAWSON STREET)

This property originally formed part of that portion of the farm Rustenburg that was purchased from Casper Lotter in 1859 by the Dutch Reformed Church.

The double-storey, windmill and dam date from the same period and were presumably originally part of a farmstead. The property was purchased in 1921 by the state as a residency for the local Magistrate and was donated to the Municipality of Pearston for museum purposes in 1984.

PEDDIE

The town developed around Fort Peddie, a frontier post established in 1835. It was named after Lieutenant-Colonel John Peddie, who led the 72nd Highlanders in the Sixth Frontier War (1834–1835) against the Xhosa. The town attained municipal status in 1905.

HISTORIC CAVALRY BARRACKS AND STABLES

This military building complex was erected in 1840 and, until 1862, served as an important centre for, *inter alia*, the Cape Mounted Riflemen and the Dragoon Guards (7th Regiment) during the Seventh Frontier War (1846–1847). Thereafter, some of the military buildings were used as the Residency until about 1900 when a new Residency was built. A part of the barracks was used as a Postmaster's house at one stage.

WATCHTOWER (ON RIDGE OVERLOOKING PEDDIE)

This square, double-storey stone watchtower was built in 1841. Watchtowers were part of a system of forts on the Eastern Cape frontier, although they were mostly signal towers for sending signals by means of bonfires to other watchtowers to ward off attacks. This tower was fairly large and intended for defence.

PORT ALFRED

The town was founded in 1825 and was originally named Port Frances. In 1860 it was renamed Port Alfred in honour of Queen Victoria's second son, Prince Alfred. The town attained municipal status in 1894.

HISTORIC OLD RAILWAY STATION

This station building, which dates from the early 1880s, was presumably erected by George Pauling, a local Railway Engineer, for the firm R Firbank & Company, to whom the building contract was granted. The building is not only closely associated with the history of the Kowie Railway Company and its successor, The Kowie Railway Syndicate, but also forms an integral part of the present railway system between Port Alfred and Grahamstown.

SETTLERS METHODIST CHURCH (BATHURST STREET)

The original Settlers Church on this site was built in 1823 at the instigation of Reverend William Shaw. It was constructed of stone with a clay floor, thatched roof and clay pulpit. It was destroyed by fire in 1846 during the War of the Axe and thereafter rebuilt. In 1925 a committee was formed to raise funds for the restoration of the church, which was completed in 1938.

WHITE GABLES DWELLING (15 PARK STREET)

This early Victorian dwelling, with its impressive triangular front gables, dates from the 1830s and was erected by Captain Thomas Cowderoy. Two murals in the billiard room are also noteworthy.

PORT ELIZABETH

The city grew around Fort Frederick, a military station established in 1799, but rapid development only occurred with the arrival of the 1820 Settlers. It was named Port Elizabeth in 1820 by Sir Rufane Donkin (1772–1841), Acting Governor of the Cape, after his wife Elizabeth Frances, who had died two years previously in India. Port Elizabeth attained municipal status in 1868 and became a city in July 1913.

ATHENAEUM (BELMONT TERRACE)

This late Victorian building, with impressive neoclassical elements, was designed by George William Smith. It comprises two sections that were opened in 1896 and 1901.

CASTLE HILL MUSEUM (FIRST HOUSE) (CASTLE HILL)

The house, 7 Castle Hill, was built in 1825 for the Reverend Francis McCleland, first Colonial Chaplain in Port Elizabeth. It is an excellent example of an early nineteenth-century townhouse in the Eastern Cape, among the earliest substantial buildings to be erected at Algoa Bay and evidently the oldest dwelling. It houses an antique collection and memorabilia of furniture, porcelain, silver and paintings.

CITY HALL (MARKET SQUARE)

This impressive City Hall was completed in about 1862, although the clock tower was only added in 1883. Its neoclassical style impressed many travellers and writers in the nineteenth century and is today still regarded as one of the most imposing buildings of its kind in South Africa. It was gutted by fire in 1977, leading to an ambitious restoration programme.

CORA TERRACE (1, 3, 5, 7, 9, 11, 13)

These houses in Cora Terrace are outstanding examples of Victorian architecture, contributing to the traditional aspect of this particular section of Port Elizabeth. They are situated on land granted in 1831 to Henry Watson Henderson, who was later killed in the Sixth Frontier War in 1834. His widow married Joseph Smith and these houses, with curved pane tops, were built from 1856 onwards. Cora Terrace was named after Joseph and Elizabeth Smith's daughter, who died at sea in 1861.

DONKIN RESERVE (WHITES ROAD)

This open area was established by Sir Rufane Donkin as a shrine to his late wife. The inscription on the pyramid reads: 'One of the most perfect human beings, who has given her name to the City below, who is mourned by the husband whose heart is still wrung by undiminished grief.'

DONKIN STREET VICTORIAN TERRACED HOUSES
(31, 33, 34, 35, 37, 39, 41, 45, 47, 49, 51, 53, 55)

These houses, built between 1860 and 1880, are integrated as a single unit, yet each house is lower than the preceding one. The whole street has been declared a National Monument.

DOUBLE-STOREY LATE-VICTORIAN SEMIDETACHED HOUSES (38, 40, 42, 44, 46, 48, 50, 52, 54, 56, 58 NEWINGTON ROAD)

These houses form part of a unique terrace consisting of a row of identical late-Victorian double-storey, semidetached houses that were erected at the turn of the nineteenth century and have since remained unaltered.

DOUBLE-STOREY SEMIDETACHED HOUSES
(21, 23, 25, 27 DONKIN STREET; 14 CONSTITUTION STREET; 8, 10 WHITLOCK STREET)

These houses, with their Victorian and Georgian features, were erected shortly after the turn of the nineteenth century. Those in Donkin Street, opposite the Donkin Reserve, form part of a unique row of terrace houses in Victorian style.

DOUBLE-STOREY VICTORIAN SEMIDETACHED HOUSES (8–10 BIRD STREET)

These Victorian houses date from the 1860s. Their whitewashed wooden trelliswork and verandahs supported by cast-iron columns form an impressive façade.

FEATHERMARKET HALL BUILDING (BAAKENS STREET)

This hall, incorporating the original plan by Sir Wolfe-Barry of London in the later plans of architect WH Miles, was erected during 1883–1885. Ever since it was opened on 10 December 1885 by the Governor, Sir Hercules Robinson, as auction premises and a storage facility for the ostrich feather industry, the building has played an important role in the commercial and cultural history of the city.

FLEMING HOUSE (20 BIRD STREET)

The site incorporates the original section of the Manor House, together with the garden and boundary wall fronting onto Bird Street. It was built in 1851 by William Fleming in the Regency style with a verandah showing Chinese influence. The interior features a remarkable cast-iron spiral staircase.

FORT FREDERICK (BELMOST TERRACE)

Built in 1799 and named after The Duke of York, this fort was built by troops sent to Algoa Bay to prevent a possible landing of French troops to assist the Graaff-Reinet rebels during their dispute with the Cape Colony. The fort contains a powder magazine and a guardhouse, which was originally defended by eight 12-pounder guns.

HOLY TRINITY ANGLICAN CHURCH AND CHURCH HALL (HAVELOCK STREET)

Built in 1866, this Anglican church is a good example of the neogothic revivalist style. It was built from stone and has a slate roof. The present church is a restored and enlarged version of the original building, which was destroyed in part by a fire in 1897. The church hall has the same basic design as the church, although it is older.

HORSE MEMORIAL AND GRANITE PLINTH (JUNCTION OF CAPE AND RUSSELL ROADS)

The Horse Memorial consists of life-sized bronze figures of a horse about to quench its thirst from a bucket held by a kneeling soldier. The inscribed granite plinth on which it stands incorporates a drinking trough at the base. This memorial, designed by Joseph Whitehead and cast in bronze by Thames Dillon Works, Surrey, England, was unveiled on 11 February 1905 by the Mayor of Port Elizabeth, Mr Alexander Fettes. The monument commemorates the horses that suffered and died during the Anglo-Boer War (1899–1902).

JEWISH PIONEERS MEMORIAL SYNAGOGUE (RALEIGH STREET)

Designed by architect Orlando Middleton, this is a fine example of Art Nouveau-inspired architecture. It was constructed by Jacob Kohler & Sons and is the oldest surviving synagogue in Port Elizabeth. The synagogue was consecrated on 11 December 1912 by the then Chief Rabbi, Dr JL Landau.

MARKET SQUARE

This square forms an important part of the historic centre of Port Elizabeth.

MEMORIAL CAMPANILE (JETTY STREET)

Situated at the original harbour entrance, this brick structure was completed in 1923 to commemorate the landing of the 1820 Settlers.

MIRACLE CANNON (KING GEORGE VI ART GALLERY, 1 PARK DRIVE)

This bronze land cannon, now known as the Miracle Cannon, was salvaged from the wreck of the Portuguese galleon *Sacramento*, near Cape Recife.

OLD DWELLING SECTION OF THE SHARLEY CRIBB NURSING COLLETE (58 PARK DRIVE)

Plans for this two-storey home were submitted in February 1897 by Alfred Smith. The architect was George William Smith and the builder, Lennox Mackay. In 1908 the Smith family returned to England, and in 1923 the house became the Park Hotel.

This hotel was described in 1930 by an advertisement as 'South Africa's newest and most up-to-date hotel'. In 1949 the property was purchased by the Cape Provincial Administration and became a nurses' home, library and administrative office for the training college. The house retains its original fabric and is most characteristic of the period in which it was built.

OLD ERICA GIRLS' SCHOOL BUILDING (RICHMOND HILL)

Designed by the architect W White-Cooper and built by HJ Beckett in typically Dutch-style architecture with Art Nouveau decorations, the building was officially opened by the Superintendent General of Education, Dr Thomas Muir on 4 November 1903.

OLD GREY INSTITUTE RECTOR'S HOUSE AND HALL (BELMONT TERRACE)

The establishment of the Grey Institute is closely associated with the introduction of organised education in the Cape Province under the administration of Sir George Grey. The buildings are in neogothic style and form an essential part of the appearance and character of the historic core of Port Elizabeth.

OLD HARBOUR BOARD BUILDING (STRAND STREET)

The Harbour Board building, also known as the White House, is proclaimed on account of its outstanding Art Nouveau architecture. It was erected in 1904.

OLD POST OFFICE (FLEMING STREET)

This impressive building, reminiscent of a Rhineland castle, was designed in 1897 by HS Greaves of the Public Works Department of the Cape Colonial Government and was erected by J Kohler & Sons. Although only fully completed in 1902, it was opened to the public on 25 June 1900. With its prominent tower of 41.45m, it forms an integral part of the architectural environment around Market Square, which is the most significant open space in the Port Elizabeth city centre.

OPERA HOUSE (DONKIN STREET)

This building in late-Renaissance style based broadly on the Doric Order, was designed in 1891 by GW Smith, a prominent Port Elizabeth architect. It was built by the firm Small & Morgan. The Opera House was opened on 1 December 1892 by the mayor, J McIlwraith, and councillors of Port Elizabeth.

PEARSON CONSERVATORY (ST GEORGE'S PARK)
This impressive conservatory, with its Victorian characteristics, was designed and erected by Boyd & Son of Paisley, Scotland. The dismantled intersections were transported to Port Elizabeth and were re-erected under the supervision of Mr Fraser of Boyd's. The building was officially opened by John X Merriman on 12 September 1882, and is named after HW Pearson, Mayor of Port Elizabeth.

PRINCE ALFRED'S GUARD, DRILL HALL (PROSPECT HILL)
Opened in 1880, this historic building has been the headquarters of the Prince Alfred's Guard ever since, and is now also a museum. Unlike other South African units which, until the proclamation of the Republic, may have had bestowed upon them titles linked with royalty, the designation 'Prince Alfred's Guard' sprang from a duty performed by the unit when it provided a special escort for Prince Alfred during his visit to Port Elizabeth in 1860.

PRINCE ALFRED'S GUARD MEMORIAL (ST GEORGE'S PARK)
The memorial is one of the largest and heaviest architectural products in the Victorian idiom, and was manufactured by the Saracen Foundry of Walter MacFarlane, Glasgow, Scotland.

The structure is a fitting tribute to the memory of the officers and men who made the supreme sacrifice in the Ninth Frontier War (1877), War of the Guns (1880–1881), Langeberg (Bechuanaland) Campaign (1897) and the Anglo-Boer War (1899–1902). In the First World War they saw no active service as a regiment, but many served as volunteers in other units. In the Second World War they left for Egypt as a regiment of the 11th Armoured Brigade in the 6th South African Armoured Division.

PUBLIC LIBRARY (GOVAN MBEKI STREET)
The erection of this library was made possible by a donation from the Estate of William Savage and a subsidy from the Colonial Government. The building was designed by William Cheers and was officially opened on 29 July 1902. The style of the library is late Victorian and is a mixture of Gothic and classic characteristics.

ROBIN HILL COTTAGE (1 HARRIS STREET)
The original title deed of this single-storey wood-and-iron building, with four end gables, was issued on 18 December 1878 in favour of Maryanne Davidson. The house remained in the Davidson family for 110 years and is one of the few perfectly preserved Victorian cottages still in existence in Port Elizabeth.

STERLEY COTTAGES (10 AND 12 CASTLE HILL)
These typical Settler cottages date from about 1840 and were originally the properties of Constable Sterley. Together with the adjacent historic house at 7 Castle Hill, these buildings form an interesting architectural complex.

TS LANHERNE BUILDING (HUMEWOOD ROAD)
This impressive Victorian house was erected in 1894 for RH Hammersley-Heenen, Resident Engineer and General Manager of the railways. During the Second World War it served as a convalescent home for soldiers, sailors and airmen. In 1960 it was sold to the Municipality of Port Elizabeth, which in 1967 leased the property to the International Youth Hostel Association. In 1979 the Naval Cadet Corps took over the base. The majestic Norfolk pines alongside the building were cultivated from seeds obtained from the Canary Islands.

TWO HISTORIC TIMBER COTTAGES
(49 HAVELOCK STREET)
These two timber cottages were built in 1856 by John Wood, a carpenter, on the Grey Institute quitrent land.

WEGSPRINGHUIS, ALSO KNOWN AS HILLSIDE HOUSE (14 BIRD STREET)
A Victorian building dating from the early nineteenth century, this property was granted to George Daniel Diesel in 1824.

WINDY RIDGE (24 NEWINGTON ROAD)
This is one of the best examples of authentic Victorian architecture in Port Elizabeth, and typical of townhouses built in the 1880s.

QUEENSTOWN

The town was founded by Sir George Cathcart in 1853 and named after Queen Victoria of England. It attained municipal status in 1855.

FAÇADE OF TOWN HALL (CATHCART ROAD)
This sandstone building was designed by the architect Sidney Stent and was erected by the building contractors Male & Kirton. The cornerstone was laid on 24 May 1882 by the wife of Mayor DS Barrable.

HEXAGON
The Hexagon, with its six streets radiating outwards from the centre of Queenstown, was designed as a defence measure, to provide a clear firing line and easy access. It has remained the focal point of the town plan.
  The idea of this hexagon-shaped plan originated with Commander TH Bowker, whose memorandum on the granting of farms and the establishment of Queenstown was accepted in 1853 by Sir George Cathcart, then Governor of the Cape.

OLD MUNICIPAL MARKET BUILDING
(4 ZEILER STREET)
One of the oldest buildings in Queenstown, the market was built shortly after the erf was purchased by W Wright for that purpose, and continued to be used as such until 1983.

QUEEN'S COLLEGE (HISTORIC PORTIONS)
(BERRY STREET)
The original part of this school was designed in 1897 and the cornerstone of the main entrance was laid on 15 September 1897. Queen's College was extended in 1914, 1919 and 1920.

QUEENSTOWN FRONTIER MUSEUM
(NAUDE STREET)
This museum, originally erected in 1868 as a primary school, is an outstanding example of a Victorian school building.

RHODES

Formerly named Rossville after the Reverend David Ross (1863–1908), a Dutch Reformed minister stationed at Lady Grey for the whole of his active life, the small town was renamed after Cecil John Rhodes (1853–1902). The latter had an avenue of pine trees planted in the main street.

OLD PRIMARY SCHOOL BUILDING
(VISSER STREET)
This U-shaped school building, with its Cape Dutch elements, is built of local dolerite stone. In 1970 the school was closed and the property was sold in 1986.

RIEBEECK EAST

Founded on the farm Mooi Meisjes Fontein in 1842, this small town was named after Jan van Riebeeck (1619–1677), first Dutch Commander at the Cape.

MOOIMEISIEFONTEIN (DISTRICT)
This farm was the home of Voortrekker leader Piet Retief from 1814–1836. He sold half of the farm in 1829, and this was where Riebeeck East was established.

SALEM

The town was founded as a settlement of the Sephton party of 1820 Settlers. Its biblical name was taken from Psalm 76, and means peace, in commemoration of the settling of a feud between religious sects.

CHURCHES OF 1832 AND 1850 (MISSION VILLAGE)
The cornerstone of the first church was laid on 1 January 1822 and inauguration took place on 31 December 1824. It was demolished in 1832. The neogothic replacement's cornerstone was laid on 18 July 1850. The church is closely associated with the 1820 Settlers, as well as the role of Methodism in South Africa.

HISTORIC HOMESTEAD (FARM DEVONSHIRE)
This is a single-storey Settler-type farmhouse built in 1832 by Richard Gush on the original allotments granted to Hezekiah Sephton, leader of the Salem party of 1820 Settlers.

UPPPER CROFT DWELLING
A Georgian double-storey, the house was built c.1832 by William Carey Hobson, a British Settler, and was part of his estate until 1913. It was occupied by Samuel Best Shaw, principal of the Salem Academy (1856-1863) and is one of the oldest Settler homes in the district.

SEYMOUR

Established in 1853 and named after Lieutenant-Colonel Charles Seymour, Sir George Cathcart's military secretary, Seymour was originally the military post, Eland's Post.

SUNDIAL (THE RESIDENCE)
The sandstone sundial was erected by D Cross on the site of Eland's Post in 1839. A section of the fort was converted into a residency for the local Magistrate. The sundial was presented to the Port Elizabeth Museum in 1922 but was returned to Seymour in 1933. It is mounted on a stone pedestal, with the dial protected from the elements by a thick sheet of glass.

SIDBURY

Sidbury Park was one of the earliest and most prosperous sheep farms, originally called Soetemelksfontein. It was founded by Lieutenant Richard Daniell, RN, and named after his home in England.

ST PETER'S ANGLICAN CHURCH (DISTRICT)
The cornerstone of this building was laid by Colonel John Hare, acting Lieutenant-Governor of the Cape, on 31 October 1838. The church, with its neogothic and neoclassical characteristics, was erected by a certain Sandford of Grahamstown and the first services were held on 5 May 1841, even though the building had not been completed. It served as shelter for the local congregation during the Seventh (1846–1847) and Eighth (1850–1853) Frontier Wars. Many well-known Settler names appear on the headstones in the churchyard.

SOMERSET EAST

Laid out on the farm Somerset and founded in 1825, the town was named after Lord Charles Henry Somerset (1767–1831), Governor of the Cape Colony from 1814–1826. The town attained municipal status in 1837.

154 CHARLES STREET
This property, which was granted to J van Dyk on 1 September 1825, was one of the first lots

to be allocated immediately after the founding of Somerset East on Lord Charles Somerset's old experimental farm. The historic buildings date from the early 1830s.

DUTCH REFORMED CHURCH (NEW STREET)
The enlargement of this church, the original sections of which date from the 1830s, was planned by Charles Otto Häger in 1870. Consecrated on 17 November 1871, the rebuilt church is predominantly neogothic in style.

GILL COLLEGE (NEW STREET)
The property comprises the original College building built in 1869 (library), College House built in 1892 (the senior boys' hostel) and the Old Bellevue Seminary (girls' high school). The college was established in 1869 through a bequest of Dr William Gill (1795–1863) as a high school and university training centre for boys. It was originally intended as a university for the Eastern Cape but, owing to strong opposition from the newly formed Rhodes University College, it was unable to meet the regulation that limited university college status to institutions with over 75 matriculated pupils. In 1903 it became a high school only. Gill College was one of the first institutions of higher education to admit women. However, in 1928 it once again became a boys' school until the amalgamation with Bellevue Girls' High School in 1965, becoming coeducational once more.

HISTORIC DWELLINGS (36, 38, 41 PAULET STREET)
These three properties granted to Jan Jonathan Durandt, William MacDonald MacKay and Robert Robinson respectively, were three of the first lots to be allocated immediately after the founding of Somerset East. The buildings on the properties date from 1825–1830. Also of interest is the fact that William MacDonald Mackay was the first and only Landdrost of Somerset East.

HISTORIC GEORGIAN DWELLING (89 PAULET STREET)
The core of this house, which is predominantly in the Georgian style, presumably formed part of the original homestead of Somerset's experimental farm that was divided in 1825, and that formed the centre of the present town of Somerset East. The house is one of the oldest buildings in the area.

HOPE CONGREGATIONAL CHURCH AND PARSONAGE
(CNR PAULET AND BEAUFORT STREETS)
The property on which this church complex is situated was bequeathed to the London Missionary Society in 1842 by Dorothy Edwards, widow of Reverend John Evans of Cradock. The Victorian parsonage dates from 1825–1830 and the neogothic church was erected in 1844.

OLD OFFICERS' MESS (45 PAULET STREET)
This Georgian double-storey building was originally erected in 1815 by Lord Charles Somerset for officers and men who were stationed on the eastern frontier. Later it became the Battis Private Hotel and then the Battis family home until 1917. It is now the Walter Battis Art Gallery.

OLD PARSONAGE (BEAUFORT STREET)
Now the Somerset East Museum, this double-storey Georgian building was built c.1820, and served as headquarters for the Somerset Experimental Farm. From 1825–1829 it became the Drostdy, after which it was transferred to the Wesleyan Church. From 1834–1944 the property belonged to the Dutch Reformed Church and was used as a parsonage.

STEYNSBURG

The town developed around the Dutch Reformed church, which was built in 1872.

Steynsburg was named after Douwe Gerbrandt Steyn, grandfather of President Paul Kruger. A village management board was created in 1874.

PIONEER HOUSE (FARM BULHOEK)
This pioneer house is one of the best existing examples of a typical 'trekboer' house, and dates from 1817. Elsie Steyn, President Kruger's mother, grew up on this farm.

STEYTLERVILLE

The town was founded on the farm Doorspoort in 1876 and was named after Reverend Abraham Isaac Steytler (1840–1922), minister of the Dutch Reformed Church and Moderator of the Cape Synod (1909–1915). It attained municipal status in 1891. Steytlerville is a 'dry' town, ie no liquor may be sold there.

DUTCH REFORMED CHURCH
(SAREL CILLIERS STREET)
Designed by the architect FW Hesse and constructed by HH Moon & Ledbury of Cape Town, the church is situated on the original town square. It is a prominent landmark and is still in its original state. This neogothic church building was inaugurated on 30 May 1907.

STUTTERHEIM

The town was established in 1857 around the Bethel Mission Station and was named after Major-General Baron Carl Gustav Richard von Stutterheim (1815–1871), Commander of the British-German Legion. It attained municipal status in 1879.

BARON VON STUTTERHEIM MILL
This double-storey stone building, known as Baron von Stutterheim Mill, was erected by HJ Adkins, official contractor of the British-German Legion Military Settlers, during the years 1860–1861, on the instruction of Major-General Baron Richard von Stutterheim.

CHURCH AND MANSE OF MGWALI MISSION STATION (DISTRICT)
Mgwali Mission, unique in the annals of African missionary endeavour, was the first mission station in the nineteenth century to be governed by an African. The early buildings were erected in 1857 but a new complex was added in the 1880s. The latter includes a boarding house, a magnificent example of late Victorian educational architecture. The manse has retained the original fireplaces in the dining room and bedroom and the kitchen has its original range and Dutch oven. The church is a large, rectangular, neoclassical ediface with a portico and rear extension. The original pulpit remains. There are commemorative plaques in Xhosa to Reverend Tiro Soga, who first translated the Bible into Xhosa.

Mgwali remains a testimony to Reverend Soga, a remarkable man with many firsts to his name. He was the first African to be awarded a degree, the first to be ordained a minister in a Protestant church, the first African missionary in South Africa and the first Xhosa hymnologist. He was also a well-known journalist and pioneer of the African Nationalist Movement. Educated at Lovedale, he furthered his studies in Glasgow and Edinburgh, where he trained for the ministry. There he married a Scottish woman, Janet Burnside, and brought her back to South Africa.

FORTIFIED HOUSE (GANGERS' COTTAGE NO 17)
(EAST LONDON AND QUEENSTOWN RAILWAY)
This fortified house is one of the only remaining examples of a series of similar structures that were built during the Ninth Frontier War (1877–1878) to protect the railway line between East London and Touws River.

TARKASTAD

Laid out on the farm Boschfontein in 1862, Tarkastad was named after the Tarka River. The town attained municipal status in 1883.

OLD DUTCH REFORMED CHURCH PARSONAGE
(17 GREY STREET)
This parsonage was built in 1864, soon after the arrival of the Reverend JGS de Villiers, the first Minister of Tarkastad. This double-storey building has a unique wrought-iron verandah.

UITENHAGE

Founded on the loan farm of Elizabeth Scheepers, Uitenhage was named, in honour of JA Uitenhage de Mist (1749–1823), Commissioner-General from 1803–1804 by the Governor, JW Janssens. The town attained municipal status in 1841.

BLENHEIM HOUSE (4 BAIRD STREET)
This imposing dwelling, with its Cape Dutch features, was originally erected in 1815 as a single-storey building. In 1903 an upper storey and a wood-decorated verandah were added.

CAPE DUTCH HOMESTEAD (34 CUYLER STREET)
Uitenhage has three remaining Cape Dutch houses, two of which are in Cuyler Street. Erected in 1817, there was great concern when the neighbouring house was demolished and a garage erected on the site. This house then became environmentally more important and in 1988 was declared a Provisional National Monument to secure its existence.

CUYLER MANOR HOMESTEAD (DISTRICT)
The site incorporates the section of the original Cuyler Manor farm with the historic dwelling, as well as the visitors' house, coach house, wagon house and mill house. This predominantly Cape Dutch-style homestead was erected in 1814 by Colonel Jacob Glen Cuyler, Landdrost of Uitenhage, who was closely associated with the settlement of the British Settlers in 1820.

DUTCH REFORMED CHURCH HALL
(112 CALEDON STREET)
This fine building was designed in 1818, but was only completed in 1843. It served as the Dutch Reformed church until 1927, when it became the church hall.

DWELLING HOUSE (21 CUYLER STREET)
The original part of this rectangular house, with its straight end gables, dates from about 1840, and the rear of the building was added in 1880. With Cape Dutch and Georgian elements, it is one of the oldest dwellings in Uitenhage.

MUIR COLLEGE BOYS' PRIMARY SCHOOL
(PARK AVENUE)
Built in the late nineteenth century, the original section of Muir College was designed by William White-Cooper, a prominent architect of the region who earned a reputation as a designer of institutional buildings. It is of great architectural value as it is the only example of his work. Together with the Edward VII post box in the grounds, it forms an integral part of the architectural and historic character of the area.

NEOCLASSICAL FAÇADE OF THE ORIGINAL OLD TOWN HALL (25 MARKET STREET)
Designed by the architect Richard Wright and constructed by the builders Grant & Downie, the original Town Hall's cornerstone was laid on 11 April 1881 by Mayor Edward Dobson, and it was officially opened on 7 August 1882. The cornerstones of two new municipal buildings were laid on either side of the Town Hall on 1 July 1952, and the rear portion of the Town Hall rebuilt. The new complex, incorporating the façade of the original Town Hall, was officially opened on 2 December 1955.

OLD DROSTDY (50 CALEDON STREET)
The designer of the Drostdy building was the architect ML Thibault. Construction started in 1804 and was completed in 1810. Today the Drostdy forms part of Uitenhage's historic core.

OLD MAGISTRATES OFFICE BUILDING COMPLEX (CALEDON STREET)
This building, with its impressive blend of facebrick and plaster with elaborate detailing, was designed by RE Wight and built in 1897 to accommodate the court house and post office. The dominant feature of the building is a massive clock tower, named the Victoria Tower in honour of Queen Victoria's Diamond Jubilee.

OLD RAILWAY STATION (MARKET STREET)
This railway station, which was erected in 1875, is the original terminus building of one of the earliest railway lines in South Africa. The double-storey Gothic-style structure has always been known as the Doll's House. The railway station closed down in 1951.

SCHEEPERS HOUSE (11–13 CUYLER STREET)
This property was registered in the name of GS Scheepers in 1815. He was the son of Gert Scheepers, on whose farm the town of Uitenhage was established. The house was built by CM Luyt, Scheepers' son-in-law.

SETTLER COTTAGE (23 CUYLER STREET)
The land on which this cottage stands was originally granted to Joshua Norton in 1826. This elongated cottage, with its two end gables, was presumably erected shortly thereafter. This area incorporates some of the town's oldest surviving residential structures.

SITE OF ANGLO-BOER WAR CONCENTRATION CAMP
This site was in use from April to October 1902, and was one of the last of about 50 concentration camps that were established during the Anglo-Boer War by the British. Mainly women and children from the Free State were housed here in corrugated-iron houses. What was probably the house of the Camp Superintendent, other material remains and the graveyard still exist today.

VENTERSTAD

The town was laid out in 1875 and was named after the owner of the land on which it was established, Johannes JT Venter. It attained municipal status in 1895.

DUTCH REFORMED CHURCH (16–18 VAN WYK STREET)
The Gereformeerde congregation at Venterstad was established on 26 June 1875 and this rectangular church building in the neogothic style was taken into use on 13 March 1877. The town developed from the congregation and was originally managed from the church. The first Gereformeerde mission action in South Africa had its origin here as well.

NORTHERN CAPE

The largest region in geographical terms, the Northern Cape covers 30 per cent of South Africa, stretching from the Namaqualand seaboard in the west to Kimberley in the north-central part of the country. Much of the region's history revolves around the discovery of copper and diamonds. However, the Northern Cape remains the least developed region in South Africa.

BARKLY WEST

This town was originally established in 1869 as a camp for alluvial-diamond diggers and was known as Klipdrift, but was renamed Barkly West in 1870 after Governor Sir Henry Barkly. During the Anglo-Boer War (1899–1902) the town was occupied by Boer forces for four months, and was temporarily renamed Nieuw Boshof. It attained municipal status in 1881.

BRIDGE AND TOLL HOUSE OVER VAAL RIVER

Built in the last quarter of the nineteenth century as a private undertaking, this bridge and toll house played an important part in the development of the region beyond the Vaal River. The bridge was designed by James Ford and built by Fairbank, Panling & Co. of London, while the steelwork was executed by Westwood Bailie & Co. and transported by ox-wagon from Colesberg.

The Vaal River Bridge was opened on 24 June 1885 by the wife of James Hill, a senior member of the Cape Legislative Assembly for Barkly West. In 1938 when the commemorative ox-wagon trek passed this way, it was renamed Magrieta Prinsloo Bridge.

CANTEEN KOPJE NATURE RESERVE

In 1867 after the first diamond had been found in Hopetown, others were found along the Vaal River. By 1869 alluvial-diamond-bearing gravels were discovered at Canteen Kopje, and in 1870 a dispute arose over the ownership of the diamond diggings. One of the interested parties, England, appointed John Campbell as Magistrate. In effect, he represented British administration in the area that was to become known as Griqualand West.

Canteen Kopje also yields evidence of prehistoric man's occupation. Early Stone Age implements have been discovered, together with fossilised remains of numerous animals.

DUTCH REFORMED CHURCH (MOLTENO STREET)

The foundation stone of this church was laid by the Reverend FWR Gie on 15 December 1906. Designed in free-Renaissance style, the completed sandstone building was consecrated on 14 December 1907. Its original pulpit, benches, rafters and pressed-steel ceilings have remained intact.

OLD MAGISTRATE'S COURT
(CNR PRETORIUS AND CAMPBELL STREETS)

Built mainly of Ventersdorp lava and forming an integral part of the history of the old Republic of Klipdrift (now Barkly West), this court building was completed in 1897. The contractors were Messrs Grant & Downie.

ST MARY'S CHURCH

St Mary's church was the first permanent church building erected in the Klipdrift area after the discovery of diamonds here in 1869. The foundation stone was laid in February 1872 by Sir Henry Barkly, and the church was consecrated on 24 November 1872.

BRANDVLEI

Brandvlei attained municipal status in 1962.

DUTCH REFORMED CHURCH
The foundation stone of this neogothic church was laid on 15 July 1905. The building was completed and inaugurated at the end of 1905.

CALVINIA

Established on the farm Hoogekraal in 1851, Calvinia was named after the religious reformer, John Calvin (1509–1564). The town attained municipal status in 1904.

DUTCH REFORMED CHURCH (DORP STREET)
The foundation stone of this building was laid on 30 September 1899 and the church was inaugurated in November 1900. This imposing neogothic cruciform church, designed by John Gaisford, constitutes a vital architectural element in the historic centre of Calvinia.

DUTCH REFORMED CHURCH AND CHURCH SQUARE (NIEUWOUDTSVILLE DISTRICT)
The location of this church, with its long, axial entrance avenue, is one of a few 'nagmaal saamtrek' (communion gathering) places still remaining. Built in 1907 of dressed stone and symmetrically designed in neogothic style on a Greek-cross plan, the church has a large clock tower centrally placed over the entrance.

T-SHAPED DWELLING AND ADJACENT BUILDING (42–44 HOOP STREET)
The erf was transferred to Abraham van Wyk on 24 December 1853 and the original T-shaped Cape Dutch house was probably built by him. It was one of the gable houses built adjacent to the Dutch Reformed church, and is one of the few original houses left in Calvinia.

TOWN HOUSE AND ALL OUTBUILDINGS (63 WALTER STREET)
The elongated, rectangular mid-nineteenth-century dwelling with a T-shaped extension has an exterior timber staircase that provides access to a loft. This property was sold in 1990 and was converted into a guesthouse, and the 'nagmaalkamers' in the outbuildings are now used as guest accommodation.

CAMPBELL

The town was established by missionary George Bartlett of the London Missionary Society, and was first known as Knoffelvallei, and then Grootfontein. It was renamed Campbell after John Campbell (1766–1840), Director of the London Missionary Society, who inspected the society's stations in the Cape between 1812–1814.

MISSION STATION (DISTRICT)
This site was one of the earliest centres of Christianity north of the Vaal River, and was visited by such early travellers as William Burchell, John Campbell, George Thompson, Dr Andrew Smith and Dr David Livingstone.

CARNARVON

Carnarvon was laid out in 1860 on land belonging to the Rhenish Missionary Society. It was originally known as Harmsfontein and then Schietfontein, and was renamed in 1874 after Henry Howard Molyneux Herbert (1831–1890), the Earl of Carnarvon and British Colonial Secretary. The town attained municipal status in 1882.

CORBELLED HOUSE COMPLEX
(FARM T'KOKOBOOS)
The first T'Kokoboos corbelled hut was built in 1851. The name probably comes from the San name for a type of Karoo bush, which grows in the district. T'Kokoboos is one of only two dated corbelled sites in the district.

CORBELLED HOUSE COMPLEX (KONKA)
Including two huts and a dry-stone walled sheep kraal, the complex was built in three stages: the first structure is a rectangular hut, the second a circular hut and the third development was the incorporation of both corbelled structures into a mid-twentieth-century farmhouse.

CORBELLED HOUSES (STUURMANSFONTEIN)
Probably built in the 1850s, these peculiar corbelled houses are examples of the ingenuity of the first settlers in this area, and are important relics of the cultural and national architectural history of South Africa.

DAM WALL AND TOWER (VANWYKSVLEI DAM)
Vanwyksvlei dam was built between 1882 and 1885. The land surveyor, Garwood Alston, who surveyed the dam terrain, is presumed responsible for building the dam. With a length of 311m, a height of 9.7m and a high-water mark of 8.2m, the dam has a tower with five steel sluices on the water side. Two staircases (exterior and interior) provide access to the tower, and there is a bridge between the tower and the dam wall. Vanwyksvlei is one of the oldest of the large dams in South Africa, and is an excellent example of the engineering capability of an earlier age.

DUTCH REFORMED MISSION COMPLEX
(UNIE PLEIN)
The site consists of the present church building, old mission school, present parsonage, old parsonage and a pre-primary school.

The first church is still in use and celebrated its 150th year in 1997. During the Anglo-Boer War (1899–1902) the church was used as a military hospital.

KAROO-STYLE DWELLING (14 NEW STREET)
The property was originally granted on 22 February 1875 to PGM Jacobs, who was presumably responsible for the construction of this typical flat-roof Karoo-style house.

'SVENSKDO' (11 CHURCH STREET)
Situated opposite the Dutch Reformed church, this property was purchased by ED Adriaanse in 1863, and it can be assumed that he built the original Karoo-style house. There is a loft door with ladder and an 'abbakagel', a stable room and a coach house.

COLESBERG

Colesberg was established in 1830 as Toverberg, and was named after the nearby hill. Renamed after Sir Galbraith Lowry Cole (1772–1842), Governor of the Cape Colony (1828–1833), it attained municipal status in 1840.

BELL STREET HOUSES
(NOS. 303, 304, 305, 306, 307, 308, 310, AND REMAINDER OF ERF 330)
These square houses, representative of early Karoo-style architecture, have beautiful cornices and interesting fanlights above the doors.

CONISTON HOUSE (3 VENTERHOEK STREET)
Coniston House, a double-storey Georgian-style dwelling, was erected for Thomas Plewman in 1853 by Mason Marthinus Johannes Smit and carpenter Frederick Waldeck. Discussions held by Lord Loch and his entourage on the Second Swaziland Convention were held in the dining room.

DOUBLE-STOREY GEORGIAN DWELLING AND OUTBUILDINGS (3 D'URBAN ROW)

This property, with its double-storey Georgian house, forms an integral part of the historic core of Colesberg. The house dates from the 1830s, while the stables and rondavel-shaped building at the rear are presumably much older.

DOUBLE-STOREY WAREHOUSE (BELL STREET)

This square, double-storey warehouse is the only remaining example of its kind in Colesberg. Together with the other historic buildings in Bell Street, it forms a unique architectural and historic group.

DUTCH REFORMED CHURCH
(8 CHARL CELLIERS STREET)

The original church's foundation stone was laid by WC Rhyneveld, Civil Commissioner of Graaff-Reinet, on 29 November 1830, and the church was opened on 2 April 1832. Construction on a new church began in September 1861. The foundation stone was laid on 17 February 1864 and the church opened in August 1866. During 1925 and 1926, a church tower was added.

FLEETWOOD RAWSTONE HOUSE (NEW STREET)

Named after Fleetwood Rawstone, an ex-army officer who went to Colesberg with Adolph Albert Ortlepp in 1804, this property was transferred to Ortlepp in 1860, who sold it to James Murray, a farmer from Noupoort, in the same year. It is a single-storey Karoo-Georgian structure with a flat roof, cornice and parapet.

HISTORIC HORSE MILL
(COACH HOUSE, TOWN CENTRE)

Built by JD du Plessis in 1891 on the farm Sewefontein, the horse mill was donated by Annie van der Linde, a daughter of Du Plessis, to the Historical Society of Colesberg, after which it was dismantled and slowly rebuilt at the historic coach house in the town. Still operational, the mill has a teak wheel and is one of the few complete horse mills remaining in South Africa.

HISTORIC HOUSE (BELL STREET)

This house is representative of early Karoo architecture, and with the adjoining houses in Bell Street, forms an interesting historic group.

KEMPER MUSEUM (RHYNEVELDT SQUARE)

First the Colesberg Bank and later the Standard Bank, the building was completed in 1862. From 1939-1976 it housed the municipality, and currently houses the Kemper collection of Anglo-Boer War memorabilia, and fossils.

OLD HOMESTEAD AND THRESHING FLOOR
(FARM HEBRON)

The site includes the old part of the original house and 'stoep', but excludes the garage, a later addition. Hebron is one of the oldest farms in the area, and the old house is an outstanding example of vernacular architecture. The threshing floor is an interesting relic of its time.

CONCORDIA

Established in the early 1800s by the Rhenish Missionary Society, this small town was taken over by the Nederduitse Gereformeerde Mission in 1863. Concordia takes its name from the nearby copper mine discovered by Albert von Schlicht in 1940.

ORBICULE KOPPIE

This koppie of concentrated orbicules is of scientific value in the study of rock types in the earth's crust. The orbicules are typically dioritic with a pegmatitic matrix and show signs of indentation and flattening. The koppie outcrops in the Archaean Complex, Kheis System, and is possibly of metamorphosed origin.

DANIELSKUIL

A rich diamondiferous pipe was discovered by Thornton Fincham on the farm Brits, in 1960. This was later sold to De Beers Consolidated Mines and called Finsch Mine. There are also asbestos mines and a lime quarry in the vicinity.

ANGLO-BOER WAR BLOCKHOUSE
A dry-stone-walled circular blockhouse is the only remaining one of five such structures erected by the British garrison stationed there during the Anglo-Boer War (1899-1902) under the command of Captain George Cullum.

FIRST AND SECOND DUTCH REFORMED CHURCHES
The cornerstone of the first Nederduitse Gereformeerde church at Danielskuil was laid on 17 December 1894 and the building was consecrated in 1896. A rectangular stone church, with a vestry to one side, it was erected largely through the efforts of Johannes Roux of the farm Boplaas, and his brother-in-law, Jonas.

The Reverend Brink laid the cornerstone of the second, larger church on 13 October 1923. The builder was Mr Scribante of Olifantshoek, and building material was reportedly brought from Kimberley by ox-wagon. This church was replaced by a larger church in 1964. The original two neogothic stone churches are now used as church halls.

DE AAR

The town was laid out on the farm De Aar in 1902, and developed around the station that was established there in 1881. It attained municipal status in 1904.

OLIVE SCHREINER HOUSE (9 GRUNDLING STREET)
The well-known author Olive Schreiner (1855-1920) and her husband SC Cronwright-Schreiner lived in this house from 1908 to 1913. It was here that she completed her book *Women and Labour*, and wrote two articles for special occasions entitled, *Thoughts about Women*, and *Closer Union*.

ST PAUL'S CHURCH
(CNR ALIDA AND FRIEDLANDER STREETS)
This neogothic church was erected in 1894 and inaugurated on 3 July 1895 by Bishop Gibson of Cape Town. During the Anglo-Boer War (1899-1902) the church was mainly used by British troops.

FRASERBURG

The town was laid out in 1851 on the farm Rietfontein, and was named after Reverend Colin Fraser, President MT Steyn's father-in-law, and the elder, Gerrit Jacobus Meyburgh.

OLD DUTCH REFORMED CHURCH PARSONAGE
This house, with its predominantly Cape Dutch characteristics, was designed by the architect HJR Burnett and was completed in 1856.

OLD ST AUGUSTINE'S ANGLICAN CHURCH
Built in 1870, the church is now known as the Afrikaanse Protestante Kerk.

'PEPERBUS' (OR PEPPER-BOX)
The so-called Peperbus was built in 1861 by Adam Jacobs, according to a plan by the Reverend Bamberger. The building is architecturally interesting, with its hexagonal shape that gradually merges into a hexagonal dome and a bell tower.

GARIES

The village's name derives from a Hottentot word 'tharies', the name of a grass that grows in the valley.

ROCK FORMATION KNOWN AS THE 'LETTERKLIP'
This unique rock formation was fortified and occupied from 1901–1902 by the British forces during the Anglo-Boer War. Various regimental badges and officers' names are engraved on the rock face.

GORDONIA

Formerly known as Korannaland, this district was named after Sir Gordon Sprigg, who served four terms of office as Prime Minister of the Cape Colony between 1878 and 1892.

OLD MISSION CHURCH BUILDING (FARM RIETFONTEIN)
Building commenced on 13 October 1889 and was completed on 15 April 1890. The church was inaugurated on 1 May 1891 by the President of the Rhenish Missionary Society in South West Africa (now Namibia).

REBELLION TREE (FARM VANROOISVLEY)
It was under this camel thorn tree that General Manie Maritz openly declared rebellion against the government of South Africa on 9 October 1914.

GRIQUATOWN

The town was founded in 1802 as the London Missionary Society's mission station, Klaarwater. Renamed Griquatown by the Reverend John Campbell (1766–1840) in 1813, after the Griqua tribe that lived there, it attained municipal status in 1910.

MARY MOFFAT MUSEUM (MAIN ROAD)
This was previously the London Missionary Society mission station founded in 1803. Dr Robert Moffat visited Griquatown in 1821, and his daughter Mary (wife of David Livingstone) was born in this house.

MOFFAT'S PULPIT (NATIVE CHURCH)
Dr David Livingstone, Dr Robert Moffat and Andries Waterboer (Griqua leader) all preached from this pulpit. Made by Robert Moffat during his stay in Griquatown in 1820 when he stayed for a few months to assist Reverend H Helm while on his way to Kuruman, the pulpit is made of packing cases and local timber.

OLD RESIDENCY (MAIN STREET)
This dolomite building is said to have been erected by convicts from Kimberley in the 1880s. The first resident was JJ Christie, Resident Magistrate of Griquatown between 1880 and 1890. This is the oldest government building in the town.

HANOVER

Laid out on the farm Petrusvallei in 1854, the town was named after Hanover in Germany, from whence came the parents of Gert Gous, the owner of the farm. It attained municipal status in 1885.

CAMDEBOO HOUSE (4 RHYNEVELD STREET)
Currently used as a museum, Camdeboo House dates from the early eighteenth century and is presumed to have been the property, belonging to Gert Gous, on which Hanover was established. Although a corrugated-iron roof was added and the floor plan was changed considerably, the alterations haven't detracted from the character of the house. The building is an integral part of Hanover's historic nucleus.

CAPE DUTCH HOUSE (11 CHRISTOFFEL STREET)
Regarded as one of the most impressive houses in Hanover, this house was probably built in the early 1860s, when imported Oregon pine first became available in the Cape. The building has two Cape Dutch end gables – most unusual for this area.

DUTCH REFORMED CHURCH (CHURCH STREET)
Under the chairmanship of Dr Andrew Murray, the church authorities of Graaff-Reinet decided on 15 October 1856 to establish a parish at Hanover, and the first church was built in 1859. That was demolished in 1906 and the cornerstone of the new church was laid on 30 November 1906. It was taken into use in November 1908. Little has been altered in this neogothic cruciform-shaped church, and it is still painted in the original light-green shade. Noteworthy is the pulpit, which can seat 12 ministers simultaneously.

HERBERT

This district was named after the British Colonial Secretary, Henry Howard Molyneux Herbert, Earl of Carnarvon.

GLACIAL PAVEMENTS
(FARM BLAAUWBOSCHDRIFT AND BUCKLANDS)
Glacial pavements at Blaauwboschdrift and Bucklands, like those at Nooitgedacht in the Kimberley area, furnish evidence of a completed glacial cycle and isostatic movements that accompanied the glaciation and deglaciation of a continent and its adjacent seas.

HISTORIC ANGLO-BOER WAR BLOCKHOUSE
(RIET RIVER)
This blockhouse was erected by the Royal Engineers in 1901 on the south bank of the Riet River to secure the rail bridge and drift across the nearby Modder River. The name of the Prince of Wales' Leinster Regiment (Royal Canadians), which was stationed here from December 1901, still appears on the walls.

HOPETOWN

The town was founded on the farm Duvenaarsfontein in 1854, and was named after the Auditor-General and Acting Secretary of the Cape, Major William Hope. It attained municipal status in 1858.

OLD WAGON BRIDGE (OVER ORANGE RIVER)
Manufactured by Bailie & Company in Scotland and shipped to Cape Town, the wagon bridge was taken to Hopetown by rail and ox-wagon, and erected in 1878. It was of strategic importance during the Anglo-Boer War.

RUINS OF JACOBS' HOUSE (FARM DE KALK)
In 1867 Schalk van Niekerk noticed the 'pretty stone' found by young Erasmus Jacobs and used by children as a plaything. It proved to be the first authenticated diamond found in South Africa, and became known as the Eureka. It was purchased by De Beers Consolidated Mines in 1966 and presented to Parliament.

KAKAMAS

An irrigation settlement was established here in 1898 by farmers who were left destitute by the severe drought of 1895–1897 and the rinderpest epidemic of 1897. The town was laid out in 1931 and attained municipal status in 1964.

BATTLEFIELD
On 4 February 1915, during World War I, an attack by German troops on forces of the Union of South Africa took place on this terrain. In 1960 a monument in honour of the German casualties was erected here.

MUSEUM BUILDING (VOORTREKKER STREET)
Originally Kakamas' old power transformer building, it was built in 1914 by AB Hangartner, a Swiss craftsman. The building is designed in the form of an ancient Egyptian temple, and its façade bears the following inscriptions: 'Kagamas' and 'Anno Dom MCMXIV'.

WATER FURROWS, TUNNELS AND DRY-STONE WALLING, NORTH FURROW (BAVIAANSKLOOF)
When the settlement of poor farmers arrived in Kakamas in 1898, they dug canals and laid out farms. Although rainfall in the area is erratic and scanty, water and rich mud brought down by the Orange River ensure the fertility of the soil. It was necessary to divert water from the river for irrigation. The sites include tunnels, sections of canals and dry-stone walling of the north furrow, which was started in 1908.

WATER WHEEL NEAR DUTCH REFORMED CHURCH PARSONAGE
Situated on the canal near the parsonage and designed by Piet Burger, this historic water wheel was erected at the Kakamas Settlement. It is one of the few examples of its kind left.

WATER WHEELS (ERVEN 103, 1057, 68, 1467)
These four historic water wheels, situated along the northern furrow of the irrigation canal at the Kakamas South Settlement, are identical. Ingeniously designed, the wheel directs the course of the water by means of pulleys. Moving water turns the wheel while a series of buckets scoop water and empty it at a collection point ready for distribution.

KEIMOES

Situated on the north bank of the Orange River, this town takes its name from the Nama words 'gei', which means 'great', and 'mûs', which means 'fountain'. Keimoes attained municipal status in 1949.

DUTCH REFORMED MISSION CHURCH
Also known as the 'Witkerk', this Dutch Reformed Mission church dates from 1889 and was built under the supervision of Reverend CHW Schroder. It is typical of late nineteenth-century vernacular church architecture.

WATER WHEEL
This water wheel is one of a few of its kind remaining in South Africa. Designed by Piet Burger, one of the first colonists in the area, it is mounted on a furrow on the canal and operates by means of a series of pulleys in much the same manner as those at Kakamas. The wheel is still in excellent condition and is a well-known landmark on the canal at Keimoes, in front of a beautiful vineyard.

KENHARDT

This town was founded in 1876 along the Hartbees River. Although the origin of its name is unknown, Kenhardt was named by a group of policemen who were sent to the area to capture a party of rustlers. The town attained municipal status in 1909.

DUMORTIERITE OCCURANCE (FARM N'ROUGAS NORTH)
This type of occurrence, named after Eugene Dumortier, the nineteenth-century French palaeontologist who discovered it, is a hard, fibrous, blue or green mineral, consisting of hydrated aluminium borosilicate.

OLD LIBRARY
Erected in 1897, this building is a typical example of a pioneer house. As one of the oldest buildings in Kenhardt, it is of great historical importance to the area.

KIMBERLEY

The city developed from the diamond mining camp that was formerly known as Vooruitzicht, Colesberg Kopje and De Beers New Rush. It was renamed Kimberley in 1873 in honour of the Earl of Kimberley, and attained municipal status in 1877, and city status in 1912.

ALEXANDER MCGREGOR MEMORIAL MUSEUM (10 CHAPEL STREET)

Built in 1907, this imposing double-storey building was designed by the architect Carstairs Rogers on the instruction of Margaret McGregor, as a memorial to her husband, Alexander, a diamond pioneer and the Mayor of Kimberley in 1886. The building was presented in trust to the City of Kimberley.

ALFRED BEIT HOUSE

Alfred Beit House was built as a hostel for the Kimberley Girls' High School, possibly by Timlin, and named after Sir Alfred Beit. The large double-storey Victorian building has a stone foundation and is constructed of Kimberley redbrick in Colonial bonding.

ARMAGH (40 MEMORIAL ROAD)

Armagh was designed by Carstairs Rogers in 1901, and built by George Wright for Robert Hugh Henderson, who leased the property from De Beers Consolidated Mines for 21 years. Henderson was mayor during the siege of Kimberley. The double-storey is an example of Kimberley consolidation-phase architecture.

BEACONSFIELD LIBRARY BUILDING (CENTRAL ROAD)

The Beaconsfield Library has been housed in this building since its foundation in 1889.

BEACONSFIELD POST OFFICE (CENTRAL ROAD)

According to historical records from 1884, the present post office was originally erected as a court and magistrate's office. The building is a good example of a double-storey Victorian structure, built of blue Kimberlite stone, and with a corrugated-iron roof and verandah. Together with the adjoining old police station, and the public library directly opposite, it forms a complex. The cornerstone was laid in 1881, but the building was only completed in 1888.

CHAPEL (KIMBERLEY HOSPITAL)

This interdenominational chapel at the hospital is proclaimed a monument to commemorate the pioneer work of Sister Henrietta Stockdale in the training of nurses, and in recognition of the nursing profession in South Africa. Sister Henrietta was born in England and trained as a nurse in London. On her arrival in South Africa in 1847, at Port Elizabeth, she travelled by ox-wagon to Bloemfontein to work at St Michael and All The Angels, later returning to England to complete her training. She returned to South Africa in 1878 to become matron at St John's Cottage Hospital, Bloemfontein, and in 1879 she became matron of Carnarvon Hospital in Kimberley, which at the time had nine beds.

During the eight years of her work there, the hospital increased its capacity to 160 beds. A small chapel and a nurses' home were also erected and it was there that she started training nurses. The chapel was converted into four extra rooms. Sister Henrietta raised funds for a new chapel, and when completed, it was initially used as an Anglican church, but later became interdenominational.

It was through the work and efforts of Sister Henrietta that, in 1891, the Cape government recognised nursing as a profession and established a register of nurses. Although she retired in 1895 as matron, Sister Henrietta continued to train nurses and midwives until her death in 1911.

DE BEERS CONSOLIDATED MINES LIMITED

The seven properties listed below, together with the historic buildings thereon, are not only closely associated with the founding and growth of De Beers, the largest diamond mining company in South Africa, but also form the nucleus of De Beers Conservation area. The buildings are characteristic of the late Victorian era.

✢ General Manager's House (13 Lodge Road)

- Rockmount House (20 Carrington Road)
- De Beers Mining Company Offices and Old Rhodes Boardroom (Warren Street)
- De Beers Head Office (Stockdale Street)
- The Old Stable (Stockdale Street)
- De Beers Benefit Society Building (Stockdale Street)
- The Consolidated Building (Stockdale Street)

DOORNLAAGTE ARCHAEOLOGICAL SITE (DISTRICT)

This proclaimed area is an archaeological site of exceptional importance where evidence has been found of human occupation between 50 000 and 100 000 years ago. Discovered by a bulldozer driver, the quarry was opened in 1960. The driver noticed the first shaped, stone artefact as well as many others, reporting his find to the Alexander McGregor Memorial Museum. Four archaeologists went to the site in 1963, examining an area of 15m x 6m, which revealed 2 000 stone artefacts. Excavations showed that generation after generation of man had lived here for thousands of years.

DUGGAN-CRONIN BANTU GALLERY (12 EGERTON ROAD)

This magnificent old Victorian dwelling, formerly known as The Lodge, was designed by the architect Sydney Stent. It was built in 1899 as the residence of John Blades-Currey, manager of the London & South African Exploration Company.

The building was taken over by De Beers Consolidated Mines in the same year and used as a guest house until 1937. Thereafter, it was converted into an ethnographic museum to house the collection of photographs of the Bantu, San and Hottentot peoples and their way of life, taken by AM Duggan-Cronin, The collection now forms part of the McGregor Museum complex.

DUNLUCE MANSIONS (10 LODGE ROAD, BELGRAVIA)

A late Victorian mansion with a magnificent wooden, decorated verandah, Dunluce was designed in 1897 by DW Greatbatch for Gustav Bonus, a member of the diamond syndicate. John Orr, a well-known merchant, lived here from 1903 until his death in 1932. Thereafter Dunluce was occupied by his family until 1975, when Barlow Rand Limited bought, restored and donated it to the McGregor Museum.

DUTCH REFORMED MOTHER CHURCH (NEWTON)

This historic church building was built in three stages. The original church was designed by the Reverend JD Kestell, who was minister in Kimberley between 1882 and 1893. The building was dedicated on 29 May 1886.

DWELLING (14 WEST CIRCULAR ROAD)

The ground on which this corrugated-iron house stands, was granted to Octavius Cornelius Broomhead on perpetual quitrent of one Pound Sterling in May 1878. The present owners bought the property in 1968 for 200 Pounds Sterling.

EDWARDIAN DWELLING (7 LODGE ROAD)

Designed in 1906 by the well-known architect DW Greatbatch, this single-storey Edwardian house was built for Ernest (later Sir) Oppenheimer in 1907. Harry Oppenheimer was born here in 1908. On an original L-shaped floor plan, the house was constructed of Kimberley redbrick with a high-pitched corrugated-iron roof, later replaced with tiles. The verandah and front of the house rests on round concrete pillars, while the windows are hinged and the four-panel front door has a half-moon fanlight.

FAÇADE OF THE 1897 MCGREGOR MUSEUM BUILDING (2 EGERTON ROAD)

This Victorian building, designed by the architect DW Greatbatch, was erected in 1897 as a recuperative hotel and was known as the Kimberley Sanatorium. In 1908 De Beers Consolidated Mines changed the name to Belgrave Hotel, which it remained until 1931. From 1933 to 1971 the building was used as a Catholic school after, which it was transferred to the McGregor Museum.

FIRST SEVENTH-DAY ADVENTIST CHURCH
(CNR BLACKING STREET AND DYER PLACE)
This church is the original Seventh-Day Adventist church in South Africa and was started by Pieter Wessels of the farm Benoudheidsfontein in 1885. When diamonds were discovered on his farm he sold it to The De Beers Company and used the money to promote the interests of his church, hence this corrugated-iron church.

FORT KUMO (42 CARRINGTON ROAD)
Kumo was the first house built in Carrington Road, and was completed in 1898. Situated on the outskirts of Kimberley, the house was besieged during the early stages of the Anglo-Boer War, and was converted into a fort manned by soldiers. During the siege an underground bunker was constructed on the grounds. As the sole survivor of many structures of its kind constructed at the time, the bunker is of significant historic importance.

GLACIAL ROCK FORMATIONS
(FARM NOOITGEDACHT)
On a section of ground (about 171.306ha), approximately 4 567.2m south of the Vaal River and just east of the old homestead, the boundaries of which are demarcated by suitable beacons, are excellent examples of glacial pavements. These erratics (pieces of rock that differ in composition and shape from the rock surrounding them, having been transported from their place of origin, usually by glacial action) scratched the rock surfaces they passed over, and are now exposed.

GRAVE OF SOLOMON TSHEKISHO PLAATJE
(GRAVE 11, LUTHERAN BLOCK C,
ROW 1, WEST END CEMETERY)
Solomon Plaatje was the first General Secretary of the African National Congress. He was born in Boshof in 1875 and died in 1932 in Pimville.

HISTORIC DWELLINGS
(18, 20, 22 AND 24 ELSMERE ROAD)
This impressive row of houses, with Victorian and Edwardian features, forms an integral part of the architectural street scene of Elsmere Road, and is an attractive architectural unit.

HISTORIC MINING SCHOOL BUILDING
(HULL STREET)
The historic mining school building was erected in 1899 in the late Victorian style to house the first technical training school for the mining industry in South Africa. It is, therefore, closely associated with the development of the mining industry.

JACK HINDON OFFICERS' CLUB
(FORMERLY OLD ALEXANDERFONTEIN HOTEL)
(DANIE THERON COMBAT SCHOOL,
ALEXANDERSFONTEIN)
This magnificent building, with Victorian and Edwardian features, was designed as a hotel in 1900 by the well-known architect Daniel Westwood Greatbatch. The building was completed in 1902 and enlarged in 1907 by the addition of an extra wing. The hotel, which was closed in 1939, was taken over by the South African Defence Force in 1967, and converted into an Officers' Club.

KIDDIE HOUSE (11 CURREY STREET)
Kiddie House was erected for the internationally known baker, AC Kiddie, in 1910. The double-storey manor house, in Edwardian style, has a galvanised-iron roof and decorated varandahs on both storeys.

KIMBERLEY AFRICANA LIBRARY
(DU TOITSPAN ROAD)
Officially opened on 23 January 1887 by Justice Lawrence, Chairman of the Building Committee, the Library was designed by RE Wright of the Public Works Department and built by Messrs Westlake & Coles, and Smith & Bull. When a cottage that stood behind the library was demolished in 1928, 731 carats of diamonds were extracted. The Library's share of the proceeds of the sale amounted to 2 321 Pounds Sterling. Following a three-year break from 1983 to 1986 for alternations and restoration, the building was taken into use as the Kimberley Africana Library.

KIMBERLEY BOYS' HIGH SCHOOL
(MEMORIAL ROAD)
The cornerstone of the school was laid on 8 April 1913 by the then Governor-General of the Union of South Africa, the Earl of Gladstone. Designed by DW Greatbatch, the building was constructed by Church & McLauchlin, and exemplifies a high point in Kimberley's architecture. It was taken into use in January 1914. With a symmetrical façade, the Cape Dutch gabled, double-storey building is flanked on both sides by a single-storey wing. Ionic pillars adorn the main entrance.

Situated alongside the main building, the memorial library is designed in similar vein, also with a symmetrical façade and an orange-tiled roof. The cornerstone was laid on 6 February 1955 by the principal, LM Dugmore. It was erected as a memorial to old boys of the school who died in both world wars.

KIMBERLEY BOYS' HIGH SCHOOL SPORTS PAVILION
The cornerstone of this building was laid on 8 September 1905 Colonel D Harris. Built with a corrugated roof, the sports pavilion has a symmetrical façade, comprising a verandah with cast-iron pillars connecting an extension on either side of a double-storey. Both the extensions and the main section are adorned with triangular gables. Originally the clubhouse of the Pirates Club, the pavilion was acquired by the school in 1919.

KIMBERLEY CLUB BUILDING
(70–72 DU TOITSPAN ROAD)
The historic Kimberley Club was used by many celebrated civic and military dignitaries during their visits to Kimberley. They include Cecil John Rhodes, Sir JB Robinson, Sir Ernest Oppenheimer, Dr Harry Oppenheimer, Lord HH Kitchener, General JDP French and Viscount BL Montgomery.

The club has also been honoured with visits by the British Royal family, including the Duke of Connaught (1906), the Prince of Wales (1925), Prince George (later Duke of Kent, 1934), as well as King George VI, Queen Elizabeth and the Princesses Elizabeth and Margaret (1947).

KIMBERLEY GIRLS' HIGH SCHOOL BUILDING COMPLEX (RENDELSHAM ROAD)
The Edwardian school complex was designed by the architect DW Greatbatch and erected by the builder J Newton. Construction began after 1906 and was completed and opened in 1913. The terracotta work was carried out the by firm Church & McLaughlin. The adjacent psychologist's offices, a later addition to the school, are built in the same style.

KIMBERLEY MASONIC TEMPLE
(DU TOITSPAN ROAD)
The foundation stone of the temple was laid with full Masonic ceremony on 10 October 1888, and the dedication ceremony was conducted on 15 August 1889. Designed by HA Reid, this building is a superb work of neoclassical architecture.

KIMBERLEY REGIMENT DRILL HALL (PARK ROAD)
Constructed in 1892 in the Kimberley Public Gardens as the Art Gallery of the 'South African and International Exhibition', this is the only exhibition building still in existence. Later in 1892 the Kimberley Rifles acquired the building. The Kimberley Regiment was formed in 1899 from the Diamond Field Horse and Kimberley Rifles, with Lieutenant-Colonel Finlayson as Officer Commanding.

LINDOW HOUSE (11 LODGE ROAD)
This Edwardian dwelling was erected by DW Greatbatch in 1910 for Herbert Harris, son of Sir David Harris. During World War I, when Sir Ernest Oppenheimer was the target of anti-German demonstrations and sentiment, due to his origins, he took refuge in this house.

MARKET SQUARE AND CITY HALL
Market Square was the centre around which the city of Kimberley grew. It was the scene of many important events in the history of the city, as well as of South Africa and Zimbabwe (formerly Rhodesia).

In 1871, after the discovery of gold, Market Square became a tent town of diamond diggers; many illicit diamond deals were transacted here in which the notorious Scotty Smith figured. It was also here that diamond magnate Barney Barnato sought the votes of the farmers of the district when he stood as a candidate for parliament.

The town hall and square was a place of refuge for the women and children when Kimberley was besieged during the Anglo-Boer War (1899–1902), and also where General French was welcomed when the town was relieved. Expeditions to Stellaland, Goshen and Rhodesia departed from this square, and it was those expeditions that lead to the annexation by Britain of those territories.

The city hall was designed by FC Rogers in the neoclassical style and was completed in September 1899. Together with Market Square it forms an important historical and architectural group.

MEMORIAL TO PIONEERS OF AVIATION (FARM ALEXANDERSFONTEIN)
The memorial to the pioneers of aviation was erected on the site of the original airfield, where Cecil Compton Paterson established South Africa's first flying school in 1913. Of the first ten pupil pilots, only five passed. These flyers became the first pilots of the newly formed South African Aviation Corps, which was the forerunner of the South African Air Force. The memorial consists of a symbolic monument designed by AP du Toit and replicas of the first hangar and Compton Paterson biplane.

OLD CIVIL COMMISSIONER'S RESIDENCE AND OUTBUILDING (5 BENNET STREET)
Designed by HS Greaves in 1881, the residence was built in 1883, and extended in 1903 with a free-standing two-roomed building.

OLD COURT BUILDING (CNR TRANSVAAL ROAD AND SOUTHEY STREET)
The seat of the High Court of Griqualand West was moved from Barkly West to Kimberley during 1876. Originally placed in the Mutual Hall, the court was later moved to a wood-and-iron building on the eastern boundary of the site where the present building stands. This shanty was described by *The Diamond News* of 26 April 1881, as 'a collection of hovels so disreputable and dilapidated in appearance that they cannot fail to attract the attention of the passer by. Probably the first impression which a stranger would form is that the construction in question were the former stores of some bankrupt trader...'. Work commenced in haste in 1884, and the building was ready for use two years later.

PUBLIC UNDENOMINATIONAL SCHOOL COMPLEX (LANYON TERRACE)
After a meeting held on 25 November 1886 with a proposal that 'Public Undenominational Schools should be established in Kimberley', it was decided to establish boys' and girls' first class schools, as well as a kindergarten (1903) for children from three years of age. This site was granted by the government in 1887, and building commenced soon after. A teachers' hostel was also built in 1904.

ROCK ENGRAVINGS (FARM DRIEKOPSEILAND)
Well-known for its singular geometrical rock engravings, this site in the Riet River bed is also of great importance geologically. The rocks on which the engravings occur are pavements that were formed and scraped millions of years ago by a glacier moving over them. Over 3 000 rock engravings, estimated to be 800 to 2 500 years old, are predominantly abstract of entopic design, and are thought to relate to San religious experiences.

RUDD HOUSE (5 LOCH ROAD)
Built during the late 1880s, the house was formerly known as The Bungalow until it changed hands in 1896 when it was transferred to Charles Dunnell Rudd. When De Beers Mining Company was formed in 1880, Charles Rudd was chairman and managing director, and his friend Cecil Rhodes was secretary.

RUGBY HOUSE (88 ROPER STREET)
Although the property was first transferred to WM Willis in 1884, it wasn't until 1928, after it was bought by Frederick James Dobbin in 1918, that a house was built there. Dobbin was a well-known South African international rugby player, and his love for the game extended even to the house; both the window in the front door and the roof of the entrance gateway are shaped like rugby balls.

SECRETARIUS FARMSTEAD (DISTRICT)
This homestead is a rare blend of pre-Victorian and Victorian rural architecture in the Kimberley area. The farm was purchased by the Berlin missionary Carl Lorenz Theodor Radloff in 1864 and the farmhouse was built by his son, Adolf Reinhard Radloff, in 1867. Two wings were added c.1885, and a large wagon house, stables and a workshop were built about the same time as the house. A separate cottage was built c.1900 and the dairy c.1908.

SHOOTING BOX COMPLEX (FARM VOGELSTRUISPAN, ROOIPOORT)
The tender from Messrs John Dickson & John A MacKenzie of Kimberley, 'for the erection of a shooting lodge, ranger's cottage and stables at Rooipoort farm', was accepted by Gardner Williams, General Manager of De Beers, on 13 February 1899. Over the years, directors of the company have entertained visitors at the shooting box, including Sir Walter Hely-Hutchinson, Earl Grey, Lord Buxton, and the Earl of Athlone and Princess Alice.

SOLOMON PLAATJE HOUSE (32 ANGEL STREET)
This property was owned by Solomon T Plaatje, a leader who achieved much in education, and was the first black author to write a novel in English in Africa. The Bridge Educational Centre, run by the McGregor Museum, provides displays on the history of Plaatje and other African writers.

ST ALBAN'S CHURCH (TAKOON SQUARE)
The foundation stone was laid on 3 October 1886 by the Bishop of the time, Dr Bruce Knight. Within four months the church, consisting of the nave, baptistry, porch and belfry with bell, was completed. A vestry was added in 1888 and a new belfry was erected in due course. The church was extended to its present dimensions in 1913.

STAR OF THE WEST (NORTH CIRCULAR ROAD)

The Star of the West has its origins in the early days of the dry diggings on the diamond fields of Griqualand West. Richard Preston was granted a perpetual quitrent on 9 July 1878, he already had a licence granted on 21 March 1877. In 1881, Preston sold to George Wrigley, who subdivided the plot, selling this lot to Maurice Zimmerman. When Zimmerman sold it by auction in 1897 it was described as 'the well-known canteen, The Star of the West, built of iron and wood...'. Ernst Martienssen bought the Star of the West in 1900 and erected the current building. Plans were drawn up by Rogers & Ross, dated 1903, and it is assumed that construction started shortly thereafter.

THE CORNER BUILDING
(CNR DU TOITSPAN AND CHAPEL STREETS)

Following a devastating fire and the subsequent destruction of the building, the property was bought by Percy George Croxford in 1907 and a new double-storey building constructed with the second storey façade containing many decorative elements. The frontage is the last surviving example of a Victorian brass-framed and curved-glass shop front in the city centre.

THE HONOURED DEAD MEMORIAL AND
THE LONG CECIL CANNON, SITED IN A SACRED
CIRCLE (FARM BULTFONTEIN)

This memorial was designed by Sir Herbert Baker at the request of Cecil John Rhodes, who had, since the siege of Kimberley, considered erecting a memorial in honour of the residents of Kimberley who died during the Anglo-Boer War (1899–1902). In Greek classical style, the memorial is based particularly on the Doric temples and vaults that Baker visited during an overseas trip. The Long Cecil Cannon next to the memorial was designed by the engineer Labram, during the siege of Kimberley.

TRINITY METHODIST CHURCH (CHAPEL STREET)

The foundation stone of this church was laid on 7 March 1906 by HA Oliver, MLA and CW Compton. The church's gothic exterior and interior detailing is typical nineteenth century ecclesiastical architecture in England. The building is a historic landmark in Kimberley.

UNION MASONIC LODGE (4 FREE STATE ROAD)

Free Masonry was established in the diamond fields during the early 1870s. The Union Lodge was founded by a warrant granted by the Grand Lodge of Scotland; the founding ceremony took place on 7 April 1886 in the Good Templars' Hall. The cornerstone of this building was laid on 18 December 1886 and the inauguration was on 28 January 1887.

KURUMAN

This town was laid out in 1887 and attained municipal status in 1916. The exact origin of its name is unknown.

HISTORIC KURUMAN EYE SITE
(VILLAGE COMMONAGE)

This is the source of the Kuruman River, where water gushes out of a dolomite cave. The fountain supplies enough water daily for the needs of the town, and for irrigation. Even before 1800, white settlers knew about the 'eye'.

LONDON MISSIONARY SOCIETY CHURCH
(MOFFAT CHURCH)

Built by Reverend Moffat in 1820, the church was completed in 1838. Not only did Moffat preach here until 1870, but it was also here that he translated the Bible into Tswana.

MOFFAT AND HAMILTON MISSION HOUSES AND
COACH HOUSE (MISSION STATION)

The Moffat and Hamilton mission houses and the coach house, together with the already proclaimed mission church, form the nucleus of the famous Kuruman Mission Establishment. As Robert Moffat and his wife arrived in the area in the early 1820s, these buildings must have been built some time thereafter.

WONDERWERK CAVE (PORTION OF THE FARM WITH THE CAVE THEREON, WONDERWERK)
The Wonderwerk Cave extends 40m into the Rooiberg range, and is 12m to 24m wide. It has a depth of 140m. Artefacts discovered in the cave date from the Early, Middle and Late Stone Age.

LELIEFONTEIN

The town was established in 1816 on land granted to Hermanus Engelbrecht. It was named after arum lilies growing at the spring.

METHODIST CHURCH AND MANSE
Erected in 1855, this was the third church to be built at the Leliefontein Mission Station, founded by Barnabas Shaw in 1816. The predominantly neogothic-style church and the manse form an important historic and architectural complex.

MAGERSFONTEIN

BATTLEFIELD
The well-known Battle of Magersfontein took place here on 11 December 1899 during the Anglo-Boer War. Major-General AG Wauchope and his men were subjected to heavy fire from the Boers under the command of General JH de la Rey, suffering heavy losses as a result. There are nine memorial sites on the battlefield, including a Celtic cross erected in memory of the Highland Regiment casualties, a granite memorial to Scandinavians fighting on the side of the Boers, and a marble cross recording Guards Brigade losses.

NOUPOORT

The town was laid out on Hartebeesthoek farm, a portion of the farm Caroluspoort. Its name means 'narrow pass', and relates to the poort through the nearby Carlton Hills. The town attained municipal status in 1942.

ANGLICAN CHURCH
This neogothic stone church was erected in 1901 by British troops who had their headquarters at Noupoort, and is closely associated with the history of the town.

HISTORIC OLD ANGLO-BOER WAR BLOCKHOUSE (HOSPITAL HILL)
Noupoort was the site of a large military camp and hospital during the Anglo-Boer War (1899–1902). A large concentration camp site for Boer captives was also established in the area. As elsewhere, the British forces built a blockhouse to protect the town and railway routes, yet unlike other blockhouses of the time, the Noupoort fortification on Hospital Hill did not follow regulation norms for construction. The high, circular stone, with its corrugated-iron roof, roughly plastered exterior and shooting holes, remains fundamentally unaltered.

OKIEP

This small town was established in 1862 after copper was discovered here. Its name is derived from the Hottentot language and means 'big brackish place'.

HISTORIC CORNISH PUMP ENGINE COMPLEX
The complex consists of an engine, a Cornish pump, mineshaft and furnace. This unique pump engine, typical of those invented by Thomas Newcomen of Cornwall in 1712, was used to pump water from the O'Kiep Mine during the period 1882–1929. The pump engine was restored in 1965–1968.

HISTORIC OLD SMOKESTACK MONUMENT (FARM BRAKFONTEIN)

This smokestack dates from 1880 and was erected by the Cape Copper Mining Company to provide energy to the nearby pumping engine to pump water from the mine shafts. In 1952 it was declared a national monument in memory of the Pioneer Copper Mine in Namaqualand.

OLD MESSELPAD PASS (ON THE DIVISIONAL ROAD 2952)

Constructed between 1867 and 1869 by convicts, this road was built to transport copper from the Cape Copper Mining Company to Hondeklip Bay. The pass is supported by a series of masonry walls.

STEAM LOCOMOTIVE *CLARA* (O'KIEP COPPER COMPANY MUSEUM)

Clara was one of the last remaining steam locomotives used for conveying copper ore on the historic rail section from O'Kiep and Nababeep to Port Nolloth. The locomotive was used from 1890 to 1941.

PELLA

Pella was established in 1806 by the London Missionary Society. In 1869 it was taken over by the Rhenish Missionary Society, and then by the Roman Catholic Church in 1874. The biblical name is appropriate as it served as a refuge for the inhabitants of the London Missionary Society's station near Warmbaths when it was destroyed by Jager Afrikaner and the Khoekhoen.

BUILDING COMPLEX OF PELLA ROMAN CATHOLIC MISSION STATION

In 1812 the London Missionary Society established a mission here, but after the murder of a minister and his entire family, the mission was abandoned. In 1844 German missionaries from the Rhine Missionary Society continued the missionary work. By 1874 the Lutheran Mission was taken over by the French Lyonese Africa Mission. The beautiful cathedral was built with only the aid of an encyclopaedia. Over a period of seven years, the church with its arches, domes and columns reminiscent of the Roman-Gothic style, was completed. On 15 August 1885 the church was blessed by Bishop Rooney, fellow Bishop of the Cape, and put into service.

PHILIPSTOWN

This town was established on the farm Rietfontein in 1863, and was named after Sir Philip Edmond Wodehouse (1811–1887), Governor of the Cape Colony from 1861 to 1870. It attained municipal status in 1876.

REFORMED CHURCH

Following a proposal by Ds AA de Kock in 1873 that a new church be built, a Mr Robinson of Colesberg was commissioned to draw up plans. The cornerstone of this classical church was laid on 30 September 1876, and the building was completed in December 1878, and consecrated on 10 January 1879. What makes it architecturally interesting is that it is based on a basilica plan, rather than the usual cruciform design. The well-known Afrikaans writer and theologian, Jan Lion Cachet, spent part of his ministry (1875–1883) at this church.

POFADDER

The Inland Mission station was founded here in 1875, and was named Pofadder after Klaas Pofadder, a Korana Chief. The town was laid out in 1917 and renamed Theronsville, but the name Pofadder was restored in 1936, when it was proclaimed a township.

DUTCH REFORMED CHURCH (NAMIES)

This impressive church building, which was officially consecrated in May 1922, is closely associated with the establishment and history of the Dutch Reformed Church congregation (Namies) in Pofadder.

POSTMASBURG

This town was originally called Sibiling, a mission station of the London Missionary Society. It then became a Griqua village with the name Blinkklip. In 1890 it was renamed after Reverend Dirk Postma (1818-1890), the founder of the Reformed Church. The town attained municipal status in 1936.

OLD STECULARITE MINE (GATKOPPIES)

Situated approximately 5km northeast of Postmasburg, the mine is one of the oldest landmarks in the Northern Cape, and was visited by W Somerville and PG Borcherds in November 1801. The latter described it as 'a cave abounding in red earth mixed with mica and iron-ore.

'The natives dig this out and besprinkle themselves with the powder after besmearing themselves with grease, which gives their bodies a reddish shining colour.' Other visitors to the mine were H Lichenstein (1805), W Burchell (1812) and J Campbell (1814), who wrote of the mine as 'a kind of Mecca to the Natives around, who are constantly making pilgrimages to it'. Another visitor was J Backhouse in 1839.

PRIESKA

ANGLO-BOER WAR BLOCKHOUSE (PRIESKA HILL)

This blockhouse was built in 1900 by British soldiers to secure their position in Prieska. The hexagonal structure is a good example of the craftsmanship of British soldiers during the Anglo-Boer War.

RICHMOND

Richmond was founded in 1844 on the farm Driefontein and was named after the Earl of Richmond, father-in-law of Sir Peregrine Maitland, Governor of the Cape from 1844-1847. It attained municipal status in 1844.

'DE OUDE DAK' (237 PAUL STREET)

Although the style of this impressive, rectangular Cape Dutch style house is unique, it is the interior that is most important. Built in 1846, the house has yellowwood ceilings and floors, and the doors are stinkwood with yellowwood panels.

DUTCH REFORMED CHURCH (LOOP STREET)

An imposing structure, with its neogothic elements, this church was designed by JL Leeb. The woodwork was undertaken by C & R Stevens and the construction by Joseph Sandilands. Ds JF Berrange laid the cornerstone on 28 October 1844, and the church was consecrated on 28 February 1847. The original organ was donated by the Leeb brothers in 1865.

ROODEKLIPHEUVEL

OLD HORSE MILL (FARM RIETHUIS)

Originally situated on the farm Koenoep, also in Namaqualand, the mill was moved by the current owner's father to its present site. Riethuis itself was built as a station between Springbok and Hondeklipbaai at a time when this was a busy route for the transportation of copper from Springbok to the coast. In 1865 it was decided to build a 25km stretch of railway line from Hondeklipbaai to Riethuis but the line was never built. Shortly after, Port Nolloth was chosen as the harbour from which copper would be exported.

In the arid parts of this region where streams

were unreliable or non-existent, horse mills were used till late in the twentieth century. In very good condition, this mill still has a leather wheel that was used to drive the mechanism.

SPRINGBOK

Springbok was founded in 1862 as a copper-mining town and was originally named Springbokfontein, but was shortened to Springbok in 1911. It attained municipal status in 1933.

ALL SAINTS ANGLICAN CHURCH
(NAMAQUA STREET)
Designed and erected by Reverend WJR Morris, this church was first used on 5 December 1865 after the foundation stone had been laid on 10 November 1864. Consecration was done by Bishop Robert Gray on Ascension Day in 1866.

DUTCH REFORMED CHURCH
This impressive church of dressed stone was built in 1921 by the builder FW van den Houven. Dr WP Steenkamp, well-known theologian, physician and parliamentarian, was the driving force behind the programme to build it.

FIRST NEDERDUITSE GEREFORMEERDE KERK AND THE SYNAGOGUE
(SYNAGOGUE STREET)
This oblong stone building was erected in 1877 and was the first Nederduitse Gereformeerde church in Springbok. It was restored in 1899 and served as a church building until 1921. The adjacent Synagogue was erected by M Klawansky in 1929. Both buildings were acquired by the municipality of Springbok in 1982 to be used as museums.

OLD COPPER-SMELTING OVEN CHIMNEY
Although Simon van der Stel visited the copper mountains in 1685 and took samples of the ore for smelting purposes, it was not until 1840 that the first ore was mined, smelted and exported from Springbok. From 1853 until 1863, copper mining flourished here and in 1866 a copper-smelting oven was built by the Cape Copper Company for the reduction of low-grade ore. The chimney of this smelting oven still remains.

VAN DER STEL'S COPPER MINE
This piece of land, which was owned by the O'Kiep Copper Company Limited, contains an original mineshaft sunk by Commander Simon van der Stel on an expedition to the copper mountains in 1685. The date, and probably other inscriptions on nearby rocks, are of the same period. There were originally three shafts sunk.

STEINKOPF

Established as a missionary station by the London Missionary Society, this small town was originally known as Kookfontein. The mission station was later taken over by the Rhenish Mission, and named after Reverend Dr Steinkopf.

OLD RHENISH MISSION CHURCH
Building of the rectory started in 1847 but progress was slow due to a shortage of money for stone and labour. Shortly after completion in 1849 the house was damaged by fire and was only restored two years later. It houses the town museum.

STRYDENBURG

The town was laid out on the farm Roodepan in 1892. Its name, which means 'place of strife', is taken from the quarrel that preceded the selection of the town's site. Strydenburg attained municipal status in 1914.

KAROO-STYLE COTTAGE (67 VAN WYK STREET)
This erf was sold to Hendrik Johannes Liebenberg by the Strydenburg Committee on 13 May 1893, and it appears likely that Liebenberg built this fine example of a Karoo house prior to his death in 1898.

REFORMED 'KRUISKERK' (LIEBENBURG STREET)
Designed on a simple T-shape, this church building has a symmetrical façade and a corrugated-iron roof. An extension in the centre of the façade houses a vestry, and the building has triangular gables.

A number of members of the Strydenburg NG Kerk, decided on 26 April 1897 to break away on principles of dogma and formed the first Gereformeerde Kerk onder die Kruis in South Africa. On 10 September 1898, this church was taken into use. Each family in the parish supplied their own bench, beginning a tradition that was maintained for many years whereby members had their own seats.

SUTHERLAND

The town was laid out on the farm De List in 1858 and was named after Henry Sutherland (1790–1879), minister of the Dutch Reformed Church in Worcester from 1824 to 1859. It attained municipal status in 1884.

DUTCH REFORMED CHURCH AND CHURCH HALL
The well-known Cape architect Charles Freeman designed this church, and John Delbridge was the builder. After the cornerstone was laid on 8 May 1899, it was planned to consecrate the church in October 1900. However, during the Anglo-Boer War the church was used as a school and later as a fort and barracks for British troops, delaying the consecration until April 1903. The cornerstone of the hall was laid on 12 May 1906, and the building was consecrated in 1907. The cruciform church and hall were both constructed of granite, and the church itself has a four-cornered steeple with a pointed peak.

UPINGTON

Developed from the mission station Olyvenhoutsdrift, founded in 1871, this town was renamed in 1884 in honour of Sir Thomas Upington (1844–1898), Prime Minister of the Cape Colony from 1884 to 1886. It attained municipal status in 1898.

DUTCH REFORMED CHURCH
This neogothic church, designed by the firm of architects FW & F Hesse of Cape Town, was erected in 1911 and was officially inaugurated on 13 April 1912.

HISTORIC WATER MILL
Built in 1870 by Reverend Christian Heinrich Wilhelm Schröder, an NG Kerk missionary, this water mill was constructed after the completion of the irrigation canal in Upington. It comprises a double-storey building with a wooden overshot mill wheel.

MUSEUM COMPLEX (SCHRÖDER STREET)
This was the old Nederduitse Gereformeerde mission station and clock tower known as Olyvenhoutsdrift, founded in 1871 by the Reverend Christiaan Schröder. The church and the old Schröder parsonage date from 1875 and 1883 respectively. This complex was recently restored and converted into a museum by the Municipality of Upington.

PALM TREE LANE
This magnificent lane of full-grown palm trees on the well-known 'Eiland' stretches over a distance of 1 041m. Planted by the Department of Water Affairs in 1903, it is reputedly the longest such lane in the southern hemisphere.

ROMAN CATHOLIC CHURCH
A neogothic church with an impressive bell tower was built during the years 1942–1949 by Father Karl Simbeuner and Brother Hugo, aided by children and the inhabitants of Upington.

VICTORIA WEST

This town was laid out on the farm Zeekoegat in 1844. Although named Victoria in 1844 after Queen Victoria, the West was added in 1855 to distinguish it from Victoria East. The town attained municipal status in 1858.

DUTCH REFORMED CHURCH (CHURCH STREET)
Constructed in 1846 by Cormack & Pringle, manure (the only available fuel) was used to bake the bricks of this church. The original thatched roof was replaced with slate tiles and a tower was added early in the twentieth century. Among the earliest personalities to preach at this church was Reverend Henry Carl Vos Leibrandt, historian and Cape archivist.

VOSBURG

This town was founded and laid out on the Vos family farm in 1895, hence its name. Vosburg attained municipal status in 1897.

DUTCH REFORMED CHURCH (CHURCH STREET)
The architect WH Ford designed this neogothic church building, which was erected by the builders Keating & Company. The foundation stone was laid on 27 November 1909 and the church was inaugurated on 17 September 1910.

WARRENTON

Laid out on the farm Grasbult in 1884, Warrenton was named after Sir Charles Warren (1840–1927). The town attained municipal status in 1948.

ANGLO-BOER WAR BLOCKHOUSES
Between 1 January 1900 and 31 May 1902, the Royal Engineers, commanded by Lieutenant-Colonel CD Learoyd, constructed 388 blockhouses in the Kimberley area. Of these, 16 were built near Warrenton Station, half of them permanent masonry structures. Four masonry blockhouses have survived; three are of simple rectangular design with corrugated-iron saddle roofs, while the fourth, larger structure has a square plan with pyramidal roof.

WILLISTON

Williston developed from the Rhenish Mission Station Amandelboom, which was established in 1845. In 1919 it was renamed after Colonel Hampden Willis, Colonial Secretary of the Cape Colony in 1883. The town attained municipal status in 1881.

CORBELLED HOUSES: ARBIEDERSFONTEIN, BRANDWAG, GROOTFONTEIN, GORRAS AND SCHUINSHOOGTE
These peculiar corbelled houses are examples of the ingenuity of the first settlers in this area, and are important relics of the architectural, cultural and national history of South Africa.

DUTCH REFORMED CHURCH
After the cornerstone was laid on 12 November 1912, this neogothic church was completed by the builder Van der Hoven in 1913 from locally-procured stone and other material. It was officially consecrated on 31 August 1913 by the Reverend SH Kühn.

HISTORIC STRUCTURES
(FARM JAN KLAASLEEGTE)
The site incorporates a large corbelled house, a small corbelled house, a bucket pump, a stone cattle kraal and a shepherd's house. They form a unique architectural complex.

WESTERN CAPE

This is the oldest part of the old Cape Province. Since the 1994 demarcation of provincial boundaries, the region includes Cape Town and the Peninsula; the Boland; approximately half of South Africa's western seaboard; the south coast to Plettenberg Bay; and a substantial area of the Great Karoo. It was here that European Settlers first encountered the indigenous peoples of South Africa in the seventeenth century.

AMALIENSTEIN

A former mission station of the Berlin Missionary Society, Amalienstein was established in 1816 and was later named after Frau Amalie von Stein, a great benefactress of the Society.

EVANGELICAL LUTHERAN CHURCH COMPLEX

In 1817 the Berlin Missionary Society sent PJ Joubert as a missionary to Doornkraal; he changed its name to the biblical Zoar. The community built a mill, a smithy and a church, prospering under the guidance of Reverends Gregorowsky and Radloff. An adjoining farm, Elandsfontein, was bought with a bequest from Frau Amalie von Stein, and the mission was renamed after her. On 17 September 1853 a larger church was inaugurated.

ARNISTON (WAENHUISKRANS)

Possibly the only town in South Africa with two official names, Arniston is named after the British troopship Arniston, *wrecked here in 1815, and Waenhuiskrans, a large cavern visible at low tide, where, it is claimed, a span of oxen and a wagon could easily turn.*

FISHERMEN'S COTTAGES

There are several of these cottages in this picturesque fishing village. They have been inhabited by fishermen and their families since about 1820 and are predominantly in the vernacular architectural style. Waenhuiskrans is the only existing fishing village of its kind in South Africa.

BEAUFORT WEST

The town was established in 1818 on the farm Hooivlakte, and was named by Lord Charles Somerset, Governor of the Cape (1814–1826), after his father, the Duke of Beaufort. It became the first municipality in South Africa in 1837.

CLYDE HOUSE AND TWO ADJOINING BUILDINGS (25 DONKIN STREET)

These three buildings all possess predominantly Victorian characteristics and form a unique architectural complex in the historic core of Beaufort West. The double-storey Clyde House is particularly noteworthy and was erected in about 1845 by Dr James Christie.

CORBELLED HOUSE (VLIEËFONTEIN, DISTRICT)

This corbelled house is a good example of the type of vernacular architecture developed by pioneers of this area in the nineteenth century.

DUTCH REFORMED CHURCH (DONKIN STREET)

Architecturally excellent, this church was built in 1826–1831 and enlarged in 1892 and 1894.

HISTORIC GIRLS' PUBLIC SCHOOL (CHURCH STREET)

The original Girls' Public School building was opened in October 1879 and an east wing was added in the same year. It is a fine example of Victorian public architecture and a building of considerable importance in Beaufort West.

HISTORIC RING WALL TOGETHER WITH THE CAST-IRON PALINGS AND THE ORNAMENTAL ENTRANCE GATES FROM BIRD STREET (OLD CEMETERY)

The original portion of this ring wall dates from 1857 and was erected when the Nederduitse Gereformeerde church cemetery was laid out. A joint fundraising campaign by the Dutch Reformed and Anglican congregations in 1887 enabled them to extend the ring wall to include the Anglican cemetery.

MATOPPO HOUSE (7 BIRD STREET)

This Georgian house was built by JJ Meintjies, Magistrate of Beaufort West from 1834 to 1857. He also used it as the second 'drostdy' of the town and, as such, it played an important role in the town's early history.

OLD CYPRESS TREE (BIRD STREET)

This cypress tree is the only one remaining of about 25 similar trees planted in the original Dutch Reformed Church cemetery in 1834.

OLD DUTCH REFORMED MISSION CHURCH AND PARSONAGE (89–91 DONKIN STREET)

This mission church, the foundation stone of which was laid on 4 May 1871, was completed in December 1872 by building contractor Adriaan Ventura. The Reverend Paulus Teshe was the main driving force behind its erection. The early nineteenth-century parsonage was enlarged in 1914 by the Reverend AH Barnard, and was the birthplace of well-known heart surgeons, Professor Chris Barnard and Dr Marius Barnard.

OLD LIBRARY BUILDING (CHURCH STREET)

This impressive Edwardian building, with its neoclassical features, was erected by Matthew Deas, master builder of Beaufort West. The front gable bears the date 1906.

OLD TOWN HALL (87 DONKIN STREET)

Built in 1865–1866, this was the first town hall erected in South Africa.

PEAR TREES (DONKIN STREET)

These two trees were planted in 1850 and 1860.

BETTY'S BAY

This small town was named after the daughter of Arthur Youldon, Director of Hangklip Beach Estates, who established Betty's Bay in the late 1930s.

'BLAAS 'N BIETJIE'

This property was bought in 1961 by Dr HF Verwoerd (1901–1966), former Prime Minister of South Africa from 1958 until his assassination, who planned the house himself in a modern style. A milkwood thicket is situated on the erf.

BLANCO

The town was founded on the builder's camp in 1847 during construction of the Montagu Pass between 1844 and 1847. It was first known as White's Villa, after the engineer Henry Fancourt White, but was later changed to the name Blanco. The only hop farms in South Africa are situated here.

FANCOURT (MONTAGU ROAD)

This house was built by the engineer Henry Fancourt White after his retirement in 1860. After his death in 1866, it changed hands several times and in January 1903 it was bought by Henry's son, Montagu White who partly rebuilt the house on the original foundations. Following Montagu's death in 1916, there were several owners and the homestead became dilapidated. Dr Rowland Anthony Krynauw purchased the property in 1958, restoring it to its original beauty.

BREDASDORP

This town was established in 1838 on the farm Lange Fontein, and was named after Michiel van Breda (1775–1847), a member of the Cape Legislative Assembly from 1838, who became the first mayor of Cape Town in 1840. It became a municipality in 1917.

ANGLICAN RECTORY AND HALL
(CNR INDEPENDENT AND DIRKIE UYS STREETS)
The rectory and the former Anglican church (now a hall) date from the earliest years of the town. The rectory is a fine old Cape thatched house, now the Bredasdorp Museum.

DE HOOP HOMESTEAD
(DE HOOP NATURE RESERVE)
This farmstead consists of five historic buildings that date from approximately the late eighteenth century. The group of buildings, with its large 'werf' and surrounding ring wall, forms a unique historic and architectural complex.

MOUNTAIN VIEW (KREUPELHOUT DRIVE)
This site includes the property and its historic oblong house in predominantly Cape Dutch style. It dates from approximately 1840.

RHENOSTERKOP FARM (DISTRICT)
This property is situated on the coast in the so-called Duineveld region, and features large numbers of milkwood trees. As such, it is of considerable importance both as a natural resource and from an ecological viewpoint. There are also four historic buildings in vernacular style on the property, which form an imposing architectural complex. The oldest house dates from the middle of the eighteenth century, and is built partly from wood salvaged from wrecks.

SPRINGFIELD FARM (DISTRICT)
Originally part of the farm Zoutpansberg, which had already been granted in 1747, Springfield farm came into existence with the former's subdivision in 1896.

TWO VERNACULAR-STYLE HOUSES
(LOURENS STREET)
These houses, in typical vernacular style, date from the middle of the nineteenth century. Together they form an interesting unit and an important architectural element in Bredasdorp.

WHITE MILKWOOD TREE
(FARM RHENOSTERFONTEIN)
This white milkwood (*Sideroxylon inerme*) is reputed to be between 600 and 1 000 years old, and is regarded by experts as being the largest identified example of its species.

CALEDON

First settled in 1715 and known as Zwarte Berg, the town was renamed in 1813 after the Earl of Caledon, Governor of the Cape from 1807–1811. It attained municipal status in 1884.

ANGLICAN CHURCH (PRINCE ALFRED STREET)
This stone church with stained glass windows was designed by Sophia Gray. The foundation stone was laid in 1850, and the church was consecrated in 1855 by Bishop Robert Gray.

BATH RIVER BRIDGE (MILL STREET)
This bridge was erected in 1866 by the Public Works Department, of which MR Robinson was

the engineer, and J Jardine the contractor. Together with the Lourens River Bridge (Somerset West) and the Buffelsjacht River Bridge (Swellendam), it formed part of the well-known 'wagenweg' between Cape Town and the Overberg.

DOUBLE-STOREY GEORGIAN TOWNHOUSE (DONKIN SQUARE)

This double-storey dwelling was built in the middle of the nineteenth century, shortly after the boom in Caledon due to the merino industry. Although many of the larger houses in the town date from this period, the Georgian style is uncommon.

TOWN HALL (PLEIN STREET)

The town hall is an Edwardian double-storey building. It was designed by W Black and completed in 1906.

VICTORIAN HOMESTEAD (24 MILL STREET)

Standing on a property that originally formed part of erf 632, which was granted to Andries Otto in September 1813, this Victorian dwelling was constructed c.1890, and is one of the best examples of Victorian architecture in Caledon.

CALITZDORP

Calitzdorp was established in 1821 as a settlement of the Dutch Reformed Church on land donated by Frederik Calitz, after whom the town was named. The town became a municipality in 1911.

DUTCH REFORMED CHURCH (ANDRIES PRETORIUS STREET)

Built predominantly in the Byzantine-Revival style, this sandstone church replaced the original Dutch Reformed Church building of 1857. It was inaugurated on 26 April 1912 by Reverend WA Joubert.

CAPE AGULHAS

This is the southernmost tip of the continent of Africa. Early Portuguese seafarers called it Agulhas – Portuguese for needles – as they noticed that their compass needles showed no magnetic deviation when passing this point.

CAPE L'AGULHAS LIGHTHOUSE

Completed in 1849, this lighthouse is the second oldest existing structure of its kind in South Africa, contributing significantly towards reducing the number of shipwrecks on the most dangerous part of the South African coastline. A circular tower, with a height of 19.81m, is flanked by the former living quarters.

CAPE TOWN

Cape Town was established as a halfway-house settlement by Jan van Riebeeck in 1652 to service passing ships of the Dutch East India Company. The name Cape Town was applied in the middle of the eighteenth century. In 1796, during the first British occupation of the Cape, the first municipal body, the Burgher Senate, was created. An amended Municipal Ordinance was passed on 13 January 1840, which constituted the Municipality of Cape Town.

BELVEDERE BUILDING (CNR BOUQUET AND ST JOHN STREETS)

Situated on land originally belonging to the Lodge De Goede Hoop, this Victorian building traded as the Belvedere Hotel until 1968, when it was expropriated by the state. It forms an important part of the architectural character of the historic Stalplein and surrounding buildings.

BERTRAM HOUSE (HIDDINGH HALL CAMPUS, ORANGE STREET)

Bertram House is probably the only surviving example of the brick houses of the English-

Georgian style. It was built during the first quarter of the nineteenth century. The plan is a symmetrical arrangement on either side of a central axis formed by a combination of porch, hallways and staircases. It is now a museum.

BLUE LODGE HOTEL (206–208 LONG STREET)
This impressive late Victorian building forms an integral part of the architectural character of Long Street, a part of Cape Town that has, to a large extent, retained a uniformity of character.

CAPE HERITAGE HOUSE BUILDING
(CNR CHURCH AND BURG STREETS)
This fine Edwardian commercial building, with shops and office accommodation, was designed in 1900 by architect E Seeliger, for the jeweller I Mendelsohn. Originally known as Mendelsohn's Building, the four-storey building currently houses the Cape Heritage Trust.

CARL HERMANN BUILDING
(5 CORPORATION STREET)
Built in palazzo style, this Edwardian building is a fine example of an early twentieth-century trading house. It was erected in 1904 for William Irvin on land originally belonging to the VOC Hospital and later the military barracks. It belonged to Carl Hermann from 1947 until 1984.

CHURCH SQUARE (BOUNDED BY PLEIN, SPIN AND PARLIAMENT STREETS)
Although possibly laid out in about 1679 by Jan van Riebeeck, official references to Church Square are encountered from 1703. It was the open ground of the Groote Kerk, which still abuts it. In its centre is a statue of Jan Hendrik Hofmeyr. On a traffic island in Spin Street is an inscription marking the site of the old 'slave tree', under which slaves were sold. Diagonally opposite the square was the Dutch East India Company's Slave Lodge, later the Old Supreme Court, and now a museum of cultural history.

CITY HALL (BOUNDED BY DARLING, PARADE, LONGMARKET AND CORPORATION STREETS)
The foundation stone of this building was laid on 29 August 1900 by Thomas Ball, Mayor of Cape Town. It was designed in the Italian-Renaissance style by HA Rein & FG Green, and built of sandstone by the builders T Howard & JG Scott. Its clock tower features a clock with a similar design to Big Ben, only half its size. The building was completed in 1905. The first council meeting held here was on 27 July 1905.

CLOCK TOWER (TABLE BAY HARBOUR)
Characteristically Gothic, this Victorian clock tower was erected as a signal tower in 1883.

COOWATOOL ISLAM MOSQUE (LOOP STREET)
The Indian community in Cape Town adhering to the Islamic faith resolved in 1892 to erect a mosque, which was officially opened on 19 March 1893. It has a central tower surrounded by a double catwalk.

CORNICE AND PEDIMENT OF ORIGINAL HERTZOG BUILDING (131 BREE STREET)
In the cornice and pediment there is a sculpture designed by the well-known Cape architect Anton Anreith. It is the only remaining example of such embossment on a building in Cape Town, of which there were formerly at least 20. The lower of two original figures has disappeared, but the top figure of Mercury is visible. The dwelling was demolished in 1971.

DOUBLE-STOREY HOUSE
(158 BUITENGRACHT STREET)
This property was originally granted to JJ Theron in 1811; the house was presumably built by him in the early nineteenth century. It was known as the Nova Scotia Hotel by 1861. It is a typical Cape double-storey townhouse, with a balcony, boasting predominantly Cape Dutch and Georgian features.

DUTCH EAST INDIA COMPANY'S GARDEN
(FROM ORANGE STREET, DOWN GOVERNMENT AVENUE TO THE TOP OF ADDERLEY STREET)

The oldest garden in South Africa, it was established in 1652 by Jan van Riebeeck as a vegetable garden to supply fresh produce to passing ships.

DUTCH REFORMED MISSION INSTITUTE
(THE RESTORED 1804 SLAVE CHAPEL)
(40 LONG STREET)

The 'sendinggestig' is the oldest indigenous mission church in the country and was erected shortly after the establishment of the South African Missionary Society in 1799. The building was completed early in 1804 and consecrated on 15 March 1804 by the Reverend JP Serrurier.

Architecturally, the church is also unique in that it is the only example of a building with a pitched roof of lime concrete in South Africa. The façade of baroque characteristics and Corinthian pilasters, as well as the 1824 pulpit and the organ, are also particularly noteworthy.

EGYPTIAN BUILDING
(HIDDINGH HALL CAMPUS, ORANGE STREET)

This building was completed in 1841 for the South African College, later the University of Cape Town. It is the first building erected for higher education in South Africa, and today still serves the same purpose.

FAÇADES OF THREE HISTORIC BUILDINGS
(140, 142, 148 LONG STREET)

140: Tyne Building (c.1859) (double-storey);
142: Dorfman & Katz Building (1898) (three storey); and
148: Weiner Bakery (1902).

These three buildings, with their Victorian and Edwardian characteristics, form an integral part of the historical and architectural character of Long Street.

GEORGIAN DOUBLE-STOREY HOUSE
(122 BREE STREET)

This is one of the few remaining Georgian double-storey houses in Cape Town, and is therefore undoubtedly part of the City's architectural heritage. It's now occupied as business premises.

GRAND PARADE (BOUNDED BY LOWER PLEIN, CASTLE, BUITENKANT AND DARLING STREETS)

The Grand Parade is one of Cape Town's historic squares, and was used as a military parade ground during the eighteenth and nineteenth centuries.

GRANITE LODGE AND ADJACENT DOUBLE-STOREY BUILDING (109 HARRINGTON STREET, CNR ROELAND STREET)

This double-storey building is probably the only remaining Georgian granite-faced house in South Africa. It was originally built as a dwelling house for Sir Anthony Oliphant, Cape Attorney-General at the time. Between 1839 and 1845 it belonged to Henry Sherman, and from 1845 to 1864 to the painter Otto Landsberg. In 1864 the St George's Orphanage bought the building and the adjoining double-storey building was erected in 1915 by the firm Forsyth & Parker as an extension to the orphanage.

GREENMARKET SQUARE

The history of this square dates back to 1696 when the Burgherwacht Huys was erected here as a house to accommodate the civil guard. The first reference to the area as a square, until then nameless, dates back to 21 July 1733, after the Burgher Watch House was rebuilt in 1755. It was then known as Burgher Watch Square, thereafter Town House Square. In the early nineteenth century the square was transformed into a market place for selling vegetables, and became known as Green Market Square.

GROOTE KERK (ADDERLEY STREET)
The first church on this land was built in 1678 and was replaced by the present building in 1841. The original tower was, however, retained. The pulpit, the work of Anton Anreith and the carpenter Jacob Graaff, was taken into use in 1789.

HISTORIC DOUBLE-STOREY BUILDINGS
(76 AND 78 STRAND STREET)
These two double-storey buildings are regarded as important examples of Cape Town's early building heritage. No. 76 was probably erected soon after 1800, while No. 78 probably dates from the early eighteenth century.

HISTORIC BUILDING
(6 CHURCH SQUARE, SPIN STREET)
This predominantly Edwardian building was erected in about 1902 and the design attributed to Sir Herbert Baker. It forms an integral part of Church Square, bounded on all sides by historic buildings.

HISTORIC BUILDING (14 KEEROM STREET)
This typically Cape, eighteenth-century townhouse is situated on land originally granted to Hermanus Smuts in 1751.

HISTORIC ENTRANCE GATES AND WALLS
(SOUTH SIDE OF GOVERNMENT AVENUE)
These gates and walls are part of the improvements made to The Avenue in 1803–1804 by the well-known architect Thibault, at the instance of Governor Janssens. The lions at the gates are the work of Anton Anreith.

HUGUENOT MEMORIAL BUILDING
(48 QUEEN VICTORIA STREET)
This predominantly Edwardian building was erected by the Synod of the Dutch Reformed Church to commemorate the arrival of the French Huguenots (1688). The foundation stone was laid on 24 August 1899 and the building was officially opened on 15 October 1903. The mortal remains of President SJP Kruger lay in state here from 1 to 6 December 1904.

ICS BUILDING (FAÇADE) (10 DOCK ROAD)
The original ICS Building, designed by Charles Freeman in 1896, was damaged by fire in 1928 and then modernised by Forsyth & Parker. With its striking cast-iron verandah, the building is regarded as a Cape Town landmark, and is also a good example of early twentieth-century industrial architecture.

INN ON THE SQUARE (GREENMARKET SQUARE)
Designed by WH Grant and completed in two phases, the first section of this building on the corner of Longmarket Street was completed in 1929, and the second section was added in 1941. It was the head office of Shell Oil for many years until it became a hotel in 1980. This building, with its central clock tower, forms an important element in the architectural character of Greenmarket Square.

JAN DE WAAL HOUSE (93 BREE STREET)
Jan de Waal, born in Amsterdam, arrived at the Cape in 1715 as an employee of the Dutch East India Company. The erf on which this double-storey house stands was granted to him in 1752 by Governor Ryk Tulbagh.

The house and adjoining warehouse in Shortmarket Street are typical of eighteenth-century Cape architecture. The present Georgian windows and door replaced the Dutch-style originals during the first quarter of the nineteenth century.

KING'S BLOCKHOUSE (DEVIL'S PEAK)
This is one of three blockhouses built by General JH Craig in 1795 after the British occupation of the Cape. It is a 7m^2 stone tower with slots for guns.

KOOPMANS-DE WET HOUSE MUSEUM
(35 STRAND STREET)

Built in 1701 as a single-storey thatched house, a second storey was added later. The house was enlarged by JFW Bottiger, the owner from 1748–1771, and by Pieter Malet, who owned it from 1771 to 1793. Although some authorities ascribe the house's design in its later form to Thibault, and others to Anreith, there is no proof that either had a hand in the alterations. The cultural leader and patriotic benefactress Maria Margaretha de Wet was raised in this home. On 15 April 1864 she married Johan Christoffel Koopmans from Amsterdam, an ex-officer in the British-German Legion, hence the name Koopmans-De Wet.

LODGE DE GOEDE HOOP (STALPLEIN)

These buildings were erected in 1804, and are some of the most important examples of the collaboration of Thibault, Anreith and Schutte, the architect, the sculptor and the builder respectively, who exercised great influence on architecture at the Cape in the beginning of the nineteenth century.

LUTHERAN CHURCH AND SEXTON HOUSE
(100 STRAND STREET)

The first Dutch Lutheran congregation in Strand Street did not come into existence until 1780. This is the oldest building in South Africa used continuously as a church, and is flanked by the former parsonage (Martin Melck House) and the sexton's house. In 1774, Martin Melck, a rich farmer and businessman, built a church in Strand Street for his fellow Lutherans, but disguised it as a storehouse. When he died in 1781, the building was still incomplete. Between 1787 and 1792, radical changed were made to the building when Anton Anreith embellished it with a beautiful front gable, a lavish pulpit and other wood carvings. A vestry and tower were also added. Much of the church was rebuilt in 1818 owing to the poor condition of the walls and roof, at which time a spire was added. The sexton's house was erected in 1787.

MALAY QUARTER (BO-KAAP)

This quarter has been occupied by Cape Malay people for over a century. It stretches between Strand and Wale, and between Chiappini and Buitengracht streets. The specified sections of the Malay Quarter are interesting and historic parts of Cape Town, with a special character derived from the customs and ways of life peculiar to the Malay people. The area is also of exceptional architectural merit, with picturesque terraced houses along the cobbled lanes.

MARTIN MELCK HOUSE (96 STRAND STREET)

The eighteenth century townhouse was built as the parsonage of the adjoining Lutheran Church.

OLD ARCHIVES BUILDING
(QUEEN VICTORIA STREET)

Originally built to house the University of the Cape of Good Hope, the building was designed by W Hawke with the help of WN McKinley, and the Cape Town builder FB Smith. The cornerstone of the original block was laid on 24 February 1906 by Sir Walter Hely-Hutchinson. An annex was built in 1910 and the cornerstone of the new university hall was laid on 5 November 1910 by the Duke of Connaught and Strathearn. The entire building was inaugurated on 14 February 1913 by the then Governor-General, Viscount Gladstone of Llanark. In 1934 it was taken over by the archives, which occupied it until recently.

OLD DRILL HALL (VOLUNTEER DRILL HALL 1899)
(PARADE STREET)

The foundation of the Old Drill Hall was laid on 2 October 1884 by Thomas Upington, then

Prime Minister of the Cape Colony. It was designed by James Tennant of the Royal Engineers and a Mr Kitch was the building contractor. The building was inaugurated on 15 December 1885 by Sir John Gordon Sprigg. In 1889 the Drill Hall was enlarged to its present size by the well-known Victorian architect, Anthony de Witt of the Volunteer Engineers.

OLD LOCOMOTIVE (RAILWAY STATION BUILDING)
Made in 1859 by Hawthorne & Leith of Scotland, this locomotive was put into service in 1863 when the railway line to Wellington was opened. It was also used for the line to Wynberg, which opened the following year.

OLD NATIONAL MUTUAL BUILDING (CHURCH SQUARE)
The original core of this building, first known as the National Mutual Life of Australasia Limited, was erected in 1905 on a design of Herbert Baker and Francis Masey. Enlarged by the architects J Perry and WJ Delbridge between 1919 and 1931, the building style is eclectic, featuring both Cape-Revival style and Baker elements, with gables in the Flemish style.

OLD SUPREME COURT (ADDERLEY STREET)
This building was originally completed in 1680 as the Dutch East India Company's Slave Lodge. It was converted for use as government offices in the nineteenth century by Thibault (inspector of government buildings and architect), Anreith (sculptor) and Schutte (contractor). It now functions as the South African Cultural History Museum.

OLD TOWNHOUSE (LONGMARKET STREET, GREENMARKET SQUARE)
This building was erected in 1755 as a Burgher Watch House, and was used in succession by the Burgher Senate and Municipality of Cape Town until 1905. It was given by the City of Cape Town to the Union Government, who restored it under the direction of architect JM Solomon. It houses the Michaelis Collection, a permanent exhibition of seventeenth-century Dutch and Flemish paintings.

ORIGINAL HOUSES OF PARLIAMENT (CNR ADDERLEY STREET AND GOVERNMENT AVENUE)
The cornerstone of this building was laid by Sir Henry Barkly on 12 May 1875. It was to have been built according to plans of architect C Freeman, but was ultimately completed in 1884 using the plans of HS Greaves and J Wichcord. The building was first used at the opening of Parliament on 15 May 1885. A new House of Assembly, the lobby and additional offices were constructed after the establishment of the Union in 1910, and further extensions followed in 1927, 1937, 1960 and 1964.

RIEBEECK SQUARE
This square has been in existence since the eighteenth century. It was first known as Boerenplein, then Hottentot Square, and finally renamed Riebeeck Square in the 1860s. It was here that farmers outspanned their wagons and off-loaded their products.

ROBBEN ISLAND EMBARKATION BUILDING AND QUAY (V & A WATERFRONT)
This embarkation building forms an integral part of the historic and political significance of Robben Island. It was erected to serve as the departure point for the island when the latter was used as a prison from 1960.

ROELAND STREET GAOL (ROELAND STREET)
Only the façade and stone boundary walls of the original gaol, built on this site during 1855–1858, remain. The gaol was demolished in the late 1970s, but it was agreed that because of its landmark quality and architectural and historic

interest in terms of the Victorian prison ethic, the Roeland Street façade and stone boundary walls be retained as part of the Western Cape's Archives Building.

RUST-EN-VREUGD (78 BUITENKANT STREET)
Built by the notorious Fiscal Willem Cornelis Boers, who acquired the estate in 1777, this double-storey Cape Dutch townhouse, built in Rococo style, is the only one of this style that has survived in South Africa. The Rococo style of the mid-eighteenth century favoured non-geometrical, often asymmetrical flowing forms that blend from one detail to the next.

ST GEORGE'S GRAMMAR SCHOOL BUILDING (1904) (QUEEN VICTORIA STREET)
This double-storey building (as well as the adjacent St George's Cathedral) was designed by Herbert Baker, replacing the original school established in 1858. The Grammar School was originally founded in 1848 and, although the school has moved premises to Mowbray, it remains the oldest private school in the country.

ST STEPHEN'S CHURCH (RIEBEECK SQUARE)
This is the oldest theatre building in South Africa. It was built for that purpose during the first British occupation by the Governor, Sir George Yonge, on what is now Riebeeck Square, opening on 17 November 1800. It was taken into use as a church and school in 1839.

SHORTMARKET STREET (108)
This building, clearly visible on a large panorama of Cape Town by F Schumacher dated 1776–1777, is typical of buildings erected towards the end of the Dutch period. It contains both Dutch and Georgian detailing.

SOUTH AFRICAN LIBRARY (GOVERNMENT AVENUE)
This building was designed by WH Kohler in neoclassical style. The foundation stone was laid by Sir George Grey in 1858, and the building was officially opened by Prince Alfred in 1860.

SPOLANDER HOUSE (CNR DORP AND PENTZ STREETS, MALAY QUARTER)
Stylistically this building appears to date from about 1830, but documentary evidence indicates the existence of a building on the site as early as 1818. It is one of the last early nineteenth-century buildings within Cape Town that has retained an original thatched-roof line. A landmark in the area, it is sometimes referred to as the gateway to the Bo-Kaap.

STONE WALL WITH BUILT-IN 'VR' POST BOX (BUITENGRACHT STREET)
This stone wall was built from Wale Street to Carisbrook Street with money from the tram company, when in 1902, after experiencing problems with the existing tramway system, the Cape Town City Council made Buitengracht Street available for an extension to the tram line. The rare post box with the monogram 'VR' was built into the steps in the wall at the corner of Buitengracht and Buiten streets. A prototype of this post box was designed in London by WT Allen between 1881 and 1904.

TABLE MOUNTAIN (TABLE BAY TO HOUT BAY)
Table Mountain is 1 113m at its greatest elevation (Maclear's Beacon). There are four faces to the whole massif: the north face, which is the well-known 'table' overlooking Cape Town, Devil's Peak on the east, and Lion's Head on the west. The west face comprises the Twelve Apostles overlooking Camps Bay and the Atlantic.

From north to south the main buttresses are Kloof (above Kloof Nek), Fountain, Porcupine, Jubilee, Barrier, Valken, Kasteel, Postern, Wood Spring, Slangolie, Corridor, Separation, Victoria, Grove, Llandudno Peak,

Llandudno Corner and Hout Bay Corner. The southwest face overlooks the Hout Bay valley and contains the deep indentation of Orange Kloof. The east face looks out onto the southern suburbs, starting at Constantia Corner (above Constantia Nek) and terminates at the saddle between Table Mountain and Devil's Peak. Buttresses from north to south are Vaalkat, Nursery, Window, Fernwood, Protea, Wormhole, Hiddingh, Ascension and Erica.

TAFELBERG DUTCH REFORMED COMPLEX
(CNR BUITENKANT AND COMMERCIAL STREETS)
The complex consists of the church, Cornelia House and the William Frederick school building, all designed by GM Alexander. The cornerstone was laid on 19 February 1892 and inauguration of the Mission Hall, as the building was then known, was held on 27 January 1893. This predominantly late Victorian church complex is situated on property purchased by Susanna Hertzog, who donated it to the Nieuwe Kerk in a trust deed later in 1893.

TERRACED HOUSES (OSBORNE AND FRANCIS STREETS, DISTRICT SIX)
This group of Victorian terraced houses dates from c.1850 and comprises 45 two-bedroom, semidetached and attached cottages that were erected at the beginning of a housing boom that extended into the twentieth century. The community that occupied these houses survived forced removals under the Group Areas Act, which destroyed most of the remainder of District Six.

THE CASTLE OF GOOD HOPE (CASTLE STREET)
The oldest building in South Africa, The Castle is a pentagonal fortification with a moat and bastions at each corner, named after the titles of the Prince of Orange (Buren, Nassau, Oranje, Catzenellenbogen, Leerdam).

In August 1665 Commissioner Isbrand Goske chose this site as the most suitable for the erection of an imposing fortress, which, in accordance with a decision of the Dutch East India Company, was to replace the unsafe Post De Goede Hoop. It was to be built to the design of old Dutch fortifications and was measured off by Surveyor Heinrich Lacus and engineer Peter Dombaer. Erection of the five-cornered stronghold with its bastions was done under the supervision of engineer Dombaer, master mason Douwe Gerbrandtz Steyn and joiner Adriaan van Braekel. Construction began officially on 2 January 1666. Ramparts, together with the exterior walls, warehouses, residences, church hall, slave quarters and shops on the inside were completed in 1679.

Towards 1691 a traverse wall (the Kat) was built across the inner court, against which small buildings were later erected. The balcony or new Kat, from which edicts, declarations and government announcements were made, was completed in 1695.

From 1674 until the middle of the nineteenth century, The Castle was the administrative and military seat of successive governments, and the official residence of the Governor. Thereafter it served as the British Military headquarters until it was handed over to the South African government by the Imperial government in 1917.

TIME BALL TOWER (V & A WATERFRONT)
Erected in 1883, this tower was used as a repeater station for harbour signals between the Royal Observatory and Signal Hill. In 1895 it was raised from 5.18m to 10.36m. The ball, which was hand operated at first, was electrified in 1903 and was replaced in 1934 by radio signals.

TUYNHUYS (GOVERNMENT AVENUE)
The original part of this residence was commissioned as a small summer house by

Commander Isbrand Goske in 1674, and was turned into a guest house in 1679. From 1750 onwards, Tuynhuys was used as a residence or official offices by virtually all the Cape Governors, as well as Governors-General and State Presidents.

TWO FACADES OF THREE-STOREY BUILDING
(71 ROELAND STREET, CNR BUITENKANT STREET)
Designed by architect William Black, this three-storey building was erected c.1900 for Hoffmann & Company. It is a transitional design between Edwardian and Beaux Arts, and forms a part of the historic character of Roeland Street.

VICTORIAN AND EDWARDIAN BUILDINGS
(44 LONG STREET)
The Young Men's Christian Association (YMCA) in Cape Town was founded on 24 August 1865. The original building was designed by the architect C Freeman, and was erected for the YMCA in 1883.

Extensions, including an additional building, were undertaken in 1900 in accordance with the plans of architect John Parker and the present foundation stone was laid by His Excellency the Governor Sir Alfred Milner on 4 October 1900. It is now the South African National Parks Building.

VICTORIAN DOUBLE-STOREY SHOP BUILDING
(173 BREE STREET)
In its present form this Victorian double-storey shop building, with cast-iron balcony, dates from the end of the nineteenth century.

YWCA (78 LONG STREET)
The Young Women's Christian Association was founded in 1886. This four-storey Victorian building was rebuilt in 1903 by J Parker of the firm Forsyth & Parker, and was dedicated to the memory of Minnie and Maria, daughters of JA Bam, who died in Germany.

CAPE TOWN SURROUNDS

Bantry Bay
Previously called Botany Bay, Bantry Bay is an extension of Sea Point.

DOUBLE-STOREY SEMIDETACHED HOUSE
(38 QUEENS ROAD)
This double-storey Victorian terraced house originally formed part of the Le Sueur Estate and was built by a Mr Fisher. It forms part of an important group of six Victorian buildings. The first owner was AW Snashall, who took transfer on 21 September 1894.

PUBLIC OPEN SPACES: (1) BANTRY BAY TO SEAPOINT, (2) BETWEEN NETTLETON ROAD AND THE SEA BETWEEN BANTRY BAY AND CLIFTON
The mountain and coastline from Bantry Bay to Clifton form part of an impressive landscape that is highly regarded worldwide, and is a most valuable tourist attraction.

Bellville
Originally named Twelve Mile Stone (after its distance from Cape Town), Bellville was named in 1861 after Charles Davidson Bell, Surveyor-General of the Cape from 1848–1872. Bellville became a municipality in 1940.

CAPE FLATS NATURE RESERVE (UNIVERSITY OF THE WESTERN CAPE, MODDERDAM ROAD)
This nature reserve of over 20ha provides a haven for rare and typical flora and fauna of the Cape Flats. It is a unique conservation project and offers opportunity for research into diseases and propagation of Cape flora.

XII MILESTONE AND OIL LAMP
(CNR VOORTREKKER AND DURBAN ROADS)
The milestone consists of a solid rectangular block of blue stone with a triangular top and Roman numerals 'XII' engraved on the face.

The old Victorian lamp is a hexagonal cast-iron lamppost with a four-sided lantern mounted thereon, and crowned with a solid-cast Newel decoration. This beacon, indicating the distance to Cape Town, was erected when the hard surface road over the Cape Flats was constructed in 1849. The settlement that developed to the north was known for a considerable time as Twelve Mile Stone, until its official proclamation as Bellville in 1861. The milestone was moved from its original position next to the historic Maitland Road, now Voortrekker Road, to this site in 1958.

Bloubergstrand

This area takes its name from a nearby hill, the scene of a battle in 1806, which heralded the second British occupation of the Cape. Blaauwbergstrand, is the original Dutch name.

ONS HUISIE (STADLER ROAD)
The property of the Stadler family for many years, this cottage is a typical example of the simpler form of vernacular architecture found on the coastal areas of the Western Cape. Periodic additions, plain side gables and the oven of this cottage are especially noteworthy.

Brooklyn

KLEIN ZOAR (WEMYSS ROAD)
According to its structure and architectural features, this pioneer house probably dates back to the eighteenth century. Tradition has it that Klein Zoar was originally the homestead of Wolraad Woltemade, the local hero who in 1773 rescued 14 people from the grounded ship, *De Jonge Thomas,* before perishing while trying to save more lives.

Camps Bay

The name derives from a sailor, Ernst Friedrich von Kamptz, who came to the Cape in 1778 and married the widow Anna Wernich, owner of the farm Ravensteyn that adjoined the bay.

CAPE OF GOOD HOPE NATURE RESERVE (CAPE POINT)
The Cape of Good Hope was discovered by Portuguese navigator Bartholomeu Dias in 1488, after which Sir Francis Drake described it as 'the fairest cape we saw in the whole circumference of the earth'. The 7 759ha reserve has been set aside to protect the indigenous flora and fauna of the area.

LAND ADJOINING EARLE'S DYKE
This area is declared to preserve the natural beauty of the surrounding environs.

Claremont

The suburb is named after a large estate in the area, bought by Charles Blair in 1823, who named it Claremont. The area gained municipal status in 1886 but was incorporated into the municipality of Cape Town in 1913.

ARDERNE PUBLIC GARDENS (MAIN ROAD)
These gardens were established by Ralph Henry Arderne in 1845, and with the help of his son Henry Matthew, he developed them into one of the most important gardens of the Victorian era. They are of great botanical, scientific and environmental importance.

CONGREGATIONAL CHURCH (MAIN ROAD)
The original part of the church building dates from 1877, while the church itself is closely associated with the history of the southern suburbs of Cape Town.

HERSCHEL MONUMENT (GROVE AVENUE)
This monument marks the site where Sir John Herschel stood a six-metre reflecting telescope from 1834 to 1838. The distinguished astronomer, working at his own expense, conducted research that marked the beginning of a new epoch in the astronomy of the southern hemisphere.

KIRSTENBOSCH NATIONAL BOTANICAL GARDENS
Situated on the eastern slopes of Table Mountain, Kirstenbosch is South Africa's premier botanical garden. Its name most probably derives from the Kirsten family, who owned a house on the property, the ruins of which may still be seen at the top of the chestnut avenue. There are still some Spanish chestnut trees near these ruins.

The land originally belonged to the Dutch East India Company, its forests providing timber for shipbuilding and other purposes. Kirstenbosch remained government property until 1811 when various sections were granted to colonial officials such as Colonel Christopher Bird. On his property was a spring, converted to a little oval bath, known as Lady Anne's bath.

In 1823, Kirstenbosch reverted to the government and it was assigned to DG Eksteen, who built a homestead there. Many of the old oaks and plants in the garden date from the period of his family's occupation. In 1895 Kirstenbosch was bought by Cecil Rhodes as part of a scheme for preserving these slopes of Table Mountain and Devil's Peak as a national park. After his death, Kirstenbosch fell into a state of neglect until 1913 when it became the site of the National Botanical Gardens.

ST SAVIOUR'S CHURCH AND CEMETERY
(BOWWOOD ROAD)
The nucleus of this neogothic church was designed and erected by Sophia Gray in 1850. A bell tower, two bays for the nave and a north-west porch were added in honour of Bishop Gray and his wife Sophia who died in 1872 and 1871 respectively. Further additions were made in 1903 and 1953.

VAN RIEBEECK'S HEDGE
(KIRSTENBOSCH NATIONAL BOTANICAL GARDENS)
On 12 July 1660 Jan van Riebeeck ordered the planting of a hedge. With the help of sailors from the wrecked French ship *La Marichal*, the ground was prepared, the object being to prevent Hottentots from stealing cattle. The hedge can be seen in Kirstenbosch National Botanical Gardens, on the hilltop above Bishopscourt, formerly Van Riebeeck's farm, Bosheuvel.

VREDENHOF (KEURBOOM ROAD)
This double-storey Edwardian mansion was built on land originally forming part of the Keurboom Estate, which was granted to JA van Schoor in 1893. The house was designed by architect John Parker and erected in 1907 for Christiaan Ludolf Marais.

Clifton
This is a residential suburb on the Atlantic coastline below Lion's Head.

CLIFTON SCENIC RESERVE
The extent of the reserve is approximately 12.245ha, between Victoria Road and the sea, from Fourth Beach to Camps Bay.

Clovelly
A seaside resort on False Bay, Clovelly is close to the northern side of Fish Hoek.

'THE HOMESTEAD' (MONTROSE ROAD)
The original portion of 'The Homestead', the oldest house in Clovelly, dates from the early nineteenth century. Additions to the rear of the house were effected during the 1870s and the verandah was added in the twentieth century.

Constantia
Constantia was originally over 763ha in extent, and was granted to Governor Simon van der Stel on 13 July 1685 by Hendrik Adriaan van Reede tot Drakestein, Lord of Mijdrecht, visiting Commissioner of the Dutch East India Company. During the eighteenth and nineteenth centuries it was subdivided into six farms.

Named Constantia by Van der Stel after the daughter of Commissioner Rijckloff van Goens, who made the original grant, the estate was divided after Van der Stel's death in 1712 into three parts and sold. These were called Groot Constantia, Klein Constantia and Bergvliet.

ALPHEN MANOR HOUSE (CONSTANTIA ROAD)
An area of 29 630ha, the Alphen property was granted to Theunis van Schalkwyk in 1714. The historic homestead dates back to the middle of the eighteenth century, although the upper storey was only added later. Alphen is a square double-storey manor house with a beautiful pediment and exceptional front door.

GOEDGELOOF (AVENUE PROVENCE)
This homestead is a typical example of a pioneer home in the Constantia Valley, which has, with time, undergone stylistic changes. The rectangular historic part of the house probably dates from the eighteenth century after two Beck brothers acquired the property in 1728. During the late nineteenth century the house was partly Victorianised.

GROOT CONSTANTIA (CONSTANTIA ROAD)
The site incorporates the consolidated area of Groot Constantia State Estate including the Groot Constantia manor house and Hoop op Constantia manor house, homesteads and all outbuildings. The Groot Constantia State Estate previously formed part of the farm Constantia, which was granted to Simon van der Stel in 1685, and was subdivided after his death in 1712.

The farm Constantia, with its Cape Dutch manor house, was acquired in 1885 by the Colonial Government as an experimental wine farm. Since 1975 the farmlands of the farm Hoop op Constantia, as well as a portion of the farm Nova Constantia, have been purchased by the state.

The original Cape Dutch Groot Constantia manor house, which was built by Simon van der Stel in 1692, was destroyed by fire on 19 December 1925, but was restored in 1926–1927 by the architect FK Kendall.

The Cape Dutch manor house known as Hoop op Constantia (formerly Klein Constantia) is a U-shaped house with only three gables. The Groot Constantia manor house presently houses a section of the South African Cultural History Museum.

NOVA CONSTANTIA (NOVA CONSTANTIA ROAD)
Nova Constantia originally formed part of the Groot Constantia Estate and the house probably dates from the first quarter of the nineteenth century. The homestead is U-shaped and is regarded, mainly because of its impressive gables and its setting, as one of the finest examples of a Cape Dutch house.

ORIGINAL BERGVLIET FARMYARD
(HOMESTEAD AVENUE)
The Cape Dutch house on this historic farm dates from 1769. A ring wall and outbuildings were erected in the middle of the nineteenth century. Bergvliet Farm originally formed part of Simon van der Stel's farm, Constantia.

STEENBERG FARMSTEAD (TOKAI ROAD)
Steenberg (previously Zwaanswyk), which was granted to Katarina Ustings in 1688, was one of the first farms in the region. The Cape Dutch homestead was erected in about 1740. A verandah and outbuildings date from the beginning of the nineteenth century.

TIMOUR HALL MANOR HOUSE
(TIMOUR HALL ESTATE)
This historic building is built in an interesting mixture of eighteenth- and nineteenth-century architectural styles. The large property on which it stands also contributes considerably to the character of the urban area in which it is situated.

Durbanville

Laid out in 1806 and first known as Pampoenkraal, the area was renamed D'Urban in 1836, and changed yet again to Durbanville in 1886. It attained municipal status in 1901.

ALL SAINT'S ANGLICAN CHURCH COMPLEX (BAXTER AVENUE)

The site incorporates the All Saints Anglican church, the old parsonage, the new parsonage, the church hall, and the garden of remembrance. The complex, of which the church and the older parsonage are predominantly in the Victorian style and date from 1860, is clearly associated with the history and development of Durbanville.

DUTCH REFORMED CHURCH (WEYERS STREET)

The foundation stone was laid on 1 April 1825 and the church was consecrated on 6 August 1826. The T-shaped church building was enlarged between 1890 and 1891, according to plans by the architect Charles Freeman.

KING'S COURT (2–4 CHURCH STREET)

This Victorian double-storey was built in 1894 by the owner J King, Chairman of the Pampoenkraal (later Durbanville) Council and mayor of Durbanville from 1901 to 1906.

OLD MILL KNOWN AS ONZE MOLEN (CENTRAL PUBLIC OPEN SPACE)

Onze Molen was recorded in 1850 as only the second tower mill in the Malmesbury district. It was erected in 1840 and served as a windmill until after the turn of the nineteenth century, when the mechanism and top portion of the mill were removed, and the remaining structure was used as a horse mill.

The windmill was restored in 1984 by the Natal Building Society and now forms a focal point of a new housing scheme, also known as Onze Molen.

RUST-EN-VREDE COMPLEX (WELLINGTON ROAD)

The Rust-en-Vrede building complex, which dates predominantly from the mid-nineteenth century, reflects a harmonious blend of Cape Dutch, Georgian and Victorian architectural elements. Since its erection the complex has served as a prison, magistrate's court, school, town hall and private residences. The Durbanville Municipality, which acquired the property in 1978, restored the complex in 1980 and converted it into a cultural centre.

Fish Hoek

First settled in 1818, the town was laid out in 1919 on the farm Vischhoek and became a municipality in 1940. The area is well known for the discovery of the fossilised skull of the Fish Hoek Man, dating back some 10 000 years.

COTTAGES (60, 62 SIMONSTOWN ROAD)

The original section of these two cottages date from 1919, and were built as seaside cottages by affluent residents of Cape Town. Additions were made as and when necessary.

FARM KNOWN AS OLD HOMESTEAD (KOMMETJIE ROAD)

It is possible that Johannes Bruyns was responsible for the erection of the T-shaped homestead in 1759. The dwelling represents an important link with the early settlement of the southern part of the Cape Peninsula.

Gardens

It is assumed that this suburb was given its name because of its situation on a section of Van Riebeeck's original Company's Garden, which it still adjoins.

BELLEVUE PROPERTY AND STRUCTURES THEREON (UPPER KLOOF STREET)

This property formed part of the first gardens planted by Jan van Riebeeck in Table Valley.

The Cape Dutch gable house with its Georgian elements dates from 1855 and still retains the reed ceiling construction of the original house erected in 1760.

BO-TUIN (HOF STREET)
Bo-Tuin was a section of the historic old farm Leeuwenhof, and was built in about 1820.

DOUBLE-STOREY CAPE GEORGIAN TERRACE-HOUSES
(31 BARNETT STREET AND 14 WANDEL STREET)
These double-storey Cape-Georgian terraced houses were erected by William James Hadfield in 1886.

DOUBLE-STOREY HOUSES
(46, 48, 56 BARNET STREET)
These three double-storey houses form an integral part of a row of six similar late-nineteenth-century terraced houses, with Georgian and Victorian features.

DOUBLE-STOREY VICTORIAN DWELLING HOUSE
(7 GLYNVILLE TERRACE)
Glynville Terrace was built on part of the farm Krynauw se Hof. The original row of detached single-storey houses was designed by the architect H Rowe-Rowe, and built by one Glynville during the mid-nineteenth century. Several of the houses were later extended. This house is the biggest and most impressive and is situated on a corner that completes the terrace.

DOUBLE-STOREY VICTORIAN SEMIDETACHED
HOUSES (135–137 AND 139–141 HATFIELD STREET)
This row of Victorian double-storey semi-detached houses was presumably erected in 1881 as part of a speculative housing development scheme. The properties on which the houses are situated originally formed part of the farm Welgedaan, which had been allocated to Gerrit Vreeburg in 1707.

GARDENS COMMERCIAL HIGH SCHOOL
(PADDOCK AVENUE)
The property on which this school is presently situated initially formed part of the farm Uitvlucht, granted to N van Wielen in 1732. This building has been used for educational purposes since 1944.

GEORGIAN HOUSE (5–7 WANDEL STREET)
The original section of this house was reputedly an outbuilding of the Van Breda household on the farm Oranjezicht, and dates from the 1730s. The building was rebuilt during the early nineteenth century by D Krynauw, who acquired the property in 1816.

GEORGIAN TERRACED HOUSES
(14, 16, 18, 20, 22, 24 DUNKLEY STREET)
These houses form an integral part of the property known as Dunkley Mews, consisting of a row of seven Georgian double-storey terraced houses with a corner shop at each end. They were built by WJ Hadfield in 1886 on properties bought from JG Borcherds in 1883.

LEEUWENHOF (HOF STREET)
In 1693 Governor Simon van der Stel granted Guillaume Heems, a burgher councillor, the loan of a piece of land on the mountain side. An attractive home was built during the time of the fiscal Joan Blesius, who became the owner of Leeuwenhof in 1697. In the eighteenth century it changed owners several times.

During the tenure of Johan Christiaan Brasler (1764–1788), Leeuwenhof was rebuilt, and during the ownership of Captain Johannes Zorn (1799–1836) it reached its greatest extent. Succeeding owners included Sir Christoffel Joseph Brand, Speaker of the Cape Legislative Assembly (1864–1888) and father of Johannes Henricus Brand, President of the Orange Free State; Petrus Johannes Kotzé (from 1848 to 1881), a member of the Cape Legislative

Assembly, Mayor of Cape Town and father of Sir John Gilbert Kotzé, Chief Justice of the Transvaal Republic and Judge of the Appeal Court of the Union of South Africa.

PJ Kotzé and subsequent owners cut up the land until 1936 when the Cape Provincial Administration bought the property. Resulting from the acquisition of adjoining premises, Leeuwenhof is now more than twice as large as it was when the Administration bought it.

LEINSTER HALL AND OUTBUILDINGS
(7 WELTEVREDEN STREET)

Leinster Hall was built in the 1850s by Sebastiaan Hofmeyr, on a plot which previously formed part of the farm Weltevreden. The original part of the outbuildings was erected simultaneously. Leinster Hall, with its predominantly Georgian characteristics, its noteworthy garden and its Victorian verandah, is one of four remaining historic manor houses in this region of Cape Town.

MOUNT NELSON HOTEL (ORANGE STREET)

The site pertains to historic outbuildings, ie the laundry complex and a kettle chimney. The laundry was probably designed by the architectural firm of Dunn & Watson, and was constructed shortly before 1898 under the supervision of the architectural firm of Herbert Baker. It still receives water directly from the Waterhof Fountain and is an excellent example of nineteenth century utility architecture.

The high kettle chimney is situated behind the laundry and is regarded as one of the few remaining structures of its kind.

Opened in 1899 by the Castle Steamship Company headed by Sir Donald Currie, the Mount Nelson was designed by English architects and managed by a Swiss expert, Emil Cathrein. The hotel attracted an exclusive clientele from the outset. During the Second Anglo-Boer War (1899–1902), it became the unofficial headquarters of the British army, while also harbouring prosperous refugees from the Witwatersrand.

PRESBYTERIAN CHURCH (151 HATFIELD STREET)

This building was designed in 1901 by John Parker, and constructed by McAllister & Company. The cornerstone was laid on 28 August 1901 by Lord Alfred Milner, and the church was consecrated on 11 October 1903. Inside is a War Memorial, designed by Alexander Forsyth and unveiled on 27 February 1921 by Field Marshall Earl Haig.

RAVENSWOOD HOUSE (HATFIELD STREET)

Ravenswood House is the only known example in Cape Town of the late Classical Georgian architectural style of the beginning of the nineteenth century.

This double-storey building was probably erected between 1817 and 1835 by MA de Kock as one of a series of houses for letting, and is situated on a section of the former Welgedaan property which was granted to GD Vreeburg in 1707.

SEMIDETACHED DOUBLE-STOREY VICTORIAN HOUSES (79, 81 KLOOF STREET)

The site of these Victorian double-storey terraced houses originally formed part of the old garden farm Leeuwenrust, which belonged to J Faure and was subdivided in 1880. They are thought to have been built by G Goodman, who bought the property in 1897.

THE WALLS OF THE TWO RESERVOIRS
(BELOW DE WAAL PARK)

The oldest and smallest of these two reservoirs was designed in 1847 by the Superintendent of Water Works, Mr Chisholm, and completed with a capacity of 11.4 megalitres in 1852. Due to necessity, a second reservoir with a capacity of 54.4 megalitres, was completed in 1860.

**VAN RHEEDE VAN OUDTSHOORN TOMB
(IN LANE OFF FAURE STREET)**
This burial vault is one of the few remaining historic links with the well-known Van Rheede van Oudtshoorn family, and is all that remains of the original Saasveld complex built by William Ferdinand van Rheede van Oudtshoorn in Kloof Street between 1791 and 1804.

VICTORIAN HOUSE (3 FAURE STREET)
This house, with its impressive cast-iron verandah, dates from the late nineteenth century and is an excellent example of late Victorian architecture.

VICTORIAN HOUSE (7 UNION STREET)
This impressive house, with its unusual hexagonal turret that surmounts the front verandah, was presumably erected in 1895. Its magnificent marble fire places are an exceptional feature.

VICTORIAN HOUSE (5 UPPER UNION STREET)
This house, which was originally a single-storey building, was enlarged in 1912 when a second storey was added. It forms a significant part of the architectural character of Union Street.

WATERHOF (HOF STREET)
Waterhof was originally a part of Leeuwenhof, but became a separate property in 1782. The house was probably built in 1785 or 1786 and is one of the historic eighteenth-century houses on the slopes of Table Mountain.

WELGEMEEND (CAMP STREET)
This was the historic home of the Hofmeyr family. In 1693 four hectares of land were granted to Andres de Man, Secunde under Simon van der Stel. It was acquired by Bartholomeus Bosch in 1769, whose widow, in 1772, married Jan Hendrik Hofmeyr, progenitor of the Hofmeyrs and supervisor of the Company's Station at Groote Schuur. In 1789 Stephanus J Hofmeyr, great-grandfather of 'Onze Jan' Hofmeyr, inherited the property. The oldest part of the house was built in the eighteenth century and enlarged by Stephanus. He built the homestead in its present form at the end of the eighteenth century. Welgemeend remained in the Hofmeyr family until 1944. It was purchased by the Cape Education Department and Jan van Riebeeck High School was built.

ZORGWYK HOUSE (36 BREDA STREET)
This house, built predominantly in Georgian style, was originally the homestead of the loan farm Zorgwyk. The house, which is indicated on a map of 1820, is one of the few homesteads of the early loan farms in the Upper Table Valley that have survived.

Glencairn
Local legend has it that a Scot from the original Glen Cairn named this suburb. It is said that he wandered about the valley playing his bagpipes.

WELCOME COTTAGE AND ADJACENT DWELLING HOUSE (GLENOAK ROAD)
This property originally formed part of a loan farm granted to Johannes Henricus Brand in 1811 and the houses are closely associated with his family. He was a member of the Court of Justice, his son Christoffel was the first Speaker of the House of Assembly, his grandson Johannes Henricus was President of the Orange Free State and his great-grandson was the well-known aviator Sir Quintin Brand.

Green Point
An independent municipality in 1839, it was reconstituted in 1859 and absorbed into the municipality of Cape Town in 1913. The promontory itself was named in 1675, and is said to be the second oldest English place name in South Africa.

DE GOEDE VERWACHTING (19 CAVALCADE ROAD)
This is a fine example of an early nineteenth century house at the Cape.

FORT WYNYARD (FORT WYNYARD ROAD)
The fort was erected in 1860 near the site where the Dutch East India Company Battery 'Kyk en de Pot' stood. The latter was dismantled between 1825 and 1827. The fort was named after Lieutenant-General RN Wynyard, the Lieutenant-Governor of the Cape Colony, and was reorganised in 1890.

GREEN POINT LIGHT HOUSE (100 BEACH ROAD)
Built and probably also designed by Hermann Schutte, this lighthouse is the oldest of its kind in South Africa. Construction began in 1821 and the lighthouse was officially opened on 12 April 1824. It originally consisted of a tower surmounted by two lanterns. The present light was erected in 1856, improved in 1906 and electrified in 1929. Standing 19.81m above high water, it has an intensity of 850 000 candles and a range of approximately 25.46km. A foghorn was installed in 1926.

GROVE HOUSE (4 GROVE ROAD)
This house in its present form dates from the late nineteenth century, and is a good example of Victorian architecture.

NEW LABORATORY BUILDING COMPLEX AT FORT WYNYARD
Used to manufacture ammunition during British rule in the early nineteenth century, three of a original eight buildings, which were ringed by a wall, still remain. They were constructed in the vernacular style, using local building materials such as stone and lime.

NEW SOMERSET HOSPITAL (BEACH ROAD)
The declaration is for the original section of the hospital as it existed in 1878, excluding later additions. The New Somerset Hospital was opened in 1862 and was the first hospital where doctors were trained in South Africa. It played an important part in the history of medical practice in South Africa.

VAULT OF WOUTERSEN-WESSELS FAMILY (WESSELS ROAD)
The architecture is most interesting and there is reason to believe that it is the work of the well-known architect Hermann Schutte. Some prominent citizens have been buried here, including Advocate ML Wessels, brother of Sir John Wessels, former Chief Justice of the Union of South Africa.

Hout Bay

The name, which means 'wood bay', was given to the area a year after the landing of Van Riebeeck in 1652, on account of the fine forests encountered here.

EASTERN BATTERY, BLOCKHOUSE AND EAST FORT (CHAPMAN'S PEAK)
The East Fort consisted of a powder magazine and water cistern on the ground floor, an officer's quarters on the first floor, and wooden balconies and musket posts on the upper floor. The blockhouse, cookhouse and battery were below the road. The cookhouse was built during the first British occupation of the Cape (1795–1802) and included a Dutch oven for baking. The men's barracks and lieutenant's quarters are on the upper level of the road and were built in 1797.

KRONENDAL (MAIN ROAD)
Although the farm had been in existence since the late seventeenth century, the H-shaped Kronendal, one of the finest Cape Dutch houses in the province, was only built in 1800 by Johannes Guillham van Helsdingen. During the nineteenth and twentieth centuries the

estate changed hands frequently. After the threat of being damaged by a scheme to widen the road, the house was saved by being proclaimed a national monument.

LONG KLOOF (MAIN ROAD)
Long Kloof dates from the late nineteenth century, and was originally a wine cellar on the farm Moddergat, owned by PJ Boonzaaier. After the farm's subdivision in 1946, the building was used as a farm stall.

OAK VILLA COTTAGE (BAVIAANSKLOOF ROAD)
The core of this fisherman's cottage, in typical vernacular style, dates from the 1850s. Additions were made in 1878.

WESTERN BATTERY (1781),
PUMPHOUSE AND OLD CANNON
(AT THE HARBOUR, AT THE FOOT OF HANGKLIP)
The ruins of the fort, built in 1781, are situated on land granted to officers of Her Majesty's Ordinance on 25 November 1844. Canons can still be seen here today.

Kalk Bay

This village developed around a small military outpost situated here in 1795. Its name is taken from lime kilns established here in the seventeenth century. Kalk Bay became a municipality in 1893 and was incorporated into Cape Town municipality in 1913.

SCHOONZICHT (204 MAIN ROAD)
This early twentieth-century Edwardian double-storey beach house borders on the old False Bay coastal road.

WAVE CREST (181 MAIN ROAD)
This residence was built up from two of the earliest cottages in Kalk Bay, the first of which was erected in 1846. The two cottages were joined and Victorianised in about 1890, and a second floor and verandah were added later. The house displays an interesting combination of Georgian and Victorian features.

Kenilworth

It is assumed that this suburb was named after the site of the ruined Kenilworth Castle in Warwickshire, England, also the setting of the novel *Kenilworth*, by Sir Walter Scott.

ASCOT HOUSE AND OUTBUILDINGS (2 ASCOT ROAD)
After this property was transferred to Henry Cloete in 1900, a house and outbuildings were built in the Arts and Crafts style espoused by Herbert Baker. Ascot is an fine example of stately, domestic Edwardian architecture, with characteristic bay windows, gable detail and red roof tiles. The interior also reflects elements of its former style, such as oak window ledges, wainscoting and a billiard room with the original table.

BEAU SOLEIL MANOR HOUSE AND ADJACENT
COACH HOUSE (SALISBURY ROAD)
The original section of this double-storey manor house, with its neogothic and Victorian characteristics, was built in 1877 by Dirk Cloete. Further additions, as well as the red brick coach house with its elegant rustication, were made at the end of the nineteenth century.

PELYN DWELLING HOUSE (ASCOT ROAD)
This house was designed and built by the architectural firm Baker & Masey in the neo-Tudor Arts and Crafts style. It was bought in 1906 by the well-known architect FK Kendal, who named the house Pelyn after the Kendall estate in Cornwall, England. Kendall resided in this house until his death in 1948.

STELLENBERG (STELLENBERG AVENUE)
One of the most historic and beautiful of all the Cape Dutch houses, this building dates from the second half of the eighteenth century.

Historic figures such as Frans van der Stel, Commissioner de Mist, Rhenius, Robert Clive of India, Lord Macarthy and Sir James Craig are all associated with the history of Stellenberg.

VICTORIAN DOUBLE-STOREY HOMESTEAD
(15 ALEXANDRA AVENUE)
This impressive dwelling house, dating from the last decade of the nineteenth century, is an excellent example of a Victorian double-storey, bay-window house. It forms a significant part of the architectural character of Alexandra Road.

Maitland
This suburb was named after Sir Peregrine Maitland (1777–1854), Governor of the Cape from 1844 to 1847. It became an independent municipality in 1902, but was incorporated into the Cape Town Municipality in 1913.

OUDE MOLEN (ALEXANDRA CARE AND REHABILITATION CENTRE)
This windmill, noteworthy for its bullet-shaped tower, was built in 1780–1782 for the Burgher Council, and was originally known as Die Nieuwe Molen. It is the oldest structure of its kind in South Africa. In 1807 it was acquired and restored by the burgher Kassien Dekenah, and remained in his family's possession until 1847. In 1901, the property with the mill, was bought by the Colonial Government for the establishment of a hospital, later known as the Alexandra Institution. In 1928 it was converted into a church, and at present serves as a music room.

Milnerton
This area was laid out on the farm Biesjeskraal in 1902 and was named after Sir Alfred Milner (1854–1925), Governor of the Cape Colony from 1897 to 1901, and High Commissioner until 1905. Milnerton became an independent municipality in 1955.

OLD MUNICIPAL HALL (JANSEN STREET)
This unique hall, later known as the Casino, dates from 1904 and was originally erected as a concert and dance hall. In particular, the special sunken dance floor is noteworthy.

OLD WOODEN BRIDGE OVER LAGOON
(WOODBRIDGE ISLAND)
This bridge has, until recently, been in constant use since its construction in 1901 by the Royal Engineers to provide entrance to a cannon trench. It is made of Jarra wood and is the only one of its kind in South Africa.

Mowbray
The suburb was first named Drie Koppen (three heads) after the heads of three slaves who were executed for murder in 1724, and impaled here. It was renamed Mowbray by the estate owner, who emigrated from Melton Mowbray, in Leicester, England. It became a municipality in 1890 and was incorporated into the Cape Town municipal area in 1913.

DE MEULE HISTORIC HOMESTEAD
The site includes the outbuildings and ring wall, Mostert's Mill, a threshing floor and entrance gates to Welgelegen. The residence, probably the oldest remaining building on Welgelegen, was acquired by J van Reenen in 1756. It displays a combination of architectural styles, including Cape Dutch and Arts and Crafts.

DOUBLE-STOREY VICTORIAN HOUSES
(2, 4, 6, 8 ,10, 12 GROVE ROAD)
These identical semidetached houses, are part of a unique block of two terraced rows. Dating from the 1880s, they have magnificent cast-iron verandahs and balconies.

MOLENVLIET HOUSE (MOLENVLIET ROAD)
This property originally formed part of the farm Koornhoop, which was granted to Thieman

Hendricks in 1661. The predominantly Cape Dutch house was formerly a barn for the Westoe building complex and dates from the early nineteenth century.

MOWBRAY TOWN HALL (MAIN ROAD)
This impressive Town Hall, with its Flemish-Renaissance features, was designed by the architect JC Tully of Tully & Waters and was erected in 1900.

THE KOORNHOOP DOVECOT (DIXTON ROAD)
This double-storey structure with six arches and a pediment between the side gables of two barn-like buildings has a width of 9.37m and is approximately 7m high. The upper section contains about a hundred small pigeon nests formed in the thickness of the wall and the lower section provides for a number of arched fowl nests of plastered brickwork. The dovecot was built in the eighteenth century on the historic farm Koornhoop, which was laid out with the introduction of the Free Burgher System in 1657.

VICTORIAN DOUBLE-STOREY HOUSES
(1, 3, 5, 7, 9, 11 ALBERT ROAD)
These houses form part of a unique block consisting of two terraced rows of identical late-Victorian double-storey, semidetached houses that date from the 1880s. The first and last houses in Albert Road have ornate triangular pedimented gables and cartouches, while the other houses are without gables.

WELGELEGEN HOUSE (RHODES AVENUE,
UNIVERSITY OF CAPE TOWN CAMPUS)
The original house on the historic Welgelegen property was drastically altered from 1899–1902 according to designs by Sir Herbert Baker. The rebuilt house in pseudo-Cape Town style was made available by Cecil Rhodes to the Curry family in perpetuity.

WELGELEGEN CEMETERY
At the end of the Van Reenen family's occupation of the farm in 1827, this graveyard formally became the family burial place of Gysbertus van Reenen and Sybrand Mostert, and their descendants. There are more than a hundred members of the two families buried here, and many in unmarked graves.

WESTOE CAPE DUTCH DWELLING (WESTOE ROAD)
This property, which came into the possession of Francois Pieter De Necker in 1785, originally formed part of the farm Koornhoop. The Cape Dutch house, known as Westoe, was erected shortly after by De Necker, and was restored in 1967. The outbuildings date back to the nineteenth century.

Muizenberg
Muizenberg developed from a cattle post to a military outpost and winter anchorage of the Dutch East India Company in 1743. Originally called Steenberghoek, the present name is taken from Wynand Willem Muijs who was the sergeant in charge of the military post in 1744.

DE POST HUYS (MAIN ROAD)
This building was originally erected in February 1673 by the Dutch East India Company as a military observation post. It was later used as a civilian dwelling and was owned by Sir JB Robinson from 1915–1929.

HISTORIC RAILWAY STATION (MAIN ROAD)
This impressive building, surmounted by a clock tower was built in 1912–1913. It was officially opened on 7 June 1913 by the Minister of Railways & Harbours, Mr Henry Burton, and is a fine example of Edwardian architecture.

LABIA MUSEUM (198 MAIN ROAD)
In 1901 Clifford Hume Knight bought this property and built the house. It was bought in

1939 by Countess Ida Labia. The large house is reminiscent of a Venetian 'palazzo' and is in the neo-Renaissance style.

LONG COTTAGE (248 MAIN ROAD)
The original section of this thatched-roof house was presumably erected as a fisherman's cottage c.1856. This predominantly vernacular-style building was enlarged to its present size shortly after the turn of the twentieth century and is unique in this area.

MAIN ROAD (190–194, THE FORT; 196, CANTY HOUSE; 252, WATERGATE)
These properties not only form an integral part of the only remaining concentration of early twentieth-century Edwardian beach houses in South Africa, but also border on the historic old False Bay coastal road.

OLD MAGISTRATE'S COURT (184 MAIN ROAD)
The cornerstone of this building was laid in April 1910. It has a sandstone foundation similar to that of the adjacent building, and with the old Police Station, De Post Huys and the Labia Museum, they form an impressive architectural complex.

OLD POLICE STATION (186 MAIN ROAD)
Constructed in c.1910, the old Police Station is built mainly in the Cape-Revival style, with Flemish influence in its uncommonly high gable.

RHODES COTTAGE (MAIN ROAD)
Only the second house to be built in Muizenberg, in 1868, the Rhodes Cottage Museum was restored by De Beers Consolidated Mines Limited to mark the centenary of the company in 1988. Cecil John Rhodes died here on 26 March 1902, and after his death it was left in the care of his manservant, Tony de la Cruz, until 1904. It was then boarded up until 1932 when it was given to the Northern Rhodesian Government (now Zambia) as a rest and rehabilitation centre for civil servants. In 1937 it was handed back to South Africa. The museum was opened by the then Mayor of Cape Town, Mr Sonnenberg, in 1953.

VERGENOEG HOUSE (1 ROYAL ROAD)
This impressive double-storey beach house, with its gables in the Flemish-Revival style, was designed by Sir Herbert Baker. It was built in 1903 for Alpheus Williams, the General Manager of De Beers Consolidated Mines.

Newlands

The suburb's name is taken from the new garden (lands) laid out by Governor Van der Stel for Burghers of the Dutch East India Company in 1700.

BOSHOF HOUSE (BOSHOF AVENUE)
The property on which this house is situated originally formed part of the historic Boshof farm owned by Alexander van Breda. The original section of the building dates from the early nineteenth century, and was enlarged and Victorianised during the 1840s.

HISTORIC VINEYARD HOTEL (COLINGTON ROAD)
The original section of the Vineyard Hotel was built in the Adam style between 1799 and 1800 by Andrew Barnard and his wife, Lady Ann, as a country residence. It was named The Vineyard by the Barnards. The natural beauty of the grounds still reflects the traditional rural characteristics of Newlands.

JOSEPHINE MILL (BOUNDARY ROAD)
This water mill, situated on the site of an earlier mill built by Johan Frederick Dreyer in 1818, was erected in 1840 by Jacob Letterstedt, a Swedish immigrant and 1820 Settler. It was named after Crown Princess Josephine, later Queen of Sweden. The taller extension was

erected sometime between 1863 and 1881, to house the steam mill. Anders Ohlsson & Company leased the property from 1888 until 1896, when Ohlssons Cape Breweries purchased it. Kate van der Byl, owner of the adjoining mill house, bought the mill in 1931 and her niece, Myra East, donated it in 1975 to the Historical Society of Cape Town, which restored it between 1975 and 1987. Still operational, this water mill's wrought-iron wheel is virtually intact, and is the only remaining example of its type in South Africa.

LETTERSTEDT BUILDING, MALT HOUSE AND KILN AT OHLSSONS BREWERY (BOUNDARY ROAD)
Construction of the first brewery on this site, initiated by Jacob Letterstedt, was completed in 1859. In 1888 the Mariendahl Estate was leased to another Swede, Anders Ohlsson, who replaced some earlier buildings with new malting facilities and a kiln, which were in turn replaced by the pneumatic maltings of 1903. These buildings were restored and now house a museum for the early history of beer brewing.

LONG COTTAGE (NEWLANDS AVENUE)
The Newlands House Estate originally formed part of the historic estate that was established in 1751 by Governor Ryk Tulbagh. Long Cottage first formed the slave quarters and chicken coop of Newlands House, but was later converted into a home.

MILL HOUSE (BOUNDARY ROAD)
This Georgian double-storey Mill House was erected by Jacob Letterstedt in the 1840s. Together with the garden it forms an integral part of the historic Josephine Mill Complex. It was formerly the engineer's cottage.

MOUNT PLEASANT (10 NEWLANDS AVENUE)
This property was purchased in 1883 by F Centlivres, who built this castle-like house. A symmetrical, double-storey building, it is primarily neogothic in style. It was at one stage the residence of the German Consul and High Commissioner to South Africa.

RED HOUSE (HIDDINGH AVENUE)
The rear part of the Red House is believed to have been built before 1729, while the remainder definitely dates from the early nineteenth century. Red House is consequently one of the oldest houses in Cape Town's southern suburbs.

ST ANDREWS CHURCH (PALMBOOM ROAD)
This attractive little church has considerable architectural merit. Designed by Sophia Gray, it was built in about 1857.

Noordhoek
This area was first settled in 1743 after land was granted to the widow of Frederik Russouw by Baron GW van Imhoff. It is assumed that the name originates from 'Norwegian Corner' (Noorhoek) as the nearby mountains used to be known as the Mountains of Norway.

DE GOEDE HOOP ESTATE
This estate originally formed part of the property known as Noordhoek and was purchased in 1913 by the mining magnate and governor of the former Rhodesia, Sir Drummond Chaplin, as a retirement dwelling. The foundation stone of the pavilion dwelling in the Beaux Arts style was unveiled in 1923 by Prince Arthur, Duke of Connaught, and the building completed in 1925.

Observatory
This suburb was named after the Royal Observatory built here in 1821.

GROOTE SCHUUR HOSPITAL
(FOOT OF DEVIL'S PEAK)
The site includes the east façade of the original Groote Schuur Hospital, together with the

incinerator tower, the palm court, and the operating theatre in which the first heart transplant was performed by Professor Chris Barnard on Louis Washkansky in December 1967. In March 1923 the government granted the extreme northern side of the Groote Schuur Estate, which Cecil Rhodes had bequeathed to the South African nation, to the University of Cape Town for the establishment of a medical school and hospital. Colonel DJ Mackintosch of the Western Infirmary, Glasgow, provided expert advice on the layout of the hospital and laboratories. Construction commenced on 20 January 1931 under the supervision of the Department of Public Works architect JS Cleland. The inauguration ceremony took place on 31 January 1938 with the first Governor-General of the Union of South Africa, Sir Patrick Duncan, officiating.

THE ORIGINAL VALKENBERG HOSPITAL BUILDING COMPLEX (1899)

The site consists of the administrative block (exterior and interior), courtyards, external façades, designated blocks, a stores building and a laundry. In 1881 the remainder of the 200-acre farm, Valkenberg, was bought by the Colonial Government to erect a reformatory. In 1891 the reformatory was moved to Tokai and the first mental patients were transferred to Valkenberg from Robben Island. By 1892 the Colonial Secretary, JW Sauer, approved the erection of a new mental hospital of 250 beds. Construction work was started in 1895 and completed in 1899. As such, Valkenberg was the first mental asylum in the country designed according to modern principles.

VALKENBURG HOMESTEAD AND CEMETERY

This Cape Dutch residence is one of the oldest farmhouses situated along the Liesbeeck River. The original section of the house dates from 1770 and was built by Cornelis de Waal, who bought the property in 1746. The house was enlarged in 1820 and 1830 and was later Victorianised by the addition of a verandah. The extensions were probably made by Cornelis Mostert, who acquired the farm early in the nineteenth century. Valkenburg was subdivided after his death and this area, with the main homestead, subsequently became part of the Valkenburg Institution. The residence had fallen into disuse by 1970, and since then, its structural condition has deteriorated substantially. The site, with the original house, outbuildings and cemetery, was transferred to the Cape Town City Council in 1985.

WRENSCH HOUSE BUILDING COMPLEX
(77 LOWER WRENSCH ROAD)

This building complex, with its Cape Dutch, Georgian and Victorian features, forms a unique architectural unit. The main building and some of the outbuildings date from the last quarter of the eighteenth century.

Oranjezicht

This suburb was named after the homestead of D Loubser, who bought the farm in 1709. It overlooked the Oranje bastion of the Castle.

DE WAAL PARK (CAMP STREET)

The park was laid out through the endeavours of David Christiaan de Waal, Mayor of Cape Town from 1889–1890. It was opened in 1895 for the use of the general public.

DOUBLE-STOREY LATE-VICTORIAN DWELLING
(1 BELVEDERE AVENUE)

This late-Victorian double-storey villa was built shortly after the turn of the nineteenth century.

DOUBLE-STOREY VICTORIAN HOUSE AND PROPERTY (7 BELVEDERE AVENUE)

This double-storey house was erected soon after the turn of the nineteenth century.

Cast-iron decorations on the verandah and balcony, as well as those on the boundary wall, are typical of the late nineteenth century.

DOUBLE-STOREY VICTORIAN HOUSE
(15 BELVEDERE AVENUE)
This imposing dwelling, with its late Victorian features, was erected at the turn of the century and is one of the earliest dwellings in Belvedere Avenue, itself an architecturally important area of Orangezicht.

EDWARDIAN DOUBLE-STOREY MANOR HOUSE
(21 BELVEDERE AVENUE)
This impressive double-storey manor house was erected shortly after the turn of the century, and is an excellent example of Edwardian architecture. It also has neoclassical and Victorian features.

GATEWAY AND WALLS, ST CYPRIAN'S SCHOOL
(GORGE ROAD)
The gateway and walls date from the end of the eighteenth century, and are situated on a section of the historic Nooitgezicht property. Because of their impressive architectural style, it is often stated that they were designed by Louis Michel Thibault.

MOLTENO POWER STATION
The Molteno Power Station was erected in 1894 and was originally known as the Graaff Electric Light Works, after DP de Villiers Graaff. It was the first hydroelectric power plant in the country, and was later converted to steam. As this power station could not meet the ongoing demand for electricity, the Central Electric Light Station was erected on the beach at Rogge Bay.

MURITAI HOUSE (22 ROSEMOUNT AVENUE)
This property originally formed part of the Oranjezicht Estate, which was acquired by a syndicate known as Oranje Zicht Estate Limited, in 1901. It was designed by the architect WS Law for AM Davidson, and submitted to the Cape Town City Council in 1903.

RHEEZICHT DWELLING HOUSE (GORGE STREET)
Rheezicht forms part of the property allocated to JJ Tesselaar in 1771. The original house was commissioned after 1782 by A van Breda.

TOWN FOUNDATIONS (UPPER ORANGE STREET)
The remaining section of the well-known Oranjezicht Estate dates from the era of the Van Breda family, who owned this farm for nearly 200 years. The main fountain, or Stadsfontein, as it was known, was covered with a vault in 1813. Another larger, vaulted collection point under the main fountain was built for all the fountains in 1853. From the latter, a wooden pipeline led to the proclaimed swing pump in Prince Street. This fountain originally played an important part in supplying water to Cape Town. There is also a structure that served as a chlorinating room, an old 1800 outbuilding, a bell cage from the old slave bell (c.1775), an old gateway and various garden walls. The farmhouse was demolished in 1957.

VICTORIAN VILLA (6 BELLEVUE STREET)
This Victorian villa was designed and erected in 1903 by E Seeliger for John Heinrich Dehning. The site originally formed part of Bellevue, one of the oldest farms in the Upper Table Valley.

VILLA CATHARINA (1 ROSEBANK PLACE)
This Victorian double-storey, semidetached house forms an essential part of a row of linked townhouses dating from the late nineteenth century.

WOLSELEY HOUSE (22 SOPHIA ROAD)
This property originally formed part of the Rheezicht Estate, which was subdivided in 1894. It was designed in the early Edwardian style by architect C Hawkins for W Schreiber in 1903.

Parow

Parow was established in 1901 and was named after a German ship captain, Johann Henrich Ferdinand Parow (1833–1910), who was shipwrecked at the Cape in 1865, and who became the owner of the land on which the town was laid out. Parow attained municipal status in 1939.

DOUBLE-STOREY DWELLINGS
(64, 66 HOPKINS STREET)

These two impressive double-storey houses, with their Edwardian and Victorian features, were erected in 1910 by George Thomas Hopkins. The magnificent cast-iron verandah and balcony at No. 66 were presumably added by Johannes Petrus Serenus du Toit, the next owner, who bought the property in 1917.

HISTORIC VAULT (MEIBOOM AVENUE, PLATTEKLOOF EXTENSION NO.3)

This crypt was presumably commissioned by Gustav Greffrath, to whom the farm Platkloof was transferred on 15 December 1843. The date 1862 appears on the front of the rectangular crypt.

Pinelands

The town was laid out on a section of the Uitvlugt Forest Reserve in 1919 and was the first 'garden city' in South Africa. It was here after the Anglo-Zulu War of 1879 that King Cetshwayo was detained. Pinelands became a municipality in 1948.

THE MEAD AND MEADWAY

This area was laid out in 1921 and the first house, 5 Meadway, was completed in 1923. Part of the Uitvlugt Forest Reserve, the area was donated by the state to the Garden Cities Trust, shortly after it was formed in 1918 by the Honourable Richard Stuttaford. The Mead and Meadway were developed in accordance with the original layout of Pinelands, prepared in 1919 by Thompson, Hennel & James, architects of London. They were associated with the first two garden cities established in the UK, through the efforts of Ebenezer Howard, a forerunner of contemporary town planners and the originator of the new town and garden city concepts.

The Pinelands layout plan was the first town planning scheme prepared in South Africa. It formed the basis for South Africa's first and subsequent town planning legislation. The Mead and Meadway and their buildings were proclaimed in 1982. Meadway, together with the road reserve called Meadway and the open space known as the Mead, are declared areas.

Plumstead

This suburb was developed in 1823 around the site of an old Dutch East India Company military camp.

MEYERSHOF (MEYER STREET)

This farmhouse stands on land that formed part of the property awarded to Joseph Sagers in 1814. It was named after Dr Heinrich Meyer, who purchased the property in 1885.

Robben Island – World Heritage Site

Honoured as one of South Africa's first three World Heritage Sites proclaimed in December 1999, Robben Island joins the likes of the Great Wall of China, Great Zimbabwe, the Taj Mahal, the Great Barrier Reef and the Grand Canyon. The island was first used by the Dutch East India Company (VOC) as a vitualling station, and later became an asylum (until 1913) and a leper colony (until 1931).

During World War II it played a key role in the defence of Cape Town, and during the 1950s it was controlled by the South African Navy. In 1969 control of the island was taken over by the

Department of Correctional Services, and it was during this time that Nelson Mandela and other political prisoners were imprisoned here.

OLD RESIDENCY AND PARSONAGE
These buildings were erected before 1894 to serve as residences for the Commissioner and the clergyman respectively. The façades and ground plans of the two structures are very similar, and their projecting wings and bay windows are noteworthy. Local chipped stone was used as building material. Both buildings display aspects of the social, religious and administrative activities that took place on Robben Island during its turbulent history.

Rondebosch

The suburb was known as 't Ronde Doorn Bosjen during Van Riebeeck's time and was so-named after a round clump of thorn trees that grew on the banks of the Liesbeeck River. The first free burghers settled here in 1657. Rondebosch was proclaimed a municipality in 1886, but was incorporated into the municipal area of Cape Town in 1913.

GLENARA RESIDENCE (BURG STREET)
This impressive Victorian double-storey house was designed by the architect AW Ackerman and built by one, Mannix, for Lewis Anthony Vincent from 1882–1883. It has been used as the official residence of principals of the University of Cape Town since 1925.

GROOTE SCHUUR MANOR HOUSE
(GROOTE SCHUUR ESTATE)
Cecil John Rhodes purchased this property in 1891 and named it Groote Schuur. The house was redesigned by Herbert Baker according to instructions from Rhodes, who bequeathed the estate to the South African nation. Since 1910 it has been used as an official residence of prime ministers and presidents of South Africa.

KLEINE SCHUUR MANOR HOUSE
(GROOTE SCHUUR ESTATE)
The history of Kleine Schuur is closely associated with the VOC and the outpost located on the estate. The property was sold in 1791 by the VOC to HC Herholdt. In 1912 GFA Pigot-Moodie sold Kleine Schuur, Westbrooke and the surrounding land to the state.

RONDEBOSCH COMMON (CAMPGROUND ROAD)
This land served as a camping ground for Batavian and British troops during the eighteenth and nineteenth centuries. Later it was reserved for the use of the public for recreational purposes.

RONDEBOSCH FOUNTAIN (MAIN ROAD)
A well-known landmark in Rondebosch, the 'fountain' is actually a drinking trough. Dating back to 1891, it consists of a circular iron drinking trough, legs in the shape of horses' hooves, and a pole, topped by a lantern.

RUSTENBURG HOUSE (MAIN ROAD)
Built in about 1657 with a second storey added in c. 1780, the house was destroyed by a fire in the nineteenth century, and later rebuilt.

ST PAUL'S ANGLICAN CHURCH (MAIN ROAD)
The land on which this church building was erected was granted by Sir Lowry Cole on 30 August 1832. The original neogothic church was opened on 16 February 1834 and a gallery was added in 1845. Thereafter the church was considerably enlarged and the original church incorporated into a new building, which was completed in October 1854. Further additions were made in 1857, 1858 and 1909.

UNIVERSITY OF CAPE TOWN: HISTORIC MIDDLE AND UPPER CAMPUS (RHODES ESTATE)
The site incorporates the Jameson Memorial Hall, its podium and two flanking buildings (the

Students Union and the Jagger Library) but excluding extensions to the rear of the colonnade linking these buildings to the Jameson Memorial Hall, the Jameson Memorial Hall steps (from the podium to the residents road), the Arts Block and the Mathematics Block, the resident forecourt, two residences (Smuts Hall and Fuller Hall), the open fields (at present rugby fields), together with their connection across Rhodes Drive to the Summer House.

The Summer House (also known as Belvedere), was built c.1760 by the Dutch East India Company (VOC) on the Rustenburg Estate, and is probably one of the oldest existing buildings in South Africa. It was reconstructed by Sir Herbert Baker in 1894 and forms the focal point of an avenue of oak trees running up the hillside from the Rustenburg House, which on the instigation of Cecil John Rhodes, was replanted with plumbagos, japonicas, jacarandas and turkey oaks. Part of this walk remains and is known as Japonica Walk. The Summer House and Japonica Walk lie on the main axis around which the campus of the University was planned.

The Woolsack Residence, with its mixture of Cape Dutch and neoclassical features, was rebuilt by Sir Herbert Baker on the instruction of Cecil John Rhodes, for use by poets and artists. Rudyard Kipling and his family stayed here during the summers from 1900–1907. The property was transferred to the University in 1980. This unique group of buildings in the Classical Revival style, together with the open spaces, constitute the original campus plan designed by the architect JM Solomon in 1918.

WESTBROOKE (GROOTE SCHUUR ESTATE)

Both Groote Schuur and De Onder Schuur (now Westbrooke) were favourite places of Cape governors during the nineteenth century. They leased them during the summer months to avoid the heat of the town. In 1821 De Onder Schuur was sold to Egbert Andreas Buyskes, and in 1832 it was bought by Judge William Westbrooke Burton, who named it Westbrooke. In 1838 he sold it to Abraham de Smidt, the then owner of Groote Schuur. In 1912 it was sold to the state.

Rosebank

Until 1953, Rosebank was originally the site of the Agricultural Show of the Western Province. It was incorporated into Cape Town in 1913.

VREDENBURG HOUSE
(13 VREDENBURG CRESCENT)

The land on which this Cape Dutch house was erected was originally granted in 1785 to Andries Daniel Grove, owner of the adjacent farm Rijgersdal. The T-shaped house was probably built by Grove shortly thereafter. It is one of the oldest existing original farmhouses in the vicinity of Rosebank.

WHITBY HOMESTEAD (3 BARRY LANE)

This property previously formed part of the farm Zorgvliet, and was bought by Reverend TL Hodgson of the Methodist Church in 1839 for the construction of a church and vicarage. The church was completed in 1845 and the vicarage, with its Cape Dutch and Victorian elements, presumably dates from the 1840s. The vicarage was inhabited by several ministers from 1840 to 1864.

Sea Point

The name dates from 1776 when Sam Wallis and his men camped here to avoid an outbreak of smallpox in Cape Town. A municipality was established in 1839, but it was incorporated into Cape Town municipality in 1913.

ELLERSLIE GIRLS' HIGH SCHOOL BUILDING COMPLEX (355 MAIN ROAD)

This school was founded in 1899 after the purchase of the Ellerslie Estate. Originally a

Cape Dutch house was utilised until a single-storey school building designed by John Parker was completed in 1901. Further additions followed in 1906, with a top storey added in 1913. The original Cape Dutch house was demolished in 1935 and a new double-storey building erected.

SALISBURY HOUSE (5 BELLEVUE ROAD)
This double-storey Victorian semidetached house was designed in 1895 by Austen Cooke for Mrs RCE Bell, and built shortly after. The name dates from the transferral of the property to Miss E Alderslade on 12 June 1924.

Simonstown

The town was officially established in 1743 and was named after Simon van der Stel, Commander of the Cape from 1670 to 1691 and Governor of the Cape from 1691 to 1699. In 1687 he recommended to the Dutch East India Company to use Simonstown as the winter anchorage as it was more sheltered than Table Bay. It was the Royal Navy's South Atlantic base from 1814 to 1957, when it was handed over to the South African Navy. The town attained municipal status in 1883.

ADMIRALTY HOUSE (ST GEORGE'S STREET)
This house, which dates from the middle of the eighteenth century, became admiralty property in 1814. Rear Admiral Sir Jahleel Brenton was the first of many admirals to live here. The building was changed considerably in 1863.

ALBERTYN'S COTTAGE (KING GEORGE WAY)
A small rectangular cottage, built by Alexander Tennant between 1799 and 1801, this is a local example of an early English-style building.

BAY VIEW HOUSE (132 ST GEORGE'S STREET)
This double-storey building with its Georgian and Victorian features dates from 1803.

CHURCH OF ST FRANCIS OF ASSISI
(COURT ROAD)
This church was completed in 1837 and consecrated on 30 July 1837.

DE BEERS BUILDING (88 ST GEORGE'S STREET)
This sandstone building, which dates from 1902, was designed by Sir Herbert Baker for Cecil Rhodes' De Beers Cold Storage Syndicate, as a meat outlet in Simonstown. Used by the company's successor, Imperial Cold Storage & Supply Company, from 1903–1921, it was then sold to the Standard Bank of South Africa, who used the building as a branch office until 1974.

DIE STEM PARSONAGE (CHURCH STREET)
This double-storey building was erected in 1815 by the building contractor Herman Schutte. The verandah was added in 1820. It was here that the music for the national anthem, *Die Stem van Suid Afrika*, was composed in 1919 by the Reverend ML de Villiers. It now houses a museum of national emblems.

DUTCH REFORMED CHURCH (CHURCH STREET)
The foundation stone of the Dutch Reformed Church building was laid on 10 December 1855, and the building itself was consecrated on 10 December 1856. The church is closely linked to the history of Simonstown. Music for the national anthem was composed in 1919 in the adjoining parsonage, by the then minister, Reverend ML de Villiers.

HUGO FAMILY VAULT AND CEMETERY (MAIN ROAD)
Built for Field-Cornet Pieter Francois Hugo and his family, the graveyard has a simple plastered and lime-washed vault with a saddle roof and straight end gables with decorative moulding. The inscribed date above the arched entrance is 1860, which is probably the year in which the vault was built.

IBEKA (CORNWALL ROAD)
This land was one of the original erven granted in Simonstown. It was first acquired in 1817 by PJ Truter, the collector of customs, who probably built the house, later called Ibeka. In 1868 it was sold to the British War Department, and served as a garrison officers' mess until 1921, after which it was used to house military and naval personnel.

MARTELLO TOWER (MARTELLO ROAD)
The Martello Tower was erected in 1796 on Sir James Craig's orders, to improve Simonstown's defence system. It is claimed that this is the oldest British structure of its kind in the world and the first building to be erected after the first British occupation of the Cape. The 7.62m tower is circular, with a 1.83m-thick wall.

MAST HOUSE AND LEAN-TO STRUCTURE (NAVAL MUSEUM)
In 1814 it was decided to move the Royal Naval establishment from Cape Town to Simonstown. Numerous buildings were erected by the Royal Engineers, one of which was the Mast House, for producing sails, as well as the storage of boats, sails, masts and spares. It was also used for servicing the Royal Navy's sailing vessels. Mast House consists of two linked double-storey barns of considerable length to accommodate sails and masts.

NINE-INCH MLR-CANNON (MIDDLE NORTH BATTERY)
Manufactured by the Royal Gun Factory, Woolwich, this 12-ton cannon was first issued on 18 May 1881 and installed in its present position c.1895. It played an important role at this military base until 1906.

OATLANDS HOUSE (DISTRICT)
This house, formerly known as the Government Garden House and later as the Commandants' House, probably dates from the end of the eighteenth century. Its inhabitants included Colonel John Graham and Captain (later Colonel) Henry Somerset. The name Oatlands was given to the property by Somerset.

OLD MAGISTRATE'S OFFICES AND RESIDENCE (MAIN STREET)
This building was erected in 1776 with Christoffel Brand as its first occupant. Admiral Lord Nelson is presumed to have been one of the first visitors at the residence after his arrival in Simonstown on 21 May 1776. Towards the end of the eighteenth century, it was used as a naval hospital. From 1814, when Simonstown became a separate district, it served both as a courtroom and magistrate's residence. It now houses a museum.

OLD STABLES AT OATLANDS HOUSE
The old stables, also known as the guard house, were originally erected in the eighteenth century as stables for the well-known Oatlands property. Shortly after the second British occupation of the Cape it served as a guard house for some time.

PALACE BARRACKS
Palace Barracks is an architecturally outstanding late-eighteenth century building. It was probably built in 1785, and since 1886 has served as a military barracks and later as a naval officers' mess.

STUDLANDS (ST GEORGE'S STREET)
This building was built as a wine house or tavern in 1779 by JP Eksteen, and is probably the oldest building of its kind in South Africa.

UNION TAVERN AND STABLES (SMITH'S LANE)
The Union Tavern was erected as a public house in 1801 by Johannes Bissinger, and was later also used as a hotel.

YARRA YARRA (ST GEORGE'S STREET)
The grounds on which these two predominantly Victorian semidetached houses are situated, originally formed part of the Studlands property, granted to JP Eksteen on 5 May 1779 for the erection of a wine house. Owner Jan Gysbert Hugo erected the houses according to an 1897 design by JE Vixseboxse.

St James
The name of this small town was taken from the St James Church constructed in 1874.

BEACH HOUSES (20, 22, 32, 92 MAIN ROAD)
These houses are an integral part of the only remaining concentration of twentieth-century Edwardian beach houses in South Africa.

BRAESIDE (3 BRAEMER ROAD)
This double-storey house also forms part of the concentration of early twentieth century Edwardian beach houses (see above).

CORRIEMAR HOUSE (4 MAIN ROAD)
The site includes a homestead and a stone wall along the road. Originally a fisherman's cottage that was later extended, the house stands on a piece of land first granted to JH Muller.

GREYSTONES (10 MAIN ROAD)
This double-storey early twentieth-century Edwardian beach house borders on the old False Bay coastal road.

SEA FEVER (82 MAIN ROAD)
The original part of this picturesque thatched cottage presumably dates from the late eighteenth century.

STONEHENGE (36 MAIN ROAD)
This double-storey beach house dates from the 1920s and is predominantly in the Italian style, with Art Deco characteristics.

VILLA CAPRI
The original section of this house was built in approximately 1795. At one stage a whaling station was based on the property.

Tamboerskloof
This residential suburb is situated on the slopes of Signal Hill and Lion's Head, extending downwards from Kloof Nek. The origin of the name, Tamboerskloof, which means 'drum gorge', is not clear. A concentration of German-speaking immigrants in the area over the years has lent it a particular character.

AMMUNITION MAGAZINE (MILITARY ROAD)
Constructed in c.1893, this good example of late-nineteenth century military architecture forms an integral part of the British fortifications of the Cape Colony. The magazine was used to store ammunition. Markings on the timber floors, indicating the position of the containers, are still visible.

DEVONSHIRE VILLA (33 CARSTENS STREET)
This dwelling, which is an excellent example of late-Victorian architecture, was erected in 1893–1894 by WM Cook, an affluent Cape Town draper and silk merchant who named the property Devonshire Villa.

RUIMZICHT HOUSE (10 MILNER ROAD)
Dating from the 1890s, this double-storey building is predominantly in the late-Victorian style. Noteworthy are the ornate front and side gables, as well as the cast-iron decorations on the façade.

SILVER KNOWLES HOMESTEAD (20 BROWNLOW ROAD)
The house was designed and erected by HT Jones for a Mr Hosking in 1902. The verandah ornamentation and three original marble fireplaces are especially noteworthy.

VICTORIAN DOUBLE-STOREY BUILDING
(31 CARSTEN STREET)
This double-storey dwelling, with its Victorian and Jugendstil features, dates from the 1880s, and was presumably erected by CG Prince.

VICTORIAN HOUSE (14 KOHLING STREET)
Predominantly Victorian in style, the cast-iron ornamentation on the ceramic saddle roof, the verandahs, the boundary wall and gates of this double-storey dwelling are noteworthy. It also forms a significant component of the architectural scene of Kohling Street.

Three Anchor Bay
Dating back to 1661, the name could possibly refer to anchors securing chains stretched across the bay for defence purposes.

DUTCH REFORMED CHURCH AND PARSONAGE
(MAIN ROAD)
This church building was officially opened on 9 July 1879 by Dr Andrew Murray. Only eight months later, on 10 March 1880, the secession of the congregation from the Groote Kerk took place. The stained glass windows date from 1885 and the embattled tower from 1903.

Tokai
The land was first granted in 1792 to Jan Andreas Rauch, a German tradesman who named his estate Tokay, possibly after a well-known wine centre in Hungary. The estate passed into the hands of the Eksteen family in 1802 and was bought by the Cape Government in 1883 as a forest reserve and nursery.

HISTORIC SANDSTONE CHAPEL
(NEAR PORTER REFORMATORY SCHOOL)
This predominantly neogothic sandstone chapel probably dates from the 1890s. It forms an integral part of the Porter Reformatory, which was established here in 1880.

TOKAI ARBORETUM (SPAANCHEMAT ROAD)
The South African Forest Industry had its beginnings on this site when Joseph Storr Lister, Conservator of Forests of the Western Conservancy of the Cape Colony, laid out this impressive arboretum in 1885. It is well known by botanists, horticulturists and silviculturists for its large variety of indigenous trees.

TOKAI MANOR HOUSE (TOKAI ROAD)
Built shortly after 1792 by Rauch, and designed by the architect LM Thibault, the house was bought by the Cape Colony Government in 1883. In 1919 the Porter Reformatory for coloured youths took over the buildings.

Woodstock
First named Papendorp, the suburb was renamed Woodstock when it became a municipality in 1881. It was incorporated into Cape Town's municipality in 1913.

MELBOURNE TERRACE (1, 3, 5, 7, 9, 11, 13)
The land on which these houses are built was granted to Bernardus Josephus van der Sandt in 1844. Built by GA Gamans, this row of seven late-Victorian terraced houses was designed by Marie Welch, who bought the property in 1900.

ROODEBLOEM COMPLEX (ELSON STREET)
This historic complex of buildings, of which the core of the original dwelling house dates from the eighteenth century, was built on land first granted in 1666 to Hendrick Lacus. The buildings are at present used by the Ruth Prowse Art Centre.

THE FRENCH REDOUBT (TRAFALGAR PARK)
This formed part of the line of fortifications built by the French Garrison in 1786 around Cape Town. The forts remained in use until 1827, but this is the only one remaining. It is also known as The Frederick William Redoubt.

TRAFALGAR PARK
(CNR VICTORIA AND SEARLE STREETS)
This fortress was hastily built in 1781 when an attack by British forces on the Cape was expected. A conical kiln, probably for brick-making, was added some 50 years later.

TREATY TREE (SPRING STREET)
On 10 January 1806, the articles of capitulation of the Battle of Blaauwberg, were signed here at 'Treaty House'. The house was demolished in 1935, but tradition has it that the treaty was signed under this milkwood tree.

Wynberg

The suburb's name derives from a vineyard planted here in 1658 by Jan van Riebeeck. Wynberg became an independent municipality in 1886, but was incorporated into the municipal area of Cape Town in 1927.

CAPE EDUCATION MUSEUM (9 ALIWAL STREET)
The original part of this building was erected in 1854, and the Industrial School for Girls, which was established in 1836 (due to the efforts of Lady Elizabeth D'Urban, wife of the then Cape Governor) was moved to these premises. The original T-shaped building had a thatched roof, but in 1911 it was sympathetically enlarged in Edwardian style by the architectural firm, Forsyth & Parker. The Cape Education Museum is currently housed in the building.

DUTCH REFORMED CHURCH
(CNR CARR HILL AND DURBAN STREET)
A Dutch Reformed Church was built here in 1831. In 1899 it was replaced by the present fine building.

FIVE HISTORIC BURIAL VAULTS
(DUTCH REFORMED CEMETERY)
This site includes the burial vaults of JF de Wet, AJ Truter, J Meyer, Von Landsberg and J Letterstedt, as well as the family grave of Dr Philip Eduard Faure, Maria Koopmans-de Wet and George McCall Theal. The delimited area also includes 11 burgher graves and the cypress avenue that leads to the burial vaults.

GLEBE COTTAGE (WATERLOO ROAD)
This building dates back to the beginning of the nineteenth century, and was used *inter alia* for military purposes, as well as a church, a school and a funeral parlour.

HAWTHORNDEN HOUSE (HERSCHEL WALK)
Although the core of this double-storey house probably dates from 1653, it was rebuilt in its present French-Victorian style in 1881, by Captain John Spence.
  Sir JB Robinson bought Hawthornden in 1891 and lived there until his death in 1927. Count Natale Labia, grandson of JB Robinson, donated Hawthornden to the Cape Provincial Administration in 1978, but retains the use of the house during his lifetime.

HISTORIC OLD WYNBERG VILLAGE
The following properties form an integral part of the historic old Wynberg Village, which is an area of considerable character, as well as historic, architectural and environmental importance. It is one of the few areas close to the city of Cape Town that has retained its historic character.
+ Albert (5 Victoria Street)
+ Ashleigh Cottage (Lonsdale Street)
+ Bell House (Roos Lane)
+ Boot Inn (6 Standard Lane)
+ Carr Hill (No 1)
+ Casa Nara (Wolfe Street)
+ Chelsea Cottage (307 Moore Road)
+ Chelsea Cottages (3, 5, 7, 9 Moore Road)
+ Church Hill (Young Lane)
+ Clarence (3 Victoria Street)
+ Clover (Wolfe Street)

- Cnr Durban Road and Wolfe streets
- Cnr Wellington and Coghill
- Cnr Wolfe and Kemp streets
- Cnr Wolfe and Lonsdale streets
- Cnr Wolfe and Van Riebeeck streets
- Coach House (Piers Road)
- Coach House (Riebeeck Street)
- Coghill Road (24, 47)
- Delfshaven (Waterloo Road)
- Drew House (Cnr Durban Road and Victoria Street)
- Dunkling (3 Wolfe Street)
- Durban House (32 Durban Road)
- Durban Road (8, 9, 11, 13, 15, 18–20, 45, 48, 49, 51, 59, 60, 65)
- Elim Row (68, 69)
- Erin Cottage (Wolfe Street)
- Falcon House (21 Durban Road)
- Fig Tree Cottage (Cruse Lane)
- Forrester Inn (Durban Road)
- Good Hope Cottage (7 Durban Road)
- Hodi Mihi (Carr Hill)
- Ido Ville (34 Durban Road)
- In Fin Art Shop (Cnr Wolfe and Durban roads)
- Ivanhoe Cottage (Lonsdale Street)
- Kent and Albany (4–6 Victoria Street)
- Klein Maynard (Wolfe Street)
- Kleine Oude (Cnr Carr Hill and Durban Road)
- Laundry Cottage (Durban Road)
- Leather Bottle (7 Standard Lane)
- Little Marlow (Wolfe Street)
- Long Cottage (53 Durban Road)
- Lonsdale Street (No 9)
- Lord Nelson's Cottage (7 Lonsdale Street)
- Mega Cottage (Lonsdale Street)
- Mercury House (Riebeeck Street)
- Moore Road (No 4)
- Mortimer Road (No 7)
- Oak Cottage and The Cottage (Durban Road)
- Old Bakery (23 Durban Road)
- Osborne House (Wolfe Street)
- Oude Wynberg Stadhuis
- Parboo Building (Wolfe Street)
- Petersklip (Piers Road)
- Pink Cottage (Young Lane)
- Prince Alfred Arms (4 Durban Road)
- Prince Alfred Cottage (6 Durban Road)
- Quellerie Cottage
- Railway Station (Station Road)
- Rembrandt (9 Victoria Street)
- Riebeeck House (Riebeeck Street)
- Riebeeck Street (3, 4, 5)
- Shirley Cottage (Lonsdale Street)
- Somerset House (Wolfe Street)
- Spes Bona (Cnr Durban Road and Victoria Street)
- Standard Lane (1, 2, 3, 4, 5)
- The Armoury (Wolfe Street)
- The Muse (3 Wolfe Street)
- Unicorn House (Cnr Victoria and Durban Streets)
- Victoria Cottage (7 Victoria Street)
- Waterloo Close (9 Durban Road)
- Waterloo Edge (Cnr Young Lane and Durban Road)
- Waterloo Road (7, 37, 45)
- Wellington Road (23–25, 34–36)
- Withens (3 Carr Hill)
- Wolfe Street (6, 15, 50).

MONTEREY HOUSE (KLAASENS ROAD)

Monterey, originally known as Oosterzee, was built by PAM Cloete shortly after the Anglo-Boer War (1899–1902). In 1928 it was sold to an American, Hugh Tevis, who spent approximately 237 000 Pounds Sterling on alterations, and converted the existing building into a neo-Tudor mansion.

From 1951 to 1976, the house served as a private preparatory school for boys, under the name Monterey. It was restored in 1982 by the Seardel Investment Corporation, and converted into the company's headquarters.

OFFICERS' MESS (MILITARY CAMP)
The officers' mess was built in about 1880 or earlier, and is at the heart of the Wynberg Military Camp, which already existed in 1797.

PRINCE ALFRED HOUSE (WATERLOO STREET)
This double-storey house is built in Georgian style and dates from the 1850s. It is one of the most important houses in the historic centre of Wynberg.

TENDERTON DWELLING HOUSE (60 DURBAN ROAD)
This U-shaped house was originally in the Cape Dutch style, but sections of it date from the second half of the nineteenth century when it was greatly Victorianised. The property was originally part of the Vredenhof farm, and was allocated to William Hawkins on 8 April 1856.

TROVATO MANOR HOUSE (44 COACH ROAD)
An impressive manor house with late-Victorian and neoclassical elements, Trovato was built in 1898–1902 for Carl Jeppe, appointed Consul General for the Transvaal in Cape Town in 1898. The house was designed by Herbert Baker.

VICTORIAN DWELLING HOUSE (14 LANGLEY ROAD)
With its predominantly late Victorian elements, this dwelling was erected at about the turn of the nineteenth century, and forms an integral part of the architectural character of Langley Road and the historic core of Wynberg.

VREDENHOF (59 DURBAN ROAD)
Mostly Victorian in character, this property originally formed part of the farm Vredenhof and was transferred to Jan Zeeman in 1827. The original section of the house was presumably erected shortly afterwards and later enlarged.

WINTHROP BUILDING (8 DURBAN ROAD)
This U-shaped house, with its thatched hip roof, dates from 1830 and is one of the oldest houses in the historic nucleus of Wynberg. It originally served as a military mess, but was owned by the Grossouws from 1921 to 1985.

Zonnebloem (District Six)
This area is famous for its colourful history and forced removals of the population in the 1960s to the Cape Flats. It's roughly bounded by the railway, De Waal Drive, Canterbury Street and Scott Street. Originally called Zonnebloem, it became known as 'District Six' from its municipal ward status. By the 1840s, the Buitenkant ceased to mark the city limit, and artisans and small businessmen of all races moved into the area. Over time, the suburb became overpopulated and slum conditions prevailed.

MORAVIAN CHURCH AND PARSONAGE (MORAVIAN HILL)
This property was bought by the Moravian Missionary Society in 1885. The Georgian double-storey house that was on the property was erected in 1850 and was used as a parsonage. The neoclassical church was completed in 1886.

ZONNEBLOEM COTTAGES (CAMBRIDGE STREET)
These farm labourer cottages were Victorianised in the early nineteenth century and, together with the Zonnebloem College Complex, form an integral part of the historic area within the city of Cape Town.

CERES
Established in 1854, Ceres became a municipality in 1964. It was named after the Roman goddess of agriculture.

BAIN'S KLOOF PASS
The pass stretches from the Divisional Council boundary on the Paarl side to the Darling Bridge on the Ceres side. Andrew Geddes Bain discovered the kloof in 1846 when the Colonial

Secretary, John Montagu, was searching for a direct route through the mountains between Cape Town and the new Mitchell's Pass. Montagu accepted the route for his highway and named it Bain's Kloof. Bain commenced construction work in February 1849, and the pass was opened on 12 September 1853 by the Chairman of the Central Road Board, PB Borcherds.

BOPLAAS (FARM KOUE BOKKEVELD, DISTRICT)
This farm has been in the possession of the Van der Merwe family since 1743, and is well known in Afrikaans literature through the works of IW van der Merwe (Boerneef). The buildings date mostly from the beginning of the nineteenth century, and form a unique and almost unspoilt example of an old-fashioned farmyard.

EDWARDIAN DWELLING (EXCELSIOR FARM)
This house with its impressive verandah was erected from 1910–1914, and is predominantly in the Edwardian style. A nearby, elongated thatched-roof building is an excellent example of a vernacular Koue Bokkeveld structure.

KAROOPOORT OUTSPAN (R46 FROM CERES)
Karoopoort was a well-known and popular outspan for early travellers to the north. It was described, among others, by the travellers Lictenstein and Burchell at the beginning of the nineteenth century. There are also three historic buildings on the site that probably date from the middle of the nineteenth century.

NOOITGEDACHT FARMHOUSE (DISTRICT)
This farmhouse is an important and typical example of the traditional building style of the Koue Bokkeveld.

OLD TOLL HOUSE (MICHELL'S PASS, NEAR CERES)
The old toll house was built shortly after the completion of Michell's Pass in 1848. Charges were collected on animals and vehicles from 1 January 1849. Once Michell's Pass allowed easy access from the Cape to the north, particularly after diamonds were discovered, the toll house played an important role.

VERLORENVLEI HISTORIC FARMSTEAD AND OUTBUILDINGS
(R46 TOWARD TOUWSRIVER, DISTRICT)
This farm previously formed part of the original farm Verlorenvallei, granted to Schalk Willem Pienaar in 1833. The H-shaped dwelling dates from 1827 and was presumably erected by Pienaar. The outbuildings, which date from the early nineteenth century, are also of interest.

CITRUSDAL

This town was established by the Dutch Reformed Church in 1916. Its name is derived from the word citrus, relating to the orange groves in the surrounding areas. It attained municipal status in 1957.

ORANGE TREE (FARM GROOT HEXSRIVIER)
According to historical records, orange trees grew in the vicinity of Citrusdal as early as 1777. Botanists think it likely that this orange tree is more than 200 years old.

CLANWILLIAM

This town was originally named Disselsvlei, after the farm of Jan Disselsvlei on which the town was laid out. It was renamed by Sir John Cradock, Governor of the Cape (1811–1814), after his father-in-law, the Earl of Clanwilliam. The town attained municipal status in 1901.

DIE ERF (PARK STREET)
This Cape Dutch house accommodated a Drostdy official shortly after the establishment of a sub-Drostdy at Clanwilliam in 1808.

DUTCH REFORMED CHURCH (MAIN ROAD)
The church building was designed in neogothic style by Carl Otto Häger (1813–1898), the well-known architect. He also supervised its erection, which was completed in about 1864.

IRISH SETTLER COTTAGE (MAIN ROAD)
This Irish Settler cottage dates from the early nineteenth century and represents the vernacular building style used by Irish Settlers in the 1820s.

OLD MAGISTRATE'S OFFICE (2 PARK STREET)
On 1 February 1808 the Earl of Caledon, then Governor at the Cape, approved the establishment of Clanwilliam as a sub-Drostdy of Tulbagh. DJ van Ryneveld, the first Deputy Landdrost, was appointed and took up residence at 3 Park Street.

OLD PRISON BUILDING (MAIN ROAD)
This Georgian building, the core of which was probably erected as early as 1808, is a predominant architectural feature in the historic core of Clanwilliam. It now houses the publicity office and the Clanwilliam Museum.

OLD RESIDENCY OF THE DEPUTY LANDDROST (3 PARK STREET)
This building was erected in the 1820s as a dwelling for the Deputy Landdrost. It is in the Cape Dutch style and is T-shaped. The building is one of the oldest dwellings in Clanwilliam.

ST JOHN'S ANGLICAN CHURCH AND PARSONAGE (MAIN ROAD)
This neogothic church building, designed by Sophia Gray, was erected in 1865, on the remains of an earlier Settler church. The building was inaugurated in 1866 by Bishop Gray. The Parsonage, which presumably dates from the 1840s, is an exceedingly beautiful old Cape thatched cottage.

DAL JOSAFAT (DISTRICT PAARL)

The name is of biblical origin, from Joel (Jehoshaphat).

CAPE DUTCH HOUSE (FARM AMSTELHOF)
This Cape Dutch house in its present form dates from the second half of the nineteenth century, as is evident *inter alia* from the date, 1856, on the front gable, the plain style of the gable and in Victorian influences.

GOEDE RUST, NON PARIELLE AND ROGGELAND FARMS
The site incorporates this consolidated farm, formerly known by each of the names mentioned above, and all historic buildings thereon. The farms Non Parielle and Goede Rust were originally granted in 1690, and Roggeland in 1693.

These three farms remained in the hands of the French Huguenots and their descendants for centuries. There are approximately 14 historic buildings in the Cape Dutch or Victorian style, the most important of which have already been restored. The Huguenot cemetery on Non Parielle is also of interest from a cultural history point of view.

HISTORIC DWELLING (FARM KLEINBOSCH)
The farm Kleinbosch was granted to the Huguenot progenitor Francois du Toit. The H-shaped house was erected by his grandson, Guillaune. The date 1792 appears on the concavo-convex front gable.

HISTORIC VLAKKELAND FARMSTEAD (ONDER DAL JOSAFAT)
This Cape Dutch complex, inclusive of the surrounding ring wall, presumably dates from the years 1790 to 1800, and was previously the farmstead of the farm Vlakkeland, which was granted to Huguenot Jean Roux in 1694.

HUGUENOT MEMORIAL SCHOOL (REMAINS OF) (FARM KLEINBOSCH)

In 1881 the Genootskap van Regte Afrikaaners decided to establish the Huguenot Memorial School. The building was erected in 1882–1883 and served as a school until 1910. It was originally a Georgian double-storey building and was the first school to use Afrikaans as its medium of instruction.

KLEINBOSCH CEMETERY (KLEIN DRAKENSTEIN AREA)

This cemetery was laid out in about 1700 by the Huguenot Francois du Toit on his farm Kleinbosch. Three of the founders of the Genootskap van Regte Afrikaners, namely Reverend SJ du Toit, DF du Toit and PJ Malherbe are also buried here.

MALHERBE HOUSE (FARM KLEINBOSCH)

This Victorian house dates from the middle of the nineteenth century and was originally the dwelling of Petrus Jacobus Malherbe, the founder member of the Genootskap van Regte Afrikaaners.

ONDERDAL SCHOOL BUILDINGS (ROGGELAND ROAD)

The Onderdal School was founded in 1847. Building work on the new school commenced late in 1854, and the building was inaugurated on 31 May 1855. It was officially opened on 5 June 1855 and was used until 1968 when it was finally closed. Founder members of the Genootskap van Regte Afrikaaners also received instruction here.

SCHOONGEZICHT FARM (DE HOOPSTEUN ROAD, DISTRICT)

This property was granted in 1694 to Abraham Vivier, and was sold in 1723 to Francois du Toit. The original section of the house was erected in 1717, while the front gable dates back to 1826. The H-shaped Cape Dutch house has impressive gables, windows and casements, as well as a beautiful interior.

VALENCIA FARM (WINDMEUL AREA, DISTRICT)

Valencia, formerly known as Naauwbepaald, first formed part of the well-known Huguenot farm Kleinbosch, granted to Francois du Toit in 1692. The present homestead dates from about 1818, and was erected by Daniel Francois du Toit. It was changed from its original Cape Dutch style to a Georgian appearance in about 1855. The Cape Dutch outbuilding bears the date 1801 on the front gable, and was presumably the original dwelling on the farm.

DARLING

This town was laid out in 1853 and was first named Groene Kloof. It was renamed after Sir Charles Henry Darling, Lieutenant-Governor of the Cape (1851–1854) and attained municipal status in 1955.

GROOTE POST FARM

In 1752 Groote Post was already one of the largest and most important farms in the vicinity of Malmesbury. The impressive homestead and outbuildings date from the early nineteenth century and from 1814–1827 it was the country house of Lord Charles Somerset. The farm was divided into seven sections in 1827, after which the section with the main homestead, named Groote Post, belonged to several well-known families such as the Versters and the Duckitts.

ZWARTLAND SURVEY BEACON (FARM KLIPVLEI)

The pyramid-shaped, sandstone beacon with a mounted platinum pin forms the Western Terminal Point of Sir Thomas Maclears' Zwartland Survey Base Line, laid in 1840 to 1841. It is closely associated with the development of surveying in South Africa.

DE DOORNS

The name of this town is taken from the farm De Doorns boven aan de Hex Rivier, which existed here as early as 1725. The area became a municipality in 1951.

DE DOORNS HISTORIC CAPE DUTCH FARMHOUSE
The farm De Doorns, which was granted to Gabriel Rossouw in 1759, is one of he oldest farms in the Hex River Valley. The original section of this Cape Dutch house, which dates from approximately 1796, was enlarged to its present H-form by Pieter Jacobus de Villiers shortly after 1818. The rear gable bears the date 1823.

DE RUST

This small town was laid out on the farm De Rust in 1900.

DUTCH REFORMED CHURCH AND OLD CHURCH HALL (LE ROUX STREET)
This cruciform church, with neogothic characteristics, was designed by the architect George Wallis of Oudtshoorn. The cornerstone was laid on 28 November 1900 by the Reverend J Beyers, and the building was officially inaugurated on 28 November 1902. An impressive pulpit, designed by another architect, JE Vixseboxse, and installed in 1911, is also noteworthy. The old hall, which was erected in 1904, was used as a school from 1904–1913. At present it serves as the Church Hall.

MONS RUBER ESTATE WINE HOUSE (FARM RIETVLEI)
Strategically situated on the route between Mossel Bay and Beaufort West, this was originally the old toll house situated on the Olifants Drift. With the diamond rush of the 1870s, traffic between Mossel Bay and Kimberley was greatly increased, and the Rietvlei toll became a lively outspan. Later the post coach changed horses here, enabling passengers the opportunity to rest. The building eventually became known as the Kantien (bar) until its closure, probably soon after 1913.

SCHOEMAN HOUSE (FARM RIET VALLEY)
This homestead, which was constructed mainly in the vernacular style, dates from the 1850s. It is presently inhabited by the third generation of the Schoeman family and has been changed according to the needs of successive owners. Most of the original yellowwood ceilings and floors in the house have remained intact.

VREDELUS FARMHOUSE
After JJ Schoeman and SPD le Roux purchased the farm De Rust in 1899 and donated land to the local congregation for a church, development on the remainder of the farm was postponed for more than two years on account of the Anglo-Boer War.

WATERMILL (FARM VOËLGESANG)
This historic old double-storey water mill, with its enormous iron wheel, dates from the 1890s.

ELIM

This small town was founded in 1824 in the Bredasdorp district by German missionaries, the Herrnhuters (Moravian Brethren) and takes its name from the biblical name Elim, meaning 'haven of peace'. It was chosen because of the fountains in the area, which the Moravians related to Exodus 15:27, 'And they came to Elim where were twelve wells of water and threescore and ten palm trees; and they encamped there by the waters'.

ELIM MISSION STATION
The site incorporates the church, parsonage, shop, mill, original farmhouse and houses inhabited by the shop manager, minister and

deacons. The historic Mission centre of Elim dates from 1824 when the Moravian Church purchased the farm Vogelstruis Kraal, and laid out the Mission Station. The farmhouse was adapted as a parsonage and, with economic growth, a mill was built towards 1830.

The thatched-roof church was originally erected in 1835 and enlarged in 1865. The church clock was manufactured in Germany in 1764. Chandeliers, installed in 1835, were originally oil lamps and in 1973 were converted to electricity. The 200-year old organ, purchased from the Dutch Reformed church in Three Anchor Bay, was made in Germany and has 531 pipes. A weather vane features an angel, a reminder of the coming of Christ.

The old windmill dates back to 1828 and was used until October 1972. The Rembrandt Tobacco Corporation assisted with the restoration of the MillHouse in 1974, as well as the mill wheel in 1990, so that the mill could fulfil its historic function once more. It is the largest wooden water-mill wheel in the country, and still mills wheat with stone grinders. The original shop which was built in 1898 is still operational.

Elim features a Slave Monument, dedicated to the emancipation of slaves on 1 December 1938. One house remains in Elim with an original dung floor, which must be repolished every eight days. Graves of the German missionaries can still be seen at Heer-en-Bos.

FAURE

A small village, Faure is an important junction with main roads branching to Cape Town, Bellville, Stellenbosch and Somerset West. It is also situated on the railway line from Cape Town to the Strand.

MEERLUST FARM (DISTRICT)
This well-known farm was granted in about 1693 to Henning Huysing (originally Husing), who later became one of the wealthiest cattle farmers of the Cape settlement. He apparently built the original T-shaped house c.1702. Johannes Albertus Mijburg became the owner of the farm in 1757 and it is still in the possession of the Myburgh family. In 1776 the main homestead was enlarged in Baroque style, to its present H-shape. The wine cellar, stables, dovecot, sundial, slave bell chair, family graveyard, old slave quarters and a long row of buildings in which craftsmen and slaves practiced their respective trades, are also worth mentioning.

VERGENOEGD FARMSTEAD (DISTRICT)
The property was originally granted to Pieter de Vos in 1696. The earlier section of the H-shaped dwelling house with its impressive gables, probably dates from the middle of the eighteenth century.

FRANSCHHOEK

The town's name, which literally means 'French Corner', was given on account of the French Huguenot refugees who settled here in 1688. The town was established in 1860 and attained municipal status in 1881.

CAPE DUTCH MANOR HOUSE (FARM BURGANDY, ORIGINALLY NAMED BOURGOGNE)
Built on a farm originally allotted to Pierre, one of the three original De Villiers brothers in 1694, the original homestead is much altered. The concavo-convex front gable of this H-shaped Cape Dutch manor house bears the date 1791, when it belonged to Jacob Marais. The house itself forms an important part of South Africa's architectural heritage.

DUTCH REFORMED CHURCH (HUGUENOT STREET)
This church, with its neogothic and Cape Dutch architectural features, was built at the instance of Reverend PN Ham, shortly after the local

congregation had broken away from the Paarl congregation in 1845. The oldest part of the church building was erected in 1846–1847, and was officially consecrated on 18 April 1847. The north and south wings were added in 1883.

DUTCH REFORMED CHURCH CEMETERY (HUGUENOT FARM)

This was the first town cemetery in Franschhoek. Land was divided from the old Huguenot farm, La Cotte, and in 1847 a Dutch Reformed church, together with a cemetery was established here.

DWELLING (43 HUGUENOT STREET)

This property previously formed part of the farm La Cotte, which was originally granted to the French Huguenot Jean Gardiol in 1713. The house, with its predominantly Cape Dutch features, was presumably erected in 1850.

JAN JOUBERTGATS BRIDGE (FRANSCHHOEK PASS)

This bridge was built by the Royal Engineers, and assisted by soldiers of the South African Corps as part of the first hard road over the Franschhoek Mountains. It was completed in 1825 and, except for a new surface, is one of the earliest bridges in South Africa.

LA MOTTE (DISTRICT)

This farm was the headquarters of the extensive Franschhoek plantations when three farms of the same name were granted to free burghers in the same district in the late seventeenth century. It was originally granted to a German Settler, Hans Hendrik Hattingh in 1695. In 1752 it came into the possession of Huguenot Gabriel du Toit, and in 1815 to another Huguenot descendant, Gideon Jacobus Joubert.

LA PROVENCE (MAIN ROAD)

This imposing house, one of the best known Cape Dutch houses, was probably built by Peter de Villiers, who bought the farm in 1756. The H-shaped building has beautiful gables, bearing the dates 1800 and 1815 respectively. The site includes a smaller dwelling on the Paarl side, and a store house on the Franschhoek side of the main dwelling, which, together with a rectangular piece of land form an integral part of the main dwelling.

LATE-VICTORIAN HOUSE (9 HUGUENOT ROAD)

This impressive bay-window house was erected in 1898 by JP de Villiers. It is predominantly late Victorian in style and forms an important part of the architectural character of Huguenot Road.

GENADENDAL

Established as a mission station in 1737 by the Moravian missionary Georg Schmidt, this small town was originally named Baviaanskloof. It was renamed Genadendal (Vale of Grace) in 1806.

HISTORIC CORE OF THE MORAVIAN MISSION STATION

The Genadendal Moravian Mission Station is the oldest mission village in South Africa. When Georg Schmidt was not allowed to continue his work, he returned to Europe in 1744. In 1792 missionaries H Marsveld, D Schwinn and JC Kuhnel resumed work at Baviaanskloof, and by 1802 the settlement was the largest in the Cape Colony. Buildings within the historic core date from the eighteenth and nineteenth centuries, and are predominantly in Cape Dutch and vernacular styles. A bell in the churchyard was presented to the Mission Station in 1793. It was placed in position in 1798, after permission to use it had been obtained from the authorities at the Cape. It is suspended between two pillars surmounted by an arch. The old mill was restored in 1990–1992.

OLD BRIDGE OVER THE RIVIERSONDEREND
This bridge, the first over the Riviersonderend, was built in 1819–1820 by the Moravian Missionary JD Beinbach and members of his congregation. Two pillars were added in 1823.

GEORGE

The town was proclaimed George Town in 1811 after King George III of England, who had donated a Bible to the church. George became a municipality in 1884.

CRADOCK PASS (OUTENIQUA MOUNTAINS)
Construction of this pass, named after the Governor, Sir John Cradock, commenced in 1812 under the supervision of three contractors, PA Matirz, F Trenk, and S Muller. The pass, which is approximately 8km in length, is 969.5m above sea level at the highest point, and was completed in 1815 (*see also* Montagu Pass).

DUTCH REFORMED CHURCH COMPLEX
(COURTNAY STREET)
The site includes the youth house (1812), the parsonage, the long building (1821) and the old cemetery. This property, which was established in 1812, originally extended over an entire block. The mother church (1842), together with the abovementioned buildings, all date from the early nineteenth century.

GEORGIAN HOUSE (33 LANGENHOVEN STREET)
This impressive double-storey building, with its Georgian features, was erected in about 1840. In 1982 it was restored and converted into offices.

HISTORIC PRISON BLOCK BUILDING (1861)
(ON THE SITE OF DE BULT HIGH SCHOOL, LANGENHOVEN STREET)
This building is an important example of a typical nineteenth-century gaol built in the Georgian style. It was George's second gaol (1861–1911), but was later used as one of the first industrial schools established to address the issue of poor whites in South Africa, following the Anglo-Boer War (1899–1902), as well as the formation of the Union of South Africa (1910).

MILL RIVER HOMESTEAD (FARM EENSZAAMHEID)
This house is typical of the vernacular-style architecture of the Langkloof. The first person to settle on the Moelenrivier loan farm in the Langkloof was a miller, Pieter Terblanche. Part of the present house and the mill were already in existence when the farm was bought by PJ Taute in 1815. Boer commandos encamped here during the Anglo-Boer War. The author Pauline Smith, who knew the Tautes, wrote her book, *The Beadle,* during one of her visits here.

MONTAGU PASS
Montagu Pass, which replaced the older Cradock Pass, was built after 1843 by the engineer Henry Fancourt-White. It was named after the Colonial Secretary, Sir John Montagu, who officially opened the pass in December 1847. The smithy also dates back to the days of the construction of the pass.

OLD OAK TREE (IN FRONT OF THE OLD KING EDWARD VII PUBLIC LIBRARY)
This tree was planted in 1811 by Landdrost van Kervel. Now known as the Slave Tree because of the old chain and lock embedded in the tree trunk, it is said to be the biggest oak tree in the southern hemisphere.

OLD STONE BRIDGE (MONTAGU PASS)
The attractive arched stone bridge over the upper reaches of the Malgas River in the Montagu Pass was part of the original construction of the pass, opened by Sir John Montagu in 1847.

SECTION OF OLD MAIN ROAD BETWEEN GEORGE AND KNYSNA
The 11km section of road stretches from a point opposite the turnoff to Saasveld College at the intersection with the main road from Hoekwil and Wilderness, and includes the bridges over the Kaaimans, Silver and Touws rivers. The picturesque gravel road meanders through indigenous forest and has been used since the nineteenth century. For years it was the main road to the east. Bridges over the Silver and Kaaimans Rivers replaced earlier structures and were built in 1903 and 1904 respectively.

ST PAUL'S CHAPEL CHURCH
This building was erected in 1855 and for many years served as a school and church for the coloured community of St Marks.

TOLL HOUSE (MONTAGU PASS)
This toll house dates back to the middle of the nineteenth century and from here, at the bottom of the Montagu Pass, a toll was collected after the pass was opened for traffic in 1849.

VAN DE GRAAFF'S BEACON
This stone beacon bearing the crest of The Netherlands and the monogram of the Dutch East India Company, is housed in the public library. A replica of which is housed in the South African Museum in Cape Town.

GREYTON

This small town was established in 1854 and was named after Sir George Grey (1812–1898), Governor of the Cape Colony from 1854–1859 and 1860–1861. It attained municipal status in 1910.

GEORGIAN HOUSE (MARKET STREET)
This dwelling house has an interesting combination of vernacular and Georgian characteristics and dates from the mid-nineteenth century. The single-storey rear section probably predates the original grant of land in 1839.

THE POST HOUSE (MAIN STREET)
Originally built in 1860 to serve as the village post office, it is one of the oldest buildings in Greyton. Presently used as a country inn, the post box can still be seen in the front room.

GROOT DRAKENSTEIN

This region near Paarl was named after Hendrik Adriaan van Rheede tot Drakenstein, High Commissioner in 1687.

BELLINGHAM FARM
The imposing Cape Dutch homestead dates from the seventeenth century. Surrounded by beautiful landscaped gardens, it is bordered by eighteenth century outbuildings and ring wall. There is also a magnificent collection of antique furniture and objets d'art. Bellingham House has been bequeathed to the nation by Bernard and Fredagh Podlashuk.

BOSCHENDAL HOMESTEAD (FARM CHAMPAGNE)
This farm, originally granted to the Huguenot Jean Le Long in 1685, became the home of Jacques de Villiers and his wife Marguerite Gardiol. Their grandson, Paul, built the historic manor house in 1812 and the farm remained in the De Villiers family until 1879. The H-shaped manor house, outbuildings and ring wall form a unique Cape Dutch architectural group.

CAPE DUTCH HOUSE: WATERGAT
(BIEN DONNE EXPERIMENTAL FARM)
The asymmetrical house was presumably erected in 1863 by CF Beyers. The gable depicts the simple lines of the penultimate phase of the Cape Dutch architectural style.

LA RHONE HOMESTEAD

The original grant of this farm, made in 1691, was to a Huguenot, Jean Garde. From 1702–1902, however, the farm saw a succession of different owners, with the result that it has close historic ties with families such as the Malans, Jordaans and Haupts.

It was from the Haupt family that Cecil John Rhodes acquired the farm in 1902, since when it has remained the property of Rhodes Fruit Farms (now Anglo American Farms). The extent of Garde's house is marked today in a building used as a tap-room, by windows specially built to the original proportions.

The manor house dates from the third quarter of the eighteenth century, when the farm belonged to Pieter and Magdalena Joubert, and has been preserved virtually intact, including most of the original interior woodwork. H-shaped and gabled, La Rhone overlooks a vast courtyard flanked by widely and systematically spaced outbuildings, among them a cellar with a gable dated 1837. With its outbuildings and ring wall, the house forms a unique and important Cape Dutch architectural complex.

HAARLEM

This town was laid out in 1856 by JC Taute, and was subsequently taken over by the Berlin Missionary Society in 1860. Even though the mission station was known as Anhalt-Schmidt, after the place in Moravia from where the missionary Schmidt had originated, the village itself was named Haarlem.

HISTORIC LUTHERAN MISSION CHURCH
This church, built in the shape of a Greek crucifix, was erected between 1877 and 1880 and is one of the few churches in South Africa built in this style.

HEIDELBERG

Laid out on the farm Doornboom in 1855, the town was named after Heidelberg in Germany. It became a municipality in 1862.

DUTCH REFORMED CHURCH (CHURCH SQUARE)
The cornerstone of this impressive cruciform church was laid on 13 February 1913, and the building was officially inaugurated on 7 March 1914. It was the third church to be erected on this site since the founding of the Dutch Reformed congregation in Heidelberg in 1855.

HISTORIC HOMESTEAD (FARM KROMBEKSRIVIER)
This farmhouse, built predominantly in the Cape Dutch style, was erected in about 1740–1744. The Krombeksrivier homestead is not only one of the oldest farmhouses in the vicinity, but also one of the earliest outspans on the road to the Eastern Frontier.

HOMESTEAD (FARM LIZMORE)
The core of this Cape Dutch homestead dates from the 1750s. Additions were made in the 1840s after which it remained unaltered. Since then, Lizmore has been in the possession of the Barry family for five generations.

SOUTHEY'S ARMS (FARM GLAMORGAN)
This T-shaped thatched dwelling dates from about 1870, and was reputedly erected by Andrew Geddes Bain during the construction of the Tradouw Pass. It was named after Richard Southey, then magistrate of Swellendam.

HERMANUS

Originally named Hermanuspietersfontein after the Dutch teacher who found a water spring here where he watered his sheep, the town was established in 1855. It attained municipal status in 1904, when the name was also shortened to Hermanus.

CYPRESS TEA GARDEN (NOW BURGANDY RESTAURANT, MARINE DRIVE)
This building initially consisted of two stone-and-clay fishermen's cottages built in the vernacular style by Swedish boat builder, John Louis, later known as John Wessels, in 1875. A cypress tree donated to Wessels by a certain Overbeek was planted in the front garden and became a landmark until it was destroyed in a storm many years later. In 1914 Miss Bubery from England bought the property from Wessels and started the Cypress Tea Garden. It is one of the oldest buildings in Hermanus, and in certain sections the original floors and windows still exist. In 1968 a committee was formed to save Cypress Building from being demolished.

OLD FISHING HARBOUR INCLUDING THE OLD SEA WALL
Hermanus owes its origin to the local fishing industry. For more than a century the old harbour served fishermen and the community, and it is still a spectacular attraction.

HEROLDS BAY

This small town, originally known as Sandstrand, was named after the first Dutch Reformed minister of George, TJ Herold (1812–1823).

CAVE ADJACENT TO KLAMARNI DWELLING
This cave is of considerable scientific value owing to the recent discovery of deposits of stone artefacts and faunal remains.

HOTAGTERKLIP

Situated near Struisbaai, Hotagterklip is one of a number fishing villages on the Cape coast characterised by whitewashed cottages with thatched roofs, half-doors and great chimney stacks.

HISTORIC FISHERMAN'S COTTAGES
This impressive architectural complex consists of nine fishermen's cottages, all examples of the traditional vernacular style.

KNYSNA

This town was established in 1882 when the two hamlets of Melville (1825) and Newhaven (1846) amalgamated. It attained municipal status in 1881. Knysna occupies the site of the estate of George Rex (reputed son of George III and Hannah Lightfoot) who lived on his farm Melkhoutkraal from 1804 until his death in 1839.

BELVIDERE MANOR HOUSE (BELVIDERE)
In October 1831 George Rex bought the farm Uitzicht, renaming it Belvidere. This Georgian manor house, with yellowwood ceilings and floorboards, was built by a Scottish officer, Thomas Henry Duthie, as a home for his bride Caroline, the third daughter of George Rex.

HOLY TRINITY CHURCH AND CEMETERY (BELVIDERE)
This imposing little church was erected by the enthusiasm and financial assistance of Thomas Henry Duthie. The foundation stone was laid on 15 October 1851, and the church was consecrated on 15 October 1855 by Bishop Gray. It is designed in a typical Norman style of the eleventh and twelfth centuries.

KNYSNA HEADS
This area is of importance because of its natural beauty. Two large sandstone cliffs, at the exit of the Knysna lagoon guard the passage to the sea.

MATJIES RIVER CAVE
A human skull (of a Bushman) was discovered here by Professor TF Dreyer of Bloemfontein in

December 1927. He found that the cave had been occupied by different ethnic groups at different periods, and named four different layers that underlined his theory: Bushman, Myilus, Wilton and Burnt.

Professor AJD Meiring wrote a thesis, entitled 'The Wilton skulls of the Matjies River Shelter', in 1937.

The National Museum in Bloemfontein started excavations and established beyond any doubt that the Matjies River deposit was rich in prehistoric remains. Some 200 human skeletons were recovered, and over 30 000 stone artefacts and other remains, revealing evidence of the peoples of the shelter. This cave is one of great archaeological importance and has yielded considerable collections of Stone Age remains.

MILLWOOD HOUSE (QUEEN STREET)

This historic cottage, built of wood and corrugated iron, is the only building that remains from the time of the discovery of gold at Millwood. The latter was proclaimed a gold field in 1886.

OLD GAOL (CNR CHURCH AND QUEEN STREETS)

The gaol was the first building erected in Knysna by the Colonial Government and was erected to house convicts on their way to the concentration camp on Prince Alfred Pass. The cornerstone was laid by G Fichat on 19 February 1859. Designed mainly in Victorian style, today the building houses the Maritime Museum, the Angling Museum and the Knysna Art Gallery.

OLD ST GEORGE'S CHURCH (10 MAIN STREET)

The foundation stone of this first church built in Knysna, was laid in April 1849 by John Rex, son of George Rex, who donated the land. The church was consecrated by Bishop Robert Gray on 3 October 1855.

PUBLIC LIBRARY (MAIN ROAD)

This building, with its neoclassical elements is one of only a few remaining sandstone buildings in Knysna. It was erected in 1893 and enlarged in 1937 by the addition of a western wing.

RUINS OF ANGLO-BOER WAR FORT

The erection of this fortification, atop a commanding hill above the town, was carried out on the instructions of the commander of the town guard, Major WA Thomson. The fort faces the Heads and is possibly the reason for its name, Thomson's Folly. There was never a shot fired in anger from it. Two of the guns from the fort can still be seen in the town.

KUILS RIVER

Originally a post of the Dutch East India Company named De Cuylen, a village was established here during the eighteenth century. It was named after the river situated in the area. The town attained municipal status in 1950.

HAZENDAL FARM (BOTTELARY ROAD)

Hazendal was allotted to the Messenger of the Court, Christoffel Haasenwinkel, in 1704. The homestead, built in 1790, originally consisted of three rooms, and was later extended to an H-shape dwelling. Slave quarters, with a concavo-convex gable, date from 1781. A shed was built in 1780, and a wall dating from 1791 is still intact. Hazendal was sold to Izaak Daniel Bosman in 1831, and today, five generations later, still belongs to the Bosman family.

HISTORIC MILESTONE XV
(HOUSED IN THE FOYER OF THE MUNICIPALITY)

This elongated milestone made from sandstone with the Roman numerals 'XV', presumably dates from the late eighteenth or early nineteenth century, and was previously situated on the road between Bellville and Kuils River.

MOOIPLAAS HOMESTEAD (BOTTELARY)
This property is the remainder of the farm Rozendal, granted to C Hazenwinkel in 1727. The Cape Dutch dwelling on the farm was built by JC Bosman and its neoclassical gable bears the date 1833.

ZEVENFONTEIN FARMHOUSE, NOW CALLED ZEVENWACHT (OFF VAN RIEBEEK ROAD)
This fine old Cape house with its attractive front gable and garden wall was built in about 1800.

LADISMITH

Originally named Lady Smith, after the wife of Cape Governor Sir Harry Smith (1787–1860), the town was established on the farm Elandsvlei in 1852. To avoid confusion with Ladysmith in Natal, which was established in 1850, the name was changed to Ladismith. A municipality was instituted in 1862, and an elected municipal council installed in 1903.

ALBERT MANOR (44 ALBERT STREET)
This T-shaped single-storey house was reputedly built at the turn of the nineteenth century by Mr Rowan for MC van Tonder, a farmer from Buffelskloof. There is also a coach house, now used as guest rooms.

EVANGELICAL LUTHERAN CHURCH COMPLEX (CHURCH STREET)
This complex, in typical neogothic idiom, dates largely from the 1860s. The buildings are closely associated with the history of the Evangelical Lutheran Church, formerly known as the Berlin Missionary Society.

OAKDENE DWELLING HOUSE (CHURCH STREET)
This stately double-storey house was erected by the immigrant Heinrich Wilhelm Becker in 1876. He was Mayor of Ladismith for an unbroken period of 32 years.

OLD DUTCH REFORMED CHURCH
This church, consecrated on 13 May 1874, was designed and built in neogothic style by the well-known architect Carl Otto Häger.

OLD WESLEYAN CHURCH (BECKER STREET)
The cornerstone of this mainly neogothic church was laid on 13 September 1906 by HW Becker, Mayor of Ladismith. In the 1960s it was transferred to the Dutch Reformed Church and by 1979 the Congregation of Christ bought the property and restored it. The building was put into use again on 1 September 1979.

THATCHED COTTAGE (58 CHURCH STREET)
This cottage, predominantly in the vernacular style, was erected in the mid-nineteenth century. It presumably served earlier as a caretaker's cottage for the Oakdene property.

VICTORIAN DWELLING HOUSE (19 QUEEN STREET)
Built in 1894, probably by JA Neft, this mainly late Victorian double-storey house forms an integral part of the architectural street scene of Queen Street and the historic core of Ladismith.

LAINGSBURG

Named after John Laing, Commissioner of Crown Lands in the Cabinets of Sprigg and Rhodes, the town was established on the farm Vischkuil aan de Buffels Rivier in 1881, and became a municipality in 1906.

BLOCKHOUSE (GEELBEK RIVER)
This blockhouse was built by the British during the Anglo-Boer War (1899–1902), to guard the bridge over the Geelbek river.

DUTCH REFORMED CHURCH AND CHURCH HALL (VOORTREKKER STREET)
The original church building, built on the farm Vischkuil by SG Greeff at his own expense, was

consecrated on 13 July 1881. In 1881 Greeff donated the church, together with four erven for building a parsonage. Since the consecration of a new church by Reverend A Morrees in 1905, the old church has been used as a church hall. The new church is a cruciform stone structure with a pitched roof and neogothic embellishments. The complex is surrounded by unique iron railings and gates.

LANGEBAAN

The town was founded in 1870 and its name refers to the long stretch of beach.

DUTCH REFORMED CHURCH AND PULPIT (OOSTERWAL STREET)

The church, with its neogothic features, was donated in 1872 as a chapel of ease to the Parish of Hopefield by a member of the congregation, William van der Byl. The building was taken into use on 1 April 1872. The yellowwood pulpit was made in 1721 by Adam Albertyn, progenitor of the Albertyn family in South Africa, for the Dutch Reformed Church in Stellenbosch. It was donated to the Zoutrivier (now Hopefield) congregation in 1853, from where it was transferred by ox-wagon to the Langebaan church in 1878. It is undoubtedly the oldest existing pulpit in South Africa.

OESTERWAL

Bordering on the Langebaan Lagoon, the farm Oesterwal, with its springs of fresh water was a favourite port of call for ships and vessels during the seventeenth and eighteenth centuries as this was the only source of fresh water in the area. The house and adjacent outbuildings, which date from the eighteenth century, served as the Colonial Residency for the Saldanha Bay area from 1821 to 1849. The homestead, which has since been subdivided, was restored in 1960 and named Oesterwal.

VOC BEACON (FARM GEELBEK)

This black slate stone beacon with the inscription 'G.V.O.C.' chiselled thereon was presumably erected in 1785 by Governor Cornelis Jacobus van der Graaff to indicate the western boundary of the Cape.

MACASSAR

This area has been developed since 1964. Macassar is situated near the mouth of the Eerste River, at the Strand.

KRAMAT OF SHEIK YUSSUF

Sheik Yussuf (1626–1699), an Islamic priest, was the brother of the Sultan of Macassar, ruler of the state of Gowa on the island of Celebes. Yussuf supported his father-in-law against the Dutch East India Company in the struggle to gain a trade monopoly. Fearing his influence, the Company imprisoned him in the Castle of Batavia and then banished him to Ceylon in 1684. Later, he was sent to the Cape, where he arrived on 31 March 1694 aboard *De Voetboog* and accommodated at the Castle. He was later settled at the mouth of the Eerste River on False Bay. Macassar Beach is named in his honour.

MALGAS

A ferry operates across the river between Bredasdorp and Heidelberg at Malgas. When Swellendam was at the height of its prosperity, considerable trade was carried on from Port Beaufort up the Breede River to Swellendam. Malgas was the main inland centre for small vessels using the river.

DUTCH REFORMED CHURCH

This attractive stone church dates from the middle of the nineteenth century when Malgas was a flourishing inland harbour on the Breede River.

MALMESBURY

Named by Sir Lowry Cole, Governor of the Cape Colony (1829–1834), after his father-in-law, Sir James Harris, first Earl of Malmesbury, this town was established in 1829 and became a municipality in 1896.

BOKKERIVIER FARM (BOKBAAI)

The farm Bokke Rivier is world renowned for the Bokbaaivygies, nemesias and a wealth of other flowers and wildlife that flourish there. The farm buildings of Buck Bay are of outstanding historic and aesthetic values.

CAPE DUTCH HOUSE (FARM LANGRIETVLEI)

This T-shaped Cape Dutch house, with its impressive concavo-convex gables, was probably erected in 1789. At that time the property belonged to Jacob Laubscher, who, according to Lichtenstein, was one of the most prosperous men in the colony.

COMMUNION WELL
(SITUATED IN THE PREMISES OF LEWIS STORES)

This well is one of three similar wells erected in 1751 for the use of communicants on the Church Square adjoining the original church at Malmesbury. It is now exhibited in this store.

DUTCH REFORMED CHURCH BUILDING AND RING WALL (CHURCH STREET)

This neogothic church building was officially opened on 13 September 1860. The tower, which was added in 1864, collapsed in 1877, and was rebuilt in 1880. The church is closely associated with the establishment of the Swartland congregation, as well as the founding of the town of Malmesbury itself.

EASTERN TERMINAL POINT BEACON
(EENDRAG FARM)

One of the tasks undertaken between 1841 and 1848 by Sir Thomas Maclear, the astronomer at the Cape, was to survey an area from Cape Agulhas to Namaqualand for the purpose of determining the size and shape of the earth. Several of his beacons, which were stone pyramids, were later replaced by standard concrete pillars and incorporated in the trigonometrical survey of South Africa. This beacon is the Zwartland baseline survey.

GEELBEK HOMESTEAD (FARM GEELBEK)

Geelbekfontein, now known as Geelbek, was originally a quitrent farm and was used for several years as a livestock station by the Cape brandy retailer, S Verwey. Geelbek was granted to his widow Aletta van As after his death in 1744. The homestead is thought to have been erected by Alexander van Breda, as the initials 'AvB' and the date '1860' appear on the front gable. The main house now forms part of an extended farmyard that has been restored and rehabilitated as part of the West Coast National Park.

KLAVERVALLEI FARM (DISTRICT)

This farm is closely associated with the establishment of the wool industry in South Africa in the late eighteenth century. In 1795 S Valentyn came to Klavervallei with two pure-bred Spanish merino rams, where he conducted breeding experiments with Cape ewes. The homestead is an incomplete H-shape, but different stages of development are still visible; the main T-shaped section certainly predates the 1815 grant of the farm to W Duckitt.

LANGEBAAN ROAD FOSSIL SITE
(FARM LANGEBERG, DISTRICT)

The Langebaanweg quarry preserves a wider range of mammals than any other fossil site of similar age in the world. The Varswater section yielded 200 vertebrate and invertebrate species and a further 100 species have been identified from other parts of the mine. The fossils were first discovered in the course of phosphate mining operations in the late 1950s. Professor R Singer and later, Dr QB Hendey arranged that the fossils be removed by hand from the excavated material. During the 1960s and 1970s Dr Hendey undertook controlled excavations and published a number of scientific papers describing the fossils.

MUSEUM (1 PROSPECT STREET)
Designed by architect B Goldman, this building was built in 1911 as a synagogue after the local Jewish community established the Malmesbury Ohel Jacob congregation in 1904. It was later transferred to the municipality as the museum of local history, and the contribution of the Jewish community is portrayed here.

NEW APOSTOLIC CHURCH
(CNR VOORTREKKER ROAD AND RAINER STREET)
This neogothic church, designed by Sophia Gray and consecrated in 1859 by Bishop Robert Gray, served the Anglican community until 1975 when a new church was consecrated in Wesbank. The property was sold to the New Apostolic Church.

VICTORIAN DOUBLE-STOREY HOMESTEAD
(14 FAURE STREET)
This magnificent Victorian double-storey house was built at the turn of the nineteenth century with material imported from abroad.

MAMRE

Moravian missionaries were inspired by Genesis 13:18, 'Then Abram removed his tent, and came and dwelt in the plain of Mamre, which is in Hebron, and built there an altar unto the Lord', in naming this town.

MORAVIAN MISSION STATION
The site includes the school building, the old farmhouse (the 'Langehuis'), the storekeeper's house, a store, a shop, the church and the historic section of the present school. This mission station is an important place of interest both because of its history and its architectural beauty. It was founded in 1808 by Moravian missionaries on the site occupied by the Dutch East India Company's military outpost, 't Groenekloof, from 1701–1791. The original buildings are virtually unaltered; the old farmhouse (now a parsonage) still has its 'holbol' (concavo-convex) gable and thatched roof, and certainly predates 1770. The original gable of the church building bears the date 1818, but was slightly altered later. The restored old mission store is now a restaurant.

WATERMILL
The historic water mill, dating from about 1840, is an important part of the existing building complex. It was restored and is now a museum.

MATJIESFONTEIN

The township was established in 1883 by James Logan as a health resort for those suffering from lung complaints. During the 1890s it was visited by various celebrities including Lord Randolph Churchill (father of Sir Winston, the sultan of Zanzibar, Olive Schreiner and Cecil John Rhodes. Matjiesfontein was the first village in South Africa to have waterborne sewerage, and the first to be lit by electricity. The London lampposts imported by Logan still line the streets. In 1968 David Rawdon, a Stellenbosch hotelier, bought the entire village from John Buist, grandson of Logan, and started to preserve its Victorian charm.

MATJIESFONTEIN CEMETERY
(FARM PIETERMEINTJIESFONTEIN)
The graves of James Logan and his family are among those buried in this cemetery. The obelisk

on the hillside commemorates Major-General AG Wauchope of the Royal Highlanders, who died in action during the Battle of Magersfontein in 1899, and JM Grant, District Engineer of the Cape Government Railways.

MATJIESFONTEIN VILLAGE
(WITH THE VICTORIAN BUILDINGS)
The mid-Victorian houses beside the railway station in the Great Karoo have been aptly described as 'straight from a Dickens' novel'. As little as possible in the village has been changed except that the public buildings are transformed into utility buildings and recreation facilities have been added. David Rawdon took over almost 30ha of village land, on which stood the hotel, town hall, police office, magistrate's court, shop and about 15 dwellings. During the Anglo-Boer War (1899–1902) it served as the headquarters of the Cape Command, and 12 000 troops camped around the village.

RAILWAY STATION BUILDING
This building, erected in 1893, forms an integral part of the late-Victorian hamlet, Matjiesfontein. It replaced the original building of 1877 and was erected to serve passengers with meals as trains of the time did not have dining cars.

MCGREGOR

Originally Lady Grey, but to avoid confusion with Lady Grey near Aliwal North, the town's name was changed to McGregor after Andrew McGregor (1829–1918), the Dutch Reformed minister from the church in Robertson (1862–1902). It attained municipal status in 1907.

COTTAGES (MILL STREET)
Named Bradshaw, Elim, La Motte and Mamre, these new-vernacular-style guest cottages have thatched roofs and plastered finishes.

DIE TREIN (VOORTREKKER STREET)
This interesting architectural group of buildings consists of four attached houses in the vernacular style. The oldest part is about 100 years old. Other parts were added from time to time.

DOUBLE-STOREY DWELLING (MILL STREET)
Designed with parapet and monopitch roof, the first floor of this house has two openings with wooden doors.

DUTCH REFORMED CHURCH
(VOORTREKKER STREET)
The foundation stone was laid in 1904 by dominee Andrew McGregor. This architecturally interesting church building, in the neogothic style, forms an essential part of the historic core of the town.

HARMONY COTTAGE (BARRY STREET)
Harmony Cottage is a new plastered cottage with monopitch roof.

HISTORIC RHEBOKSKRAAL (DISTRICT)
This gabled house dates from the eighteenth century, and is one of the best examples of the last phase of Cape Dutch architecture. Additionally, this house has typical Georgian and Victorian characteristics, such as the interesting annex and fanlights.

LABOURERS COTTAGES (LONG STREET, KEERON STREET, SECOND AVENUE, AND LADY GREY)
This strategically situated site forms an integral part of the historic core of McGregor. The 28 housing units were erected in 1976 in the traditional vernacular style, by means of a subsidy from the National Monuments Council.

LADY GREY COTTAGE (VOORTREKKER STREET)
This T-shaped vernacular cottage with reed thatch has a hooded gable over the front door, and straight end gables.

MERCURY HOUSE (CNR BREE AND GREWE)
The double-storey house is a good example of the Georgian style, and forms an important element of the historic core of McGregor.

MULBERRY COTTAGE (BARRY STREET)
A vernacular cottage with reed thatch and straight end gables, Mulberry Cottage has slatted shutters on its windows.

MUNICIPAL OFFICES AND PUBLIC LIBRARY (VOORTREKKER STREET)
These offices are situated in the centre of town, and consist of a gabled house and a Georgian annex, both of which date from about 1870. The house is a representative example of the last flickering of Cape Dutch architecture, while the Georgian annex is a double storey. Together these buildings form an interesting unit and an important architectural element of the historic core of McGregor.

OLD DISUSED MILL (MILL STREET)
This stone building, with corrugated iron pitched roof, has an end gable with loft door, clad with corrugated iron. One of the few undamaged water mills in the country, the wooden mill still has its wheel and channel.

OLD MILL LODGE (MILL STREET)
These historic buildings date from the second half of the nineteenth century. The old Mill Lodge forms an important architectural part of this picturesque little town.

PEAR TREE COTTAGE (BARRY STREET)
This vernacular cottage has a reed thatch, straight end gables and an external chimney.

PEPPER TREE COTTAGE (OFF VOORTREKKER STREET)
This vernacular cottage with reed thatch has straight end gables and an external hearth.

SUMMER PLACE COTTAGE (GREWE STREET)
This double dwelling has a thatched roof and straight end gables.

SUNFLOWER COTTAGE (BARRY STREET)
This vernacular cottage has straight end gables and a thatched roof.

MEIRINGSPOORT

The pass through the Zwartberg Mountains, between De Rust and Klaarwater, was completed in 1857 and opened in 1858. It was named after Petrus Johannes Meiring.

HERRIEKLIP
CJ Langenhoven (1873–1932), Afrikaans writer, champion of the Afrikaans language and lyricist of *Die Stem van Suid Afrika* South Africa's old national anthem, chiselled the name of a well-known elephant, Herrie, from his book *Sonde met die Bure*, on this rock in July 1929. With his characteristic sense of humour he referred to it as a monument to himself.

MERWEVILLE

Established in 1904 on the farm Vanderbylskraal, Merweville was named in honour of the Reverend P van der Merwe (1860–1940), who, although the minister at Beaufort West, was also Chairman of the Church Council that decided to establish a congregation in the Koup area. A village management board was established in 1921.

DUTCH REFORMED CHURCH (161 CHURCH STREET)
This church replaced the original 1897 church building and the cornerstone was laid on 24 January 1914. Designed by the architects HH, FW & F Hesse, it was constructed by Masterson & Company.

MONTAGU

Laid out on the farm Uitvlugt before 1851, the town was named after John Montagu (1797–1853), Colonial Secretary of the Cape from 1843 to 1853. Montagu became a municipality in 1895.

CAPE DUTCH DWELLING (24 LONG STREET)
This dwelling is largely in the Cape Dutch style, with a cellar forming an integral part of the house. This property and the other historic buildings in Long Street form an important historic and architectural group.

CAPE DUTCH HOUSE (6 LONG STREET)
This rectangular thatched house, predominantly in the Cape Dutch style, dates from the 1850s.

CAPE DUTCH GABLE HOUSE (17 LONG STREET)
The front gable of this house is an excellent example of the so-called Worcester gable, and was erected in 1859.

CAPE DUTCH HOUSE (30 BATH STREET)
This house dates from 1856 and has a flat-roofed addition from the late nineteenth century. It forms a significant part of the architectural character of Bath Street and of the historic core of Montagu.

DOUBLE-STOREY GEORGIAN DWELLING (26 LONG STREET)
This double-storey building, with its typical Georgian features, dates from the 1890s.

DUTCH REFORMED CHURCH COMPLEX (13 BATH STREET)
The cornerstone of this church was laid on 1 November 1858. Completed in 1862, the building was established by Barry & Nephews, and was consecrated on 21 May 1898. The church was enlarged and altered to its present neogothic cruciform shape in 1898 and a gallery was added in 1906. The other building on this property dates from the same period as the church. Iron trelliswork around the building complex is noteworthy.

GABLED HOUSE (38 LONG STREET)
This house dates from 1858 and forms an important element in the street scene of Long Street. The dwelling has straight end gables and a plain front gable, and is a typical example of this specific phase of the Cape Dutch architectural style.

HISTORIC BUILDINGS (20, 24 BATH STREET, 33 LONG STREET, 3 PIET RETIEF STREET)
These properties form an integral part of the historic core of Montagu. The buildings situated in Long Street (the oldest street in the town) and Bath Street (the main street) date from the late nineteenth century and reflect the Cape Dutch and Victorian styles of building. The building in Piet Retief Street, with its Cape Dutch and Georgian features, was designed by the architect John Parker, and was erected in 1910 as a primary school for the town.

HISTORIC CAPE DUTCH DWELLING (21 LONG STREET)
This Cape Dutch house has a tall, moulded concavo-convex gable, and dates from the 1860s. Also noteworthy are the straight end gables and attractive fanlight.

HISTORIC CAPE DUTCH DWELLING (46 LONG STREET)
This thatched-roof house with its two plain straight end gables was built predominantly in the Cape Dutch style and dates from the 1850s.

HISTORIC CAPE DUTCH DWELLING (58 LONG STREET)
This unique complex, consisting of a rural Cape Dutch house and semidetached wine

cellar, was erected in 1871 by Francois du Toit. He was married to the daughter of Gideon Johannes Retief, youngest brother of the Voortrekker leader Piet Retief.

HISTORIC DWELLING (40 LONG STREET)
Erected by A Kriel in 1892 on the farm Derdeheuwel and used by the Kriel family as a townhouse, this Cape Georgian-style house, with crenellated balustrade and moulding, attests to master craftsmanship and, as such, forms an integral part of the historic core of the town.

JOUBERT HOUSE (25 LONG STREET)
A charming house museum, this is one of the oldest existing houses in Montagu. It was built in 1853 on a large piece of land that was originally a town farm. The thatched-roof house features a centre gable. An outbuilding is believed to have been the first town prison. Over a period of time sections of the land were sold, and by 1970 the house had deteriorated to such an extent that it was uninhabitable. In 1981 it was purchased by the Montagu Museum, and restored to its former beauty. Each room is furnished with nineteenth century antiques, in accordance with the style of a townhouse of that period. In 1880 Joubert House was the venue of a luncheon in honour of Paul Kruger and General Piet Joubert.

LATE-VICTORIAN BUILDING (42A–44 BATH STREET)
Erected by the African Bank Corporation in 1899, it was built during the formative years of The South African banking institution, and is an important link in the commercial development of Montagu.

MISSION CHURCH (41 LONG STREET)
The old mission church was built in 1907 and is of considerable interest, both from an architectural point of view and with regard to the unique street façade of Long Street. It was acquired by the municipality in the early 1970s and opened as a museum in 1975. The old organ, pulpit and christening font of the mission church were retained, and the building has been extensively restored.

T-SHAPED CAPE DUTCH HOUSE (13 LONG STREET)
This house was erected in 1854 and is one of the three oldest houses in Montagu. In June 1880 SJP Kruger and General PJ Joubert were entertained in this house.

THE PARSONAGE (9 ROSE STREET)
This parsonage was built in 1911 for Ds DF Malan, who resided there until 1913. A stately and spacious home, with its interesting architecture and historic connections with the ministry of Ds DF Malan, it is an important part of South Africa's cultural heritage.

VICTORIAN HOUSE (21 PIET RETIEF STREET)
The property on which this Victorian dwelling house is situated was originally transferred to PA Euvard on 9 November 1859, and the house was presumably built by him.

WIJNBERG (20 LONG STREET)
The original section of this double-storey Georgian dwelling was probably built by AJ le Roux shortly after the property was registered in his name in 1855. The building first comprised a three-roomed house with thatched roof, and is one of the oldest houses in Montagu.

MOORREESBURG

Laid out on the farm Hooikraal in 1879, the town was named after JC le Febre Moorrees (1807–1885), minister of the Swartland congregation (1833–1881). It attained municipal status in 1909.

CARNEGIE LIBRARY (CHURCH STREET)
This impressive building, designed by the architect NT Cowin, was erected in 1913 on land donated by the Nederduitse Gereformeerde Church, Moorresburg. Building costs amounting to 1 500 Pounds Sterling, were covered by a grant from Andrew Carnegie of Scotland, and on completion the building was named after him. The Carnegie library was established thanks to the diligence and perseverance of Miss MD Koch of the farm Biesjesfontein, who initiated the project.

ORIGINAL 1905 SCHOOL BUILDING
(CHURCH STREET)
Erected by the Dutch Reformed Church at a cost of 2 000 Pounds Sterling, this building was erected in 1905 and was the first true school building in the town. In 1906 the school opened with 209 scholars and a staff of five. Since 1962, after the transfer of the remaining scholars to the new school, the building has been used for community functions.

MOSSEL BAY

Mossel Bay was first named Aliwal, but this was later changed to avoid confusion with Aliwal North, and it was named after the bay. Founded in 1848, it became a municipality in 1852.

CAPE ST BLAIZE CAVE (THE POINT CARAVAN PARK)
This cave is an important link in the history of the indigenous people of the Southern Cape coast. It was first occupied at least 120 000 years ago by Middle Stone Age hunter-gatherers, ancestors of the San people (Bushmen). Although much of the evidence for human occupation was removed by guano diggers at the end of the last century, some original deposits still exist. Information boards in the cave describe the remaining archaeological evidence.

FOUNTAIN AND STREAM (AGUADA DE SAO BRAS)
This Portuguese name refers to the fountain and stream used by the Portuguese sailors in the fifteenth and sixteenth centuries to obtain drinking water for their ships. The fountain appears to have been modified, possibly when an aqueduct was constructed early in the nineteenth century to bring the water close to the landing place. The start of the aqueduct is still visible to the west of the fountain.

HISTORIC HOMESTEAD (LANGKRAAL FARM)
The land on which the Langkraal homestead is situated originally formed part of the farm Outeniquabosch, which was granted to Jean Charles de la Harpe in 1815. The Cape Dutch farmhouse erected by him is believed to have been enlarged during the 1840s, while the outbuilding and adjacent thatched cottage date from the 1820s.

JOINERS SHOP (MONTAGU STREET)
This imposing joiner's shop was the first building to be built of dressed Mossel Bay stone and dates from about 1898. The architect was Sir Herbert Baker, and the builder, WJ Swart. The joiner's shop is closely associated with the history of Mossel Bay.

MARKET HALL (MARSH STREET)
This impressive building was erected in approximately 1852, and forms an essential part of the historic centre of Mossel Bay.

PORTION OF ATTAQUA'S KLOOF PASS
(BETWEEN MOSSEL BAY AND OUDTSHOORN)
Attaqua's Kloof is named after the Khoi tribe who lived in the vicinity when the pass was transversed in 1689 by Ensign Isaac Schrijver and his party. It is the oldest pass in the Langeberg and Outeniqua Mountain ranges of the Southern Cape and served as the main highway to the Karoo and Eastern Cape until

about 1870. The pass is situated west of the summit of the Robinson Pass over the Outeniqua Mountains. The track is still in a good condition and follows the old wagon route, winding up through spectacular mountains and indigenous flora. Near the top is a ruined Anglo-Boer War fort, guarding the eastern approach. In many places the ruts made on flat stone surfaces by wagons can still be seen. A toll house was situated at the narrowest point of the ascent from the west.

POSTKEEPER'S COTTAGE AND MUNROHOEK HOUSES (MARKET STREET COMPLEX)

This group of houses built at Munro's Bay in c.1830 by Alexander Munro, represents the oldest houses in Mossel Bay.

PROPERTY WITH THE BARTHOLOMEU DIAS MUSEUM AND HISTORIC BUILDINGS (MARKET STREET)

The site includes a statue of Bartholomeu Dias, Portuguese navigator of 1488, a nature garden, the Padrão and Malay graves. It was in this area close to the water point or fountain that João do Nova built a chapel in 1501. He had found a message in a milkwood tree, warning him of trouble at his destination of 'Calicut', India. He was so grateful for the timely warning that he erected a small chapel or hermitage as a gesture of gratitude, making Mossel Bay the first place of Christian worship built in southern Africa.

SHELL MUSEUM (MARKET STREET COMPLEX)

This was built in 1902 as an annex of the old mill, and was mainly used as a store. In latter years Joe Shirley used the building for his plumbing business, after which it became known as the Shirley Building.

THE MILL (MARITIME MUSEUM)

Built in 1901 by EJ Meyer as a grist plant and mill, the builder was C Wilson. Reconstruction of the building as a museum began in 1987 from plans of architect G Fagan. Most of the original stone exterior was retained, but the interior was completely renovated to provide for the reconstructed historic caravel.

(A NOTE ON THE BARTHOLOMEU DIAS CARAVEL)
This is a replica of Bartholomew Dias' caravel on his epic 1488 voyage of discovery of the sea route around the shores of southern Africa. Portuguese naval architects, under the direction of Admiral Rhegheiro S de Oliveira, designed the caravel from incomplete documents as the original design and specifications have disappeared. It was built in the shipyard of Samuel & Filhos in Vila do-Condes, Portugal, and took nearly a year to complete at a cost of around R1 000 000. The ship, the *Bartholomeu Dias*, sailed from Lisbon on 8 November 1987, and arrived at Mossel Bay on 3 February 1988, exactly 500 years after the original Dias voyage, and took three months compared with six months' duration of the 1488 voyage.

THE POST OFFICE TREE
(MARKET STREET COMPLEX)

This milkwood tree is considered to be over 500 years old. Portuguese navigator Do Nova found a message in or under a tree near the watering place in 1501, and this may well be the same tree. In 1501 Pero da'Ataide, captain of a homeward bound ship of Pero Cabrals' fleet, left a message here which was found on 7 July 1501 by the outward bound ships of João do Nova. According to tradition the message was placed in an old shoe and tied to the tree. Letters can be posted in the 'old shoe' post office, which bears a special post mark. Postcards can still be stamped today.

RECONSTRUCTED GRANARY
(MARKET STREET COMPLEX)

Governor Cornelius van de Graaf ordered a granary to be built c.1787, of stone and clay with yellowwood beams and a yellowwood plank floor. A pitched roof was erected in 1814, also with yellowwood copings. It was bought by the Boere Saamwerk Beperk in 1926, and sold on 16 February 1932 to the Suid-Westelike Graan Ko-operasie, who demolished the granary in 1950-51. The old foundations were uncovered during the development of the new Bartholomeu Dias Museum Complex, and a replica of the granary, to the original specifications, was completed in 1987.

ST PETER'S ANGLICAN CHURCH
(58 MARSH STREET)
The parish of St Peter's church was established in 1855. After land was granted by the government, a chapel (also used as a school) and a residence were built. A commemoration fund was started after Bishop R Gray's death in 1874 for the erection of the present church. The nave of this large church was designed by John Welchman, and was consecrated in 1875 by Bishop West-Jones.

MURRAYSBURG

Established on the farm Eenzaamheid in 1856, Murraysburg was named after the Reverend Andrew Murray Snr, minister of Graaff-Reinet, and Barend OJ Burger, who assisted with the establishment of the town. The town became a municipality in 1883.

FAÇADE OF VICTORIAN DWELLING
(33 DARLING STREET)
This homestead was presumably erected shortly after the granting of this property to Carel Theron in 1858. It is one of the oldest houses in Murraysburg.

OLD POWDER MAGAZINE
This powder magazine was erected in 1878 on land that was granted to the municipality by the local church council in 1859. The magazine is a simple rectangular structure, with two gables on both sides and a solid copper door in front.

NAPIER

Laid out on the farm Klipdrift or Klipfontein in 1838, this town was named after Sir George Thomas Napier (1784-1855), Governor of the Cape Colony (1837-1844). Napier attained municipal status in 1938.

DUTCH REFORMED CHURCH
(SAREL CILLIERS STREET)
This cruciform church was erected in 1926. Despite a variety of architectural styles, such as the high gable walls, the building forms a harmonious unit. The Napier Dutch Reformed congregation was founded on 26 January 1848. A dwelling on the farm Klippedrift was used as a church, but in 1926 the church council resolved to build a new church, which was inaugurated on 14 April 1928.

OLD WINE CELLAR, SLAVE QUARTERS AND HOUSE
(86 SAREL CILLIERS STREET)
The former wine cellar and slave quarters on this property were originally situated on the farm Klippedrift, the first erven of which were sold on 12 April 1828. The erf containing these farm buildings was sold to I de Villiers.

OUDTSHOORN

This town was laid out on the farm Hartebeestrivier in 1847 and was named after Baron Pieter van Rheede van Oudtshoorn, who came to South Africa in 1741. He was Secunde in 1760, returning to Holland in 1766, but in 1772 was appointed Governor of the Cape. Oudtshoorn was proclaimed a town in 1863 and became a municipality in 1887.

ARBIEDSGENOT HOUSE MUSEUM
(JAN VAN RIEBEECK STREET)

On 13 June 1903 this property came into the possession of Mrs HM (Vroutjie) Langenhoven, wife of CJ Langenhoven. There was an existing late-Victorian sandstone house on the site. Here Langenhoven wrote the words of *Die Stem van Suid Afrika* national anthem in 1918 and created most of his great literary heritage. After his death on 15 July 1932, his widow lived in the house until her death on 23 May 1950. She bequeathed Arbiedsgenot to the nation.

CANGO CAVES

The entrance to the caves was inhabited by the Khoi San some 15 000 years ago. Although they never ventured into the caves they stayed here until about 400 years ago when they left. 'Cango' comes from a San word meaning 'place of water between the mountains', or 'place of wetness between the hills'. The Van Zyl Hall was discovered by a local farmer of that name. Cleopatra's Needle is 10m tall and 150 000 years old, while the Organ Pipes are 800 000 years old and the Leaning Tower of Pisa is approximately 270 000 years old.

The Double Column comprises stalagmites that grow upwards between 10 and 15mm every100 years, and stalactites, a cylindrical mass of calcium carbonate hanging from the roof, that grow 5 to 7 mm every 100 years. Obviously, growth is faster when there is more water. When complete, the double column no longer grows in length, but in width. The oldest formation is the Weeping Willow, which is over 1.5 million years old. The Botha Hall was discovered by Louis Botha in 1792.

DUTCH REFORMED MOTHER CHURCH
(CHURCH STREET)

The foundation stone of this church was laid on 15 January 1861, but because of financial and other problems it could only be consecrated on 7 June 1879. George Wallace was responsible for the building plans, although the well-known Carl Häger had to complete the building. The church was built of local sandstone in neogothic style, and has an impressive interior.

DUTCH REFORMED MOTHER CHURCH PARSONAGE (HIGH STREET)

This parsonage is a double-storey building that was constructed in the Victorian style, and was completed in 1882.

FAÇADE OF OAKDENE HOUSE
(99 BARON VAN RHEEDE STREET)

This house is one of the oldest to have remained intact since the establishment of Oudtshoorn. It was built by JH Mulder as a Nederduitse Gereformeede Church parsonage.

GOTTLAND HOUSE
(72 BARON VAN RHEEDE STREET)

Gottland House was designed in 1902 by C Bullock for CM Lind, a local lawyer of Swedish descent. It was designed mainly in the Victorian style with Art Nouveau elements, and is an excellent example of the superior quality of local architecture during the height of the ostrich-feather boom in Oudtshoorn.

GREYLANDS HOUSE (FARM DE DAM)

Constructed during 1911, Greylands is regarded as one of the best examples of the so-called 'ostrich palaces'.

HAZENJACHT FARMSTEAD (DISTRICT)

This farmhouse, with its interesting mixture of Victorian and Edwardian elements, was erected in 1914, and is one of the ostrich palaces. A section of the house was completed with cheaper materials after the dramatic collapse of the ostrich-feather market.

MIMOSA LODGE (PREVIOUSLY SLADOWSKI HOUSE) (85 BARON VAN RHEEDE STREET)

Designed by C Bullock in the Art Nouveau style in 1907 for R Sladowski, a local Jewish dealer, this sandstone building represents the culmination of the Oudtshoorn ostrich-feather architecture.

OLD BOY'S HIGH SCHOOL
(BARON VAN RHEEDE STREET)

This building, now the CP Nel Museum, dates from about 1809 and for some half a century served as a boys' school. Designed in part by Bullock and Vixseboxse, the well-known architects, it reflects the former's copiousness and the latter's Transvaal Republic influence. Especially worthy of note is the façade, with its harmonious blend of styles and its impressive dome tower. The school hall at the back of the building is, similarly, an architecturally imposing structure. The edifice as a whole is a good example of the sandstone buildings of Oudtshoorn.

OSTRICH PALACE (146 HIGH STREET)

This richly ornamented Victorian house is one of the ostrich palaces and was designed by the well-known architect Charles Bullock. It was erected during 1909–1910 for JHJ le Roux on the farm Baakenskraal at a stage when the ostrich-feather industry was at its peak. It is now the CP Nel Museum Annex.

PINEHURST ORIGINAL BUILDING
(186 JAN VAN RIEBEECK STREET)

Another of the 'ostrich palaces' built at the beginning of the 20th century, when the ostrich-feather industry reached its peak, the house was designed by the architect JE Vixseboxse and built for EJT Edmeades.

RUS-IN-URBE (VOORTREKKER STREET)

This double-storey manor house designed by Charles Bullock for James Foster, a local attorney, during Oudtshoorn's second ostrich feather boom, was constructed between 1903 and 1904. It is an example of early Edwardian eclecticism, with a variety of styles combined into one building. The stained glass windows, cast-iron fireplaces and copperware, for example, are beautifully decorated with Art Nouveau elements. It is presently the Foster Folly Guest House.

ST JUDE CHURCH (BARON VAN RHEEDE STREET)

This church, largely the work of architect George Wallis, was built in 1897. It incorporates parts of the original church erected from 1860–1863, to an adapted design of Sophia Gray, wife of the first Anglican Bishop of Cape Town. The building is closely linked with the history of Oudtshoorn and with the Anglican Church in South Africa.

SUSPENSION BRIDGE (CHURCH STREET)

The suspension bridge is 91.44m long, with a timber walkway 1.22m wide, including its 9.14m supporting towers, main cables and bridge hangers. Built in 1913–1914, it is an interesting feature in Oudtshoorn.

WELGELUK OSTRICH PALACE
(SAFARI OSTRICH FARM)

The original homestead, built in 1910 by Mr Oliver, a Belgian, is regarded as one of the finest examples of the ostrich palaces. It was sold to Joseph Lipschitz, and upon his death it went to his son Stan Lipschitz, who is still the present owner.

PAARL

The name is taken from the round granite boulder called Paarl (Dutch for pearl) by Abraham Gabbema in 1657. Paarl was founded in 1690, became a seat of magistracy in 1839 and attained municipal status in 1840.

BERGSKADUS CAPE DUTCH MANOR HOUSE (KLEIN DRAKENSTEIN)
This historic Cape Dutch manor house was probably built in 1823 by Joshua Malherbe, and has remained basically unaltered.

CAPE DUTCH DWELLING (7 DE JONGH AVENUE)
This H-shaped Cape Dutch house was erected in 1818 by Pieter Roux. Together with the other buildings in De Jongh Avenue, the house forms an important historic and architectural group.

CAPE DUTCH HOUSE (9 DE JONGH AVENUE)
This imposing Cape Dutch dwelling house, with its thatched roof and symmetric façade, presumably dates from the 1850s.

CAPE DUTCH HOUSE (10 DE JONGH STREET)
This H-shaped Cape Dutch house, with its six gables, was probably erected in 1801 by Abraham de Clercq. The property forms an integral part of the historic core of Paarl.

COMMERCIAL HIGH SCHOOL, BOYS' HOSTEL (NAMED BETHEL) (MILL STREET)
This imposing double-storey house, with its beautiful Victorian as well as Edwardian characteristics, dates from the second half of the eighteenth century. The front gable bears the date 1764.

DE KLEINE CONSTANTIA HOMESTEAD (CONSTANTIA STREET)
This Cape Dutch house with its impressive front gable bears the date 1841. It was originally the homestead of the farm De Kleine Constantia, which was granted to Johannes Philippus Minnaar on 1 July 1817 by Lord Charles Somerset. The farm was owned by him until 1845 and was used for agricultural purposes until 1972, when it was subdivided in terms of a village plan.

DIVISIONAL COUNCIL BUILDING (194 MAIN STREET)
This impressive public building, with its neoclassical elements, forms an integral part of the architectural character of Main Street. It is a harmonious blend of Cape Dutch, Georgian, Victorian and Edwardian building styles.

DOUBLE-STOREY SEMIDETACHED HOUSES (4, 5 ZEEDERBERG SQUARE)
The Victorian house at No. 4 is thought to have been in existence in 1869, but without the verandah and bow windows. The store has a loft, also in Victorian style. This property forms an important part of Zeederberg Square, which was originally used as an outspan by churchgoers at the Strooidakkerk.

DOUBLE-STOREY TOWNHOUSE (132A MAIN STREET)
This late-nineteenth-century townhouse is predominantly Georgian in style and is an integral part of the architectural character of Main Street.

DUTCH REFORMED CHURCH (STROOIDAKKERK) (MAIN STREET)
This church was consecrated in 1805, and is one of the oldest Dutch Reformed churches still in daily use in South Africa. It has a noteworthy tradition and its architectural merit is considerable.

DWELLING HOUSE (108 MAIN STREET)
This elongated house with its Victorian verandah dates from the 1850s, and was presumably a Cape Dutch House that was later Victorianised. The property forms an integral part of the historic core of Paarl.

EDWARDIAN DWELLING (40 MAIN STREET)
With its two front gables, this Edwardian house forms an integral part of the architectural character of Main Street.

FAÇADE OF LATE-VICTORIAN HOUSE
(42 MAIN STREET)
This late-Victorian-style house was erected in 1910 and forms an integral part of the architectural character of Main Street, and the historic core of Paarl.

FAÇADES OF BARCLAYS BANK BUILDING
(MAIN STREET)
With it neo-Cape Dutch elements, this building was erected in 1919. The splayed corner entrance and gable were probably added in 1940 when the building was renovated.

GEORGIAN DOUBLE-STOREY BUILDING
(60–62 MILL STREET)
Dating from about 1803, this double-storey building is mainly in the Georgian style, but also possesses Victorian characteristics.

GIDEON MALHERBE HOUSE MUSEUM
(WESTFALEN HOUSE)
In this Georgian house, then the residence of Gideon J Malherbe, the Genootskap van Regte Afrikaners was founded on 14 August 1875. The well-known printing press of the Genootskap, on which De Patriot was printed, was also housed at Westfalen for some time.

HET GESTICHT (122 MAIN STREET)
This building was erected in 1813 to serve as an 'oefeningshuis' for religious instruction, catechism classes and prayer meetings for non-whites. It is the fourth oldest church in South Africa.

HISTORIC DWELLING HOUSE (419 MAIN STREET)
This property forms an integral part of the architectural character of Main Street. The house on the plot dates from 1832.

HISTORIC FARM (NIEUWE PLANTATIE)
This property is the oldest town farm in Paarl and is one of the very few such farms remaining here. This farm makes a significant contribution to the agricultural character of the area and has been closely associated with the Bosman family, to which it belonged for over 214 years.

JOOSTENBERG
(FARM WELTEVREDEN, MULDERSVLEI)
This farm was granted to Matthijs Michiels or Michielsen, of Stockholm in 1694. The homestead was enlarged in 1752 when it was bought by Gerrit van der Bijl, who added the front gable dated 1756. As far as is known, it is the oldest Cape gable still in existence and probably the only surviving example of one consisting of five convex curves.

KLEIN VREDENBURG (155 MAIN STREET)
The dwelling is a typical Georgian double-storey townhouse which, in its present form, dates from about the middle of the nineteenth century. The group of buildings forms an integral part of the historic core of Paarl.

LABORIE CAPE DUTCH MANOR HOUSE
This historic manor house was erected before 1800, even though the front gable bears this date. It is an important example of the Cape Dutch architectural style.

LANDSKROON (DISTRICT)
The original section of this imposing Cape Dutch farmhouse on Landskroon was erected by Pieter de Villiers, who inherited the farm in 1757. One of the outbuildings bears the date 1743. This building complex is one of the oldest and best preserved farmyards in the vicinity of Paarl. The farm was first granted to Jan Holsmi in 1691 and the T-shaped house was built by the third Pieter de Villiers, whose initials, as well as those of his wife, Helena Basson, are on the main gable dated 1769.

MAIN STREET PROPERTIES
(42A, 54, 56, 58, 82, 84, 86, 88, 98, 99, 101, 103, 105, 107, 128–130, 140, 165, 167, 169, 195, 197, 199)

These properties form an integral part of the historic and architectural nucleus of Paarl. The houses on these erven, the majority of which date from the nineteenth century, are representative of the Georgian and Victorian building styles.

MILL STREET (66)

This dwelling and the attached workshop are predominantly Cape Dutch in style, and date from the middle of the nineteenth century.

MORGENZON HOUSE AND PROPERTY
(486 MAIN STREET)

This house was presumably erected before 1850. It is predominantly Cape Dutch and forms an integral part of the architectural character of Main Street.

NANTES VUE (56 MILL STREET)

Originally granted to J Colemann in 1692, the farm Nantes Vue and the associated Colonies Molen have a long and complex history. The house was previously the farmhouse on the farm Nantes Vue; and its urban erf upon which is situated all that remains of the original farm of 20 morgen. This house's exact date is unknown, but it was apparently built by PJ de Villiers between 1824–1830. The presence of Colonies Molen, a flour mill already on the farm shortly after it was first granted, however, suggests that there could have been earlier structures on the farm.

NEDERBURG HOMESTEAD (DISTRICT)

Now a famous wine-making estate, the original farm was allotted in 1791 to Philippus Bernardus Wolvaard, who built the H-shaped gabled dwelling house in 1800. The remainder of the farm has also been proclaimed a conservation area.

NOOITGEDACHT HOUSE (2 CHURCH SQUARE)

This double-storey building originally formed part of the farm Nooitgedacht. With its Victorian and Georgian characteristics, it forms an important element in the architectural image of Church Square.

OLD MAGISTRATE'S COURT (VERGENOEGD)
(188 MAIN STREET)

This building was erected between 1790 and 1800 and was used as Paarl's first Magistrate's Court. It was also a jail and a school room.

OLD WINE CELLAR (LABORIE)

This old wine cellar dates from the early nineteenth century.

OLD ZION CHURCH (ZION STREET)

The chapel of this neogothic church was erected in 1842. A bell tower was added in 1880 and an additional wing in 1881. It is closely linked to mission activities in Paarl.

PAARL MOUNTAIN COMMONAGE

The three largest boulders in South Africa, named respectively Britannia (properly Bretagne and formerly also Paarl) Rock, Gordon's Rock and Paarl Rock, tower over Paarl Mountain.

PRINTING PRESS OF THE GENOOTSKAP VAN REGTE AFRIKANERS (HUGUENOT MUSEUM)

The printing press consists of four parts: a hand-operated printing press built in 1869 by Fredrik Ullmer of London (patent 2607), a proof press, bookbinding apparatus and a wooden clamp in which the binding was finished off. The printing press contributed much to the effectiveness of the Genootskap van Regte Afrikaners, which played an important part in the history of the Afrikaans language. *Die Afrikaanse Patriot*, the first Afrikaans newspaper, was printed on it from 15 January 1876 onwards.

PROPERTIES INCLUSIVE OF THE HISTORIC BUILDINGS (MAIN, MILL AND ORANGE STREETS)

These properties form an integral part of the historic and architectural nucleus of Paarl. The houses on these erven, the majority of which date from the nineteenth century, are representative of the Cape Dutch, Georgian, Victorian as well as the Edwardian styles of building.
(Main Street: 70, 72, 74, 78–80, 92, 106, 146–148, 150–152 (Vines Café), 172, 172a, 174–186, 214, 388–390, 469; 44 Mill Street; 27–29 Orange Street)

RONWE HOMESTEAD (HUGUENOT DISTRICT)

This farm has been in the possession of the Theron family since 1763, and is at present occupied by the ninth generation of this family. The house, which was originally built in the Cape Dutch style and dates from 1812, was later Victorianised.

ROZENBURG HOUSE (2 ROZENBURG STREET)

This dwelling, with its Georgian and Victorian characteristics, was rebuilt during the 1850s to its present form.

ROSENFONTEIN (133 MAIN STREET)

This lovely Georgian house, which dates from the 1750s, is an essential part of the historic character of Main Street, as well as of Paarl itself.

SCHOONGEZICHT (52 MAIN STREET)

The farm Schoongezicht was first allocated to PC van Blommenstein in 1819. The homestead was built in approximately 1840 by J Adams and is an excellent example of a mid-nineteenth-century house with English detail. The group of buildings was initially part of an early Paarl farm, and is now located within the Paarl town lands.

SEMIDETACHED HOUSES (157–161 MAIN STREET)

These two semidetached houses form an integral part of the historic and architectural character of Main Street.

THE GYMNASIUM (MAIN STREET)

The original building of the gymnasium school was opened on 12 January 1858. The school played a leading part in the struggle for the retention of the Dutch language, as well as in the Afrikaans language movement.

TOWER CHURCH AND SEVEN SEMIDETACHED VAULTS (HOF STREET)

This imposing church building, with its 57m high tower, was designed by an architect from Sherwood, Pitts & Wood, and erected during the years 1904–1907 by the builders De Villiers, Larson & Company. The cornerstone was laid on 8 April 1905 by Dr Andrew Murray, and the church was inaugurated on 6 March 1907.

TOWN HALL BUILDING (256 MAIN STREET)

After the original Town Hall Building burnt down in 1927, one of the first Afrikaans architects, Wynand Louw, was approached to design a new town hall, the cornerstone of which was laid in 1928.

T-SHAPED DWELLING HOUSE AND PROPERTY (414 MAIN STREET)

Originally forming part of erf 4716, this property was purchased by Debora Jacoba van Boomen on 4 August 1820 from the estate of JJ Syffret. The T-shaped house that was initially erected in the Cape Dutch style, dates from approximately 1830 and was presumably built shortly after her marriage to HJ de Rubaix. De Rubaix inherited the property after his wife's death, and in 1893 it was sold from his estate to Michiel Gobrechts. He used the property partly as a tannery, and a few of the lye pits still exist. The house was subsequently Victorianised.

VICTORIAN BUILDINGS
(91, 95, 133–135 MAIN STREET)
These three properties with their Victorian buildings are typical of the architectural tradition that gives Main Street its character, and are integral to the historic core of Paarl.

VICTORIAN DWELLING (2 ZEEDERBERG SQUARE)
This dwelling house, originally erected in Cape Dutch style, was Victorianised in the 1890s. It is an integral part of the historic core of Paarl.

VICTORIAN DWELLING (3 ZEEDERBERG SQUARE)
This building, with its decorated cast-iron verandah and a portico, the original section of which dates from the 1830s, was Victorianised in 1890. The property and two adjacent buildings form a unique central unit.

VICTORIAN DWELLING (394–396A MAIN STREET)
This house dates from about 1813 and was originally erected in the Georgian style. It was Victorianised after a fire.

VICTORIAN DWELLING (2 PATRIOT STREET)
This impressive house was erected in 1905 by Wilhelm Bruckener de Villiers in late-Victorian style, and not only forms an essential part of the traditional architectural street scene of Patriot Street, but also of the historic core of Paarl.

VICTORIAN DWELLING (127 MAIN STREET)
This Victorian house, with a front gable dated 1837, forms an integral part of the historical and architectural character of Main Street.

VICTORIAN DWELLING (VAN DER POEL SQUARE)
This late-Victorian house was erected in 1900 as a mansion for wagon maker Stark.

VICTORIAN HOUSE (94 MILL STREET)
The original section of this house was initially built in the Cape Dutch style and dates from the beginning of the nineteenth century. It was Victorianised by subsequent owners.

VICTORIAN MANOR HOUSE (19 VICTORIA STREET)
This late-Victorian manor house was erected at the turn of the nineteenth century.

ZEEDERBERG HOUSE (1 ZEEDERBERG SQUARE)
This excellent example of a Georgian double-storey house was erected in 1848 by Dr Johannes Rudolph Zeederberg (1811–1881). He was the son of Cape wine trader, RL Zeederberg, and became Paarl's first district surgeon in 1848.

PACALTSDORP

Founded as Hooge Kraal by the London Missionary Society in 1818, the town's name was changed to its present form in honour of the German missionary Carl August Pacalt (1773–1818), who worked here from 1813–1818.

MISSION CHURCH COMPLEX
The church building was consecrated in 1825 and is one of the most impressive of the remaining examples of the early Gothic Revival in South Africa. Near the church, stands the original parsonage, erected in 1835, the present parsonage that dates back to 1882, and also the historic single room erected between 1813 and 1818, where the Reverend Carl Pacalt originally lived. Together, these buildings form a unique historic and architectural group.

PHILADELPHIA

Developed from a parish of the Dutch Reformed Church that was established in 1863, Philadelphia's biblical name was taken from Revelations 3:7–13.

**DUTCH REFORMED CHURCH
(NEDERDUITSE GEREFORMEERDE)**
This imposing church, the nave of which was consecrated in 1864, was enlarged in 1910 by the addition of two wings, a vestibule and the stately tower.

PIKETBURG

Laid out on the farm Grootfontein in 1835, the town's name refers to the posting of military guards (piquet or piket) against marauding Khoekhoe under Gonnema during the term of office of Governor Isbrand Goske (1672–1676). It attained municipal status in 1906.

DUTCH REFORMED CHURCH
This neogothic-style church was designed by Carl Otto Häger. The foundation stone was laid on 12 August 1880 and the building was completed early in 1882. It was officially inaugurated on 28 April 1882.

**HISTORIC KOOPMANSKRAAL HOMESTEAD
(FARM KROMMERIVIERS VALLEY)**
The Koopmanskraal homestead, together with the outbuilding in which a horse mill is located, forms a unique thatched complex that dates from the nineteenth century. The ground plan, in the shape of a rough crucifix, is more common in ecclesiastic that domestic architecture.

**HISTORIC ST HELENAFONTEIN FARMHOUSE
(DISTRICT)**
The original St Helenafontein farmhouse was presumably built in 1835 by Pierre Rocher. In the 1880s a second storey replaced the pitched roof, and the building was converted to Georgian style.

HISTORIC WATER MILL (FARM DEZE HOEK)
This water mill was erected during the years 1863–1864 by Jacob Johannes Eksteen, owner of Deze Hoek. The impressive overshot mill wheel was manufactured during the same period by Jan Dommisse.

**MORAVIAN MISSION CHURCH AND PARSONAGE
(FARM GOEDVERWACHT)**
The church and parsonage form the nucleus of this Moravian mission station, which was established shortly after 1845 on the farm Burgershoek. The Victorian parsonage was erected in 1891, and construction of the church building commenced in 1895. It is presumed that the architect, E Seeliger, who designed the church, was also responsible for the parsonage.

**NORTHERN TERMINAL OF MACLEAR'S ARC
OF MERIDIAN AND THRESHING FLOOR
(FARM KLIPFONTEIN)**
The northern terminal of Sir Thomas Maclear's Arc of Meridian represents the beginning of South Africa's primary geodetic survey, which still forms the framework for topographical mapping and all subdivisions of land. The exact position of this terminal, forming part of a current threshing floor, was established in 1990 when a large sandstone with the inscription '1838', as well as a black glass bottle were unearthed. A stone cairn has since been erected to mark the position of the terminal.

**WOBURN LODGE HISTORIC DWELLING AND BARN
(12 WATERKANT STREET)**
Woburn Lodge is situated on a section of the property purchased by Captain Montgomery Hill in 1853. He had been sent to the Cape to implement the Abolition of Slavery Act. The dwelling, probably erected by Hill, is a long structure in the shape of a barn. Woburn Lodge has a thatched roof and is the only remaining pioneer home in the central part of Piketberg.

PLETTENBERG BAY

This town was named after Joachim van Plettenberg (1739–1793), Governor of the Cape Colony from 1774–1785. Van Plettenberg erected a beacon here with the Dutch East India Company's monogram.

FOREST HALL (THE CRAGGS)
This double-storey U-shaped manor house, of which all the woodwork is indigenous stinkwood and yellowwood, was probably erected in 1864 by William Henry Newdigate, a pioneer farmer. The third son of Francis Newdigate and Lady Barbara Legge (daughter of the third Earl of Dartmouth), he arrived in Plettenberg Bay in 1845.

ROBBERG NATURE RESERVE (DISTRICT)
The archaeological sites on the Robberg Peninsula comprise a rich concentration of open sites and at least 20 caves and rock shelters with evidence of occupation during the Earlier and Middle Stone Ages. The richness of this archaeological record has long been appreciated. Artefacts from several caves were sent to the South African Museum from as early as 1880.

ST ANDREW'S CHURCH (REDBOURNE)
One of the oldest Anglican churches in the country, St Andrew's was completed in 1851 by William Henry Newdigate on his estate Redbourne. Built of broad yellowwood boarding and lined inside with brick and plaster, the original thatched-roof building was later replaced with corrugated iron and a stone foundation.

PORT BEAUFORT

A former harbour, Port Beaufort was named after the Duke of Beaufort, father of Lord Charles Somerset.

BARRY CHURCH
This church was built by the Barry family in 1849 as an interdenominational chapel for the inhabitants of Port Beaufort.

PORTERVILLE

Porterville was laid out on the farm Pomona in 1863 and was previously known as Willem's Vallei. Named after William Porter, Attorney-General of the Cape Colony (1839–1866), it became a municipality in 1903.

MUSEUM BUILDING AND CELLS (MARKET STREET)
The so-called Court Hall was erected in 1878 by the Colonial Government, and by 1881 the municipal council purchased the building. Municipal offices were housed in the eastern section of the building and the courtroom, police offices and gaol cells in the western section. The latter was rented to the state until new magistrate's and police offices were taken into use around 1940. After the removal of the municipal offices to a new building in 1967, the building was used for museum purposes.

PRINCE ALBERT

The town was laid out on the farm Kweekvallei and named after Prince Albert, Prince Consort of Queen Victoria of England.

BAVIAANSKLOOF FARMHOUSE
(5 KM OUT OF TOWN TOWARD KLAARSTROOM)
This house has fine gables, including one that bears the date 1837. The stone 'stoep' is a good example of Boland farm culture in the Karoo.

BONA VESTA (7 PARSONAGE STREET)
Originally part of the old loan farm Kweekvallei, the farm was bought by Frederick Simon Oosthuizen in 1906 from the then owner, Pieter de Wit, who erected this Victorian townhouse.

CAPE DUTCH HOUSE (2 CHURCH STREET)
This house was built in 1850 by one of the founders of Prince Albert, Jan Luttig. The verandah and the teak trelliswork were added in 1882 after Luttig was elected Member of Parliament for the Beaufort West constituency.

DENNEHOF FARMSTEAD
(CHRISTINA DE WIT STREET)
This property originally formed part of Queekvalleij, the farm owned by the De Beer family on which the town of Prince Albert was later established. The complex comprises two buildings joined by a flat-roofed section and a continuous verandah.

DUTCH REFORMED CHURCH (FARM ZEEKOEGAT)
The church was erected in 1906, free of charge, by Mr F Oosthuizen of Zwartkraal, who was also the owner of Zeekoegat. It was inaugurated on 23 February 1907 by Reverend J Wilcocks of Prince Albert, and Reverend Albertyn of Willowmore.

DUTCH REFORMED CHURCH AND PARSONAGE
(CHURCH AND PARSONAGE STREETS)
The late Victorian parsonage and the church building are situated on a section of the old loan farm Kweekvallei, which was purchased as church property after the Swartberg Ward established an independent congregation in 1847. Soon after, the first church and parsonage were completed, but less than 30 years later it was decided to build a new parsonage and church. At the inauguration on 3 April 1893 the main speaker was Professor N Hofmeyr, father of the Reverend Adriaan Hofmeyr, the local minister.

HOUSE HELMUTH (20 CHURCH STREET)
This H-shaped Victorian double-storey house was designed by Anna Luttig and was erected in 1885 by the building contractor Alfred Linder of Wynberg.

OLD DOCTOR'S HOUSE (15 CHURCH STREET)
The Cape Dutch house, erected in 1858 by Samuel Luttig, remained in the Luttig family until 1964. From 1879 to 1902 the house was let to Dr JH Mearns, and for many years thereafter it was occupied by Dr PC Luttig. Still known as the Doctor's House, it is currently used by the Dutch Reformed church as a home for the church secretary.

OLD MISSION PARSONAGE (5 CHURCH STREET)
Adorned with a typical Prince Albert front gable, the cottage was erected in 1858 by Helmuth Luttig. It was occupied by the Luttig family until 1907, when the property was purchased by the Dutch Reformed church and converted into a mission parsonage. Since 1979 it has been in private ownership.

OLD WATER MILL (ALSO CALLED ALBERTSMEULE)
(CHRISTINA DE WIT STREET)
The old water mill was built by HJ Botes in 1850, and is still in working order. Situated at the foot of the Swartberg Pass, it is an outstanding feature on this popular tourist route. The property also features the loading platform of the old water mill.

PROPERTY AND BUILDINGS (26 CHURCH STREET)
This building has been used as retail premises since 1860. Due to the gold rush in 1891 in Prince Albert, as well as the ostrich-feather boom in the Karoo and the opening of the Swartberg Pass, the economy of Prince Albert prospered and contributed to JC Forsyth having a thriving business from 1901 to 1951.

SEVEN ARCHES HOUSE (57 CHURCH STREET)
This property was purchased in 1843 by JD de Villiers, who erected a double-storey house in1865. It was bought in 1967 by Arthur Orton, who turned the adjacent hall into a shop, still known as Orton's.

ST JOHN THE BAPTIST ANGLICAN CHURCH
AND CHURCH HALL (BANK STREET)
In 1870 Bishop Robert Gray obtained two erven for the erection of an Anglican school/chapel and a residence for the priest. The Mission School, now the church hall, was built in 1871. The church was designed by G Wallis and built from 1895 to1896.

SWARTBERG HOTEL (77 CHURCH STREET)
This hotel was probably built by J Dayson, who had bought the property on 10 August 1818. This Victorian building, still in use as a hotel, played an important role, especially after the opening of the Swartberg Pass in 1888. J Haak purchased it in 1892.

SWARTBERG PASS ROAD RESERVE
The Swartberg Pass between Prince Albert and Oudtshoorn is one of the most picturesque and best known in South Africa. It is probably the masterpiece of the engineer and road builder Thomas Charles John Bain (1830–1893).

THE VALLEY KNOWN AS GAMKASKLOOF
(BETWEEN LAINGSBURG AND PRINCE ALBERT)
Colloquially known as The Hell on account of its inaccessibility, this valley is a ravine in the Swartberg Mountains through which the Gamka River flows. A road was built to it in 1963.

VROLIKHEID FARMHOUSE
This Cape Dutch farmhouse, with elements of Karoo architecture, bears the date 1821 on its front gable and forms an important link with the history of the district. The gable was a prototype for other gables in the vicinity. A brandy still, near the house, is an excellent example of its kind.

RIEBEEK-KASTEEL

This town was named in honour of Dutch commander Jan van Riebeeck.

DE OUDE KERK MUSEUM (MAIN STREET)
The cornerstone of this former church building was laid on 8 August 1855, and the church inaugurated on 4 May 1856 by Reverend JS Moorrees of the Swartland congregation. The building was restored in 1988 and subsequently opened as the museum.

RIEBEEK-WEST

This town was established as a parish of the Dutch Reformed Church in 1858 at the foot of the mountain Riebeeck-Kasteel.

HOUSE WHERE JAN SMUTS WAS BORN
Jan Christiaan Smuts, a former Prime Minister of South Africa, was born in this house on 24 May 1870. He died at Irene in 1950.

RIVERSDALE

Founded on the farm Doornkloof in 1838, Riversdale was named after Harry Rivers (1785–1861), Commissioner and Resident Magistrate of Swellendam from 1834–1841. It attained municipal status in 1849.

FRERE MASONIC LODGE AND HALL
(10 LONG STREET)
The Frere Masonic Lodge was founded in 1879. Contruction work started in 1888 and the building was officially opened on 18 December 1888. The hall was a later addition.

KAPSTYLHUISE (FARM KLEINFONTEIN, PUNTJIE)
These two 'kapstylhuise' are excellent examples of the style of construction of primitive houses adopted by pioneers in the area. In their simplest form, the Puntjie Kapstylhuise have no walls and are, in fact, nothing more than the roof of a Cape house built at ground level. Eight or more pairs of sloping poles (kapbalke) meet at the apex and are spaced at regular

intervals to cover a floor space of 7.62m x 4.88m. Each pair is joined by a tie-beam (hanebalk) and pegged to the kapbalke with wooden pegs. Battens stretch across the 'kapbalke' and bundles of reed and thatch are sewn to the battens with riempies, twine or grass rope. The ends of the 'kapstylhuise' are rounded, one end acting as a recessed entrance. Light is provided by two small windows. Each house is divided by a simple partition into a bedroom and living room. All cooking was done outside.

KLEINFONTEIN FARM
(SECTION 11, VERMAAKLIKHEID DISTRICT)
Kleinfontein, with its H-shaped Cape Dutch house, lies in a basin at the widening of the Duiwenhoks River before it makes a final bend on its course to the Indian Ocean. The unrivalled and exceptional natural beauty, together with the historic and architectural character of the homestead, makes this area unique.

TOLL HOUSE (GARCIA PASS)
Rebuilt in 1910 on the foundations of an earlier toll house, the old toll house is a remnant of a system that played an important part in the history of transportation in South Africa.

VERSVELD HOUSE (JULIUS GORDON AFRICANA CENTRE, LONG STREET)
This predominantly Georgian house was erected by Dirk Versveld (1853–1912) shortly after 1882, and donated to the City Council of Riversdale by his son Theodore, to house the Julius Gordon Art Collections. The building was restored in 1965 and converted into a museum.

ZEEKOEGAT FARM (PUNTJIE DISTRICT)
The homestead is a typical farmhouse of the eighteenth century. From here two expeditions set out in 1782 and 1790 respectively, in search of survivors of the wrecked ship, the *Grosvenor*.

ROBERTSON
Established on the farm Over het Roode Zand in 1853, Robertson was named after Dr William Robertson (1805–1879), who was the first minister of the Dutch Reformed Church in Clanwilliam, and minister at Swellendam from 1834–1871. The town of Robertson attained its municipal status in 1902.

DOUBLE-STOREY HOUSE
(58 VAN REENEN STREET)
Historic Robertson owes its architectural variety to Cape Dutch, Georgian and Victorian style houses. This Victorian, double-storey house from the late nineteenth century forms an integral part of the town's architectural heritage.

DRUID'S LODGE (MUSEUM)
(50 PAUL KRUGER STREET)
This predominantly Georgian house was probably one of the earliest houses erected in Robertson after the town's foundation in 1853. Druid's Lodge originally had Cape Dutch features, but Georgian and Victorian alterations were probably made by an English family after 1883. The typical Victorian garden is also noteworthy.

POWDER MAGAZINE (BETWEEN THE CEMETERY ON THE ROAD TO WILDSKLOOF)
Erected in 1880 by Barry & Nephews, the magazine was used for the storage of explosives until 1965.

ROBERTSON PUBLIC LIBRARY
(CNR PIET RETIEF AND SWELLENDAM STREETS)
This predominantly Edwardian building was designed by the firm Tully & Waters of Cape Town, and was officially opened on 28 December 1904. It was originally intended to commemorate King Edward VII's coronation in 1902 and to serve as a library.

VICTORIAN HOUSE (63 VAN REENEN STREET)
This house, with its impressive cast-iron verandah, was erected in 1914 and is an excellent example of-late Victorian architecture.

WOLFKLOOF FARMHOUSE
(FARM WOLVEKLOOF OOS)
A Cape Dutch house dating from the 1850s, this house is representative of the type of dwelling erected in Robertson shortly after the founding of the town in 1853.

SALDANHA

Situated north of Saldanha Bay, this town is named after Admiral Antonio de Saldanha, who was wounded here by the Khoekhoe in 1503 while taking water.

FISHERMEN'S COTTAGES
These three oval-shaped cottages were built by George Goode-Busch in 1918 and are the only remaining fishermen's cottages of this type in the vicinity of Saldanha.

SIMONDIUM

The town of Simondium was named after Pierre Simond (1651–1713), a Huguenot minister at the Cape.

BIEN DONNE FARMSTEAD (SIMONDIUM)
Now part of the Fruit & Food Technology Research Institute of Stellenbosch, this farm was originally granted to the Huguenot Pierre Lombard in 1699. The grant was for two farms, Zonder Naam and Watergat. The name, Bien Donne, appeared for the first time in 1837 when the farm belonged to the Joubert family.

HET STICHT
During the construction of this mainly double-storey school, with its variety of stylistic elements, the school board, which was founded in 1851, decided that the building should also serve as a memorial to the French Huguenots. It was designed by PAH Grove and the date 1852 was inscribed on the façade. In 1877 the outbuildings (stables, hen house and messenger's lodge) were also converted into school rooms.

SIR LOWRY'S PASS VILLAGE

Named after Sir Lowry Cole, Governor of the Cape Colony (1829–1834), the village is situated at the foot of the Hottentots Holland Mountains near the lower end of the pass.

OLD RAILWAY STATION
This building was erected shortly after the extension of the railway line between Cape Town and Somerset West to Sir Lowry's Pass Village in 1890. Earlier, the building also housed a post office. It still retains most of its original railway fittings.

SOMERSET WEST

Founded in 1822 and named after Lord Charles Somerset (1767–1831), Governor of the Cape Colony (1814–1826), this is the oldest municipality in the country, attaining such status in January 1822.

CAMPHOR TREES (FARM VERGELEGEN)
Camphor trees, native to China and Japan, were introduced to the Cape in about 1670 by the Dutch East India Company. These five trees were planted by WA van der Stel in 1700-1706.

COACHMAN'S HOUSE AND PROPERTY
(CNR ANDRIES PRETORIUS AND VICTORIA ROADS)
This cottage, in simple vernacular style, is one of several built by freed slaves in the 1830s.

DWELLING HOUSE & WATER MILL (FARM KNORHOEK)
This imposing Cape Dutch manor house together with the adjacent water mill form a unique architectural complex.

GROOT PAARDEVLEI (LOBELIA ROAD)
The farm was granted to Frans van der Stel, youngest son of Simon van der Stel, shortly after 1700. The farm was the property of Martin Melck when he died in 1871. His widow probably altered the house to an H-shape. Many of the original architectural features remain.

HISTORIC FARM MORGENSTER (DISTRICT)
(VERGELEGEN FARM, MORGENSTER ROAD)
Originally part of the farm Vergelegen granted to Willem Adriaan van der Stel in 1700, this section was purchased in 1708 by Jacques Malan after Van der Stel's recall. The erection of the main buildings is attributed to the Malan family during the last quarter of the eighteenth century.

HISTORIC GABLED HOUSE
(CNR VICTORIA AND REITZ STREETS)
This Cape Dutch house stands on land purchased in July 1818 by PH Morkel, owner of the farm Morgenster. He built the original T-shaped house, which was later extended.

LAND EN ZEEZICHT HOMESTEAD
(15 VERSTER AVENUE)
This property originally formed part of the farm Vergelegen. In 1814 it was acquired by Hendrik Hendriksz, who built the house. His family and descendants lived on the farm until 1947 and from 1951 to 1971. In 1971 the house was restored by Count and Countess Zamoyski.

MAGISTRATE'S COURT BUILDING (MAIN STREET)
Erected in 1898, this building originally housed the post office, as well as the Magistrate's Court, after Somerset West was proclaimed an Assistant Magistracy in 1892.

OLD BRIDGE OVER LOURENS RIVER (MAIN ROAD)
The road over the Cape Flats, the intervening rivers and the Hottentots Holland Mountains was gradually improved, and by 1830 the dangerous Gantow Pass was replaced by the Sir Lowry's Pass. In 1843 a Central Road Board was established, and WS Chauncey was appointed to build a hard road across the Flats. Bridges across the Eerste and Lourens Rivers were completed in 1845.

The Lourens River was first known as the Breitenbach River after a military officer from the Cape Colony who took an interest in the area. The name was changed to Tweederivier in the seventeenth century, as it was the second river crossed on the journey from the Peninsula to Sir Lowry's Pass. It was renamed the Lourens after someone of that name drowned there. The spelling subsequently changed and it was renamed the Laurans, but is once again Lourens.

OLD DOVECOT 'ONVERWACHT'
This Dovecot is a particularly good example of the dovecots often built on old farms, and is possibly the most beautiful of all the dovecots in South Africa. It is much enriched by square pilasters at the edges of the gable proper and at the front corner of each enclosure, while five plaster vases, at the apex of the pediment and at the top of each pilaster, add yet more grace, as does much ornamental moulding.

OLD DUTCH REFORMED CHURCH PARSONAGE
(LOURENS STREET)
Erected in 1819, this parsonage was enlarged and rebuilt in the Victorian style in 1848 at the request of Dr JF Reitz, after his appointment to the congregation. Thereafter it served as the parsonage until 1948, when a new dwelling was bought to serve as a parsonage, and the old parsonage was sold. The latter was restored in 1981 and is also known as the Reitz parsonage.

OLD HOTTENTOTS HOLLAND MOUNTAIN PASS (GANTOUW)

This historic pass played an important part in the development of the settlement at the Cape towards the east, and recalls the difficulties with which pioneers had to contend. Deep grooves in the rocks made by wagon wheels and slipper brakes (remskoene) can still be seen. Two old cannons used by the Dutch East India Company to announce the arrival of ships in the Cape, and to give the alarm in case of enemy attacks on the Cape, are still there.

In 1806 General Janssens retreated to this pass when he failed to conquer the British forces in the Battle of Blaauwberg.

OLD NEDERDUITSE GEREFORMEERDE KERK (CHURCH STREET)

This church was consecrated in 1820 by the Reverend Meent Borcherds of Stellenbosch, and was restored in 1863 and again in 1963. It is also the burial place of 'Onze Jan' Hofmeyr (who died in London in 1909) and other prominent South Africans.

PAARL VALLEI HOMESTEAD (DISTRICT)

The farm was granted to Frans van der Stel, youngest son of Governor Simon van der Stel, in 1699. Back and front gables were added to the house in 1800. Although it was damaged by fire early in the twentieth century, it was restored.

POLICE STATION BUILDING (MAIN STREET)

Dating from approximately 1835–1840, this building was originally used as a dwelling, and thereafter as a school, post office and library. It is now used as a police station.

PREDIKANTSPLEIN

Since the establishment of Somerset West in 1825, Predikantsplein has never been built on or cultivated, but was earlier used as a camping site on 'nagmaal' occasions. The square forms a distinctive unit with the original church at its southern boundary and the vicarage at its northern boundary.

QUINAN HOUSE

This homestead was designed and built by the firm Baker & Masey in 1901 as a residence for the factory manager of De Beers Explosive Works. The first two general managers were William and Kenneth Quinan, after whom the house was named following its restoration.

SOMERSET HOUSE (LOURENFORD ROAD)

This property originally formed part of the farm Cloetenberg, which was bought in 1709 by Catharina Cloete. The older section of the building complex dates from 1725, and the front gable of the homestead bears the date 1785.

SWEET SAFFRAN

The original section of this Victorianised house probably dates from the beginning of the nineteenth century. Sweet Saffran is situated on property that was originally granted to GF Prenger in 1779.

VERGELEGEN (LOURENSFORD ROAD)

Built by Willem Adriaan van der Stel in 1700, the old Vergelegen homestead and its estate was purchased in 1901 by Samuel Kerr, an Irishman came to South Africa and made his fortune in the diamond fields of the Orange Free State. At Vergelegen he raised his family of seven daughters and two sons. After his death in 1905, the estate was sold to Sir Lionel and Lady Phillips. Kerr is buried on the estate.

STELLENBOSCH

Although Simon van der Stel named the area of Stellenbosch in 1679 after himself, the town was only founded by him in 1685. It attained municipal status in 1840.

ACKERMANN HOUSE (48–50 DORP STREET)
This imposing architectural complex consists of a Cape Dutch house erected in about 1815, and a double-storey annex dating back to about 1860. The property is closely associated with two well-known Stellenbosch families, the Neethlings and the Ackermans. In the years that General JC Smuts studied at Stellenbosch, he was a boarder at this residence. It was here that he met Issie Krige, whose parents lived at No. 31 Libertas Parva, and who was later to become his wife.

ALMA HOUSE (129 DORP STREET)
Typically neo-Georgian, this double-storey house probably dates from the beginning of the nineteenth century.

ARCHAEOLOGICAL RESERVE
Dr Louis Peringuey made the first discovery of 'Stellenbosch' stone implements in a roadmaker's barrow pit at the Adam Tas Bridge in 1899, proving the great antiquity of man in South Africa.

BACHELORS BUILDING
(WILGENHOF) (RYNEVELD STREET)
The original section of this historic building was erected between 1786 and 1799, but was later altered into a double-storey Georgian house. Taken into use in 1903 as a boarding establishment for students, it is the oldest section of the oldest residence of the University of Stellenbosch. Many well-known personalities in South African public life lodged here during their student years.

BAKKER HOUSE (155 DORP STREET)
With its Cape Dutch and Victorian features, this cottage dates from the 1790s. Jans Bakker, a sailor who dedicated his life to missionary work, moved to Stellenbosch in 1798 and started a school for slaves in this house.

BERGVILLE (15 VICTORIA STREET)
This predominantly Victorian building consists of two double-storey semidetached houses that form an attractive architectural unit with a joint cornice and parapet wall. The building dates from the late nineteenth or early twentieth century.

BLETTERMAN HOUSE
(CNR PLEIN AND DROSTDY STREETS)
The property includes Bletterman House and the Bletterman Annex, the old college building (gymnasium) and the arts department building (cnr Plein and Ryneveld streets). The H-shaped Cape Dutch house was erected shortly after 1787 by HL Bletterman, the last Magistrate of Stellenbosch under the VOC administration. It forms part of the Dorp Museum in Stellenbosch and is furnished in the style of a typical Stellenbosch dwelling between 1750 and 1780.

BLOEMHOF GIRLS' PRIMARY SCHOOL
(RYNEVELD STREET)
Opened on 2 June 1907, this building is an outstanding example of the eclectic style of building of the late nineteenth and early twentieth century. Together with other historic buildings in Ryneveld Street, it forms a unique historic and architectural group. Today it houses the Sasol Art Museum (Eben Donges Centre) of the University of Stellenbosch.

BOSMAN HOUSE (133 DORP STREET)
This neo-Georgian double-storey house dates from the mid-nineteenth century.

BURGER HOUSE (BLOEM STREET, THE BRAAK)
Built by Antonie Fick in 1797, this house was bought by Reverend Luckhoff in 1839 and used as a parsonage. In 1952 it became state property and was handed over to the municipality for restoration.

CALEDON VILLA (7 NEETHLING STREET)
This impressive dwelling, with its Edwardian and Victorian characteristics, was erected in 1910 by the Reverend JGJ Krige of Caledon as a retirement home.

CAPE DUTCH HOUSE
(FARM CHAMPAGNE, DISTRICT)
The farm Dwars-in-den-Weg, now known as Champagne, was granted to Jacob de Wilde in 1697. A Cape Dutch house was presumably erected in 1793 by Isaac Stephanus de Villiers.

CHURCH HOUSE
(KNOWN AS 'UTOPIA') (DORP STREET)
This typical eighteenth century H-shaped gabled house was built by PJ Hartog c.1800. In 1896 the Stellenbosch Dutch Reformed Church bought the property and used it first as a hostel for seminary students, and later as an old-age home. Although spoilt by additions in the nineteenth century, it was restored in 1962.

CL MARAIS LIBRARY BUILDING
(COLLEGE SQUARE, CROZIER STREET)
Predominantly in the neoclassical and neo-Renaissance style, this impressive building was erected from 1899–1900 as a library for the Victoria College, and was the first building erected for this purpose in South Africa.

COACHMAN'S HOUSE
(ALEXANDER STREET, THE BRAAK)
On account of its architectural merit and its situation in relation to The Braak, the house is considered to be of historical value. It was built by John Georg Lankoff, a tailor, at the end of the eighteenth century.

COETZENBURG HOMESTEAD
(JANNIE MARAIS HOUSE) (DISTRICT)
The original farm was granted to Dirk Coetzee, hence the name, in 1682. In 1724 it passed to his son Gerrit, and then to several owners in succession until Petrus Johannes Marais acquired it in 1833. In 1903 the farm passed to Marais' sons FRL and JH Marais (who became the well-known MLA for Stellenbosch). In 1961 the farm was acquired by the University of Stellenbosch for sports grounds, and the homestead is the sports office of the University.

COOPMANSHUYS (33 CHURCH STREET)
This historic dwelling is a typical Georgian double-storey townhouse of the middle eighteenth century. The property forms an essential part of the traditional architectural street scene of Church Street, and also of the historic core of Stellenbosch. The ground on which the house is built was awarded to Alhardus Bartholomeus Coopman in 1713. In 1880 it was owned by Hubertus Elffers, a teacher at the local school, during which time he rented out rooms to students.

DE EIKEN (39 MARKET STREET)
For many years this was the home of Carl Otto Häger, one of South Africa's foremost church architects. Also a photographer and painter, he died here at the age of 86 in 1898. He designed the Moederkerk in Drostdy Street, and the Old Evangelical Lutheran Church in Dorp Street.

DE GOUWE DRUIF GUESTHOUSE
(110 DORP STREET)
The original part of this double-storey townhouse dates from the middle of the nineteenth century. It was later adapted to a Georgian style. The property forms an essential part of Dorp Street's traditional architectural scene.

DEVONSHIRE HOUSE (13 RYNEVELD STREET)
Situated on the oldest street corner in Stellenbosch, Devonshire House was erected c.1861. It is a double-storey townhouse in the early Victorian style.

DIACONIES REMISE (156 DORP STREET)
This site was part of the land bought by the local church in 1753 and was first used as a vicarage garden. After the Reverend Meent Borcherds moved to No. 95 La Gratitude, the plot was subdivided and sold in 1799. The house and unique gateway were built in the nineteenth century.

DIVISIONAL COUNCIL BUILDING
(BLOEM STREET, THE BRAAK)
This building, proclaimed a monument on account of its architectural merit, is an integral part of the historic nucleus of Stellenbosch.

DORP STREET DWELLING (NO. 158)
Originally part of a farm promised in 1683 to Harmen Janszoon (Potgieter), this property was owned by the church council of Stellenbosch in 1753. On the erf, which served as a garden for the new parsonage, a building had already been erected and was used by the Reverend Meent Borcherds as a cowshed. The present house is architecturally interesting, and is an important part of the Dorp Street image.

D'OUWE WERF (30 CHURCH STREET)
This property initially formed the boundary of the original Stellenbosch cemetery, which fell into disuse in 1710. In 1783 the plot was acquired by JB Hoffman, who was presumably responsible for the original Cape Dutch house. This building was thereafter used as a boarding school for many decades and by 1889, an additional storey was added, which gave the building its present imposing Georgian appearance.

DUTCH REFORMED MOTHER CHURCH
(DROSTDY STREET)
A section of this building originally formed part of the Stellenbosch cruciform church that was erected between 1719 and 1723. In 1862 the church was enlarged and altered in the neogothic style by the architect Carl Otto Häger. The church was consecrated on 31 October 1863.

EDWARDIAN SHOP AND PROPERTY
(30 ANDRINGA STREET)
The core of the original building that was erected on this plot still remains, and probably dates from the 1860s. The land was originally transferred to J van Copenhagen on 14 June 1860, and was sold on 13 May 1899 to D Bosman and G Powis.

They conducted business as Bosman, Powis & Company until 1940 when the business was purchased by the firm R Santhagens Cape (Pty) Limited. The building had been used since 1891 as a bottle store. Its present asymmetrical Edwardian appearance probably dates from the period when the firm Bosman, Powis & Company, did business here.

ELSENBERG FARM (DISTRICT)
(R44 FROM STELLENBOSCH TO PAARL)
This farm was granted to the Secunde Samuel Elsevier in 1698. In 1752 it came into the possession of Martin Melck, who rebuilt the U-shaped Cape Dutch main farmhouse in 1761. Although it was destroyed by fire in 1916 and rebuilt, the stoep, steps and end seats are original. Elsenberg is an integral part of the university's faculty of agriculture.

FAÇADE OF CROZIER HOUSE (VICTORIA STREET)
Earlier forming part of the old College Square of the Victoria College, the façade of this late nineteenth-century building has notable Victorian and Georgian characteristics.

FAÇADE OF OLD CONSERVATORY
(VAN RIEBEECK STREET)
The South African Conservatorium of Music, the first Conservatory in South Africa, was

established in 1905, with Professor FW Jannasch as director. This double-storey building is built in an interesting mixture of architectural styles.

FAÇADE OF THEOLOGICAL SEMINARY
(171 DORP STREET)
The foundations of this building date from 1686 when the first Drostdy was built there. In 1763 the building was rebuilt into an H-shape with a traditional Cape Dutch appearance. It served as a Drostdy until 1827. In 1859 it was donated to the Dutch Reformed Church and a theological seminary was opened. The building was altered to its present appearance in 1905.

FAÇADES OF VICTORIAN COTTAGES
(16, 18, 20, 22, 24, 26 CROZIER STREET)
These Victorian semidetached cottages date from the late nineteenth century.

FAÇADES OF RHENISH GIRLS' SCHOOL COMPLEX
(THE BRAAK)
This building is the third to have housed the well-known girls' school. The cornerstone was laid on 6 May 1905 by Thomas Muir, the Superintendent-General of Education, and the school was opened on 10 February 1906.

FIRST GYMNASIUM (120–122 DORP STREET)
The first permanent accommodation of the Stellenbosch Gymnasium, this building later developed into the Paul Roos Gymnasium and the University of Stellenbosch. It was established for the higher education of boys to prepare as candidates for admission to the Theological Seminary, which opened on 1 March 1866. The Seminary occupied these premises for eight years from 1 July 1866.

FLEURBAAI HOMESTEAD (DISTRICT)
(R310 IN LIBERTAS DISTRICT)
While the farm was originally granted to the Huguenot Pierre le Febre in 1695, the manor house dates from approximately 1768. Together with the outbuildings, it forms an important Cape Dutch architectural complex.

GARDEN GATEWAY (PLEIN STREET)
An original surmise that this was the gateway to the old cemetery, has proved incorrect. The land on which the old cemetery was laid out was later divided into plots and sold. The owner of this plot decided to build the gateway into his garden wall.

GATEWAY AND GATES OF THEOLOGICAL SEMINARY (DORP SREET)
The gateway and gates, erected in about 1769 as part of the Drostdy at that time, are situated on the most historic site in Stellenbosch, which has associations with Simon van der Stel. The respective Drostdy buildings were also situated here until, in 1859, they became the seat of the Theological Seminary.

GEORGIAN HOUSE (24 THE AVENUE)
Following his retirement from farming on the farm Nooitgedacht, JM Beyers settled in Stellenbosch and entered the business world in the 1880s. During this period he erected several semidetached houses in Beyers, Ryneveld and Neethling Streets, as well as The Avenue, in order to alleviate the housing shortage that existed in Stellenbosch at the end of the nineteenth century. This flat-roofed semi-detached house, with Georgian and Victorian elements, was originally a corner unit of six semidetached houses that Beyers erected on the land where his vineyards had formerly stood.

GEORGIAN HOUSE
(CNR RYNEVELD AND DORP STREETS)
This single-storey Georgian house is situated on a property that originally formed part of the 'Kolonieserwe' granted in 1693 to the local Landdrost and Heemrade. From 1702 the

property was owned by a sick-comforter, Jan Malieu. Later it was bought by the Pieter de Waal Neethling Trust Fund. Since then two theological papers have been launched from here.

GEORGIAN HOUSE (108 DORP STREET)
The original part of this historic house dates from the beginning of the nineteenth century and was later adapted to a Georgian style. It is an integral part of the architecturally and historically important Dorp Street scene.

GROSVENOR HOUSE AND ANNEX
(12 DROSTY STREET, 1–5 VAN RIEBEECK STREET)
Built in approximately 1781 on land granted to Christiaan Ludolph Neethling, the property was transferred in 1790 to Friedrich Gotthold Holtzapfel, in 1798 to Reinhard Perryn, and in 1799 to Wilhelm Herold. Herold rebuilt the house in 1803 after a devastating fire. In 1821 the house was bought by Adrian Roux, in 1845 by Eduard Hoffman, and in 1872 by Christoffel Joseph Brand, first Speaker of the old Cape Legislative Assembly (1854–1874) and father of President JH Brand of the Orange Free State.

HAUPTFLEISCH HOUSE
(ESPERANZA) (153 DORP STREET)
The erf on which this house stands was acquired by Jacobus van den Bergh in 1704. It was sold in 1812 to FJ Hauptfleisch, who probably built the house. Later, it belonged to well-known Stellenbosch families. Now used as business premises, the house is a good example of Stellenbosch architecture in the eighteenth and nineteenth centuries.

HERTE STREET PROPERTIES (8, 13, 15, 19, 21, 23, AND 6 SCHREUDER STREET)
Granted to the Landdrost and Heemraad, and to Jan Greyling in 1750, the complex is of special architectural interest and forms an essential part of the historic core of Stellenbosch.

HISTORIC BUILDINGS (37, 39, 41 HERTE STREET)
These historic double-storey houses were erected in about 1841 as residences for coloured people, as well as freed slaves and their descendants.

HISTORIC COTTAGES
(41, 43, 47, 49 DORP STREET)
These similar semidetached cottages were erected between 1817 and 1859 in the Cape Dutch style, but were later Victorianised. They form an important visual element of the historic character of Dorp Street.

HISTORIC DWELLING HOUSE (105 DORP STREET)
A typical double-storey townhouse of the second half of the nineteenth century, this historic dwelling forms an essential part of the traditional architectural Dorp Street scene.

HISTORIC FARMHANDS' COTTAGES
(DE WAGENWEG)
These farmhands' cottages date from the year 1902 and were probably designed by architect Sir Herbert Baker.

HISTORIC HOUSE (31 VAN RIEBEECK STREET)
This predominantly Victorian house dates from the beginning of the twentieth century. Owing to the property's strategic position it forms an important aspect of the townscape.

HISTORIC OLD LIME KILN (STELLENKLOOF FARM, BLAAUWKLIP ROAD) (FORMERLY NIETGEGUND)
Unique in the Stellenbosch area, this lime kiln was probably erected by Hermanus Johannes von Brakel shortly after the subdivision of the farm Rustenburg in 1790, of which Nietgegund (now Stellenkloof) was originally a part.

HOFMEYR HALL (39 CHURCH STREET)
This neoclassical hall, with its impressive Ionic temple façade, was inaugurated in October

1900. It was built for use by the Christelike Jongelieden Vereeniging and was named after Professor NJ Hofmeyr, founder of the Stellenbosch Seminary and the CJV.

IDAS VALLEY
(MERRIMAN STREET, TOWARDS KLUWER)
The first section of the valley at the foot of Simonsberg was granted in 1683 to Francois Viljoen, a French refugee who came to South Africa before the main body of the Huguenots.

JEWISH SKUINSHUIS AND CHICKEN COOP
(44 VAN RYNEVELD STREET)
Although the core of this double-storey building dates from about 1872, the façade of the house was rebuilt during the first half of the nineteenth century. Together with the historic chicken-coop, it forms a unique architectural complex.

JUBILEE HOUSE (CPWAA) (126 DORP STREET)
This double-storey building with its classical pediment dates from the second half of the nineteenth century. It forms an integral part of the historic and architecturally important street scene of Dorp Street and also of Stellenbosch.

KLEIN GUSTROUW HOMESTEAD
(FARM KLEIN GUSTROUW, JONKERSHOEK)
The farm Klein Gustrouw was granted to a freed slave, Louis of Bengal, in 1683. It is presumed that the house was rebuilt by Pieter Daniel Grundlingh, who bought it in 1817. The farm and homestead were subdivided at the end of the nineteenth century, after which one part was named Leef-op-Hoop. The homestead has undergone many changes during the years and bears testimony to the Georgian and Victorian influences on Cape Dutch buildings.

KLEIN VREDELUST (63 DORP STREET)
The first owner of this village smallholding was Jan Cornelius, known as Jan Bombam, who named his farm Libertas. It is a good example of the architecture in Stellenbosch between the eighteenth and nineteenth centuries, and is also of historic interest.

KOOPMANSKLOOF GABLED HOUSE (DISTRICT)
Erected in 1801 by Petrus Johannes Bosman, this Cape Dutch house, with its unusual double-T-shaped ground plan, stepped gables on the side and authentic Malay plaster work, is of particular architectural interest.

LAETITIA (ALEXANDER STREET, THE BRAAK)
Distinct in character and recently restored, this double-storey building was built shortly after 1803, after the great fire in Stellenbosch.

LA GRATITUDE (95 DORP STREET)
This house was built by Reverend Meent Borcherds in 1798. After serving the Stellenbosch community from 1876 to 1830, he died here in 1832.

LANZERAC COMPLEX (JONKERSHOEK)
This farm was originally granted in 1692 as Schoongezicht. Around 1830, Coenraad Fick built a manor house there in Cape Dutch style. The outbuildings are of architectural interest.

LATE VICTORIAN HOUSE
(14 VAN RIEBEECK STREET)
This late Victorian house, with its exquisite cast-iron latticed verandah, dates from the 1890s. The property forms an important element in the townscape in view of its strategic position.

LEEF-DE-HOOP HOMESTEAD (JONKERSHOEK)
A section of this impressive H-shaped historic house on the farm Leef-op-Hoop dates from the beginning of the nineteenth century. It has Georgian and Victorian features and is unique in that both the original farm and the dwelling are divided in two.

LIBERTAS HISTORIC BUILDINGS (DISTRICT)

The site includes all historic buildings and structures on the farmyard, as well as the cemetery. Although the building complex dates mainly from the eighteenth century, the farm was granted to Jan Jurgen Grimp in 1692. Adam Tas procured the farm in 1702 and lived here until his death in 1722. In February 1706 Tas was arrested here and held in custody at the Castle until he was released in April 1707, whereupon he named his farm Libertas (Tas is free). Noteworthy of the Cape Dutch building complex is the H-shaped main dwelling house with frescos by Jan Adam Hoffman in 1779.

LIBERTAS PARVA (31 DORP STREET)

Housing the Oude Meester Wine Museum, the Libertas Parva building complex is a fine example of Stellenbosch architecture in the eighteenth and nineteenth centuries, and lends a particular character to this part of the village. As the home of well-known Stellenbosch families it is also of historic value. The H-shaped house was built in 1783 by Lambertus Fick. In 1969 it was bought by the Rembrandt van Rijn Art Museum.

LOUBSER HOUSE (157 DORP STREET)

In 1820 the Stellenbosch Mederwerkende Zendelings Genootschap bought the erf on which this house stands from the missionary Meuwes Janse Bakker, to build a meeting house. When construction commenced in 1825 on The Braak, the society sold the erf to David Kinneberg, who built the house in the same year. After him the house belonged, amongst others, to Hubertus Elffers, author of Dutch school books, and later to Bob Loubser, a Springbok rugby player (1906) and later, MP for Stellenbosch. Now occupied as an office, the house is a good example of architecture in Stellenbosch between the eighteenth and nineteenth centuries, and is of historic interest.

MAIN BUILDING, UNIVERSITY OF STELLENBOSCH

This building was erected between 1880 and 1886 to provide proper housing for the Stellenbosch College. The foundation stone was laid on 22 December 1880, after which a section of the building was put into use on 15 October 1883, and the completed building officially opened on 6 November 1886. Designed by Carl Otto Häger in neoclassical style, this main building played an important role in the history of the Victoria College, and later the University of Stellenbosch.

MARKET STREET (9, 11, 13)

Architecturally interesting, this complex of houses, dating mainly from the nineteenth century, forms an integral part of the entire western side of Market Street, as well as of the historic core of Stellenbosch itself.

MERWEDA (112 DORP STREET)

This house dates approximately from 1798, and was later converted to the Georgian style.

MOEDERSLOON DWELLING (8 THE AVENUE)

Built in 1904 for the Reverend JH Neethling (1858–1904), this Edwardian villa was bought in 1950 by Miss MM Verster and named Moedersloon in appreciation of her mother.

MORKEL HOUSE (RYNEVELD STREET)

This fine eighteenth century house contains an older section, built in about 1693, which was the wine cellar of Heemraad Jan Botha. The congregation of Stellenbosch held services here from 1711–1722.

MURRAY HOUSE (11 DROSTDY STREET)

The original section of this double-storey townhouse dates from the middle of the eighteenth century. Its best-known owner was Professor John Murray, one of the first two Professors at the Theological Seminary.

NAVARRE FARMSTEAD AND ADJACENT OUTBUILDINGS (FARM MARSHDEN)
Navarre, originally the homestead on the farm Nooitgedacht granted to Daniel Josias Malan in 1796, was erected in 1814 by his son Johannes Jacobus Malan. This impressive late neoclassical gable bears his initials. The outbuildings also date from the early nineteenth century.

NEETHLINGSHOF FARMSTEAD (BOTTELARY)
This property was originally granted to Barend Lubbe in 1699. In later years it passed to the Neethling family and eventually by marriage to the Louw family. The present H-shaped gable house, with its impressive façade, was erected in 1814 by Charles Marais.

NEO-DUTCH GABLED HOUSE (5 MINSERIE STREET)
Erected in 1919 by the trader I Perel, this house is one of three similar in the street. Characteristic of a 1920s dwelling, the steel window frames were among the first to have been used locally.

NOOITGEDACHT HEERENHAUSEN FARMSTEAD (NEAR KOELENHOF)
Nooitgedacht was granted to the Heemraad Matthias Greeff from Magdeburg in 1692, and transferred to Jan Loubser in 1718. The present H-shaped house was built in 1774 by Hendrik Cloete, who later lived at Groot Constantia. With its gable of rare design, together with a slave bell and outbuildings, the house is a remarkable example of Cape Dutch architecture.

The farm also occupies a special place in the history of deciduous fruit growing, as it was here that the industry started on a large scale in 1892 when HEV Pickstone and S van Reenen planted 80 000 fruit trees which, with the aid of Cecil Rhodes, they imported from California.

OLD CAPE GRANDFATHER CLOCK
Made by Johann Michael Junck, who arrived from Germany in 1765 and died in 1771, the clock is assumed to have been made between 1768 and 1771. This magnificent clock is made of ebony, stinkwood and yellowwood and is toppped by three figures: Atlas in the centre, and an angel on either side.

OLD EVANGELICAL LUTHERAN CHURCH (DORP STREET)
Designed and erected by Carl Otto Häger, this neogothic-style building was originally used as a Lutheran church after the consecration on 28 November 1854.

OLD NECTAR FARMSTEAD (JONKERSHOEK)
This farm was originally granted in 1692 as Jan Lui. Old Nectar is architecturally one of the finest and best-known gable houses of the old Cape type. It is situated on the farm formerly known as Weltevrede and was allocated in 1685.

OLD PARSONAGE (141–143 DORP STREET)
The original sections of this Cape Dutch house date from the middle of the eighteenth century, and it was first used as a parsonage for the Reverend Meent Borcherds. The property forms an essential part of the traditional architectural street scene of Dorp Street, and also of the historic core of Stellenbosch.

OLD POWDER MAGAZINE (BLOEM STREET, THE BRAAK)
Ninety-one years after the political council decided Stellenbosch should have one, and taking six months to construct, the Dutch East India Company completed this magazine in 1777. The bell tower was added 20 years later.

OLD READING ROOM (182 DORP STREET)
This building was originally used by the College of Landdrost and Heemraden as offices. The foundation meeting for the educational institution, which was to become known as the Gymnasium, was held here in

1863. Before the completion of the Gymnasium building in 1866, the Old Reading Room was used as a school building for three months.

OLD RHENISH SCHOOL HOSTEL
(BLOEM STREET, THE BRAAK)

The Rhenish School was founded in 1860, and moved to this site in 1862. The house that stood here was gradually enlarged until the building assumed its present appearance at the end of the nineteenth century. It currently houses the PJ Olivier Art Centre of the Cape Educational Department.

OU BAKHUIS (GIRD HOUSE)
(152–154 DORP STREET)

These houses are good examples of the architecture in Stellenbosch between the eighteenth and nineteenth centuries, and are also of historic interest.

PIERNEEF MUSEUM (149 DORP STREET)

Displaying a harmonious mixture of Cape Dutch and Georgian characteristics, this house presumably dates from the beginning of the eighteenth century. It forms an essential architectural and aesthetic keystone in the historic core of Stellenbosch.

PORTION OF HISTORIC MILL STREAM

The mill stream, with water from the Eerste River, was the artery of Simon van der Stel's 'Colonie', and since the seventeenth century it has played an important role in the development of Stellenbosch. This, the first of three 'Water Koringmolens' powered by water from the mill stream, was erected in 1687.

PROTEAHOF COMPLEX
(80–120 RYNEVELD STREET)

Erected shortly after 1860, this building complex originally formed part of a housing scheme for former slaves. The cottages were restored recently.

PULPIT IN RHENISH CHURCH
(BLOEM STREET, THE BRAAK)

The Simon Pieter Christoffel Londt pulpit and lectern, made by the master carpenter Londt in 1853, is one of the most graceful to be seen. It was previously in the Moeder Kerk.

RED HOUSE (68 KAHLER STREET, IDAS VALLEY)

This impressive dwelling house, with its true Victorian features, dates from the nineteenth century, and is allegedly one of the oldest houses in Idas Valley.

RHENISH CHURCH (BLOEM STREET, THE BRAAK)

Built in 1823 by the Missionary Society of Stellenbosch as a training school for slaves and coloured people, the Rhenish Church was enlarged in 1840, and is one of the oldest mission churches in South Africa.

RHENISH PARSONAGE COMPLEX (HERTE STREET)

All the buildings of the Rhenish Parsonage complex, built on land granted to Marthinus Byleveld in 1785, date from the beginning of the nineteenth century.

The main building is the former parsonage of the Rhenish Church and dates from 1815. One of the back wings of this H-shaped parsonage is connected with another two buildings in the complex. Of these the so-called Leipoldt House, with its large proportions, dates from approximately 1832, while the third building, with its low dormer gable, was converted into a double-storey in about 1860. On one side the Rhenish Parsonage complex is enclosed by a long circular wall.

RUST-EN-VREDE WINE ESTATE
(ANNANDALE ROAD)

This farm is a section of an earlier farm, Bonte Rivier. Although a wine-cellar was built in about 1780, the H-shaped homestead, with a back gable similar to the front gable and four end gables, dates from 1825. The homestead was built by Johann Lorenz Liebentrau for his son Hendrik Godfried.

RYNEVELDHOF COMPLEX
(VAN RYNEVELD STREET)

This building complex, erected shortly after 1860, was originally part of a housing scheme for former slaves. With the redevelopment of the area from 1971 to 1973, the then Department of Community Development retained and restored this street scene.

ST MARY'S CHURCH (THE BRAAK)

This thatched Anglican church was completed in 1852, and was consecrated by Bishop Robert Gray in 1854. It was not until 1884 that the bell tower was added.

SAXENHOF (159 DORP STREET)

The site on which this house stands was granted in 1704 to Pieter Sax, who probably built the original homestead shortly after. In 1833 it was acquired by Dr J Versveld, the first doctor to be trained in South Africa. Dr JH Neethling bought the house in 1899, and rebuilt it in its present form. It is a good example of the architecture in Stellenbosch between the eighteenth and nineteenth centuries and is also of historic interest.

SCHREUDER HOUSE (RYNEVELD STREET)

This colonial house was built in 1709 by Sebastian Schreuder and is the oldest known European dwelling in South Africa.

SEMIDETACHED COTTAGE (45 DORP STREET)

Originally part of the farm Vredenlust, which was granted to Christoffel Henske in 1781, the cottage is one of a row of six similar semidetached buildings that were erected between 1817 and 1859 in the Cape Dutch style and later Victorianised.

SEMIDETACHED COTTAGES (1 VICTORIA STREET; 62 AND 66 ANDRINGA STREET)

These three Victorianised semidetached cottages were originally erected early in the nineteenth century. They form an important architectural unit and lend character to the nearby Church Square.

SEMIDETACHED COTTAGES
(25, 27, 29, 31, 33, 35 HERTE STREET)

This row of semidetached cottages, with their pointed gables, was presumably erected during the middle of the nineteenth century as accommodation for freed slaves. These properties form an essential part of the historic and architectural character of Herte Street and also of the historic core of Stellenbosch.

SEMIDETACHED HOUSE (51 DORP STREET)

Together with seven similar structures, this Victorianised house, originally built during the first half of the nineteenth century, forms an impressive street scene in Stellenbosch.

STELLENBOSCH HOTEL (160–162 DORP STREET)

This property was presented to Johannes Swart, a school teacher of the Dutch East India Company, by Governor Simon van der Stel. The surgeon Jan Cats bought the property in 1743. The original thatched-roof house was a single storey with dung floors. It was rebuilt in 1815 to its present state by the then owner, Tobias de Villiers. A redbrick Cape house, which also forms part of the Stellenbosch Hotel was built at No. 162 in c.1876 by the owner JH de Villiers.

THABA 'NCHU HOUSE (5 RATTRAY STREET)

Thaba'Nchu House, which has been restored to its original colour scheme, was built in 1900 by James Rattray, son of a British teacher brought out from England by Lord Charles Somerset. It is an excellent example of High-Victorian architecture in Stellenbosch.

THE BRAAK
The Braak is an open central square, for some time known as King's Square and Adderley Square. Its name derives from an old Dutch word meaning 'fallow land'. It was reserved in 1703 as a military parade ground for the Stellenbosch infantry and dragoons, and acquired its present form in about 1800.

TINETTA (135 DORP STREET)
Together with other double-storey houses situated at 125, 129 and 133 Dorp Street, these predominantly Georgian houses probably date from the beginning of the nineteenth century.

TRANSVALIA (125 DORP STREET)
This is a double-storey, early nineteenth-century Georgian style dwelling.

TROUT HATCHERY
(FARM ASSAGAIBOSCH, JONKERSHOEK)
In 1893 the Colonial Government hired a fish hatching site on Assegaaibosch, erecting this structure in 1894. It is a unique example of a late nineteenth-century Victorian trout hatchery.

UITERWYK DWELLING HOUSE (DISTRICT)
The property was granted in 1699 to Dirk Coetzee, and in 1791 Johannes Krige enlarged the existing house and added gables. The Cape Dutch house is H-shaped with an impressive concavo-convex front gable.

VAN DER BIJL HOUSE (37 MARKET STREET)
Part of the former Oude Molen farm, Adriaan Roux bought the property in 1806 and erected this house shortly afterwards. It has been in the Van der Bijl family since 1848.

VAN NIEKERK HOUSE (47 CHURCH STREET)
Part of Stellenbosch's historic core, this double-storey Victorian house is situated on a plot granted to Landdrost C Linnes in 1694.

VICTORIAN HOUSE (19 HEROLD STREET)
Herold Street, on which the house is situated, is named after the Reverend T Herold. The dwelling is situated on land that was formerly part of the farm Weidenhof.

VICTORIAN HOUSE (31 VAN RIEBEECK STREET)
The predominantly Victorian house dates from the beginning of the twentieth century. Because of the property's strategic position, this house plays an important role in the townscape.

VICTORIAN SEMIDETACHED HOUSE
(4 NEETHLING STREET)
With its curved verandah and cast-iron decorations, this is one of two identical late Victorian semidetached houses that are an integral part of the architectural scene of Neethling Street and the town's historic core.

VICTORIANISED HOUSES
(37 AND 39 DORP STREET)
These two Victorianised houses, originally erected during the first half of the nineteenth century, together with six other similar buildings, form one of the most charming and harmonious street scenes in Stellenbosch.

VLOTTENBURG (FARM BY-DEN-WEG, DISTRICT)
The property, together with an adjoining farm, was granted to two Huguenots, Pierre Rochefort and Gerard Hanseret, in partnership in 1707. The original section of this Cape Dutch farmhouse was presumably erected by Daniel Joubert shortly after he bought the farm By-den-Weg in 1784.

VOORGELEGEN (116–118 DORP STREET)
This property originally formed part of De Nieuwe Molen, which was granted to the Landdrost and Heemrade in 1750. In 1797 it became the property of Johannes Victor, who almost immediately erected the original H-shaped

Cape Dutch House. In the second half of the nineteenth century it was converted to a Georgian double-storey residence. Together with outbuildings and a garden ring wall it forms an outstanding group of buildings from an architectural and town planning point of view, and constitutes an integral part of the street scene of Dorp Street.

The old-world garden with its tranquil atmosphere, partly due to the Mill stream, is an aesthetic gem that fits in with the unique group of properties surrounding Voorgelegen.

VREDELUST DWELLING WITH WINE CELLAR (63 DORP STREET)

Vredelust is a good example of the architecture in Stellenbosch between the eighteenth and nineteenth centuries, and is also of historic interest.

VREDENBURG (DISTRICT) (N2 TOWARDS SPIER WINE ESTATE)

The farm Vredenburg was granted to Hendrik Elbertz in 1691. The historic dwelling built in 1789 by a later owner, Jacob Roux, is known today as Lower Vredenburg. It was restored in the 1930s. The outbuildings are very old.

WELTEVREDEN HISTORIC FARMHOUSE (DISTRICT)

Voortrekker leader Piet Retief bought this property in 1812, but went in 1812–1813 with the Stellenbosch commando to help Colonel Graham on the frontier. On his return he had the sale rescinded. One of the gables, built in 1804, of the old house bears the initials of his sister, Debora Retief. The farm is much older and is a section of Patrys Vallei where Hans Henske settled in 1688.

STILBAAI

The township was proclaimed in 1962 and attained municipal status in 1966.

FISH TRAPS (NOORDKAPPER POINT)

Intertidal fish traps, erected about 2 000 years ago by the Khoekhoe, existed at several localities along the Southern Cape coast. A few still remain. Constructed on a relatively rocky shore, the traps have low stone barriers are packed in such a manner that the incoming tide brings fish into the traps, from which they cannot escape when the tide recedes. There are 25 separate traps, each with its own name still in use and extending along approximately 600m of the shore.

HISTORIC PALINGGAT HOMESTEAD AND FOUNTAIN (PLATTEBOSCH)

Originally erected in the late eighteenth century, this house was rebuilt in 1814 by AJ de Jager after it was burnt down by Hottentots. Predominantly in Cape Dutch style, the house is still occupied by descendants of the De Jager family. The historic 'paling' fountain with its tame freshwater eels is noteworthy.

JAGERBOS HOMESTEAD (ALSO KNOWN AS JAGERBOSCH)

The Jagerbos Homestead is one of two original houses erected early in the nineteenth century by the De Jager family. A typical thatched-roof farmouse with thick walls and straight end gables, it was built by a son of the original owner of Palinggat.

STRUISBAAI

The name derives from the Dutch, 'Vogel Struijs Baay', or 'ostrich bay'.

HISTORIC OLD ANGLICAN CHURCH

This church building, with its noteworthy mixture of vernacular and neogothic features, was erected in 1892 by the Anglican Church on an erf donated to the congregation by the Van Breda family of Zoetendalsvallei.

SWELLENDAM

Established around the Drostdy in 1747, Swellendam was named after the Governor, Hendrik Swellengrebel (1700–1760) and his wife, Helena ten Damme. The town attained municipal status in 1904.

AULD HOUSE (4 VOORTREK STREET)
Auld House is a fine old Cape house with interesting associations with the historic Barry family. This rare double-T-shaped ground plan house, with unusual end gables, was built in 1802 and is one of the finest examples in the area. Its woodwork façade probably dates from after a fire in 1835. Extensions on the left of the front wing are late nineteenth century.

BUKKENBURG HOUSE
(8 HERMANUS STEYN STREET)
This late nineteenth-century dwelling, with its predominantly Victorian features, forms an integral part of the historic core of Swellendam in the immediate vicinity of the Drostdy.

CHARCOAL OVEN (FARM VOORHUIS)
This Charcoal Oven was built by Hermanus Steyn. Dating to the middle of the eighteenth century, it is the oldest known structure of its kind in South Africa.

DE KLOOF DWELLING HOUSE AND WAGON HOUSE (WELTEVREDEN STREET)
The property on which this T-shaped gable house is situated was granted to Johan Becker in 1801 by the Landdrost and Heemrade of Swellendam. The core of the house, which then consisted of a single row of rooms, was presumably built by Becker in about 1805. The house was apparently enlarged after this, to meet the needs of ensuing owners, by the addition of a further wing. The latter also has concavo-convex end gables similar to the original gables.

DROSTDY COMPLEX, VICTORIAN HOUSE
(14 DROSTDY STREET)
Reputedly a stable, coach house and saddler's dwelling serving the Drostdy, the core of this Victorianised house, originally in Cape Dutch style, dates from the eighteenth century.

DROSTDY MUSEUM (18 SWELLENGREBEL STREET)
This land formed part of the original Drostdy property that was subdivided in 1799. The house is a Georgian double-storey dating from the middle of the nineteenth century and is architecturally outstanding.

DUTCH REFORMED CHURCH BUILDING
(11 VOORTREK STREET)
The cornerstone was laid on 25 November 1910. Architecturally diverse, the church was inaugurated on 10 June 1911 by Professor CJF Muller. The decorated entrance archway and gates are all that remain of an 1802 church.

DWELLING HOUSE (11 VAN OUDTSHOORN ROAD)
This house, with its Victorian and Edwardian features, dates from the first decade of the twentieth century.

GRIER BRIDGE OVER BREEDE RIVER
Erected in the 1890s, the old road bridge is 196m in length and is carried on five large stone piers. Named after the engineer in charge of the construction, it is built of cast-iron sections manufactured in England in 1892 by Patent Shaft & Axletree Ltd.

HISTORIC COTTAGE (3 MOOLMAN STREET)
This cottage in vernacular style was reputedly one of a row of early nineteenth-century townhouses near the Dutch Reformed church.

HISTORIC COTTAGE (10 MOOLMAN STREET)
Mainly in Cape vernacular style, this cottage dates from the middle of the nineteenth century.

HISTORIC HOUSE (5 BUITENKANT STREET)
A predominantly Victorian dwelling house, with a bay window at one end and a verandah stretching around two sides, the building was erected in 1900 by a local builder named Karg.

HISTORIC HOUSE (9 MOOLMAN STREET)
This mid-nineteenth-century structure consists of two self-contained units, joined by a row of three rooms in the centre. It was reputedly part of a row of townhouses near the Dutch Reformed church.

HISTORIC HOUSES (27 BERG STREET, 10 HERMANUS STEYN STREET, 9 SIEBERT STREET AND 218 VOORTREKKER STREET)
With their Victorian characteristics, these dwellings all date from the nineteenth century or the first decade of the twentieth century, and form an integral part of the historical and architectural core of the town.

HISTORIC OLD BUFFELJACHTS RIVER BRIDGE
Building on this bridge began in 1845 but was delayed on account of the builders having to leave for the Eastern Frontier on commando. Teak from the wreck of the *Robert* was used for the structure, and it was officially inaugurated on 10 January 1852.

HISTORIC DWELLING: KLEIN DROSTDY
(12 DROSTDY STREET)
Forming an integral part of the historic core of Swellendam, this house, with Cape Georgian characteristics, dates from the 1850s.

KLIPRIVIER FARM
During the years 1833–1837 this farm was owned by Marthinus Steyn, great-grandfather of President MT Steyn of the Orange Free State, and builder of the magnificent homestead. The farm was also owned by President FW Reitz during the years 1869–1899.

KOORNLANDS COTTAGE (5 VOORTREK STREET)
This thatched cottage, with its T-shaped ground plan, was built in 1832, and in about 1855 the woodwork of the façade was Georgianised. Also typically Cape-Georgian are the double doors and fanlight.

LATE VICTORIAN DWELLING
(101 VOORTREK STREET)
Predominantly Victorian, this late nineteenth-century dwelling forms an integral part of the architectural street scene and the historic core of Swellendam.

MALTA HOUSE (9 GLEN BARRY STREET)
Originally erected as a second mill house for the nearby Drostdy, this building probably dates from the 1750s. Victorianised in about 1840, one section of the structure served as an overshot mill and the other as accommodation for the miller. The house and the adjacent late nineteenth-century outbuilding form an important architectural complex.

MAYVILLE (4 HERMANUS STEYN STREET)
This property is situated on land that originally formed part of the historic Drostdy complex. The house was built in about 1853 for the owner, Daniel de Bruyn.

MILL COTTAGE (243 VOORTREK STREET)
The nucleus of this building was presumably erected before 1840. It served as a water mill until it was converted into a house.

MOOLMANSHOF CAPE DUTCH DWELLING HOUSE
(217 VOORTREK STREET)
One of the oldest buildings in Swellendam, the oldest section of this impressive Cape Dutch dwelling was erected in 1798 by Christiaan Essenberg, a Swiss immigrant. The house was enlarged in the 1840s by JZ Moolman, and named Moolmanshof.

MORGENZON (16 VAN OUDTSHOORN ROAD)
Morgenzon is a U-shaped Cape Dutch house that was erected in about 1745 as the dwelling for the secretary of the local Drostdy. From 1855 to 1875, it was used as an exclusive school for girls.

OLD BOYS' HIGH SCHOOL
(147 VOORTREK STREET)
The land was granted in 1818 to JW van Dyk, a wagon-maker who built the house in about 1825; there was a wagon-makers' workshop in the basement up to 1870. The building was then purchased for a school and Dr DF Malan taught there in 1896.

OLD GAOL (24–28 SWELLENGREBEL STREET)
Now part of the Drostdy Museum, this Cape Dutch building formed part of the original official buildings of the Drostdy, built in 1746. The front left-hand section contains the house of the Landdrost's Secretary, and that of the Deputy Sheriff was on the right. The prison cells in the rear wings were added in about 1800.

OLD POST OFFICE (SWELLENGREBEL STREET)
This was the residence of the gaoler, who was also the postmaster, which is possibly why the post office was situated near the gaol.

OLD RESIDENCY (VAN OUDTSHOORN ROAD)
In 1839 this property was granted to Thomas Barry, who apparently built the house without delay. Afterwards, it was used as the residence of the magistrate and became known as The Residency.

OLD ST LUKE'S ANGLICAN CHURCH
(12 VOORTREK STREET)
First built as a Wesleyan mission church in 1865, this rectangular neogothic building with Cape Dutch elements is the oldest church building in Swellendam.

OSLO HOUSE (120 VOORTREK STREET)
This house, with its Cape Dutch and Victorian elements, dates from the 1850s. Flat-roofed additions at the back of the building presumably date from the last decade of the nineteenth century.

PARK VILLA HOUSE (23 VAN OUDTSHOORN ROAD)
Originally a T-shaped Cape Dutch house built in about 1802, this building was Victorianised, but still retains many Cape Dutch features.

POWDER MAGAZINE (GELDERBOOM STREET)
The simple rectangular powder magazine dates from the middle of the nineteenth century and was possibly erected by the well-known firm, Barry & Nephews.

ROSE COTTAGE (245 VOORTREK STREET)
This double-storey rectangular house, dating from about 1840, was presumably built by WM Hopley, a well-known local land surveyor.

ROTHMAN HOUSE (JVDS HOUSE AND COTTAGE)
(268 VOORTREK STREET)
The JVDS/Rothman House is a T-shaped thatched roof house with concavo-convex side and back gables, as well as a front gable on which the letters 'JVDS' and the date '1834' appear. Erected by Johannes Rothman, master wagoner and blacksmith, it is suspected that the inscription 'J(aar) V(an) D(e) S(laven)' refers to the year in which the slaves were freed. Rothman Cottage is an oblong structure with straight end gables and a hipped front gable.

ROTTERDAM CAPE DUTCH HOMESTEAD
(FARM ROTTERDAM)
The farm Rotterdam, granted to Hendrik van Volenhoven by General JH van Plettenberg in 1783, was transferred to Landdrost Anthonie Faure in 1794. The main homestead, the baroque front gable of which bears the date 1794, was erected by him.

SCHOONE OORD (1 SWELLENGREBEL STREET)
This double-storey house was built in 1853 in Cape-Georgian style and Victorianised in the late nineteenth century by the addition of a cast-iron verandah on both levels. Outbuildings, consisting of the original coach house and what is believed to have been the first bakery in Swellendam, are also noteworthy.

THE GLEN (14 GLEN BARRY STREET)
The property on which this Cape Dutch house is situated was first granted in 1799 to Johannes Matthys Ebersohn, who initially erected a T-shaped house. Jan Ferdinand Bam converted it into an H-shaped house early in the nineteenth century.

THE OEFENINGSHUIS (MEETING HOUSE)
(36 VOORTREK STREET)
Built in 1838 under the supervision of Reverend William Robertson, this Cape Dutch thatched building was built for religious and educational purposes. The glazed frame beneath the false clock in the west gable originally housed a real clock. The design of the end gables, which is peculiar to Swellendam, is noteworthy.

TOWNHOUSES (4 SHAND STREET)
Built in 1860 with slate roofs, these Cape-Victorian double-storey townhouses were the only buildings with such roofs in Swellendam. Along with a double-storey structure built in 1876, these premises were used by the farmers when they came to town every three months for 'nagmaal'.

VICTORIAN HOUSE (204 VOORTREKKER STREET)
The property on which this late nineteenth-century house is situated, originally formed part of the old Boys' High School (now Olyfkrans College). The Victorian house forms an integral part of the architectural character of Voortrekker Street.

WATER MILL (FARM RHENENDAL, DISTRICT)
The mill house is a double-storey Georgian building that dates from 1880. It is closely associated with the development of industrial architecture in South Africa, and has an overshot mill wheel.

TOUWS RIVER
Named after the river of the same name, the town was laid out in 1921 around the railway station established in 1877 as Montagu Road but renamed in 1883. Touws River attained municipal status in 1962.

ASTRONOMICAL RELICS
(IN THE GROUNDS OF THE DOUGLAS HOTEL)
Two concrete pillars, upon which these astronomical instruments were mounted, are a reminder of the British expedition that studied the transit of Venus in 1882.

TULBAGH
Laid out in 1795, the town was named after Ryk Tulbagh (1699–1771), Governor of the Cape from 1751–1771. The region was originally Land van Waveren, and this section, as a district, was named Tulbagh by JW Janssens in 1804. Tulbach attained municipal status in 1861.

On 29 September 1969 a severe earthquake seriously damaged a number of buildings, including historic houses in Church Street. With financial support from various bodies, the Tulbagh Restoration Committee restored the historic buildings in this street and acquired many of the properties in order to restore and preserve the street scene as well. The houses are mostly in the Cape Dutch and Victorian styles, and date from the late eighteenth to the late nineteenth centuries.

BALLOTINA (43 CHURCH STREET)
This house was probably designed by the well-known architect Thibault and built in 1815 for the widow of the Reverend HW Ballot. The strange geometric gable is exceptional.

BRANDY STILL (FARM SCHOONGEZICHT, DISTRICT)
This copper brandy still is one of the few remaining working stills of its kind in South Africa.

CARPE DIEM (10 CHURCH STREET)
Shortly after the property was sold in 1880 by the local church council to DH Malherbe, a Victorian style house was erected.

CHURCH STREET (12)
Built in 1754 by the district surgeon N Fuch and later owned by the church, the building served as the first school for 100 years.

CHURCH STREET (18)
This Victorian house is situated on a piece of land that was sold in 1853 to E French. It is an important architectural element in the street scene of Church Street.

CHURCH STREET (20)
The plot was originally granted in 1818 to J Marais and the original historic wagon house still exists. This property forms an important element in the street scene of Tulbagh.

CHURCH STREET (21)
Built in 1853, the house was the early childhood home of Danie Theron, the famous captain of despatch riders in the Anglo-Boer War.

CHURCH STREET (22)
This property was sold in 1796 by the local church council to J de Bruyn, when money was needed for the enlargement of the church building. The T-shaped house was erected shortly afterwards and is characterised by a concavo-convex gable.

CHURCH STREET (24)
This house was built in about 1820 by one De Lange, and is the only H-shaped gable house in the restored Church Street.

CHURCH STREET (25)
This house was built in 1814 and set a new trend as it was not based on the U-, T- or H-plan.

CHURCH STREET (26)
Built in 1796 by Jacob de Bruin, this house was later bought by the Mission Society, and from 1811 was the home of Arie Vos, who ran a mission school. It is now the home and studio of artist Christo Coetzee, who has donated the homestead to the University of Pretoria to be used as a museum after his death.

CHURCH STREET (27)
Built in 1900 by PJP Marais as a stable or coach house, this building was later bought and converted to a house by DJ Kriegler.

CHURCH STREET (28)
One of the houses built by Cosmus Rademan in 1818, this house was later sold to GM Meyer, first tollkeeper at Roodezands Kloof.

CHURCH STREET (30)
Built in the late 1700s by Cosmus Rademan, this house was bought in 1885 by HA Fagan, then owner of No. 32, for his son, Henry Allan Fagan Jnr. It remained in the family until 1903. A shop and law agency were run from the two properties. Of the five sons, Johannes was a promising composer, Gideon a composer and conductor of international standing, and Henry Allan Jnr became Chief Justice of South Africa, but died at an early age.

CHURCH STREET (32)
This building was built in 1801 and was used as the first English free school in Tulbagh from

1822. It was bought by HA Fagan Snr in 1866, and was owned by Rabbi S Hurwitz from 1912. The artist Erik Laubscher was born in this house in 1927.

CHURCH STREET (40)
This property was sold to Magteld Combrink in 1801, and she probably had the Cape Dutch house erected shortly afterwards. It is T-shaped with straight end gables and a concavo-convex front gable.

DE OUDE HERBERG (6 CHURCH STREET)
This gabled house dates from the middle of the nineteenth century and also has certain Victorian characteristics.

DE WET HOUSE (CHURCH STREET)
This house was built for Catherina Magaretha de Wet in 1812.

GABLED HOUSE (34 CHURCH STREET)
The U-shaped Cape Dutch house on this property was erected in about 1800, and has a concavo-convex gable in front.

HET LAND VAN WAVEREN (38 CHURCH STREET)
Presumably built by HJ Wydeman between 1796 and 1804, the property was once owned by G Keet, and it is a mystery how his 11 sons were accommodated in this small house. The house was partly demolished by the earthquake in 1969 and was later bought by the Restoration Committee and donated to the Municipality for use as a community art and cultural centre. It presently houses a home industry shop.

HISTORIC COTTAGE (30 VAN DER STEL STREET)
This cottage, in typical vernacular style, dates from 1822. The Drostdy and the cottage form an integral part of the historic core and character of Tulbagh.

HONEY OAK (17 CHURCH STREET)
P van der Merwe built this house in the latest fashion in 1852 for his mother. Its length was later doubled on the south side. However, with restoration, it was decided that the house would appear to best advantage in its original form and all subsequent additions were demolished.

JACKSON'S COTTAGE (DROSTDY VILLAGE)
This house was erected early in the nineteenth century in the so-called Drostdy Village, to accommodate officials of the nearby Tulbagh Drostdy. Drostdy Village was laid out in 1816.

KLIPFONTEIN FARMSTEAD BUILDING (DISTRICT)
The property was granted to Jacob de Bruin in 1818 and the main building also dates from that period. It is T-shaped with a very long front wing linking part of the outbuildings to the house.

LATE VICTORIAN DWELLING (4 CHURCH STREET)
Built in 1899 in late Victorian style by PJJ Marais, this house was a wedding present for his second wife.

MEIRING HOUSE
(CNR VAN DER STEL AND WATERKANT STREETS)
In a photograph taken as early as 1861, Meiring house was shown as having a pitched, thatched roof and a straight front gable. It was later Victorianised.

MON BIJOU (36 CHURCH STREET)
Attributed to the architect Michel Thibault (1750–1815), and built by the widow Mrs CM de Wet c.1812, this property was used as a Magistrate's Court from about 1848 for approximately five years, and also served as a school hostel for a time. Named Mon Bijou by the present owners, Dr and Mrs Silberberg, it was restored by them after the earthquake in 1969.

MONTPELLIER MAIN BUILDING (DISTRICT)
This fine example of a Cape Dutch gabled house with its concavo-convex (holbol) gable was probably built early in the nineteenth century on a farm originally granted in 1714 to Jean Joubert.

OLD CHURCH VOLKS MUSEUM (CHURCH STREET)
Until a new church was built in 1878, this old church served the congregation, after which it became a school and later, a museum in 1925.

OLD DROSTDY (DISTRICT) (VAN DER STEL STREET)
The old Drostdy is the remarkable architectural work of LM Thibault. It was completed in 1807 and served as the Drostdy until 1819.

OLD GA ZAHN CHURCH AND SCHOOL BUILDING (STEINTHAL, DISTRICT)
Built by freed slaves in 1845 under the auspices of the Reverend GA Zahn of the Rhenish Mission Society, this building represents the first school in the Breede River Valley that was associated with freed slaves . It is a simple rectangular, elongated building with thatched roof that has two hipped gables and retains its original structure of poplar beams held together with wooden pegs. The foundations are local shale-and-lime mortar with packed river cobbles and clay.

OLD MISSION CHURCH (CHURCH STREET)
The foundation stone of this church in neogothic style was laid in July 1844 and the church was consecrated on 2 April 1845. Fundraising for, and the erection of the buildings, was supervised by Reverend G Zahn. A bell tower was added after 1890.

OUDE KERK KOMBUIS (14 CHURCH STREET)
Built in 1892, this property was later owned by LJ Smith, whose son JJ Smith was to become the first Professor of Afrikaans and first editor of the *Woordeboek van die Afrikaans Taal*.

PADDAGANG (23 CHURCH STREET)
The earliest transfer of this erf was in 1795. The first 'taphuis' in Church Street was approved as early as 1821, and it is fitting that it is now run as a traditional wine house and restaurant.

PUBLIC LIBRARY
The T-shaped house, with concavo-convex front gable, was built in 1805 by Christiaan Willem Broodryk.

SCHALKENBOSCH FARM DWELLING AND OUTBUILDINGS (DISTRICT)
Dating from 1798, the main dwelling on Schalkenbosch farm is a T-shaped Cape Dutch house with a fine front gable and straight end gables. It is almost identical to the adjacent Schoonderzicht. The two historic outbuildings form an integral part of the architectural complex.

SCHOONDERZICHT HOMESTEAD AND BARN
Although the main gable of the homestead bears the date 1795, Schoonderzicht farm was originally granted to PJ Theron in 1796. A striking feature of the homestead is its concavo-convex (holbol) gable, enhanced with fine decorations.

The T-shaped house has three gables and much of the original woodwork and other materials are still intact. Historically and architecturally, the adjacent barn is an integral part of the complex.

TULBAGH HOUSE (42 CHURCH STREET)
Built in 1795 by H Vos, brother of MC Vos, the house was later bought by the Kruisvallei congregation in 1874 to serve as a parsonage. This congregation seceded from the Mother Church in 1843 after eight years of dissension in the community. The two congregations were only reunited in 1935. The building now houses business premises.

VAN DER STEL STREET (36) (DE LA REY HOUSE)
Owing to its situation and architectural merits, this historic house is an important element in the street scene in the restored part of Tulbagh.

WAGENHUYS (16 CHURCH STREET)
This oblong thatched house without a front gable is situated on land sold by the local church to a widow, Mrs SW van der Merwe and her son in 1853. The house probably dates from an earlier period.

WOLWEFONTEIN MAIN BUILDING AND BARN (DISTRICT)
This homestead, in typical Cape Dutch style, was probably erected early in the nineteenth century. Characteristic of the house is its H-shape, with a narrow opening between the main wings and a narrow overhanging roof. Adorning the house are several half-hipped gables. A barn next to the main building is an architecturally integral part of the homestead.

UNIONDALE

The name refers to the amalgamation of two villages in 1865: Hopedale established in 1856 and Lyon established in 1860. Uniondale attained municipal status in 1881.

ALL SAINTS ANGLICAN CHURCH
(VOORTREKKER STREET)
This thatched church was erected in 1874 and was consecrated by Bishop West-Jones on 8 October 1876. It is a copy in plastered brick of the stone church at Schoonberg designed by Sophia Gray.

FORT UNIONDALE
This historic fort was erected during the Anglo-Boer War (1899–1902) by the British military authorities and the so-called Town Guards for the defence of Uniondale. Four similar structures were built at the time around Uniondale but differed considerably from other forts in the Karoo and along the West Coast.

OLD DUTCH REFORMED CHURCH
(VOORTREKKER STREET)
Erected in 1862, the mainly neogothic church is closely connected to Uniondale's history.

OLD RESIDENCY (6 VICTORIA STREET)
This typical late nineteenth-century Uniondale house, with its yellowwood floors, loft, crib and stable, undoubtedly contributes to the historic character of the town.

HISTORIC BUILDINGS
(26 AND 28 VICTORIA STREET)
Dr PC Schoonees, prominent Afrikaans lexicographer and critic, was born in the cottage at 26 Victoria Street. Both cottages are single-storey vernacular structures dating from the mid-nineteenth century.

VANRHYNSDORP

Laid out in 1887, this town is named after Petrus Benjamin van Rhyn, owner of the farm on which it is situated and grandfather of politician Dr AJR van Rhyn. It attained municipal status in 1913.

BOER WAR FORT (FARM ATIES, DISTRICT)
This fort was one of five fortifications built during the Anglo-Boer War (1899–1902) by the British forces on strategic heights around the farm Aties. It is a unique example of its kind because it was constructed of local dolomite and sandstone.

CORRUGATED-IRON FORT AND DOVECOT
(FARM GRAAFWATER)
Still standing today, this rondavel-shaped corrugated-iron fort was one of similar

fortifications erected by the British forces in the Northern Cape during the Anglo-Boer War (1899-1902). The dovecot was built in typical vernacular style with a straight end gable and thatched roof.

ENGRAVINGS OF NAMES SLOTSBO, RHENIUS AND BERGH (BERGFONTEIN)

The names of KJ Slotsbo, JT Rhenius and O Bergh are engraved on a rock in this area. On 30 October 1682, a party under the leadership of Olaff Bergh left The Castle at the Cape to investigate the area from which the Namaquas brought samples of copper ore the previous year. Many early travellers visited the place after Bergh: Simon van der Stel paid a visit on 14 September 1685, and Starrenburg during 1705.

In 1712 Captain KG Slotsbo engraved his name and the year on the rock, as did Sub-Lieutenant JT Rhenius while on a cattle trade mission in 1721.

HEERENLOGEMENT CAVE HEEREN (HEERENLOGEMENT FARM – N7 TOWARDS GRAAFWATER)

The first engraved name on the wall of this historic old cave was that of Kaie Jesse Slotsbo, in 1712. In 1940, a list was compiled of all the names and initials engraved in the cave, and 174 were recorded. It must also be assumed that there were other visitors who chose not to deface the walls.

OLD IRON FORT

This old corrugated-iron fort was built by the British during the Anglo-Boer War on a farm between Graafwater and Lamberts Bay. After the war it was bought and transferred to Heerenlogement.

OLD LEOPARD TRAP

The old leopard trap is situated close to the Heerenlogement Caves.

VELDDRIFT

This town attained municipal status in 1960.

HISTORIC HOMESTEAD AND OUTBUILDINGS (FARM KERSEFONTEIN, BERG RIVER STATION)

The quitrent farm Kersefontein was granted to J Kruiwagen on 24 November 1744 and on 13 August 1770 it became the property of Martin Melck, whose family have owned it ever since. The traditional farmstead, with its Cape Dutch dwelling, encompasses a variety of outbuildings (foundry, bakery, guest house, coach house, granary, dower house containing a store, hen house and old stables, bell tower) and stables at the southern end of the farmyard. These outbuildings point, among other things, to an era when the farm was a leading stud farm and when horses used by the Green Point Tramway Company, were obtained from Kersefontein.

VILLIERSDORP

Founded on the farm Radyn in 1844, Villiersdorp was named after its founder, Field-Cornet Pieter Hendrik de Villiers. The town attained municipality status in 1901.

BO-RADYN FARMHOUSE

This historic Cape Dutch farmhouse was built in 1777, although the fine pilaster front gable, with its triangular pediment, was erected in about 1836. It was the home of the founder of Villiersdorp, Field-Cornet Pieter de Villiers.

VOLMOED

DUTCH REFORMED CHURCH (CHURCH STREET)

This neogothic church, designed by the architect J Clunis with assistance from F le Sueur, was erected by WG Olivier at his own expense on the farm Armoed and donated to the Oudtshoorn congregation. The cornerstone of this sandstone church was laid on 16 May 1910 by the Reverend

G Murray of Oudtshoorn, and the building was officially inaugurated on 25 January 1911. The Armoed congregation seceded from the Oudtshoorn Mother Church on 29 November 1921, and was renamed Volmoed.

WELLINGTON

Prior to 1838 Wellington was known as Wagenmakersvallei. It was renamed by Governor Sir George Napier after the Duke of Wellington, who defeated Napoleon at the Battle of Waterloo in 1815. Established in 1840, it became a municipality in 1873.

BLOCKHOUSE
(FARM VERSAILLES, ON BERG RIVER)
This blockhouse was built by the British during the Anglo-Boer War to protect the railway line.

CLAIRVAUX HOUSE (OFF JAN VAN RIEBEEK ROAD)
From 1892 until his death on 17 January 1917, this house was the home of the well-known theologian, Dr Andrew Murray. It was here that he wrote many of his theological books.

DUTCH REFORMED CHURCH BUILDING
(MAIN STREET)
The cornerstone of the original church building was laid on 27 June 1838 and the building completed in 1840. In 1861 it was converted into a cruciform church by the addition of two wings. The prominent tower, designed by C Freeman and HJ Jones was completed in 1891. The church building and the old market hall, which served as a council chamber in 1873 and thereafter as a courtroom, as well as the adjoining bell tower, the cemetery, and the ring wall, form a unique nineteenth-century unit.

DUTCH REFORMED MISSION CHURCH (BOVLEI)
This fine church of the congregation of Wagenmakersvallei, with its church bell, is one of the oldest mission churches in South Africa. It was consecrated in 1820 and the Reverend Isaac Bisseux ministered to the congregation from 1829 for about 50 years.

HISTORIC DWELLING HOUSE (20 BAIN STREET)
Originally serving as the first school building in Wellington, this predominantly Victorian house dates from about 1855.

HISTORIC DWELLINGS (34–35 BAIN STREET)
These two erven originally formed part of the farm Champagne, granted to the Huguenot Hercule Verdeaux in 1699. The dwellings, one of which dates from the 1830s and the other from the 1850s, were originally in the Cape Dutch style but were Victorianised during the second half of the nineteenth century.

LADY LOCH BRIDGE OVER BERG RIVER (DISTRICT)
This steel bridge replaced the original wooden bridge that was built in 1853 by Andrew Geddes Bain. It was erected in 1910 by the firm Braithwaite & Kirk. The name of the original bridge, which was named in September 1891 after the then governor's wife, was transferred to the new bridge in 1910.

MEMORIAL ARCH AT THE ENTRANCE TO VICTORIA JUBLIEE PARK (CHURCH STREET)
A commemorative arch was erected by the Municipality of Wellington in 1902 to mark Queen Victoria's diamond jubilee (1897) and the coronation of King Edward VII (1902).

OLD HUGUENOT SEMINARY
(CAMPUS OF THE TEACHERS' COLLEGE)
+ The building complex consisting of House Bliss (1904), House Murray and Goodnow Hall (between College Street, Hex Berg Road (Addy) Street and the Krommerivier).
+ The building complex of the Huguenot College, College Street, consisting of the

Ferguson Hall, Cummings Hall, House Samuel, Murray Jubilee Hall, and the College main building.

All the buildings are closely linked to Dr Andrew Murray, whose farsightedness led to the establishment of the Huguenot Seminary in 1874. The buildings also form an important link in the history of education in South Africa. The dedication of Dr Abbie Ferguson, Dr Anna Bliss, Miss Anna Cummings and those who followed them led to the establishment of the Huguenot College and the College of Education from the Seminary.

OUMA GRANNY'S HOUSE (FOUNTAIN STREET)
The property on which this building is situated was allocated to PB Marchant in 1876. Shortly thereafter it became the property of the Malherbe family. The house is an exceptional example of Victorian architecture and the wrought-iron verandah and unusual plaster ornamentation are especially noteworthy. The CP Hoogenhout collection is housed and exhibited here.

PRIMARY SCHOOL BUILDINGS (GROENBERG)
This school was built in the 1860s. CP Hoogenhout, who played an important part in the first phase of the Afrikaans movement, was a teacher there from 3 August 1874 until the beginning of the twentieth century, and much of his important work was done there. Hoogenhout was born in Amsterdam in 1843 and died in Wellington in 1922.

TWIST NIET (31 BURG STREET)
This Cape Dutch house, which bears the date 1811 on its front gable, was formerly the homestead of the farm Champagne on which part of the town of Wellington was laid out. Champagne was originally granted to the French Huguenot Hercule Verdeaux in 1699, but the house was presumably erected by Gabriel le Roux.

WORCESTER

Established on the farms Langerug and Roodewal in 1820, Worcester was named by Lord Charles Somerset, then Governor of the Cape, after his brother, the Marquis of Worcester. It became a municipality in 1842.

ACVV-DIENSSENTRUM (86 DURBAN STREET)
This Cape Dutch house, with two pedimented concavo-convex gables, dates from 1824 and was Victorianised in about 1906. It was bought by the Afrikaanse Christelike Vrouevereeniging in 1974 and restored to its original state under the direction of architect Dirk Visser.

AFRICANA MUSEUM
(CNR CHURCH AND BARING STREETS)
A typical example of mid-nineteenth-century architecture in Worcester, this building was built in 1854 by Cornelius Beck. It became the property of the Worcester Museum in 1940 and now houses the Publicity Association.

ALMARDE HOMESTEAD
(FARM SONSKYN, DISTRICT)
Almarde originally formed part of the loan farm Hartebeesrivier, which was occupied by Pieter Jacobs from the 1790s, and granted in 1845 to two Jacobs brothers, Pieter Jacobus and Stephanus Christoffel. The main homestead, with the date 1803 on the front gable, the wine cellar and thatched cottage outside the ring wall, are all predominantly Cape Dutch in style.

BAIN HOUSE (69 PORTER STREET)
Once the property of Andrew Geddes Bain, this dwelling dates from the 1840s, and has a typical late-classical Worcester main gable.

BECK HOUSE MUSEUM
(CNR CHURCH AND BARING STREETS)
This building is a typical example of mid-nineteenth century Victorian architecture in

Worcester. Erected in 1841, it was bought by Cornelius Beck in 1854, and was restored in 1970. It now houses the Beck Museum.

CAPE DUTCH HOUSE (20 FAIRBAIN STREET)
Probably built before 1865, this Cape Dutch dwelling has a neoclassical front gable that is typical of a so-called Worcester gable. Together with the adjacent restored buildings, it forms an important element in the streetscape of the older part of Worcester.

CAPE DUTCH FARMSTEAD (GLEN HEATLIE FARM)
The original part of the Glen Heatlie farmstead, with its Cape Dutch and Victorian features, was presumably erected in 1817. The building was enlarged in 1879 by Thomas Heatlie, who bought the farm in 1851 and extended it. A wagon house at the rear of the house and an old ship's bell of 1783 that hangs on a historic bell-cage are also noteworthy.

CAPE DUTCH FARMSTEAD (OLIFANTSBERG FARM, NOW KNOWN AS EIKENHOF, DISTRICT)
Erected in 1825 by Jacob de Vos, the original part of this Cape Dutch farmhouse was a simple elongated dwelling that was later enlarged to its present H-shape. The front gable bears the date 1841 and the name J de Vos.

CAPE DUTCH FARMSTEAD
(STETTYN FARM, DISTRICT)
Historic Stettyn, which has been in the possession of the Botha family since 1818, was originally granted to Jan Cloete and Jan Jurgen Radyn on 26 September 1714. The Cape Dutch farmhouse, the original section of which was built in 1777 by the then owner Schalk van der Merwe, was enlarged in the early nineteenth century by Phillippus Roedolph Botha. He was probably also responsible for the addition of the typical Worcester front gable. Although badly damaged by fire in

1930, the house was restored in 1977. A mill house, in operation until approximately 1929, was presumably erected in 1850.

CHURCH SQUARE
Church Square forms an integral part of the original town plan of Worcester as it was drawn up in 1819, and was set up as an outspan area for churchgoers. In former times the square was often used for open-air meetings of every kind, and with the surrounding buildings, it forms a historic and architectural centre. On 21 July 1919 the artist Hugo Naudé applied for permission to erect a monument in the centre of the square. The war memorial was unveiled on 7 February 1923 by HRH Prince Arthur of Connaught, Governor-General of the Union of South Africa. Over the years many other memorials have been erected.

DE DOORNS (DISTRICT)
This exceptionally fine Cape Dutch house, along with the adjacent old water mill, was built in 1790.

DIVISIONAL COUNCIL BUILDING (TRAPPES STREET)
An important part of the historic core of Worcester, this double-storey building dates from about 1860. It has typical Georgian characteristics, such as the sash windows, the cornice, as well as the proportions, size and positioning of the windows.

DOUBLE-STOREY GEORGIAN BUILDING
(66 CHURCH STREET)
This double-storey building dates from c.1840 and is predominantly Georgian in style. It forms part of the unique architectural streetscape of Church Street.

DROSTDY (HIGH STREET)
Construction of the Drostdy started in February 1823 under the supervision of Captain Charles

Trappes, first Landdrost of Worcester. It was designed by WC Jones, inspector of government buildings. Although not completed, it was occupied by the Landdrost in August 1825. The building was restored in 1977, and reopened on 10 February 1978.

DUTCH REFORMED CHURCH
(CHURCH STREET)

This neogothic cruciform church, the cornerstone of which was laid on 7 February 1831 by the Civic Commissioner of Worcester, PJ Truter, was consecrated on 3 February 1832.

DUTCH REFORMED MISSON CHURCH
(CNR ADDERLEY AND HIGHT STREETS)

The church building, the neighbouring parsonage and old school building, together with the other buildings in the so-called Rhenish Church Complex, form a unique historic and architectural group that has close links with the ecclesiastical history of Worcester.

EENSGEVONDEN DWELLING HOUSE
(SOMERSET STREET)

The original section of this predominantly Cape Dutch T-shaped house with its Jerkin Heads, presumably dates from the 1720s.

The house was rebuilt and enlarged during the second half of the eighteenth century.

GABLED DWELLING (37 RUSSELL STREET)

This house, with its fine gable, was built in 1860 and is a good example of nineteenth-century architecture in Worcester.

GERMAN EVANGELICAL LUTHERAN CHURCH
(ADDERLEY STREET)

A neogothic church, erected shortly after the establishment in 1881 of the local German Evangelical Lutheran congregation, this building was inaugurated on 14 November 1883 and a bell tower was added in 1903.

HISTORIC BUILDING
(78 STOCKENSTROOM STREET)

The property on which this house is situated was granted in 1837 to Thomas Bayley. After a subsequent subdivision, this building was probably erected during the 1870s. It is a double-storey, flat-roofed house with Georgian features and much of its original fabric.

HISTORIC CAPE DUTCH HOUSE
(24 PORTER STREET)

The land on which this house stands was granted to JF van der Graaff on 15 July 1822. The predominantly Cape Dutch house was presumably built by him in 1825, and is one of the oldest houses in Worcester.

HISTORIC EIKENBOSCH FARMHOUSE AND OUTBUILDINGS (SLANGHOEK VALLEY)

The predominantly Cape Dutch house and outbuildings are situated on land granted in 1716 to the pioneer of Goudini, Pieter du Toit.

HISTORIC GABLED HOUSES
(1–3 TRAPPES STREET)

The original section of this Cape Dutch complex, with its typical 'holbol' gable, was erected in 1820–1821, and is reputed to be the oldest dwelling in Worcester. The front section of the complex, with its typical Worcester gables, dates from the 1850s.

HISTORIC HOUSE (72 FAIRBAIRN STREET)

This dwelling in the vernacular building style, with Cape Dutch and Victorian elements, was erected by H Afrika in 1858–1859. The property forms an integral part of the architectural character of Fairbairn Street, which forms a significant part of the historic core of Worcester.

HUGO NAUDÉ HOUSE (115 RUSSELL STREET)

Erected during the first decade of the twentieth century by Hugo Naudé, the well known artist, as his home and studio, this house is predominantly in the neoclassical idiom. Naudé lived here until his death on 5 April 1941. The pedimented front gable is noteworthy.

KAAPSEDRAAI (165–165A HIGH STREET)
This property represents one of the earliest plots auctioned in Worcester in 1820. This house, with its Cape Dutch characteristics, was originally L-shaped, but later another wing was added to the eastern side.

KLEINPLASIE BUILDING COMPLEX
Comprising a farmhouse, wine cellar, coach house, slave cottage, labourers' cottages and a kraal, Kleinplasie originally formed part of the farm Roode Draai (also known as Roodewal), which was granted to Pieter du Toit (D'Oude) on 30 March 1746. In 1818 this farm and the farm Langerug were purchased for the establishment of the new town of Worcester. The homestead and outbuildings form a well-known Cape Dutch farmyard, show grounds and a restaurant.

RODEWAL (28 CHURCH STREET)
This house, with its plain pedimented front gable, typical of the predominant style in historic Worcester, dates from the 1830s. The flat-roofed extension dates from 1852.

THE OLD GAOL
Although it is more than likely that this building was erected before 1800, it was renovated in 1823 to serve as Worcester's first gaol. The renovation occurred shortly after the relocation of the magistracy to Worcester, and the purchase of the farm Langerug, on which the building was located.

TOWN HOUSE (52 CHURCH STREET)
The land on which this house stands was bought in 1837 by Wouter de Vos, and the house was presumably erected about 1850, although it is also speculated that Gabriel Afrika, who bought the property in 1884, was responsible for its construction. The house has a gable unique in Worcester, in that it is crowned with three rounded pediments.

UITVLUGT FARM (DISTRICT)
This farmstead comprises an H-shaped homestead, a wine cellar with a central gable and a flat-roofed outbuilding. The eastern gable of the homestead has the date '1824' inscribed, while the western gable (possibly an extension) has the date '1840' inscribed.

VICTORIAN DWELLINGS
(43 CHURCH STREET AND 22 FAIRBAIN STREET)
These two Victorian dwellings date from about 1850 and 1900 respectively. The former structure was originally in Cape Dutch style but was later Victorianised.

VICTORIAN DWELLING HOUSE 'AT LAST'
(162 CHURCH STREET)
The core of this impressive Victorian house was originally the first church in Worcester. The verandah with its cast-iron work, and the cast-iron crown mouldings on the roof are particularly noteworthy.

YZERFONTEIN

This fishing village, formerly Ijzerfontein, takes its name (which means iron fountain) from a spring that rises on an iron-stone formation.

LIME KILNS: FARM DE LA REY AND FARM JACOBUSKRAAL
These lime kilns, in which shells were burned, are of a similar structure and are two of a few remaining examples of open lime kilns in South Africa.

FREE STATE

Formerly known as the Orange Free State, the Free State is a province of central South Africa, between the Orange and Vaal rivers. The area was settled by the Boers in 1836 after the Great Trek and was annexed by Britain in 1848. It became a province of South Africa in 1910. Much of its economy is based on agriculture and mineral resources such as gold and uranium.

ALLANRIDGE

The town was founded in 1950 and was named after the geologist and prospector, Allan Roberts. This was the site of the first gold borehole in the Free State.

PROSPECTING BOREHOLE

The borehole played an important part in the discovery of the Orange Free State gold fields. It was on this site that the first gold prospecting borehole was sunk in 1933.

BETHLEHEM

Established on the farm Pretoriuskloof in 1860, the town was proclaimed in 1884. Bethlehem was named after the biblical town of the same name.

BETHLEHEM TECHNICAL COLLEGE
(WESSELS STREET)

The Hoër Huishoudskool President Steyn evolved from the Spinning and Weaving School established by Anna van Gent and Charlotte Theron of the Orange Free State Women's Organisation, and was inaugurated by President Steyn on 23 November 1907. It continued until 1913 when it was amalgamated with the Techniese Skool vir Meisjes and renamed Huishoudskool. The present building was erected in 1914. Since 1988 the school has been used by the Bethlehem Technical College.

CAVE WITH PREHISTORIC PAINTINGS
(FARM SCHAAPPLAATS, DISTRICT)

Rock paintings in this area reflect the religious experiences and beliefs of the San (Bushmen) whose ancestors lived here for over 20 000 years. The paintings are mainly groups of human figures with the heads of buck. They are painted in considerable detail, in white and red.

CIVIC CENTRE (20–22 MULLER STREET)

On 15 November 1859, FP Naudé wrote to the acting State President, ER Snyman, that with two partners (JC Muller and DJJ Malan) he had purchased the farm Pretoriuskloof, with the intention of building a church and establishing a town. On 27 February 1884, Pretoriuskloof was proclaimed as the town Bethlehem. In 1891 a wood-and-iron town hall was constructed, but by 1930 a new town hall was built. A second storey was added in 1950.

DUTCH REFORMED MOTHER CHURCH AND
BASUTO WAR MEMORIAL (CHURCH SQUARE)

The cornerstone of this impressive sandstone church was laid by President MT Steyn on 12 April 1910. Designed by the Reverend JD Kestell, the church was inaugurated on 18 February 1911.

The Basuto War Memorial was erected in memory of two Europeans and a Hottentot who died during an attack in the Basuto War (1865–1866).

OLD DUTCH REFORMED MISSION CHURCH
(MUSEUM BUILDING) (CHURCH STREET)

The foundation stone of this building was laid on 2 December 1906 and the church was taken into use in 1909. It was the second Dutch Reformed Mission church to be erected in the Free State.

OLD MAGISTRATE'S OFFICE (LOUW STREET)

This sandstone building, the cornerstone of which was laid on 26 January 1893 by President FW Reitz, is an excellent example of the Republican style of architecture, which was strongly influenced by the Renaissance style.

OLD MISSION HOUSE
(PRESIDENT BOSHOFF STREET)

The Mission House is significant because Reverend HA Roux was the first missionary of the Dutch Reformed Church in Bethlehem. The house is also part of the sandstone architecture of the town. Assisted by Louis Ferdinand, Reverend Roux enlarged the house in 1903. He arrived in Bethlehem on 4 October 1899, days before the outbreak of the Anglo-Boer War. Soon after the occupation of the town by British forces, Reverend Roux was taken prisoner and sent to Ceylon, and his wife and daughter sent to a Harrismith concentration camp. After his release, he returned to continue his work.

PREEKSTOEL (PULPIT ROCK)
(FARM MARWANDA, DISTRICT)

Pulpit Rock is situated approximately 3km from Bethlehem, and the name is derived from its shape. During the Anglo-Boer War (1899–1902), General Paul le Roux addressed his men and led them in prayer at this site.

PRETORIUSKLOOF NATURE RESERVE AND
WALL OF THE LOCH ATHLONE DAM

Pretoriuskloof, situated in the centre of Bethlehem and extending from the Loch Athlone dam wall to Church Street, is a reserve for birds and small game. A freshwater fountain from which the first residents drew drinking water is part of the reserve. The dam wall was built in the early 1920s and the dam was officially opened by the Earl of Athlone in 1925.

REMAINING PORTION OF HISTORIC TOWNHOUSE
(12 CHURCH STREET)

This townhouse is the oldest existing building in Bethlehem. It was common practice for affluent farmers to build a townhouse in the nearest town to accommodate the family every three months when they came to town to attend 'nagmaal' (communion), and also to buy and sell goods. This house was presumably built by Johannes Hendrik Blignaut, who took transfer of the property on 24 October 1874.

ST ANDREW'S PRESBYTERIAN CHURCH
(144 CAMBRIDGE STREET)

Early in the twentieth century, Presbyterians in Bethlehem expressed a desire to form their own congregation. In 1910 the first service was conducted in the old Magistrate's Office and on 14 September of that same year, Reverend Dower arrived in Bethlehem.

On 11 June 1913, SJ Strapp laid the cornerstone of the new church, and the consecration took place on 28 September 1913 with Reverend James McRobert officiating. The sandstone building, with pitched corrugated-iron roof, wooden floors and steel ceilings, has retained many of its traditional elements.

ST AUGUSTINE'S ANGLICAN CHURCH
(34 LOUW STREET)

Built of sandstone with a tiled roof and stained glass windows, St Augustine's church was designed by the architect CJC Bernhard and constructed by the contractor WE Barker. The cornerstone was laid on 29 February 1928 by Pavline Croisilles Belbin.

SANDSTONE WAGON HOUSE WITH LOFT
(CNR MULLER AND LANDDROS STREETS)
This sturdy sandstone wagon house, with its high-pitched iron roof and loft, was erected in 1894 by AA Baartman, builder of wagons, carts and spiders (popular American buggies known as a 'spiders' in South Africa). The adjacent outbuildings were added after the Anglo-Boer War (1899–1902).

STRAPP'S SHOP (18 CHURCH STREET)
This Victorian shop dates from the late nineteenth century, and is an excellent example of the sandstone architecture of the eastern Free State. Strapp's Shop forms an integral part of a building complex that includes the old magistrate's office as well as St Augustine's Anglican church.

THE SEMINARY (WESSELS STREET)
This impressive sandstone building was erected in 1894 by the Dutch Reformed Church, to house the girls' school known as the Seminary. Since 1903 the building has been used as a girls' hostel by the Coeducational Government School, except for a period of eight years when it functioned as Girls' Government School. It occupies an important place in the history of education in Bethlehem.

TOWNHOUSE (14 PRESIDENT BURGER STREET)
This cottage, the original portion of which was erected just after the Anglo-Boer War (1899–1902), is an excellent example of a townhouse at the turn of the nineteenth century.

BETHULIE

The town was established in 1863 and named Heidelberg, but was renamed Bethulie in 1872 after the nearby mission station to avoid confusion with towns of the same name in the Cape and Transvaal.

CONCENTRATION CAMP CEMETERY
This cemetery contains the mortal remains of 1 737 Boer women and children who died in the concentration camp established here during the Anglo-Boer War (1899–1902). Designed by J du Toit, the cemetery was inaugurated on 10 October 1966 by the State President, CR Swart.

DUTCH REFORMED CHURCH (GREY STREET)
This imposing T-shaped building, with its neogothic characteristics, is one of the oldest existing churches in the Free State. The cornerstone was laid by JH Brand on 20 March 1886, and the consecration took place on 30 September 1887. When the church was renovated in 1905, the steeple was replaced by a lighter steeple of wood and iron.

MEMORIAL AND GRAVE OF LOUW WEPENER
(FARM FELICIA, DISTRICT)
Lourens Jacobus Wepener was born in 1812 in Graaff-Reinet. In 1850 he settled on the farm De Nek in the Aliwal district. During the Eighth Frontier War (1850–1853), he exhibited leadership skills and rose to the rank of commandant. He was killed in action in August 1865 and buried on his farm Constantia. In the 1940s his remains were reburied at this site.

PELLISSIER HOUSE MUSEUM AND CEMETERY
(VOORTREKKER STREET)
Now a museum, this building was erected in 1834–1835 by the Reverend Jean Pierre Pellissier of the Paris Evangelical Missionary Society. Pellissier House is one of the oldest existing buildings in the Free State, and dates from a period when missionary work made an important contribution to the development of the area. Reverend Pellissier, his wife and their five children are buried in the graveyard behind the house.

BLOEMFONTEIN

The city of Bloemfontein was established on the farm of the same name in 1846, by Major HD Warden, who was commissioned to the area to serve as British Resident. He bought the farm from Johan Nicolaas Brits. When the Orange Free State was annexed by Britain in 1848, Bloemfontein became the seat of the new administration. Municipal status was attained in 1880.

ARTHUR NATHAN SWIMMING POOL
(FAIRVIEW STREET)

Designed by the Town Engineer HF Peet, the building was begun by Rochelle & Smith and the cornerstone was laid on 19 December 1906 by Wolff Ehrlich, Mayor of Bloemfontein. The project was completed by a Mr Becket and the swimming pool complex was inaugurated by Councillor CL Botha on 7 October 1907.

BLOEMFONTEIN TECHNICAL COLLEGE
(DOUGLAS STREET)

This site incorporates part of the original Bloemfontein Technical College, the old Grey College Building. This imposing old building, with its Flemish features, was designed by the architect WH Stucke and was erected in 1894–1895 by D Godley. The foundation stone was laid on 16 May 1894 by President FW Reitz, and the eastern and western wings were completed in 1895 and 1898 respectively.

The building accommodated Grey College until 1907, was subsequently used by the Normal College, and since 1923 has housed the Bloemfontein Technical College. The Suid-Afrikaanse Akademie vir Wetenskap en Kuns was founded here on 1–2 July 1909.

CATHEDRAL OF ST ANDREW AND ST MICHAEL
(ST GEORGE'S STREET)

Dedicated in 1866, the eastern part of this Anglican cathedral is, after the First Raadsaal and the basic core of Green Lodge, the oldest surviving, dateable building in the city. The cathedral was erected on the foundation of a small church from 1850, which was never completed, and the site was used as a sheep fold. The western extension was dedicated in 1885. Unfortunately, the bell tower, which had been added in 1906 according to plans drawn up by Sir Herbert Baker, had to be demolished in 1964 because it had become dilapidated. A new bell tower has since been erected along the same lines as the earlier one.

CITY HALL COMPLEX (PRESIDENT BRAND STREET)

The cornerstone of this impressive complex was laid on 27 February 1934 by Prince George, Duke of Kent. It was designed by Gordon Leith and erected by WF & P du Plessis. The sandstone City Hall complex was officially opened on 4 December 1936 by the Earl of Clarendon, the then Governor-General of the Union of South Africa. It forms an integral part of the architectural character of President Brand Street.

CONSPIRACY TREE (FARM ONZE RUST, DISTRICT)

Onze Rust was bought by President MT Steyn in 1897. He resided there from 1905 until his death in 1916. This wild fig tree, known as the Conspiracy Tree, was where Steyn and other prominent statesmen deliberated before the Anglo-Boer War.

CORRUGATED-IRON BUILDING
(SCHOOL OF ARMOUR, TEMPE, DISTRICT)

After the fall of Bloemfontein in March 1900, the British garrison was stationed at Tempe and Naval Hill. On 15 November 1900 the Town Council donated 300ha of the farm Boven Tempe to erect a cantonment, which included a military hospital that would accommodate 150 patients and was to be administered by the Royal Army Medical Corps.

After the withdrawal of the British garrison in 1912 and 1913, the dwellings, barracks, warehouses, offices, stables and hospital were abandoned. The site was taken over by the South African Defence Force and became a training depot. It is thought that the wood-and-iron buildings at Tempe were shipped from Burma in 1904, and transported to Bloemfontein by mule wagons.

ELIZABETH LE ROUX HOSTEL
(ORANJE GIRLS' HIGH SCHOOL, 75 ALIWAL STREET)
The foundation stone was laid in 1899. During the Anglo-Boer War (1899–1902) the building was used as a hospital, but was purchased in 1906 by the first Board of Trustees of the Oranje Girls' High School, under the chairmanship of President MT Steyn, for use as a school hostel.

FICHARDT HOUSE (40 ELIZABETH STREET)
Fichardt House is one of the best examples of a late Republican mansion in Bloemfontein. The original section of the building is presumed to have been built by Judge Reinhold Gregorowski in the late 1880s. It was purchased in 1896 by Charlie Fichardt, son of businessman Gustav Fichardt and Mayor of Bloemfontein, who was responsible for altering it to a double storey.

In the 1890s several prominent people resided in the house, including Sir Alfred Milner, British High Commissioner, President Paul Kruger, Sir Andries Maasdorp from 1902–1919, and the Chief Justice of the Appeal Court, Sir Etienne de Villiers until his death in 1947.

FIRST RAADSAAL (95 ST GEORGE'S STREET)
The First Raadsaal is the oldest surviving building in its original condition, and the only example of the Pioneer building style in Bloemfontein. Originally built in 1849 as a school by Sir Henry Warden, the British Resident, it was also used as a Dutch Reformed church and a venue for public meetings. In 1854 it became the first meeting chamber for the Orange Free State Volksraad. It was later used as a school and an Anglican church until the National Museum was established there in 1877.

FISCHER HOUSE (72 PRESIDENT REITZ STREET)
Designed by French architect HE de la Cornelliere, the first President of the Orange Free State School of Architects, the house was the home of Ella and Percy Fischer from 1910–1946. The latter was the second son of Abraham Fischer, the former Prime Minister of the Orange River Colony and member of the Union Cabinet. Percy Fischer served as Judge President of the Orange Free State Division of the Supreme Court from 1939 until his retirement in 1948. His eldest son, Bram Fischer, became a well-known figure in the Struggle for Liberation.

FOURTH RAADSAAL (PRESIDENT BRAND STREET)
The Fourth Raadsaal may be regarded as the architectural jewel of the Free State. The building was designed by Lennox Canning and the cornerstone was laid by President FW Reitz on 27 June 1890. Construction was completed in 1893. The Raadsaal reflects simplicity and dignity, and is characterised by the successful blending of Greek, Roman and Renaissance elements on the one hand, and the sandstone and red brickwork, which were characteristic of the Free State building style of the time, on the other.

FREE STATE BOTANICAL GARDENS
(RAYTON ROAD)
Established in 1967, this botanical garden is of particular scientific and environmental interest because it contains the only remaining Karoo vegetation in the vicinity where palaeoclimatologyes can be studied.

FRESHFORD HOUSE MUSEUM
(31 KELLNER STREET)

Architect John Edwin Harrison designed and built the house for himself. It was completed in 1897 during the transition between late Victorian and Edwardian periods and is typical of residences of this period in Bloemfontein.

GNOME AEROPLANE ENGINE
(MILITARY MUSEUM, FORT BLOEMFONTEIN)

The *Gnome* 7-cylinder, 50-horsepower rotary aircraft engine numbered 'Type 52 (sic)' No. 3583438 and No. 345 Moteur B Te (sic Te) SGD', was built from spare parts and donated to the National Museum by John Weston.

GREEN LODGE (HISTORIC MAIN BUILDING)
(81 ST GEORGE'S STREET)

The original section of this building dates from the 1840s and was built by Henry Green, Assistant Commissioner-General of the Orange River Sovereignty. The house was later occupied by the Reverend Andrew Murray, President MT Steyn's father, Judge AW Fawkes and, from 1925–1932, by Chief Justice Jacob de Villiers. The house was altered to its present form in the Cape Dutch idiom in 1902.

GREY COLLEGE (JOCK MEIRING STREET)

+ Andrew Murray House and Brill House – designed by Frank Taylor and officially opened on 19 December 1907 by the then Governor of the Orange River Colony, Sir Hamilton J Goold-Adams.
+ Hamilton Hall – designed by Herbert Baker and opened in 1907 by Sir Hamilton Goold-Adams, after whom the hall was named.
+ Main Building – the cornerstone was officially laid by President Reitz on 16 May 1894. The architect was WH Stucke.
+ Tuck Shop – a popular gathering place for pupils since 1908.

HERTZOG HOUSE MUSEUM
(19 GODDARD STREET)

This late Victorian house was erected in 1895 and was the home of JBM Hertzog, Prime Minister of South Africa, from 1895–1920. When he left on commando he was the Criminal Judge for the Orange Free State, and he returned as the famed general. His Education Law of 1908, which led to bilingual education, was formulated here.

The west and southeast extensions date from about 1905. After General Hertzog's departure, the house was used as a parsonage and was extensively altered until it was restored in 1983–1984 to house a museum in General Hertzog's honour.

HISTORIC TREE GARDEN
(PRESIDENT BRAND STREET, IN FRONT OF THE AFRIKAANSE LETTERKUNDIGE MUSEUM EN NAVORSINGSENTRUM)

The first two trees were planted on 24 February 1879 by President JH Brand to celebrate the 25th year of the Republic of the Orange Free State. Since then, various dignitaries have planted trees to commemorate different occasions. These include President Reitz (1890), then British Secretary of Colonies, Joseph Chamberlain (1903), Lord Alfred Milner (1905), and former Orange Free State Administrator, AC van Wyk (1979).

MILITARY MUSEUM (FORT BLOEMFONTEIN)
(CHURCH STREET)

Now totally restored, the Military Museum is situated in the old fort that was constructed in 1848 by the British garrison when the area was under British control and known as the Orange River Sovereignty. When the Orange Free State Republic was formed in 1854, the interim government decided to take over the fort, and on 11 March 1854 the British flag was raised for the last time. In 1880 the fort was upgraded and new buildings were constructed from 1880–1890. The British once again took occupation of the fort in 1900 and a section was used as a hospital. In 1904 the fort was handed over to the Orange River Colony volunteers and by December 1906, to the South African Constabulary.

NATIONAL WOMEN'S MONUMENT
(MONUMENT ROAD)

This obelisk of Kroonstad sandstone, which stands 36.5m tall, is dedicated to the memory of the 26 370 Boer women and children who died during the Anglo-Boer War (1899–1902). It was unveiled on 16 December 1913.

OLD GOVERNMENT BUILDINGS
(PRESIDENT BRAND STREET)

The Government Buildings were completed in 1877, although the Volksraad chamber had already been occupied since 31 May 1875. In 1895 the upper storey was completed, and in 1902, Sir Herbert Baker and Masey slightly altered the existing building. In October 1908 a part of the Government Buildings burned down, after which it was restored by architect Taylor to plans drawn up by Baker.

OLD PRESIDENCY (PRESIDENT BRAND STREET)

The Old Presidency stands on the site where JN Brits erected the original 'hartebeest' hut on the farm Bloemfontein. It is also the site where the British Resident, Major Warden, built his residence and where a simple Presidential Residence was built in 1861.

The present building, completed in 1866, was designed by Lennox Canning in Scottish Baronial style, but his plans were simplified for financial reasons. It was the official residence of the Orange Free State's last three presidents – Brand, Reitz and Steyn – and, until 1910, Sir Hamilton Goold-Adams, Lieutenant-Governor of the Orange River Colony.

OLD RAILWAY BUREAU (MAITLAND STREET)

This double-storey brick building, with its Victorian and neoclassical characteristics, was designed by the architect DE Wentink. The builder was H Heath. The cornerstone was laid on 7 June 1898 by President MT Steyn, and the building was occupied on 15 February 1899. The unsuccessful discussions between President Kruger and Sir Alfred Milner (with President Steyn acting as intermediary) at the Bloemfontein Convention, which was a last attempt to prevent the outbreak of the Anglo-Boer War, also took place there from 31 May until 4 June 1899.

ORIGINAL ARCHIVES BUILDING
(CNR ELIZABETH AND MARKGRAAF STREETS)

Designed by the architect JS Cleland, this redbrick building with tiled roof was the first building in South Africa constructed specifically as an archive repository. The cornerstone was laid on 22 October 1925 by the then Minister of Finance, NC Havenga.

SANNASPOS BATTLEFIELD (FARM AHMETNAGHER)

At this site along the Koringspruit, General CR de Wet, Chief Commandant of the Orange Free State Commandos, outmanoeuvred the British forces under Brigadier General RG Broadwood on 31 March 1900. The military tactics displayed here by General De Wet later became famous in military history as this battle was the first of the guerrilla phase of the Anglo-Boer War (1899–1902).

At the battlefield site there is a museum that commemorates the battle, a monument that commemorates the casualties, grave sites of the casualties of the battle, and a lookout post that overlooks the old battlefield.

SANNASPOS RAILWAY STATION

This railway station building of sandstone was completed shortly before the Anglo-Boer War

(1899–1902). Being one of only a few station buildings erected during the Republican period, it forms an important link with the Orange Free State railway system of the nineteenth century. During the Battle of Sannaspos on 31 March 1900, the building provided shelter for the Q Battery of the Royal Horse Artillery against the rifle fire of the Boer forces.

TWIN-TOWER CHURCH (CHARLES STREET)
This Twin-tower Church is closely associated with the historic past of the Free State. The congregation was established in 1848 and on 6 May 1849, four months after the foundation stone was laid by Major Warden, the Reverend Andrew Murray Jnr was inducted as the first clergyman in the school building, which was used as the church hall and later served as the First Council Chamber of the Volksraad of the Orange Free State Republic.

Although the church was only consecrated in 1852, the original building was demolished in 1878 and replaced by the present Twin-tower church on the same site. The foundation stone of the present church was laid on 10 May 1878, and the church itself was consecrated on 7 May 1880. This was the last congregation of the Reverend JD Kestell (1912–1919).

UNIVERSITY OF THE ORANGE FREE STATE

+ Abraham Fischer House – designed by Frank Taylor and officially opened on 16 October 1909, the men's hostel was one of the first two buildings erected on the site of the former Grey University College.
+ First University Building – this small redbrick building was erected at the turn of the nineteenth century to serve as additional classrooms for Grey College. From January 1904 to December 1907, the building served as the first headquarters of Grey University College.

+ Main Building – the cornerstone of this building, with neoclassical features, was laid on 19 December 1907 by Sir Hamilton Goold-Adams. It was formally opened on 16 October 1909. The north and south wings date from 1915 and 1929 respectively.

WHITE HORSE STONE
(EASTERN SLOPE OF NAVAL HILL)
This White Horse Stone was laid out during the Anglo-Boer War (1899–1902) by the garrison of the Wiltshire Regiment, stationed at Naval Hill.

BOSHOF

Boshof was established on the farm Vanwyksvlei in 1856, and was named after Jacobus Nicolaas Boshof (1808–1881), the second President of the Orange Free State (1855–1859), and founder of its civil service. The town attained municipal status in 1872.

BRITISH MILITARY CEMETERY
(FARM VENDUTIEDRIFT, DISTRICT)
This cemetery contains the mortal remains of the British soldiers who died during the Battle of Paardeberg between the British forces under Lord Roberts, and the Boer forces under General PA Cronjé, in February 1900.

PAARDEBERG BATTLEFIELD
The former battlefield and burgher cemetery on the farm Wolwekraal, together with the British cemetery and Colonel DL Hannay's grave on the farm Vendutiedrift, serve as visible reminders of this important turning point in the Anglo-Boer War. The many bomb fragments and other ammunition still to be found on the battlefield are preserved in the site museum.

POWDER MAGAZINE (TOWN COMMONAGE)
This historic powder magazine, which was designed by the architect DE Wentink in

September 1898, is an oblong building that was built of local dolerite. It was presumably erected in preparation of the impending Anglo-Boer War.

ROCK ENGRAVINGS
(FARM STOWLANDS-ON-VAAL, DISTRICT)

Most of the engravings at Stowlands-on-Vaal were done with the 'pecked' technique, in which a hard stone was used in a chopping motion to remove the outer crust of the boulder and expose the lighter-coloured rock beneath. The age of these engravings is estimated to be within the last 3 000 years. They are of a religious nature and associated with shamanism.

SITE WHERE GENERAL DE VILLEBOIS-MAREUIL WAS KILLED (FARM MIDDELKUIL)

Count Georges de Villebois-Mareuil, born 22 March 1847, was a Frenchman who served the Boer Republics with distinction during the Anglo-Boer War (1899–1902). He became a Boer General and his name was immortalised when he defended a position to his death. He was buried the following day with military honours by Lord Methuen.

BOTHAVILLE

The town of Bothaville was established in 1893 on Theunis Louis Botha's farm Botharnia, a section of farm Gladdedrift, which he purchased.

NEDERDUITSE GEREFORMEERDE MOEDER KERK CHURCH (PRESIDENT STREET)

This impressive cruciform church was designed by the architect Gerard Moerdijk, and built of sandstone by the contractors Marshall & MacIntosh. The cornerstone was laid by Ds FGT Radloff on 6 April 1918, and the church was officially inaugurated on 2 April 1920.

BRANDFORT

Brandfort was established in 1866 on the farm Keerom, but was only proclaimed in 1874. It was named after JH Brand (1823–1888), the fourth President of the Republic. Brandfort attained municipal status in 1884.

CONCENTRATION CAMP CEMETERY
(FARM LOUVAIN)

This cemetery contains the mortal remains of 1 263 women and children who died here during the Anglo-Boer War (1899–1902). The cemetery, which was designed by J du Toit, was officially opened on 22 September 1962 by President CR Swart.

CLOCOLAN

Clocolan was laid out in 1906 on the farms Harold and Rienzi, and attained municipal status in 1910. The origin of its name is obscure with the most likely suggestion, being that it is of Bantu origin.

SHELTER WITH ROCK PAINTINGS
(FARM TANJESBERG)

These paintings are aesthetically pleasing and of high quality in terms of technique and content. Eland, elephant, felines and human figures are painted in red or ochre, shading into white. The site also contains unique motifs such as cattle-like creatures, wild dogs and therianthropic (half animal, half human) creatures. Eland, usually depicted at the top in other shelters, are pictured at the bottom here.

EXCELSIOR

This town was laid out on the farms Excelsior and Sunlight in 1910. It is administered by a municipality and is the seat of an Assistant Magistrate.

OLD HOSTEL BUILDING
(TWEESPRUIT AGRICULTURAL HIGH SCHOOL)
Constructed in 1903 by the Relief Works Department of the Orange River Colony to stable horses, this sandstone building comprised quarters for a stablehand, two fodder storage rooms and a harness room. Since the opening of the Agricultural School in 1918, alterations have been made to the interior of the building to serve as a hostel.

FAURESMITH

Laid out on the farm *Sannah's Poort* in 1850 and named after Philip Eduard Faure, Moderator of the Dutch Reformed Church, and Sir Harry Smith, Governor of the Cape, the town attained municipal status in 1859.

OLD GAOL (WEST END STREET)
In 1899 four stands were purchased for the construction of a prison, warder's house and hospital. The prison is enclosed by a high wall and the cells are situated in a rectangular, dolerite building in the middle of the property. Between 1903 and 1906 a new storeroom was built and the old storeroom was converted to a cell for female prisoners. In 1907 a tender was awarded to Robert Jack of Philippolis to construct new ablution facilities. In 1907–1908, two new cells were added for female prisoners.

STANDARD BANK BUILDING
(CNR VOORTREKKER AND VAN RIEBEECK STREETS)
A branch of Standard Bank opened in Fauresmith in 1864 but closed in 1869 because the House of Assembly decided not to allow 'foreign' banks to operate in the Orange Free State without its permission. After the Anglo-Boer War, Standard Bank returned and has occupied these premises since 1919. The property was registered in 1902, but the building's architecture long predates 1919.

THREE SURVEY BEACONS (FARM RAMAH, DISTRICT)
These three beacons formed part of the boundary line between the Orange Free State and Griqualand West, which Sir Charles Warren and Jos E de Villiers established in 1876 and 1877. This marked the end of the so-called Diamond Fields Dispute.

FICKSBURG

GENERAL FICK MUSEUM (OLD MARKET SQUARE)
The sandstone building of the old Magistrate's Office Building, now known as the General Fick Museum, was completed in 1893 and is a fine example of such buildings erected in the Orange Free State during the late Republican period.

NEDERDUITSE GEREFORMEERDE MOEDER KERK
(CHURCH SQUARE)
Before the Anglo-Boer War, a decision was taken to build a church in Ficksburg, but construction only began after the war. Plans were drawn by the architect Walter Donaldson and the cornerstone was laid on 27 May 1905 by Reverend Kestell. The church was consecrated on 12 April 1907. It was dedicated to the memory of Boers who lost their lives in the Anglo-Boer War.

OLD PRISON CELLS (BRAND STREET)
A rectangular sandstone building with a flat corrugated-iron roof, the gaol has a small barred window above each of two entrance doors. The cells formed part of a prison built in 1893, but later demolished. Charles Robert Swart (later State President of South Africa), a history and Latin teacher at the high school, was arrested on 13 November 1914 for having a photograph of rebels in his possession. Because he refused to identify the rebels, he was threatened with execution. However, he was later released, ostensibly to prepare pupils for their matriculation examinations.

TOWN HALL (OLD MARKET SQUARE)
The Town Hall is a sandstone building with a pitched, corrugated-iron roof, and two small steeples. A verandah connects two sides of the building. In the 1890s the town management approached architect Walter Donaldson to submit plans for a Town Hall. The cornerstone was laid on 21 July 1897 by the Chairman of the Municipality, MI Fourie, and the building was completed before the outbreak of the Anglo-Boer War.

FOURIESBURG

Laid out on the farm Groenfontein in 1892, Fouriesburg was named after Christoffel Fourie, the owner.

NEDERDUITSE GEREFORMEERDE CHURCH BUILDING (CHURCH SQUARE)
After the original section was built in 1894, the sandstone church was enlarged in 1908 and consecrated in 1909. It is situated on the site where President Kruger, then Commandant of a Transvaal Commando, camped when he went to the aid of the 'Orange' Free State in the Basuto War of 1865.

SURRENDER HILL (FARM AMSTERDAM, DISTRICT)
After the occupation of Bethlehem by British forces, the Free State burghers withdrew to the Brandwater Basin. General CR Swart and President MT Steyn withdrew on 15 July 1900 and after their departure, the British occupied five of the six surrounding mountain passes.

Although 600 burghers managed to withdraw, the remaining commandos, under General Marthinus Prinsloo, surrendered over the last two days of July to the British force under General A Hunter. This was one of the biggest defeats suffered by the Boers during the Anglo-Boer War. Since then, the site has been known as Surrender Hill.

FRANKFORT

The town of Frankfort was established on the farm Roodepoort in 1869, and was named by Albert von Gordon, most probably after Frankfurt in Germany. It attained municipal status in 1896.

OLD MAGISTRATE'S OFFICE, POLICE STATION, POST OFFICE (VAN REENEN STREET)
Situated next to each other, these three buildings form an integral part of the architectural character of Van Reenen Street. The Edwardian Magistrate's Court was constructed between 1900 and 1910, when the Free State was known as the Orange River Colony. The Police Station is an L-shaped building, of which the date of construction is unknown. The Post Office, designed by architect HGA de la Cornelliere, has a pitched corrugated-iron roof with a Cape Dutch gable above the front entrance, and bears the initials 'ER 1', and the date, '1904'.

HARRISMITH

Harrismith was originally laid out on the farm Majoorsdrift in 1849, on a site west of the present town. Due to the lack of water, it was re-established on the present site in 1850. The town was named after Sir Harry Smith, Governor of the Cape (1847–1851), and attained municipal status in 1875.

BLOCKHOUSE (VELD FLOWER GARDEN)
The blockhouse was erected by the British during the Anglo-Boer War (1899–1902) to protect the town's water supply.

BRITISH REGIMENTAL BADGES
The three Regimental Badges of the 42nd Black Watch of Royal Highlanders and the Manchester and South Staffordshire Regiments are situated on the hills at Harrismith.

HISTORIC HOMESTEAD (FARM KERKSVLEI)

This sandstone house at Kerks Vly took four years to build. Stone was quarried locally, while the yellowwood beam ceiling and floorboards were transported by wagon from Pietermaritzburg. The inscriptions '1884 SJA Raath' and 'Kerks Vly' appear above each of the two front entrances, while the inscriptions 'SHA Raath' and 'SEJ Odendaal' (Raath's second wife's maiden name) appear above the fireplace. Of significance is that the Boer War Treaty between General Prinsloo and the British forces was signed at this house. The fact that Kerks Vly wasn't burned as other farmhouses during the war is ascribed to a portrait of Queen Victoria found hanging on the wall.

TOWN HALL (WARDEN STREET)

This impressive redbrick building was designed by the architects Price & Agupter, and was erected by the builders Kelly & Anderson of Johannesburg. The cornerstone was laid by Sir Hamilton Goold-Adams on 2 August 1907, and the Town Hall was officially inaugurated on 7 September 1908.

HEILBRON

The town of Heilbron was laid out on the farm Rietfonten in 1872, and attained municipal status in 1890. Heilbron, which means 'spring of blessing', owes its name to a particularly strong fountain that still supplies the town with water.

RAILWAY STATION BUILDING

The rectangular sandstone building, with a pitched corrugated-iron roof, was built in 1898, and is one of only a few railway stations constructed during Republican times. The first railway line in the Free State from Norvalspont to the Orange River via Bloemfontein was opened on 10 October 1890.

VEGKOP BATTLEFIELDS AND MONUMENT (VECHT KOP)

After skirmishes with small bands of Mzilikazi's Matabele, the Voortrekkers, under the command of Andries Hendrik Potgieter ,formed a laager at Vegkop, where they defeated the Matabele in a decisive battle on 16 October 1836.

WEILBACH HOUSE AND ADJACENT OLD FARMSTEAD (FARM LEEUWPOORT)

Weilbach House, the only house in the area not destroyed by British troops during the Anglo-Boer War, is a sandstone dwelling with a pitched corrugated-iron roof. A corrugated-iron verandah on three sides is supported by wooden pillars finished with woodwork depicting the Union Jack.

The name 'JC Weilbach' and the date '1894' appear above the front door. Italian tradesmen were responsible for the stonework. The old farmstead is thought to have been built in the 1870s.

HENNENMAN

Originally a railway station named Ventersburg Road, the town was renamed after Petrus F Hennenman. The town was established in 1936 on the farm Vredefontein and was first named Havengaville. It attained municipal status in 1947 under the name Hennenman.

FARMHOUSE FERREIRASRUST (DISTRICT)

A good example of late Republican architecture, this sandstone building, with corrugated-iron roof and five chimneys, has a verandah on three sides and a cellar. It was built in the 1890s for the wealthy Thomas Minter, owner of the Kaal Valley Mine. In 1910 it was purchased by Daniel Ferreira and is still owned by his family.

HOOPSTAD

This town was laid out on the farm Kameeldoorns in 1874. It was originally named Hauptstad after the surveyor AP Haupt, but was later changed to Hoopstad. The town attained municipal status in 1905.

NEDERDUITSE GEREFORMEERDE CHURCH (CHURCH STREET)

The cornerstone of this impressive cruciform church with neogothic features was laid by President FW Reitz on 6 June 1891. The building was officially inaugurated on 2 December 1892.

JACOBSDAL

Established on the farm Kalkfontein in 1859, the town was named after the owner, Christoffel Johannes Jacobs. It attained municipal status in 1860.

HISTORIC BLOCKHOUSE

Dating from 1901, this Historic Blockhouse was built of dolerite by the British. During the Anglo-Boer War (1899–1902) it formed part of a line of similar blockhouses that were erected to protect the road link between the two railway lines that ran through Kimberley and Bloemfontein.

HISTORIC SITE WITH BURGER MEMORIAL (FARM MAGERSFONTEIN)

This cemetery was laid out in 1929 on land donated by the then owner of the farm Magersfontein, George van Vuuren.

The mortal remains of burghers who died during the Anglo-Boer War (1899-1902) at the battles of Tweeriviere, Modderrivier and Magersfontein, and in the environs of Kimberley, were exhumed and reinterred in this cemetery. A memorial recording the burghers' names was erected in 1969.

NEDERDUITSE GEREFORMEERDE CHURCH (CHURCH STREET)

After the cornerstone was laid on 29 January 1878, the original part of this impressive church was completed on 29 July 1879. The building was changed to its present cruciform shape by the addition in 1929 and 1930 of the tower and transept. The completed building was inaugurated on 24 May 1930.

JAGERSFONTEIN

This town was founded on the farm Jagersfontein in 1878 and was named after the Griqua family of Evert Jagers, who owned the farm and lived at the fountain. It attained municipal status in 1904. In 1893 the 971-carat Excelsior diamond was found in the vicinity and was to date the largest white discovered. In 1895 the 637-carat, flawless white Reitz diamond was discovered.

WATER PUMPS

These 18 water pumps form part of the water supply scheme that the firm Stewarts & Lloyds installed for Jagersfontein in 1913. The pumps offered a unique solution to a freshwater supply problem experienced by many rural towns.

KERKENBERG

This mountain in the Drakensberg range was named in 1837 by the Reverend Erasmus Smit, who felt that the adjoining open spaces would serve as a suitable place of worship. When the Voortrekkers arrived in the Orange Free State, there was a dispute among them about the eventual destination of the Great Trek. Some wanted to go to the Transvaal and others to Natal. Piet Retief chose Natal.

A party of Piet Retief's trek, led by his stepson, A Greyling, formed a laager at the foot of the Kerkenberg in October 1837.

From here groups of Voortrekkers left in search of a suitable route down the Drakensberg. Piet Retief left his laager on the 7 October 1837 with 14 men to reconnoitre Natal in advance.

On 11 November Coenraad and Piet Meyer returned with the good news that they could settle in Natal and would be able to live there in peace. The news spread further and the Voortrekkers decided to go to Natal on 14 November, when the first 18 wagons descended the mountains.

RETIEF'S ROCK (FARM ABERDEEN)
It was here that Piet Retief's daughter Deborah painted the date of her father's birthday (12 November) in green on a rock in commemoration of his achievement.

KESTELL

Laid out on the farms Mooifontein and Driekuil in 1905, the town was named after the Reverend John Daniel Kestell (1854–1941), minister of the Dutch Reformed Church, author and cultural leader. It attained municipal status in 1909.

NEDERDUITSE GEREFORMEERDE CHURCH (VAN RIEBEECK STREET)
This impressive sandstone church, with Byzantine and neoclassical elements, was designed by the well-known architect Gerard Moerdijk, and erected by the builder F Barker. One of the largest sandstone churches in South Africa, it was officially inaugurated on 31 March 1928.

SANDSTONE DWELLING (2 OLIVIER STREET)
This Victorian sandstone house was probably built by Dr AC Hunter, who bought the property in 1911. It is a good example of Free State sandstone architecture.

KOFFIEFONTEIN

Situated on the Riet River, Koffiefontein was proclaimed a town in 1892. A diamond was discovered here in 1872 by a transport rider, and by 1882 four mining companies were operating in the area.

LUTHERAN CHURCH COMPLEX (FARM ADAMSHOOP)
The site of the church complex includes the graves of the slave Frederick Opperman and his son, Adam, who settled in the southwestern Free State around 1860. Before his death in 1892, Adam Opperman stated in his will that the land should remain the property of his family. On 1 April 1867, an agreement was reached between Adam Opperman and HT Langemann, the director of the Berlin Missionary Society, whereby the latter would send a missionary to Koffiefontein, and would give Adam representation and voting power in the Free State conferences of the Society. Adam Opperman in turn agreed to donate the church building and site to the Society, and to build a house for the minister.

The first minister was Ludwig Zerwick who settled on the farm Poortjiesdam in 1869. He was succeeded by Gustav Trumpelmann and the name was changed to Adamshoop. Later enlarged and used as a school, the first church was built by Adam Opperman and his helpers in the 1860s. On 1 April 1892, the cornerstone for a new church was laid by Hienrich Grutzner and the building was consecrated in 1897. The school building is built in Karoo style with a flat, corrugated-iron roof.

KOPPIES

The town of Koppies was laid out on the farm Honingkopjes in 1910, from which it also takes its name. It attained municipal status in 1926.

VREDEFORT ROAD CONCENTRATION CAMP (FARM PROSPECT)
The cemetery contains the mortal remains of approximately 800 Boer women and children who died here during the Anglo-Boer War (1899–1902).

KROONSTAD
The town was laid out on the farm Klipplaatsdrift in 1855. The origin of the name possibly derives from Kroon drift, which was named after a horse called Kroon, belonging either to Sarel Cilliers or 'Lang Adriaan', father of General JH de la Rey. Diamonds were formerly mined at the Crown Diamond Mine.

HISTORIC OLD MARKET BUILDING (CNR MARKET AND MURRAY STREETS)
The Old Market Building, with Victorian features, was presumably erected at the turn of the nineteenth century. Steel gates between the iron pillars were added in 1960. The building forms an integral part of the historic Market Square.

NEDERDUITSE GEREFORMEERDE MOEDER KERK AND SAREL CILLIERS STATUE (CROSS STREET)
The cornerstone of the church was laid on 24 December 1912 by Reverend GWB van der Linden, and the building was inaugurated in 1914. The statue of Sarel Cilliers was sculptured by Coert Steynberg and unveiled by Acting Prime Minister Klasie Havenga, on 26 December 1950.

OLD MAGISTRATE'S OFFICE BUILDING (CNR MARKET AND MURRAY STREETS)
Built in 1905, the Magistrate's Office is situated on Market Square. On 17 April 1900 during the Anglo-Boer War a court martial was held here.

Presidents Paul Kruger, Martinus Theunis Steyn, General Louis Botha, Christiaan de Wet and Koos de la Rey addressed their men here.

OLD MARKET SQUARE POST OFFICE AND PRISON CELLS (66 MURRAY STREET)
This building served as the Office of the Village Council in 1883. Thereafter it was also used as a post office, police station and Magistrate's Office. Behind the post office building are a couple of prison cells, built before 1861.

OLD TOWN HALL AND LEAPING FOUNTAIN (CHURCH STREET)
The cornerstone of the Town Hall was laid on 14 March 1903. Designed by AE Till, the building was opened on 8 June 1907 by Sir Hamilton John Goold-Adams, Lieutenant-Governor of the Orange River Colony. The hall houses the restored Municipal Council Chamber; a statue and leaping fountain were created by A Heider.

LADYBRAND
Founded on the farm Mauersboek in 1867, the town was named after Lady Catharina Fredrica Brand, wife of Sir Christoffel Brand (1797–1875), the first speaker of the Cape Legislative Assembly. It attained municipal status in 1904.

HOMESTEAD (19 PRINSLOO STREET)
This homestead is representative of the sandstone architecture that characterises the eastern Free State.

MAIN BUILDING AND SCHOOL HALL (LADYBRAND SECONDARY SCHOOL, COLLINS STREET)
The cornerstone was laid on 16 March 1904 by Hugh Gunn, Director of Education of the Orange River Colony. Architecturally, the school represents Free State Edwardian style, and is linked to the history of education in Ladybrand.

OLD MAGISTRATE'S COURT AND POLICE STATION
(CNR CHURCH AND PIET RETIEF STREETS, AND
PIET RETIEF AND JOUBERT STREETS)

After the original Magistrate's Office was destroyed by fire in 1986, the Free State Volksraad agreed to fund a new Magistrate's Office in June 1897.

The new building, in neoclassical idiom, was completed on 1 June 1898 and served as a Magistrate's Office until 1953. The police station is reputed to have been built by a Mr Paterson in 1875.

ROCK PAINTINGS
(MODDERPOORTSPRUIT, DISTRICT)

Some of these paintings have been ascribed by archaeologists to the San people, while others to an earlier period, citing chronological and regional differences among them. The earliest paintings were monochrome, the next stage bichrome, later polychrome. In the more recent paintings, subjects such as British soldiers, Voortrekkers, wagons and cattle appear.

ROSE COTTAGE CAVE
(FARM LADYBRAND, DISTRICT)

Rose Cottage Cave exhibits an abundance of rock paintings. Excavations have produced a wealth of stone tools and Late Stone Age artefacts. Rose Cottage is a rare sight and of great archaeological significance.

ST JAMES ANGLICAN CHURCH (JOUBERT STREET)

This Anglican church was designed by John Edwin Harrison and built in 1897. Consecrated by Bishop JW Hicks on 26 January 1898, it was originally known as the Douglas Memorial Church, in honour of Father James Douglas. St James is constructed of Ladybrand sandstone, with a high corrugated-iron roof, arched wooden ceiling and wooden floors. The small lead-glass windows were imported from England.

LINDLEY

The town of Lindley was laid out on the farm Brandhoek in 1875 and was named after Daniel Lindley (1801–1880), the American Presbyterian Missionary, who became the first ordained minister to the Voortrekkers in 1840. The town was donated to the Dutch Reformed Church in 1885, and then transferred to the municipality in 1891.

EARLY SOTHO SETTLEMENT
(FARM SEDAN, LINDLEY DISTRICT)

This Sotho 'living' site dates from the seventeenth century. The remains of approximately 200 prehistoric stone huts can be seen, built in a circular pattern. Separate settlement units formed part of a larger social and political group. The inhabitants subsisted on herding cattle, cultivating grain and hunting.

LUCKHOFF

Established on the farm Koffiekuil in 1892, the town was named after HJ Luckhoff (1842–1923), the Minister of Fauresmith.

HISTORIC OLD POWDER MAGAZINE

This powder magazine, which was erected during the first half of 1899, is a rectangular structure built from local dolerite stone. It was presumably erected in preparation for the impending Anglo-Boer War.

PARYS

Parys was laid out on the farm Klipspruit in 1876, and attained municipal status in 1887. The name was suggested by a German surveyor, Schilbach, who served in the Franco-Prussian War and had taken part in the Siege of Paris. He imagined a large city on both banks of the Vaal River, similar to Paris, which lies on both banks of the Seine.

NEDERDUITSE GEREFORMEERDE MOEDER KERK AND BELL CAGE (HEFER STREET)

The cornerstone of this cruciform church with neogothic features was laid by the Moderator of the Orange Free State Synod, Reverend JJT Marquard, on 14 January 1899. The building was completed shortly after the outbreak of the Anglo-Boer War (1899–1902) and was used by British troops as an observation post.

OLD MAGISTRATE'S OFFICE (LIEBENBERGTREK STREET)

Now a museum, this redbrick building was built soon after the Anglo-Boer War and dates to the period when the Free State was known as the Orange River Colony, under British rule. In 1907 a section of the building was used as a charge office by the South African Constabulary.

PETRUS STEYN

This town was laid out on the farm Petrus Steyn in 1914, and was named after the owner of the farm.

OLD PARSONAGE OF THE DUTCH REFORMED CHURCH (33 DU PLESSIS STREET)

Most of the rooms of this sandstone house, with its high-pitched roof, have their original wooden ceilings and floors. The Dutch Reformed Church of Concordia (known as Petrus Steyn since 1926) was established in 1914. Services were first held in the town hall and a house in town used as a parsonage. Designed by F Pieterse, this house was completed in 1917.

PHILIPPOLIS

Founded as a London Missionary Society station in 1823, the town was named after Dr John Philip (1775–1851), who had selected the site. It attained municipal status in 1862.

DUTCH REFORMED CHURCH

The original Griqua Mission Church stood on this ground. It was later bought by the congregation of Philippolis and used for several years. The cornerstone of this church was laid on 8 May 1869 by Reverend Colin Fraser, who also conducted the inauguration on 24 February 1871. The transepts were only added in 1885. During the Anglo-Boer War the church was occupied by British troops.

HISTORIC OLD POWDER MAGAZINE

At the end of 1861 the Griquas sold all of their remaining land in the Free State to the Free State government. The government decided to build a magazine in order to supply ammunition to the Boers. Work was completed on the magazine in January 1871.

KAROO-STYLE DWELLINGS (16 AND 24 TOBIE MULLER STREET, AND 26 KOK STREET)

These houses are fine examples of the flat-roofed style, which, from the late 1850s, replaced the houses with steep thatched roofs in the Orange Free State. They represent the most characteristic building type of the early Republican period and are examples of the earliest townhouses that have been preserved in the Free State.

KAROO-STYLE HOUSE (4 JUSTISIE STREET)

The stand on which this house was built was transferred to Jan Kok by the Griqua government on 21 November 1861. On 9 December 1861 the property was sold to AA Ortlepp & Co after which the house was built. The Karoo-style dwelling has clay walls and reed-ceiling rooms.

OLD POUND AND SURROUNDING AREA (JUSTISIE STREET)

Residents of Philippolis know the old pound as Adam Kok's livestock kraal. This is based on an assumption that the structure dates prior to 1860 when the town was in the possession of the Griquas under Adam Kok III. When James Backhouse visited the town in 1839 he sketched a structure at the foot of a hill, which is probably the pound. Built of stone, the walls are 2.5m high and 500cm wide, with wooden gates.

OLD VICTORIAN LIBRARY (JACOBSON LIBRARY)
(34 VOORTREKKER STREET)
This imposing building, with its predominantly Victorian features, dates from 1905–1906. Moritz Jacobson bought the property in 1921 and lived there until 1977, when he donated it to the municipality of Philippolis to be used as a library. In 1978 it was taken over by the Provincial Administration of the Orange Free State and restored.

VICTORIAN HOUSE AND ADJACENT WAGON HOUSE
(5 AND 7 COLIN FRASER STREET)
Christiaan van der Post, father of author Sir Laurens van der Post, bought this property with its Victorian house in 1906. Christiaan settled in the Free State during the 1870s.

REDDERSBURG

Founded on the farm Vlakfontein in 1861, the town was named after the Saviour ('Redder'). It attained municipal status in 1889 or 1894.

OLD C.N.O. SCHOOL (7 STEWIE JOUBERT STREET)
Erected to house the C.N.O. School, which opened in 1904, this building played a vital role in the history of education in the town.

OLD GEREFORMEERDE KERK
(BOSHOFF STREET)
The Reformed Church of South Africa was founded in Rustenburg in 1859, with the Reverend Dirk Postma as its first and only minister. In that same year he established seven congregations, one of which was in Reddersburg in May 1859. The church building was consecrated on 2 January 1863. It has two gables but no steeple, and is still in its original form apart from the ceilings, which have been replaced.

REITZ

The town was founded in 1889 on the farm Stampkop, which was a portion of Langspruit. Originally named Amsterdam, the town was renamed by Francis William Reitz (1844–1934), President of the Orange Free State. Reitz attained municipal status in 1903.

DUTCH REFORMED CHURCH (CHURCH STREET)
The architect of this imposing sandstone building was Wynand Louw. The cornerstone was laid on 10 August 1912 by President MT Steyn and the building was inaugurated by Reverend JD Kestell on 18 May 1914.

ROUXVILLE

Founded on the farm Zuurbult in 1864, the town was named after Reverend Pieter Roux, minister of the Dutch Reformed Church in Smithfield from 1853–1875. The town attained municipal status in 1893.

NEDERDUITSE GEREFORMEERDE KERK
(CHURCH STREET)
This impressive sandstone building, with neogothic features, was designed by Richard Wocke. The cornerstone was laid on 11 July 1879 and the building was officially inaugurated on 11 March 1881. The restored tower, which was designed by HGE de la Cornelliere, was inaugurated on 22 March 1924.

OLD TOWNHOUSE (ROUX STREET)
A good example of early Republican house construction, this sandstone house was built for Philippus Johannes Cornelis Swanepoel, a farmer in the district. He owned the property from 1867 to 1899.

SENEKAL
This town was established on the farm De Put in 1875 and was named after Frederik Petrus Senekal (1815–1866). It attained municipal status in 1886.

NEDERDUITSE GEREFORMEERDE MOEDER KERK AND CHURCH SQUARE
This historic sandstone church was designed by the architects JH & AE Till, and was built by the contractors Rowe, Marshall & Hill. The building was consecrated in 1896. The Church Square is enclosed by a wall on which fossil tree trunks were placed in the 1940s.

SMITHFIELD
Laid out on the farm Rietpoort in 1849, the town was named after Sir Harry Smith (1787–1860), Governor of the Cape Colony (1847–1852). Municipal status was attained in 1948.

FARMSTEAD AND FARM BEERSHEBA
The Beersheba Mission was founded in 1835 by Reverend Samuel Rolland of the Paris Evangelical Mission. Although very little remains of the mission, the house has a high sandstone foundation, wood-and-steel ceilings and wooden floors. The double entrance door has stained glass and lead-glass panels.

HISTORIC CEMETERY (FARM CARMEL)
Carmel was originally a mission station of the Paris Evangelical Missionary Society from 1833 to 1869. In the walled yard is a vault with the mortal remains of the French missionary, Jean Louis Prosper Lemur, who died on 12 March 1870.

KAROO-STYLE DWELLING (CHURCH STREET)
A particularly good example of the flat-roof architecture of the 1850s, this Karoo-style house comprises five rooms with wooden floors and ceilings.

RUINS OF HOUSE IN WHICH GENERAL CR DE WET WAS BORN (SITUATED ON THE FARM FORMERLY KNOWN AS LEEUWKOP, AND NOW PART OF THE FARM KLEINFONTEIN)
These ruins are all that remain of the two-roomed clay cottage in which General CR de Wet was born on 7 October 1854. The sixth of 14 children, he lived here with his parents until the age of five. De Wet fought at the Battles of Laing's Nek, Ingogo and Majuba. At the outbreak of the Anglo-Boer War (1899), he was called up, together with his sons Kotie, Isak and Christiaan.

SOUTPAN
FLORISBAD RESEARCH STATION (ARCHAEOLOGICAL AND PALAEONTOLOGICAL SITE)
This Research Station was named after Floris Venter, who opened the mineral spring near the Haagenstad salt pan.

The remains of the Florisbad cranium, were discovered here in 1932. Florisbad has yielded a large number of well-preserved fossils, of extinct and extant animals characteristic of the Late Middle Pleistocene Age to about 10 000 years ago.

One of the buildings at the research station is a two-roomed corrugated-iron house, built by Floris Venter for his mother in 1903. It has been restored and houses a site museum for the station.

SWINBURNE

OLD TOLL BRIDGE OVER WILGE RIVER
This Toll Bridge is one of two such bridges erected in the Free State. Building started in December 1883 and the bridge was officially opened on 23 July 1884.

THABA 'NCHU

Thaba 'Nchu was established in 1893 and was named after the nearby mountain, which in Sotho means 'black mountain'.

REVEREND ARCHBELL'S MISSION HOUSE
(ST PAUL'S MISSION)
After the Barolong tribe moved from Platberg to Thaba 'Nchu in 1833, the church and the Reverend Archbell's Mission House were re-erected here. His house was probably enlarged between 1836 and 1839.

MOROKA HOUSE
(RATLOU VILLAGE)
This dwelling was built in 1922 by Dr James Sebe Moroka, President-General of the African National Congress from 1949–1952. Dr Moroka was a great grandson of Moroka, the chief (1795–1880) of the Barolong tribe, who allied himself with the Voortrekkers. He defended them against the Matabele and Mzilikazi.

Educated at the Lovedale Missionary Institute at Alice in the Eastern Cape, Dr Moroka then studied at the University of Edinburgh, where he qualified as a medical doctor in 1918. He practiced at Thaba 'Nchu when he returned to South Africa.

VAN REENEN

The village was named after Frans van Reenen (1816–1914), the owner of the farm Sandspruit, who planned the route of the pass on which the road was built in 1856.

LLANDAFF ORATORY (THE LODGE)
This redbrick chapel was erected in 1925 by Joseph Maynard Matthew, at the time a Landdrost in Natal and a Roman Catholic, to house a memorial to his son Llandaff, who died during the Burnside Colliery disaster while trying to save the lives of other miners. The little church claims to be 'the smallest church in the world', and 'the only Roman Catholic Church in the world which is privately owned'. After being denied the right to place a plaque in memory of his son in other Roman Catholic churches, Joseph Maynard had this church custom built. Although it seats only eight people, it carries all the appropriate vestments.

VENTERSBURG

Ventersburg was laid out on the farm Kromfontein in 1872 and was named after the farm's owner, the Voortrekker PA Venter.

DUTCH REFORMED CHURCH (STEYN STREET)
A brick building with terrazzo finish, this church has an ironstone foundation and a steel ceiling. The cornerstone was laid on 12 June 1912 by President MT Steyn, and the church was consecrated on 18 July 1913. The original altar and baptismal font have been preserved.

LEGHOYA VILLAGE
(SANDRIVIERSHOOGTE, FARM WATERVAL)
Leghoya Village, with its characteristic corbelled huts and stone kraals, dates from the seventeenth century and is an excellent example of the architecture and way of life of the Leghoya tribe in the Free State.

OLD POLICE STATION COMPLEX
Restored and reopened as a Police Museum on 20 October 1983, this police station was probably erected prior to 1914, judging from photographic evidence. Plans for the prison

building were dated October 1898. The rondavel behind the police station is a replica of the original. The complex also includes stables with a flat, corrugated-iron roof, and a pound constructed of stone.

SITE TOGETHER WITH THE SKANSKRAAL AND VOORTREKKER GRAVE (FARM KROMFONTEIN)

This square, protective kraal was erected in 1865, under the supervision of Field-Cornet PA Venter. About 200 Basuto, who had been sent by Moshesh, Venter's friend, erected the stone walls, about two metres in height, with eight to 12 loopholes in each. The kraal was used in 1858 and from 1866 to 1868, and also served as a defence point in the Basuto Wars.

VILJOENSKROON

This town was laid out in 1921 on the farm Mahemskuil and was named after the owner of the farm, JJ Viljoen, and his horse Kroon. It attained municipal status in 1925.

FARMHOUSE AND SANDSTONE COOLING CHAMBER (FARM THORNVALE)

The farm Doorndraai was registered by Paul Michiel Botha and Theuns Louis Botha in 1865. In 1893 the farm was divided between them and Paul donated a section to his son, also Paul, in 1899. It is believed that the house and cold store were erected in 1903. Edwardian in style, the house is built of sandstone with a pitched corrugated-iron roof. The cold store is a sandstone rondavel with a thatched roof.

VREDE

The town of Vrede was founded in 1863 on the farm Krynauwslust, and was proclaimed in 1879. Its name, which means peace, was decided upon after a dispute over the site for the town had been settled.

ALL SAINTS' ANGLICAN CHURCH (70 CHURCH STREET)

This small church, with its neogothic characteristics, was built of dolerite by the builders Thomas Cowan and Alec H Doing of Harrismith. All Saints was consecrated on 9 November 1890 by Bishop GWH Knight-Bruce of Bloemfontein.

NEDERDUITSE GEREFORMEERDE KERK (CHURCH SQUARE)

The cornerstone of this neogothic, sandstone church was laid on 31 October 1885 by President JH Brand, and was inaugurated in 1887. During the Anglo-Boer War (1899–1902) the church was modified into a hospital, which was damaged by the British forces.

VREDEFORT

Vredefort was laid out on the farm Vischgat in 1876 but was only proclaimed in 1881. The town attained municipal status in 1890.

OLD POST OFFICE (15 ORANGE STREET)

To satisfy the requirements of gold diggers in the Vredefort area, a regular postal service was introduced in 1888 and a post office was erected in 1904. This Edwardian building is similar to the post office in Frankfort, designed by HGA de la Cornelliere, and it is thought that the same plan was used. Still in use today, the original building consists of a storeroom, Post Master's Office and a large chamber for the circulation department.

WARDEN

Laid out on the farm Rietvlei in 1912, the town attained municipal status in 1920. It was named after Charles Frederick Warden, Landdrost of Harrismith (1884-1900), and son of Major HD Warden.

NEDERDUITSE GEREFORMEERDE KERK AND
OUTBUILDINGS (CHURCH STREET)
This impressive building, with its 44m high clock tower, was designed by the architect F Heese and erected with the assistance of members of the congregation. The cornerstone of the building was laid on 7 February 1920, and the church was officially consecrated on 14 April 1924. This church is reputed to be the largest sandstone church in South Africa.

WEPENER

This town was named after Lourens Jacobus (Louw) Wepener (1812–1865) and attained municipal status in 1904.

JAMMERSBERGDRIFT BATTLEFIELD
(FARM ANNIEDALE, DISTRICT)
In April 1900, Colonel EH Dalgety and his Colonial Division of about 2 000 men were besieged for 16 days by General Christiaan de Wet and his superior force of almost 6 000 men. With the arrival of British reinforcements, General De Wet conceded victory and fled on 15 April 1900. The heroic manner in which the Colonial Division resisted during the siege, and the fact that Jammersbergdrift was one of General De Wet's few military defeats, makes this battlefield exceptionally important. Many of the entrenchments and other material remains are still evident at the site. There is also a monument commemorating the battle, and a cemetery.

OLD WAGON BRIDGE OVER THE CALEDON RIVER
(JAMMERSBERGDRIFT)
The location of Wepener with the Jammersbergspruit, east of the Caledon River, caused severe traffic problems in the rainy season and the town was often cut off from the rest of the Free State. A bridge was the only solution and this steel-arched bridge on sandstone was completed in 1892.

ROBERTSON CEMETERY AND CHAPEL
(FARM CEMETERY)
Four Robertson brothers and a sister came to South Africa in the 1850s and in 1884 a residence was built for two of the brothers and the sister. Although dilapidated, the house still exists. The small church has a pitched corrugated-iron roof with a wooden ceiling and floor. In the cemetery, apart from the Robertsons' graves, there is a mass grave of three officers and 25 troops of the Cape Colonial Division and Boers who were killed in action at Jammersbergdrift in 1900.

SHELTER WITH ROCK PAINTINGS
(FARM VENTERSHOEK)
These rock paintings record a scene in which the San people drive away cattle while some of their numbers fight a rearguard action against Bantu pursuers. This work can be dated to about 1821. Unfortunately, a number of the paintings have been removed, one of which is on exhibition in the Musée de l'Homme in Paris.

WINBURG

Laid out on the farm Waaifontein in 1841, Winburg attained municipal status in 1872.

BRITISH CONCENTRATION CAMP CEMETERY
Situated 2km west of Winburg, this cemetery contains the graves of Anglo-Boer War (1899–1902) concentration camp victims, as well as those of 200 British soldiers.

DUTCH REFORMED CHURCH BUILDING
(CHURCH SQUARE)
This impressive neogothic sandstone church was designed by the architects JH & AE Till and erected by the builders Rundle, Rowe & Marshall. The cornerstone was laid on 20 January 1899 by MT Steyn, President of the Orange Free State. During the Anglo-Boer War

(1899–1902) the unfinished church building was converted into a British hospital. Building work recommenced after the war and the completed church building was eventually inaugurated on 18 March 1904.

PREHISTORIC STONE HUTS (DOORNBERG, WILLEM PRETORIUS GAME RESERVE)

These stone huts are of archaeological interest and only occur in restricted areas, in particular, the northeastern Free State and Mpumalanga. Although the huts are attributed to the Leghoya people, there is still some doubt among scientists as to their true origin.

These stone huts were selected after careful investigation by experts, as they are representative of the particular features of this prehistoric architecture. Several of these huts are still in a good state of repair, while those that aren't will be restored by scientific experts.

GAUTENG

The smallest of all South Africa's provinces and originally part of the old Transvaal Province, Gauteng encompasses the capital city of Pretoria, as well as Johannesburg and the industrial region centred on Vereeniging to the south. It is dominated by a low ridge, which the early pioneers named Witwatersrand, in which the world's richest gold deposits were discovered in the 1880s. The wealth of these gold mines catapulted South Africa's industrial development to a new level.

BOKSBURG

Established on the farm Vogelfontein in 1887, Boksburg was named after Willem Eduard Bok (1846–1904), the State Secretary of the Transvaal Republic. It attained municipal status in 1905.

OLD GOVERNMENT BUILDING (CHURCH STREET)
The building was designed in 1889, two years after the establishment of Boksburg itself, by Sytze Wierda, the 'government ingenieurn' architect of the Zuid-Afrikaansche Republiek. It was intended to accommodate the Mining Commissioner, the post office and other government offices. On 15 October 1890 the cornerstone was laid by the Head of Mining, CJ Joubert. It served as a Magistrates' Office from 1901–1958.

OLD POST OFFICE
(CNR MARKET AND JOUBERT STREETS)
Although the original plans were dated 1898, due to the outbreak of the Anglo-Boer War (1899–1902), the Post Office was only completed in 1905, when it was unveiled by JF Brown, the Post-master General.

ST MICHAEL AND ALL ANGELS CHURCH
(PLEIN STREET)
This church was designed by Sir Herbert Baker in the Romanesque style. The building was consecrated in 1912.

EDENVALE

The town was laid out on the farm Rietfontein in 1903 and was most likely named after John Eden, part owner of the farm. It attained municipal status in 1942.

HISTORIC OLD HORWOOD FARMHOUSE
(HOMESTEAD ROAD)
This property was bought in 1903 by the Roman Catholic priest Father John de Lacy, OMI, on behalf of the church. After his arrival on the Rand in 1886, he applied to the government for a grant of land to establish a church, a school and houses for the teachers in the mining village of Johannesburg.

Father de Lacy was also responsible for bringing the nuns of the Holy Family order to the Rand, and was instrumental in founding Nazareth House, Marist Brothers' College and the hospital. In 1919 the property was sold to Daniel William Horwood. It appears that the farmhouse started as a small two-roomed cottage with a central hall, with later additions of a verandah and two large side wings as 'stoepkamers'.

GERMISTON

Laid out on the farm Elandsfontein in 1887, the town was known by this name until 1904, when it was officially named Germiston. The latter comes from the birthplace of John Jack, a gold mining pioneer, who came from the farm Germiston near Glasgow in Scotland. The town attained municipal status in 1903.

ST ANDREW'S PRESBYTERIAN CHURCH
(FH ODENDAAL STREET)

St Andrew's Presbyterian congregation was established in 1890 and its early history is closely interwoven with that of Germiston itself. The cornerstone of this well-preserved neogothic-style church was laid by Lord Milner on 14 March 1905. The building was officially opened on 8 October 1905 by Lord Selborne, High Commissioner for South Africa and Governor of the Transvaal and Orange River Colonies.

HEIDELBERG

Originally a trading post on the farm Langlaagte, the town was proclaimed in 1866. It was named after Heidelberg in Germany, where Heinrich Ueckermann (a trader) had been trained. The town attained municipal status in 1903.

DE RUST FARMSTEAD (BOSCHHOEK)

This unusual and well-preserved Victorian farmhouse was built by FJ Bezuidenhout, who was born on the farm Doornfontein in 1851. Shortly after the Anglo-Boer War (1899–1902), Bezuidenhout returned to his home near Standerton to find it in ruins. He then bought the farm Boschhoek from PJ du Toit. The house was designed by MCA Meischke and the builder was Johannes Joubert. Sparing no expense, Bezuidenhout imported furniture and sanitary ware from England. Although a rural country dwelling, De Rust itself compares well with townhouses of the time. The walls are decorated with embellished wallpapers and stucco work and the bathroom is a good example of the Victorians' love of luxury.

DIEPKLOOF FARM MUSEUM
(SUIKERBOSRAND NATURE RESERVE)

The farm was officially granted to JG Marais on 16 September 1859 although the main house was built in approximately 1850. The 'Seunshuis' was built in 1890 by Frans, son of JG Marais. When the farm was purchased by the Transvaal Provincial Administration as a nature reserve, the houses, outbuildings and wall were restored.

DUTCH REFORMED CHURCH (KLIPKERK,
HF VERWOERD STREET)

The cornerstone of this stone church was laid on 12 April 1890 by Piet Joubert, Commandant-General of the Zuid-Afrikaansche Republiek, and the church was consecrated on 13 March 1891. In 1909 the steeple collapsed, but was immediately rebuilt. At a meeting held in the basement hall on 24 July 1903, it was decided to establish a Volkskool. As a result of this, the present Hoër Volkskool and the Heidelberg Training College came into being.

HISTORIC DWELLING (60 STRYDOM STREET)

Built in 1875 by FK Mare, the first Landdrost in Heidelberg, this house typifies the style of rural building that started off in the farming districts of the Cape. However, this 'stoepkamer' tradition of architecture that is so characteristic of the Cape Dutch farmhouses, is rarely found outside the Grahamstown area.

HISTORIC NZASM RAILWAY STATION
(VOORTREKKER STREET)

This exceptional Railway Station Building, with its Dutch stepped gable on the street side and the decorative gable on the platform side, was opened on 10 October 1896. The guests of honour at this festive occasion were Dr WJ Leyds, State Secretary of the Zuid-Afrikaansche Republiek, and Sir D Robinson, Governor of Natal.

VOLKSKOOL (BEGEMAN STREET)
The Volkskool was founded in 1903 at a meeting held in the basement hall of the Dutch Reformed Church. The original school building was erected in 1907 in memory of the inhabitants of the district of Heidelberg who lost their lives during the Anglo-Boer War (1899–1902).

JOHANNESBURG

Founded on the farm Randjeslaagte in 1886, the city was named after Johann Rissik, principal clerk of the Surveyor-General Office of the Transvaal Republiek, and Christiaan Johannes Joubert, Chief of Mining and a member of the Volksraad. Johannesburg attained city status in 1928.

ANSTEYS BUILDING
(CNR JEPPE AND JOUBERT STREETS)
Considered a fine example of the architectural style of the 1930s, this building was erected in 1936 by Emley & Williamson.

CITY HALL COMPLEX (RISSIK STREET)
The cornerstone of the City Hall Complex was laid on 29 November 1910 by the Duke of Connaught and Strathearn, and the building was officially opened on 7 April 1915 by Governor-General Lord Buxton. It was designed in a grandiose Edwardian-Baroque style and is a good example of the pomp expected of this type of building before the First World War. Stylistically, it is strikingly counter-balanced by the adjoining Rissik Street Post Office.

CROSS ERECTED BY BARTOLOMEU DIAS
(UNIVERSITY OF THE WITWATERSRAND)
The padrão of St Gregory, which was erected by Bartolomeu Dias on 12 March 1488 at Kwaaihoek, near the mouth of the Bushman's River, is housed here. A replica of the cross stands at the original site.

CUTHBERTS BUILDING (ELOFF STREET)
Designed by Stucke & Bannister and completed in 1904, the building is typically Victorian in design and features a corner turret. The double wrought-iron verandah was added in 1928.

OLD STEAM LOCOMOTIVE: *EMIL KESSLER*
(SOUTH STATION BUILDING)
This steam locomotive operated from Braamfontein to Boksburg from 1890–1903. It was manufactured by Emil Kessler of Esslingen in Germany.

POST OFFICE (RISSIK STREET)
This building was originally designed by S Wierda, and construction work began around 1896 under the supervision of M Meischke and A Reid. The foundation stone was laid on 27 January 1897 by J van Apphen, the Postmaster General. In 1905 a fourth storey and clock tower were added in accordance with a design by the architect W Tonkin. The Post Office is the only noteworthy existing government building in Johannesburg dating from the time of the Zuid-Afrikaansche Republiek, and reflects the architectural style of the period.

POSWOHL SYNAGOGUE (MOOI STREET)
The cornerstone of this neo-Byzantine synagogue was laid on 24 August 1921. The building was erected by a community of Jews who emigrated from Poswohl in Lithuania to Johannesburg at the beginning of the twentieth century. It is also a memorial to a community that no longer exists; those Jews who remained in Poswohl perished during the holocaust of the Second World War.

RECONSTRUCTED FAÇADE OF THE FORMER
BUILDING KNOWN AS KIMBERLEY HOUSE
(44 PRITCHARD STREET)
Kimberley House was designed by Chris J Olley and was built in 1892. The entire

building was destroyed by a fire but the façade escaped damage. In 1988 Old Mutual Properties undertook to remove the façade and incorporate it into its offices to be built on the same and surrounding stands.

STEAM LOCOMOTIVE *KITTY*
(JOHANNESBURG STATION)
This well-preserved steam locomotive was manufactured in 1879 by the firm Kitson & Company of Leeds, England, and was brought to South Africa shortly afterwards for service in the Natal Government Railways. It is the oldest working steam locomotive in South Africa, and served to complete a century of service.

JOHANNESBURG SURROUNDS

Bezuidenhout Valley

Frederik Jacobus Bezuidenhout purchased the farm from the widow of BP Viljoen in 1861 and gave his name to the area.

YUKON HOUSE (33 NORTH AVENUE)
This imposing dwelling was completed c.1911 for TF Allen, the Mayor of Johannesburg (1917–1919), and testifies to the high expectations initially cherished in this part of Bezuidenhout Valley. In addition to a lavishly decorated interior, four stained-glass windows, named Commerce, Justice, Industry and Agriculture, are an exceptional feature of the house.

Braamfontein

Formerly known as Clifton, Braamfontein takes its name from the farm on which the suburb was established.

ENOCH SONTONGA MEMORIAL PARK (ENOCH SONTONGA AVENUE, BRAAMFONTEIN CEMETERY)
This park is named in memory of Enoch Sontonga, a Xhosa teacher who composed

Nkosi Sikelel!' iAfrika at the Nancefield Hostel in 1897. This song was performed at the inaugural meeting of the South African Native National Congress in 1912, and became the national anthem of the ANC in 1925. Since 1995 *Nkosi Sikelel' iAfrika*, together with *Die Stem* has become part of the dual anthem of South Africa.

OLD FEVER HOSPITAL
The site (the four remaining structures of the old Fever Hospital) was first used as a 'Lazarette' in 1893 when the ZAR was obliged to provide an isolation ward facility, other than an existing one in the gaol. One wood-and-iron building exists, which was probably part of the original establishment. After the Anglo-Boer War a number of wards were erected for patients with scarlet fever, measles, diptheria, and for observation. The main section was built in 1916 by the Union Government and by 1951 it had been increased to 85 beds.

Brixton

This suburb was named by Horace Collins, Secretary of Auckland Park Real Estate and General Manager of Paarl Central Gold Mining Company, after Brixton in South London.

COTTAGE (143 FULHAM ROAD)
Shortly after the declaration of Brixton as a township in 1904, this property was sold to Joseph Feinstein on a 99-year lease. The wood-and-iron cottage was built as a house-shop in 1904. Later, two extra rooms were added as living quarters for the shopkeeper. It is the only remaining example of a house-shop in the area.

HINDU CREMATORIUM
This was the first brick-built crematorium on the continent of Africa. The Hindu community obtained the land through the efforts of Mohandas K Ghandi. Built by Damania & Kalidas, it consists of a small barrel-vaulted

rectangular oven with an attached chimney. The old wood-burning crematorium must be preserved in accordance with the dictates and tenets of Hinduism. A gas-fired crematorium was built in 1956.

Dewetshof

Established on the farm Doornfontein and proclaimed in 1954, this suburb was named after Nicolaas Jacobus de Wet (1873–1960), Chief Justice of the Union of South Africa in 1939 and Officer Administering the Government from 1943–1945.

BEZUIDENHOUT FARMSTEAD AND THE JONKERSHUIS (BEZUIDENHOUT PARK)

Frederick Bezuidenhout, after whom Bezuidenhout Park is named, was one of the early trekboers in the old Transvaal. The two homesteads are reputedly those of Frederick and his son Barend. The original part of the house, dating from the 1850s, comprised a large room with two rooms on either side. Additions were made in 1880, 1890 and 1900.

Doornfontein

This suburb was laid out in 1887 and named after the farm on which it was established.

WINDYBROW BUILDING (PIETERSEN STREET)

Designed by William Leck in a pseudo-Tudor style, Windybrow was constructed in 1896. This historic building is one of the last remaining mansions in Doornfontein and was used *inter alia* as a homestead, an officers' mess in the Anglo-Boer War (1899–1902), and as part of the first College of Nursing in South Africa.

Emmarentia

Established on the farm Braamfontein, it was named after Emmarentia Margaretha Botha, wife of the farm's owner, Louwrens Geldenhuys. Emmarentia was proclaimed in 1937.

14 GREENHILL ROAD

Built in 1887 and completed in 1902, the house still contains its 'werfmuur', which is extremely rare and was characteristic of Cape Dutch farmhouses. This style of house was brought from the Cape by the Voortrekkers, as they 'trekked' northwards. It characterises their buildings in the areas of the former Orange Free State and Transvaal, although very few remain intact.

Forest Hill

The area was surveyed in 1897 and the suburb laid out in 1903.

HOUSE AND OUTBUILDINGS (37 CARTER STREET)

HH Bates, the original owner, purchased this property prior to the outbreak of the Anglo-Boer War. The wood-and-iron, brick-lined house dates back to 1901, and Bates lived there until his death in 1930.

Forest Town

The suburb was established on the old Sachsenwald ('wald' in German means forest) and, until about 1930, there were pine and gum plantations in this area.

MOERDIJK HOUSE (29 DURRIS STREET)

Dutch architect Gerard Moerdijk built this large cottage for himself, situated in the forest of the newly proclaimed township of Forest Town. The only changes have been the introduction of modern facilities, such as electricity and plumbing.

Hillbrow

Laid out in 1894–1895, the suburb takes its name from the fact that it lies on the brow of a low hill.

FRIEDENKIRCHE (30 EDITH CAVELL STREET)

The Friedenkirche can be described as eclectic, with both Romanesque and Cape

Dutch features. For example, a scroll on the east façade acts as a binding element between the nave and aisle, while the most typical Romanesque element is the tower, with its arched portal windows and cornice that encircles it immediately below the roof.

SA INSTITUTE FOR MEDICAL RESEARCH (HOSPITAL STREET)

The South African Institute for Medical Research (SAIMR) was established in 1912 through an agreement between the Chamber of Mines and the Union Government. Its primary task was to conduct research and, in particular, to try to reduce the high death rate from pneumonia and other diseases prevalent among mineworkers on the Witwatersrand. Research into lung and other diseases resulting from mining, was the first breakthrough for the SAIMR, and established it worldwide as an institute with a reputation for excellence in research. Investigations of dust-related diseases, particularly silicosis (miner's phthisis) helped to make underground mining less of a health hazard. Today the activities of the SAIMR include research into all the diseases that pose health problems in South Africa.

Hospital Hill

Actually a portion of Hillbrow, Hospital Hill takes its name from the Hillbrow Hospital and the old General Hospital, which are located here.

OLD FORT (KOTZE STREET)

In 1896 the government of the Zuid-Afrikaansche Republiek decided to build a fort around the existing prison, which had been built in 1892, and enlarged it in 1894, after the invasion of the Transvaal by Dr LS Jameson. The fort consisted of two bastions – one to protect the city, and the other the road to Pretoria – on which guns could be mounted. Excavations were started in December 1896 and a section was completed and ready to be garrisoned on 21 June 1897. By 12 June 1899 the fort was completed and handed over to the state artillery.

Houghton

Houghton Estate, was named after the owners of the land, Houghton Syndicate, or the Houghton Estate Gold Mine Company, which was formed by prospectors in 1889.

BEAR LODGE (17 ELM STREET)

Designed by the architect Robert Howden, the house was built in 1910 for NJ Hofmeyer, the Mayor of Johannesburg, who was later to become the first Vice Chancellor of the University of the Witwatersrand in 1930.

CULLINAN HOMESTEAD (3 ASH STREET)

Built for Sir Thomas Cullinan, this house was designed by the architects Howden & Stuart in the Art Nouveau style. The house was previously known as Mitchell House, as it was once owned by Joseph Mitchell, Chairman of Consolidated Rand Brick and Pottery.

ORIGINAL SECTION OF KING EDWARD VII SCHOOL (44 ST PATRICK ROAD)

This school was established as the Johannesburg High School for Boys towards the end of the Anglo-Boer War (1899–1902), and for a few years it was also known as the Johannesburg College. It is one of the six so-called Milner Schools founded in the Transvaal Colony during the first decade of the twentieth century. The main building was completed in 1910, and is a good example of school architecture from the Edwardian period, with pleasing proportions and finishes.

STONE LEDGE (17 ST DAVID'S ROAD)

Designed in the Arts and Crafts style, Stone Ledge was built with kopje stone that was quarried on site for one of South Africa's famous architects, FLH Fleming. He came to South Africa in 1903, joined Herbert Baker in 1904 and became a partner in the firm in 1910. Fleming was the Diocesan surveyor for Anglican churches, schools and St Mary's Cathedral in Johannesburg.

THE WILDS (HOUGHTON ESTATE)
In 1925 the Johannesburg Consolidated Investment Company Limited donated the original section of The Wilds to the Municipal Council of Johannesburg, on condition that it be kept as an open space for the recreation of the public. Since 1936 The Wilds has been planted with indigenous flora only, and has developed into what is probably the most attractive park in Johannesburg.

Jeppestown
Laid out in 1889, it was named after Julius Gottlieb Ernst Christian Jeppe (1821–1893), a partner in the company that established the suburb. It is often referred to as simply Jeppe.

DUTCH REFORMED CHURCH
(CNR CORRIE AND OP DE BERGEN STREETS)
The foundation stone of this church was laid on 5 May 1906 by General Koos de la Rey, and the building was officially consecrated on 26 January 1907. The high steeple, the stained-glass windows and the gables of the church are particularly imposing from an architectural point of view.

OLD POST OFFICE (315 MAIN STREET)
This double-storey building was erected in late 1897 and completed in 1898. The foundation stone for the post office was laid on 15 December 1897 by CF Obermeyer, Superintendent Engineer of Public Works of the Zuid-Afrikaansche Republiek. Besides the Rissik Street Post Office (1895–1898), this is the only remaining structure in Johannesburg designed by ZAR architects under the direction of Sytze Wierda.

SALISBURY HOUSE (218–220 MARSHALL STREET)
The building was originally built as three semi-detached shops on the ground floor, with two flats and rooms on the upper storey. In 1908 Alex Anderson opened a pharmacy in the corner shop and renamed the building, Salisbury House, after a teacher at St Mary's Diocesan School. It was purchased in 1974 by the Johannesburg City Council to save it from demolition, and is the only remaining example of the verandah-style in Jeppestown, a style mostly used for single-storey houses. Salisbury House was designed by architects McIntosh & Moffat and was completed in 1903. The wrought-iron work was imported from the company of Walter McFarlane of Glasgow, Scotland.

Joubert Park
Named after Commandant-General Piet Joubert of the Zuid-Afrikaansche Republiek, this was Johannesburg's first park and it has been retained as a central lung in the city.

JOHANNESBURG ART GALLERY (ORIGINAL PART)
Designed from 1910–1914 in the Beaux Arts style by British architect Sir Edward Lutyens and assisted by Herbert Baker as honorary co-architect, the building was erected under the supervision of Robert Howden. The foundation stone was laid on 12 October 1911 by HJ Hofmeyer, the Mayor of Johannesburg. The gallery, at the time still incomplete, was opened by the Duke of Connaught, Governor-General of South Africa in November 1915.

Kensington
Established in 1903, the suburb was named by the leaseholder Max Langerman, after the borough in London of the same name.

JEPPE HIGH SCHOOL FOR BOYS
(CNR GOOD HOPE AND ROBERTS AVENUES)
This well-known school occupied the present building in January 1911. The double-storey stone main building, with Edwardian and neoclassical elements, was designed by J Ralston. The War Memorial pavilion was unveiled by General JC Smuts on 14 November 1926. The entrance gates to the main building, erected in 1941, are known as the AS Dashwood Gate and the FWB von Linsingen Gate, in memory of two teachers who died in the Second World War.

LION HOUSE (20 ROBERTS AVENUE)
Designed by G McEwan and built in 1909 for G Wollacott, a master plasterer, the house's walls and fireplaces exhibit Wollacott's exceptional art as a plasterer.

SCOTT HOUSE (59 KING EDWARD STREET)
Constructed almost entirely from concrete and considered to be one of the first concrete houses built in South Africa, the house was designed and built by a Mr Scott in 1926 in the Arts and Crafts style. The architect saw the use of building materials not solely as structural, but also as an art form. Various textures and colours are achieved by the mixing of different pebbles, sand and gravel of varying sizes and colours to create unique colours and shapes.

Langlaagte
The suburb was named after the farm Langlaagte, on which George Harrison discovered the Witwatersrand gold reef in 1886.

LANGLAAGTE DEEP VILLAGE (CROWN MINES)
This village was developed in 1903–1904 after the establishment of Langlaagte Deep Limited, and is the oldest mining village in Johannesburg. Thirty-five houses of the Cornish miners' married quarters have been preserved; the majority of the houses are semi-detached and are built of semi-sundried brick-and-iron cladding with corrugated-iron roofs.

OUTCROP OF MAIN REEF GROUP OF CONGLOMERATES (MAIN REEF ROAD)
The main reef was discovered by George Harrison and George Walker in 1886 on the farm Langlaagte, which belonged to CG Oosthuizen. Oosthuizen gave them claims 19 and 21 on 12 April 1886. Shortly thereafter, between 20 September and 11 October 1886, other farms were proclaimed public diggings: Doornfontein, Driefontein, Elandsfontein, Paardekraal, Randjeslaagte, Roodepoort, Turffontein, and Vogelstruisfontein After the discovery, prospecting took place over a distance of 29km. The first stamp battery was erected in April 1887. The most important mining properties were purchased in the second half of 1886 and the first half of 1887.

Melville
Laid out on the farm Braamfontein, the suburb was named after the surveyor, Edward Harker Vincent Melville.

MELVILLE KOPPIES NATURE RESERVE
(JUDITH ROAD)
The Nature Reserve possesses beautiful scenery, as well as interesting fauna and flora and important archaeological remains. An Iron Age village was discovered here and the remains of an iron-ore smelting furnace (used for making iron for assegais), the remains of a kraal, the foundations of a hut, and kraals for cattle as well as a grain pit, can be seen.

Milner Park
The suburb was named after Lord Alfred Milner (1854–1925), Governor of the Transvaal from 1901–1905. The land was given to the Johannesburg Town Council by the Transvaal Government in 1903.

UNIVERSITY OF THE WITWATERSRAND (JAN SMUTS AVENUE)

The site includes the façade of the main building known as the Central Block. The joint architects were F Emley and Messrs Cowin & Ellis, and the builder was J Barrow, all awarded the contract for the central block, of which only the northern wing was built at the time. The foundation stone was laid by HRH Prince Arthur of Connaught on 4 October 1922, and the building was officially opened by HRH the Prince of Wales in June 1925. In December 1931 a fire gutted the entire entrance hall and the library. The damage was repaired, with Messrs Williamson & Cowin as associate architects, and Professor GE Pearse as the consulting architect. The building altered considerably from the original 1920 plan and was completed in 1940.

Newtown

Situated on the farm Braamfontein, in 1904 the area was burned down to eradicate the bubonic plague, and then rebuilt, hence its name.

COMPOUNDS AND WORKERS COTTAGES (NEWTOWN ELECTRICAL SITE)

The labour system used on South African mines led to the development of a compound system for black workers. The Newtown Compound is a U-shaped single-storey building with a courtyard and accommodation for 312 workers. Designed on the Rand Mines prototype, it was probably erected in the 1920s. There are two well-proportioned, brick Workers Cottages with corrugated-iron roofs, and influences from the Arts and Crafts movement.

Parktown

The suburb was laid out in 1902 and was home to many of the area's mining magnates. Many of these beautiful homes and architectural treasures can still be seen today.

DOLOBRAN HOUSE (16 VICTORIA AVENUE)

This house, known as Dolobran, was designed for Sir Charles Llewellyn Andersson by the firm JA Cope & Christie, and was completed in 1906. It is exceptionally eclectic in style, making an important contribution to the unique architectural character of Parktown.

DYSART HOUSE (6 SHERBORNE ROAD)

Designed by Herbert Baker, the house was erected by the contractors GW Kelly & Barrow in 1911. An excellent example of an Arts and Craft style villa, Dysart House was named by Dr JC McNab, who owned it from 1918 until 1934, and commissioned the double-storey addition on the western side.

EMOYENI HOUSE (15 JUBILEE ROAD)

This house was designed by the pioneering firm of Johannesburg architects, Leck & Emley, and was completed in 1906 for HC Hull, later the first Minister of Finance in the Union Parliament. It was designed in the neo-Queen Anne style and is one of the most outstanding examples of the elegant houses that were erected in Parktown just after the turn of the nineteenth century. As such, it makes an important contribution to Parktown's unique architectural character.

GUILD COTTAGE (GUILD ROAD)

The Guild of Loyal Women of South Africa was established during the Anglo-Boer War (1899–1902), to bring together women of Dutch and English descent. At the end of the war, these women embarked on special projects, such as the Johannesburg branch's Home for Destitute Women and Children in Eloff Street.

The property in Guild Road was later purchased and a building designed by architect J Hicks, and built by JH Sprott. The foundation stone was laid on 16 August 1907 by Lady Selborne, wife of the Governor-General of the Transvaal, and the home was formally opened on 17 December 1907. In 1982 a Roman Catholic group, The Knights of Da Gama, intervened to prevent the closure of this organisation. The Presbyterian Church took over ownership of the property in 1983 and Guild Cottage is now a home for the treatment of sexually abused children.

HAZELDENE HALL MANOR HOUSE
(ROCK RIDGE ROAD)
Built in 1903 for Charles Jerome and designed by Charles Aburrow and Philip Treeby, the house's plans were selected from a catalogue of Walter MacFarlane of Glasgow, Scotland. Oak floorboards were imported from Belgium, while the pressed ceilings came from America and the Adam fireplace from England.

NORTH LODGE (JUNCTION OF VICTORIA ROAD, TREMATON PLACE AND BLACKWOOD AVENUE)
Completed in 1906 for HS Wilson, the lodge was designed by architect Herbert J Aldwyncle, who attempted to imitate a French castle from the late Gothic period. The result was the most architecturally romantic house in Parktown. It makes an important contribution to Parktown's unique architectural character.

NORTHWARDS HOUSE
(CNR ROCKRIDGE AND OXFORD ROADS)
This mansion was designed in 1904 by Sir Herbert Baker. It is constructed of dressed mountain stone and brick and, from a town planning point of view, forms an essential part of Parktown.

PARKTOWN BOYS' HIGH SCHOOL
(WELLINGTON ROAD)
Established in 1920, the school moved to its present site in 1922 and opened in 1923. The original main building was built by the Public Works Department of the Zuid-Afrikaansche Republiek at the time of the Milner Schools.

PILRIG HOUSE (1 ROCKRIDGE ROAD)
Designed by Herbert Baker for the lawyer AE Balfour, the house was built in 1903 by pioneer master builder John Barrow. It demonstrates Baker's use of local materials and hand-crafted finishes, and also meets Milner's desire to introduce 'a better and more permanent order of architecture'.

RANDJESLAAGTE BEACON (BOUNDARY ROAD)
With the original granting of the farms Turffontein, Doornfontein, Braamfontein and Langlaagte on the Witwatersrand, a three-cornered piece of state-owned land remained and was named Randjeslaagte. This beacon marks the northern boundary of the farm and the base of the triangle formed the present Commissioner Street, where it joins Diagonal Street in the west and End Street in the east. The adjoining farmers grazed their cattle on this piece of ground until gold was discovered in 1886 and the piece of land then became the heart of Johannesburg.

A commission consisting of Christiaan Johannes Joubert and Johann Friedrich Bernhard Rissik was formed by the Zuid-Afrikaansche Republiek to lay out the plots and streets. The city was named Johannesburg after the aforementioned commissioners.

ST MARGARET'S HOUSE (3 ROCKRIDGE ROAD)
This mansion was designed in 1904 by Sir Herbert Baker. In 1930 and 1937 further additions were made, which were designed by Baker's former partner, FLH Fleming. The house, which is built of dressed mountain stone, is situated in a spacious garden and forms an essential part of the urban planning that gives Parktown its character.

STONE HOUSE (5 ROCK RIDGE ROAD)
This house, which Sir Herbert Baker designed for himself in 1902, contributes to Parktown's

exceptional architectural character. The fine craftsmanship, as well as the use of natural building materials, render it a splendid expression of the Arts and Crafts architectural trend in South Africa.

SUNNYSIDE PARK (2 YORK ROAD)

This building was designed by Frank Emley in 1895 in the neo-Queen Anne style, for the American mining engineer, H Jennings, employed at Rand Mines. During the Anglo-Boer War, Lord Milner moved into Sunnyside Park and retained it as his official residence until he left. His successor, Lord Selborne, only used Sunnyside Park in the summer months, as he had moved the official High Commissioner's residence to Pretoria.

THE PINES HOUSE (9 GORDON HILL ROAD)

This building was designed by JC Watson and completed in 1906 for the firm Fraser & Chalmers Limited, to accommodate its General Manager, WE Park. Architecturally, the house is a good example of a Johannesburg Edwardian edifice. Its unique design displays uninhibited confidence, featuring many bold and violent contrasts. It makes an important contribution to the architectural character of Parktown.

'THE VIEW' HOMESTEAD (11 JUNCTION AVENUE)

Designed by the architect Aburrow and built in 1897 by Thomas Cullinan, a master builder, as his own home, this house remained the family home until the death of Lady Cullinan in 1963.

Randburg

Proclaimed in 1959, Randburg was named after the Witwatersrand.

WINDMILL AND ADJACENT SUNKEN GARDEN (22 PATRICK STREET, OLIVEDALE EXT 2)

Built from a magazine picture by Italian prisoners of war, the windmill was presumably one of the few working windmills in the Transvaal as it channelled water through irrigation furrows. The sunken garden next to the windmill was built by the same prisoners.

Richmond

This suburb was laid out on the farm Braamfontein in 1896.

HOUSE (33 LANDAU TERRACE)

An impressive wood and iron dwelling, unlike the usual houses in Johannesburg in the early days, this house was not a prefabricated building, and was designed by the architect Herbert A Goodman in 1903 for the firm Kühler Henderson & Co. Erected shortly after the turn of the nineteenth century, the first occupant was Mr Gau, then H Coetze (1909–1914), followed by a member of the horse artillery, EJ McSweeney. F Kühler bought the house in 1924 and lived there until 1948.

Saxonwold

Laid out and proclaimed in 1925, Saxonwold was named after Sachsenwald, Germany (Saxon Forest). The name also originates from the pine and gum trees planted here in the 1890s by Eduard Lippert from Sachsenwald, on the Eckstein Mining Group property.

VILLA D'ESTE MANOR HOUSE (82 JAN SMUTS AVENUE)

Designed by the South African architect Gordon Leith and built in 1923, this house was first owned by a Mr East. It is thought that Leith was inspired by the pavilions designed by Pellegrini of the Villa D'Este at Cernobbio on Lake Como, Italy.

Selby

The suburb was established on the farm Turffontein in 1928, on the property of Old Village Main and Ferreira Gold Mines. It was named after Paul Selby, manager of the Robinson Gold Mine (1877–1940), and later manager of Ferreira Deep Mine (1926–1927).

OLD CROWN MINES HEAD OFFICE BUILDING COMPLEX (5 PRESS AVENUE)
The site consists of the RMP Head Office Building, the adjacent Records Office, the Assay Personnel Office, the Assay Conference Hall and Office, and the old chimney situated nearby. Designed by Herbert Baker, the complex was built in 1909 after the amalgamation of eight mining companies, when Crown Mines was founded. In 1977 Crown Mines ceased operations and Rand Mines Properties Limited adapted the building as its head office in 1978.

Sophiatown

The suburb was laid out on the farm Waterval in 1903 by H Tobiansky and named after his wife, Sophia. Sophiatown was a black township until 1955, when the inhabitants were forcibly moved to Meadowlands and other new townships, in terms of the Group Areas Act. It was rezoned for whites and renamed Triomf. More recently the name Sophiatown has been readopted.

BELL TOWER OF CHRIST THE KING ANGLICAN CHURCH (RAY STREET)
Designed by the architect FLH Fleming, Christ The King church was consecrated by Bishop Clayton on 8 September 1935 and its distinctive bell tower has been a landmark ever since. This church is closely associated with the Black Liberation Movement of the 1950s and the history of Sophiatown, in which Father Trevor Huddleston (later Bishop) played a significant role. After Sophiatown was rezoned as Triomf, the building was taken over by a Pentecostal church body, but was restored to the Anglican diocese of Johannesburg in recent times.

HOUSE OF DR AB XUMA (73 TOBY ROAD)
The property was formerly known as the house of Dr Alfred Bitini Xuma, who was born in the Transkei c.1893 and died in Soweto in 1962. He was elected Vice-President at the Bloemfontein founding conference of the All African Convention on 16 December 1935, and was also President-General of the African National Congress from 1940 to 1949.

ST JOSEPH'S HOME FOR CHILDREN
(CNR GOOD AND HERMANS STREETS)
All three buildings were designed by the Diocesan architect, FLH Fleming. The first stone of the Boys' House was laid in October 1922 and the home was opened in June 1923. Originally known as St Joseph's Home for Coloured Children, it was founded as The Diocesan Memorial to the coloured men of the Transvaal who made the supreme sacrifice in the (1914–1918) war as part of the 1st Cape Corps which serviced in East Africa and Palestine.

Soweto

Laid out on the farms Diepkloof, Doornkop, Klipriviersoog, Klipspruit and Vogelstruisfontein, this township is made up of 26 separate satellite cities. The name is derived from South Western Townships.

MANDELA HOUSE
(NGAKANE STREET, ORLANDO EAST)
This was the former home of past President Nelson Mandela. Mandela was born on 18 July 1918 into the Royal House of the Tembu, in what was then the Transkei. He spent two years at Fort Hare studying law before he was expelled for his part in a student protest.

He then went to Johannesburg and at first studied law by correspondence and then at the University of the Witwatersrand. In 1952 Mandela worked with Oliver Tambo in a legal practice in Johannesburg. He left the country in

1962 and began preparation for guerrilla warfare, undergoing a course in Algeria. He returned to South Africa on 20 July of that year, and was arrested on 5 August.

It was during his marriage to Nomzamo Winifred Madikizela in 1958, until the Rivonia Trials of 1964 (interspersed with periods spent underground), that Mandela lived in this house in Orlando East, which has since become a museum.

Troyeville

Laid out on the farm Doornfontein in 1891, the suburb was named after the surveyor, GA Troye (1860–1930).

GHANDI HOUSE (19A ABLEMARLE STREET)

The site is the house of Mohandas Karamchand Ghandi (1869–1948), better known as 'Mahatma' (Great Soul). Mahatma came to South Africa in 1893 to handle the legal affairs of an Indian-based trading company.

At this time the Natal Government was introducing laws that would affect the Indian community, which led him to remain in Natal to lead the political struggle. He founded the Natal Indian Congress in 1894, and developed his philosophy of passive resistance (satyagraha). In 1914 Mahatma and General Jannie Smuts reached agreement on Indian rights in South Africa, which led to the Indian Relief Act of that year. After this he returned to India and spent 30 years in opposition to British rule, and led India to full independence.

JOHANNESBURG EAST GEREFORMEERDE CONGREGATION CHURCH HALL (PRINCESS STREET)

The cornerstone of this hall, designed by G Fleming with neogothic elements, was laid in October 1898 by FW Reitz, State Secretary of the Zuid-Afrikaansche Republiek and former State President of the Orange Free State. The building was inaugurated on 11 December 1898. In 1920, the Malvern Afrikaans Medium School was opened here and church services were also held. By 1923 it was bought by the congregation and used as a place of worship until 1950.

Waverley

Waverley was laid out on the farm Syferfontein in 1903.

WAVERLEY HOUSE (5 MURRAY STREET)

This Victorian double-storey, free-style house was designed by the architect JA Cope-Christie and built in 1904 for Arthur E Page, owner of the Flower Foundation Clubs.

Westcliff

Named for its rocky, hilly aspect, Westcliff adjoins Parktown and like the latter, was laid out for the well-heeled.

GLENSHIEL HOUSE (WOOLSTON ROAD)

This imposing building was designed by Sir Herbert Baker and his partner, Fleming. It was built between 1909 and 1910 for Lieutenant-Colonel William Dalrimple (later Sir William). Glenshiel is known as one of Sir Herbert Baker's larger houses. The original stables were later converted into a separate dwelling.

Yeoville

The suburb was established in 1892 and named after Thomas Yeo Sherwell (1851–1924), the manager of City Deep Gold Mines and also the township owner.

HOUSE HAINS (34 BECKER STREET)

Designed by the architect JA Cope-Christie, the house was built in 1903–1904 for Henry Hains, an auditor accountant who came to the Rand in 1888.

KEMPTON PARK

Founded on the farm Zuurfontein in 1903, this town was named by the owner of the farm, Karl F Wolff, who originated from Kempten, Germany. It acquired municipal status in 1942.

HISTORIC BUILDINGS OF ESSELEN PARK TRAINING CENTRE COMPLEX (FARM WITFONTEIN, DISTRICT)
The site consists of the main Administration Building, Railwayman's Inn, 'Murasie' (between the aforementioned buildings), the Shop, Coach and Rail Restaurant, the main Restaurant and kitchen, Sportman's Bar, Sports School of Excellence, Port Captain's Lodge and the old Park Station.

The foundation stone was laid on 10 December 1943 by FC Sturrock, then Minister of Railways & Harbours. It was named after a former commissioner, Louis Esselen. The first group of trainees enrolled on a course on 14 August 1947.

KRUGERSDORP

Krugersdorp was laid out on the farm Paardekraal in 1887, and was named after Stephanus Johannes Paulus Kruger (1825–1904), President of the Transvaal from 1883 to 1900. It attained municipal status in 1903.

BLOCKHOUSE (HEKPOORT)
The blockhouse was built in 1901, during the Anglo-Boer War (1899–1902), by Major-General G Barton.

BLOCKHOUSE (VOORTREKKER SQUARE, (MONUMENT TOWNSHIP)
This stone blockhouse, with its own distinctive design, was also erected by the British occupying forces during the Anglo-Boer War (1899-1902). These blockhouses were built as a defence counter to the operations of the burgher forces, in and outside the two Boer republics, both of which had already been annexed.

ISAAC EDWIN STEGMANN NATURE RESERVE (DISTRICT)
This site includes the Sterkfontein Caves – a World Heritage Site. The Sterkfontein hominid fossil site, also known as the Cradle of Humankind, comprise some of the most valuable evidence about the origin of humans, underpinning the claim that Africa is the origin of humankind.

In 1947, the discovery by Dr Robert Broom of the skull of 'Mrs Ples' (*Plesianthropus transvalensis*) created a worldwide sensation. It was the first complete skull of *Australopithecus*, a distant relative of modern *Homo sapiens*, who lived on the Highveld more than 2,5 million years ago. In 1994 the 'Little Foot' bones from a 3,3 million-year-old hominid were discovered, and in 1998 a discovery was made of the almost complete skeleton and skull of an 'ape-man'.

OLD NZASM STATION BUILDING (GEORGE NORTON STREET)
This Railway Station Building with its richly decorated gable was completed in 1896 for the Nederlandsche Zuid-Afrikaansche Spoorweg-Maatschappij (NZASM). It is one of only a few elegant railway station buildings erected for the NZASM.

PAARDEKRAAL MONUMENT (MARKET STREET)
Designed by Sytze Wierda and built by WY Veitch, this monument was completed on 27 November 1890. It was unveiled on 16 December 1891 by President Paul Kruger and commemorates the hoisting of the Republican flag, which signalled the start of the First War of Independence (1880–1881).

PALAEONTOLOGICAL SITE WITH THE ZWARTKRANS CAVE (DISTRICT)

This cave is well-known for its early hominid remains. Fossils were first discovered here in 1948 by Dr R Broom and Dr JT Robinson of the Transvaal Museum. Since then numerous individuals *australopithecine* (*Paranthrohus* or *Australopithecus robustsus*) have been found, together with sparse remains of *Homo* species, formerly known as *Telanthropus capensis*. Zwartkrans is thus the only known cave site where two hominid species occur together. The age of the Zwartkrans fossils is unknown but, by comparing the fauna and stone structure with dated equivalents in East Africa, correlation with Bed II at Olduvai is suggested. The date may therefore be between 1,7 and one million years.

TOWN HALL (COMMISSIONER STREET)

The foundation stone was laid in 1907 by the Earl of Selborne, High Commissioner of South Africa and Governor of the Transvaal and Orange River Colonies. The building was opened in 1908 by General JC Smuts, Colonial Secretary of the Transvaal.

OBERHOLZER

Laid out on the farm Wonderfontein No. 65, the town was named after the owner, Hendrik Oberholzer. It was proclaimed in 1939.

IRON AGE REMAINS (GATSRAND)

This area contains important subterranean and surface remains of the Iron Age, and is of great ethnological value.

PRETORIA

The city of Pretoria was founded on the farm Elandspoort in 1855 and was named after the Voortrekker leader Andries Wilhelmus Jacobus Pretorius (1798–1853). It was also known as Pretoria Philadelphia, Pretorium and Pretoriusdorp. Pretoria attained city status in 1931.

ANTON VAN WOUW HOUSE
(299 CLARK STREET, BROOKLYN)

The sculptor Anton van Wouw was born in Driebergen, Netherlands in 1862 and died in Pretoria in 1945. He settled in Pretoria in 1890, and was commissioned by Sammy Marks to create a monumental statue of Paul Kruger, which now stands in Church Square, Pretoria.

ASIATIC BAZAAR WITH MARIAMMEN TEMPLE
(SIXTH STREET)

The Mariammen temple is the oldest existing Hindu temple in Pretoria. This imposing 'gopuram' (lord Ram temple) was erected in 1939 and is believed to be the largest of its kind in South Africa.

AUSTIN ROBERTS BIRD SANCTUARY
(BOSHOFF STREET, NEW MUCKLENEUK)

This unique sanctuary, where over 170 different species of birds have already been recorded, provides a protected roosting place and breeding ground for thousands of birds within the city of Pretoria. It is also an attractive green area within the built-up suburb of New Muckleneuk. Austin Roberts (1883–1948) joined the staff of the Transvaal Museum in 1910, where he remained in charge of the bird and mammal collection until his death. He was the author of over 120 scientific papers and articles, and of the two standard works, *The Birds of South Africa* (1940) and posthumously, *The Mammals of South Africa* (1951).

BARTON KEEP DWELLING (JACOB MARÉ STREET)

According to V Allen, this Victorian dwelling was erected in 1888. The original owner was EF Bourke, later the first Mayor of Pretoria. Barton

Keep is one of two remaining examples of the elegant houses that characterised this part of Maré Street during the late nineteenth century.

BURGERS PARK (JACOB MARÉ STREET)
This park, the history of which can be traced back to 1874, is the oldest park in Pretoria and forms an important green lung in the centre of the city. It was laid out around 1890 and, with its wrought-iron bandstand, caretaker's cottage, kiosk and the nearby Melrose House, it forms an important Victorian unit in Pretoria.

CAFÉ RICHE BUILDING (CHURCH SQUARE)
Designed by the architect Frans Saff and built in the Art Nouveau style, this was the first building in Pretoria with sculptures, executed by Anton von Wouw in collaboration with Frans Saff. The main character sculptures are an owl on the top gable and a relief of the Roman god Mercury, the 'messenger of the gods'.

Situated on a corner plot north of the Law Chambers and near the shopping complex of Lohner, a watchmaker, it became the Post Office Bar in 1889, run by EH Clarke. Thereafter it went through a series of business changes. In 1905 it was demolished and the Reserve Investment Building was built with the Café Riche on the ground floor.

DEFENCE HEADQUARTERS
(1–15 ARTILLERY STREET)
These 15 historic houses were built during the 1890s by the government of the old Zuid-Afrikaansche Republiek as homes for officers and non-commissioned officers of the Staatsartillerie. The houses form a unique architectural and military history complex.

'DIE VESTING' AND BLOCKHOUSE
(VOORTREKKERHOOGTE)
'Die Vesting' is one of the largest wood-and-iron houses remaining in Voortrekkerhoogte, and was erected by the British military authorities shortly after the Anglo-Boer War (1899–1902). Since the beginning of the twentieth century it has accommodated several high-ranking defence force officers, including the famous Sir Pierre van Ryneveld. The nearby blockhouse possibly dates from the Anglo-Boer War and is one of the few remaining examples of a wood-and-iron blockhouse.

DUTCH REFORMED CHURCH
(CNR KIRKNESS AND DELY STREETS, SUNNYSIDE)
The architect Gerard Moerdijk was contracted to design plans for a building of which the façade would be similar to most of the churches already built by various other congregations. The builder was J Coenen. The cornerstone was laid on 30 April 1927 and the church was taken into use in 1928. Of particular historic interest is the church bell, with the words 'Anna Domini 1887, Gloria in Exelsis Deo', inscribed. Manufactured by F Otto Hemelingen, near Hamburg, Germany, it is the same bell that was on the old church on Church Square, completed in 1888. Designed in neoclassical style with a Byzantine interior, this Moerdijk church is one of his most beautiful.

DWELLING (115 CHARLES STREET, BROOKLYN)
This impressive manor house is an excellent example of the early architecture of Brooklyn, and was one of the first houses to be erected in the area. It combines Georgian and Art Nouveau building styles, featuring lead-glass windows, copper door plates and wooden fireplaces with mother-of-pearl marquetry.

ERASMUS CASTLE (ERASMUSRAND)
Although it is uncertain who the fist owner was, documentary evidence exists that Carel Jacobus Erasmus, son of Daniel Jacobus Erasmus of the farm Doornkloof, settled at Garsfontein in 1860. According to legend,

Carel Erasmus traded the farm for a pair of corduroy trousers and a 'fresh' horse. He built a 'hartbeeshuis', and later a typical farmhouse based on early Transvaal farmhouse styles. In 1903 his son Jochemus built Erasmus Castle. The architect was a Hollander, Van der Benn, and the builder an Italian, G Montbello. A harmonious composition of neogothic, Edwardian and Art Nouveau architecture, it is thought to be the only castle-like building erected on a Boer farm at the beginning of the last century.

FAÇADES OF MAIN BUILDING AND WARDS A, 2B, C, D, 2A AND B OF WESKOPPIES HOSPITAL (KETJEN STREET)

This complex of seven Edwardian buildings (construction of the oldest commenced in 1904 and was completed in 1907) forms an orderly and imposing group in a tree-filled setting. Weskoppies Hospital is the oldest psychiatric hospital in the old Transvaal; it admitted the first patient in 1892 and is today the largest hospital -of its kind in South Africa.

GENERAL SMUTS HOUSE (DOORNKLOOF, IRENE)

In 1908 General Smuts built this house known as the Big House. The wood-and-iron building is of historical interest as it was originally an officers' mess at Lord Kitchener's headquarters at Middelburg (Transvaal). Over the years, rooms were added and verandahs enclosed. It is a large house with 11 bedrooms. As Field Marshall, the Right Honourable Jan Christiaan Smuts, second Prime Minister of the Union of South Africa and a prominent figure in world affairs, lived in this house for a considerable part of his adult life. It was the only permanent home he knew after he left his father's farm.

GEREFORMEERDE CHURCH – PAUL KRUGER CHURCH (CHURCH STREET WEST)

The cornerstone of this church building, which was designed in the style of the seventeenth century Dutch Renaissance, was laid on 10 October 1896 by State President SJP Kruger. On Christmas day 1897, the building was taken into use with an inaugural speech by Professor J Lion-Cachet. As a member of the parish, President Kruger visited the church regularly.

GROOTKERK (BOSMAN STREET)

The cornerstone of this building – designed by Klaas van Rijsse, Kraan & Weijers in Dutch Renaissance style – was laid by General Louis Botha on 11 May 1903. The church was inaugurated on 30 September 1904 when Reverend Andrew Murray delivered the first sermon. Several historic events have taken place here, including the swearing in of Advocate CR Swart as the first State President of the Republic of South Africa in 1961.

HAMILTON PRIMARY SCHOOL (CNR VISAGIE AND PRINSLOO STREETS)

This historic school building was completed in 1899 as the home of the Staatsmeisieskool. In 1902 the High School for Girls was opened in the building and in 1930 it became the present Hamilton Primary School.

HISTORIC OLD CORRUGATED-IRON HOUSE AND ADJACENT OUTBUILDING (17 BEN VILJOEN ROAD, VOORTREKKERHOOGTE)

When Lord Kitchener took over the British High Command from Lord Roberts, he had his head office in India dismantled and shipped to South Africa. In 1921 the building was taken over by the Union Government and it served as a lieutenants' and captains' mess. In 1924 it was enlarged and used as a home for senior officers.

HISTORIC MAIN BUILDING (SOUTH AFRICAN ARMY COLLEGE, VOORTREKKERHOOGTE)

The cornerstone of the South African Army College, which was designed in the so-called Blockhouse style, was laid by Lord Kitchener on 12 June 1902. It was the first permanent building in Roberts Heights (now Voortrekkerhoogte) and served as a recreation centre for soldiers. When the South African Military School, forerunner of the present-day South African Army College, was founded in 1920, it was accommodated in this building.

HOMESTEAD
(1225 FELIX STREET, MOUNTAIN VIEW)
This Victorian house, built of red clay bricks, was probably built in about 1902. The extension of Mountain View, on which the homestead is situated, was formerly known as Selborne Park, as Lord and Lady Selborne lived here until 1910 during his term of office as High Commissioner in South Africa and Governor of the Transvaal and Orange River Colony. When the Union came into being, he was succeeded by Lord Gladstone.

KLAPPERKOP FORT (FARM GROENKLOOF)
Klapperkop Fort was built in 1897 to protect the southern approach to Pretoria against surprise attacks from hostile elements on the gold fields of the Witwatersrand. Building was expedited as a result of the Jameson Raid and completed in January 1898. During World War II and until 1950 it was used for storing ammunition.

KIRKNESS HOUSE
(225 POMONA STREET, MUCKLENEUK)
The house was built by John Johnston Kirkness, who came to South Africa at the age of 22 years in 1879. He was born on the Orkney Islands and died at age 82 on 13 June 1939 in Pretoria.

KRUGER CHAIRS
(IN PAUL KRUGER GEREFORMEERDE CHURCH, CHURCH STREET WEST)
According to tradition, these chairs were used during church services by President SJP Kruger and his wife Gezina. The chairs are symbolic of Kruger's religious devotion and an intimate reminder of the influence that his Christian principles had on the Government of the Zuid-Afrikaansche Republiek.

LAERSKOOL OOS-EIND
(70 MEINTJIES STREET, TREVENNA)
Founded in 1897, the Laerskool Oosteind is the oldest existing school in Pretoria. After the Anglo-Boer War (1899–1902) it became one of the leading CNE schools in the old Transvaal. Occupied in January 1901, the original section of the present school was probably designed by Kraan & Weijers, and erected by GJ Dorlas.

LANDING SITE OF THE *VOORTREKKER*
(EXPERIMENTAL FARM OF THE UNIVERSITY OF PRETORIA)
This site was part of the old Koedoospoort aerodrome where Lieutenant Colonel Pierre van Ryneveld and Flight Lieutenant Quinton Brand landed for the first time in the Union of South Africa, on 17 March 1920, during their epic flight of 46 days from London to Cape Town. They were the first people to fly from London to Cape Town and the last leg of the flight was completed in the aircraft named *Voortrekker*. Both Van Ryneveld and Brand were knighted for their contributions to aviation.

LAW CHAMBERS (CHURCH SQUARE)
Designed by Philip Carmichael & Murray for the African Board of Executors, this is the second oldest building on Church Square. Construction began in 1890 and the foundation stone was laid by Commandant-General Piet Joubert. As the building was later used by lawyers, it acquired the name Law Chambers.

LIBERTAS MANOR HOUSE (BRYNTIRION)
This was the official residence of the Prime Ministers of South Africa. The architect was Gerard Moerdijk and it was completed in 1940

at a cost of 68 000 Pounds Sterling. Built in the old Cape Dutch style, it was named after Libertas, near Stellenbosch, by Issie Smuts, wife of General JC Smuts, then Prime Minister of the Union of South Africa. Issie was born at Klein Libertas in Stellenbosch.

LION BRIDGE (CHURCH STREET EAST, ARCADIA)
Lion bridge was designed by the Department of Public Works of the Zuid-Afrikaansche Republiek under the leadership of Sytze Wierda. It was built by JJ Kirkness, and officially opened by President SJP Kruger on 11 June 1894. It is the oldest existing bridge over the Apies River and the only remaining bridge in the centre of Pretoria dating from the days of the ZAR.

MANALA SITE (WONDERBOOM)
Known as 'Komjekejeke', the site was home to Captain Silamba, one of the most important Ndebele chiefs. He received the ground shortly after the Wallmannsthal Mission was established in 1873, from Reverend Knothe, a missionary with the Berlin Missionary Society. Given to Silamba and the Manala (Manala-Ndebele) tribe, the kraals and stone walls are mostly ruins, used as an open-air museum.

MEA VOTA HOUSE (RISSIK STREET, SUNNYSIDE)
A Westernberg and C van der Made, engineers employed by the Nederlandsche Zuid-Afrikaansche Spoorweg-Maatschappij, built this imposing Victorian residence around 1899 for their own occupation. It is one of the last remaining examples of the mansions that characterised this part of Pretoria in the 1890s.

MELROSE HOUSE (JACOB MARÉ STREET)
This is a good example of a Victorian manor house. The Treaty of Vereeniging was signed in its dining-room on 31 May 1902, bringing the Anglo-Boer War to an end.

MODEL SCHOOL
(CNR SKINNER AND VAN DER WALT STREETS)
In accordance with the education policy of the Zuid-Afrikaansche Republiek, the establishment of schools was, generally, left to parents, but would be subsidised by the government. As an exception, a few schools, of which the Staats Model School is one, were established by the government. It opened in 1893, but was only properly housed in this building in 1897.

MOERDIJK DWELLING
(274 POMONA STREET, MUCKLENEUK)
Gerard Moerdijk (1890–1958), the well-known Dutch-born architect, moved to Pretoria in 1924 and designed this house for his own use. He lived here from 1925 until 1950. It is of exceptional architectural importance as Moerdijk used it to demonstrate various construction and detail techniques.

The house is built from stone hewn from the environment, to which Moerdijk added a number of different wood types in order to achieve various effects. Every room displays a different patterning of the wooden floor blocks. An outstanding feature of the house is its entrance hall that boasts a large escalator handmade from solid Rhodesian teak. The house is designed to be symmetrically sympathetic to the Union Buildings.

NATIONAL CULTURAL HISTORY AND OPEN-AIR MUSEUM (BOOM STREET)
The cornerstone of this museum was laid on 22 July 1899 by Dr Mansfield, Director of Education. It was completed in 1902 and officially opened by the Lieutenant-Governor Sir Richard Solomon on 15 December 1904. The building comprises 16 exhibition halls, which contain a remarkable collection of historic and cultural objects connected with South Africa's history.

NEDERDUITSE-HERVORMDE CHURCH BUILDING (DU TOIT STREET)

The cornerstone of this Dutch-Renaissance-style church was laid on 18 July 1904 by General Louis Botha, and the building was taken into use on 24 February 1905. It is the oldest Nederduitse-Hervormde church building in Pretoria and its history is closely interwoven with the history of the development of the Afrikaans sister churches in the Transvaal.

NZASM RAILWAY LOCOMOTIVE AND COACH (PRETORIA STATION)

NZASM Locomotive No 242 was made in 1897 by the Nederlandsche Fabriek vir de Nederlandsche Zuid-Afrikaansche Spoorweg-Maatschappij. Private Coach No 18 was built by JJ Beijnes of Haarlem in 1897 and was used by GAA Middelburg, Director of NZASM. Both the locomotive and the private coach are important links in the history of the South African railways.

OLD AGRICULTURAL PUBLICATIONS BUILDING (VERMEULEN STREET)

This building was erected by EP Grant in about 1904 to accommodate his general merchants business. The eclectic façade, comprising several classical elements, is unique in the centre of Pretoria.

OLD ARTS BUILDING (UNIVERSITY OF PRETORIA)

The old Arts Building is architecturally noteworthy. Two foundation stones were laid on 3 August 1910 by Viscount Gladstone. The contractor was JJ Kirkness and the building was completed in 1911.

OLD GOVERNMENT BUILDINGS RAADSAAL (CHURCH SQUARE)

Completed in 1892, this old government building housed the Volksraadsaal of the Zuid-Afrikaansche Republiek.

OLD MAIN BUILDING VETERINARY RESEARCH INSTITUTE (ONDERSTEPOORT)

This building was designed by the Transvaal Colony's Department of Public Works and was completed in 1908 as the centre of the then bacteriological laboratory at Onderstepoort. Today it is the historic core of what is regarded as one of the largest and most important veterinary institutes in the world. It is also a living monument to Sir Arnold Theiler, pioneer in the field of veterinary research, and a famous veterinarian of this time.

OLD MERENSKY LIBRARY BUILDING (LYNNWOOD ROAD, UNIVERSITY OF PRETORIA)

Since 1920 there had been attempts to establish a library building at the University of Pretoria. After a donation of 500 Pounds Sterling per annum for a period of five years was received from the renowned mining geologist, Dr Hans Merensky, construction began in 1937 on the Merensky Library.

The cornerstone was laid by General JC Smuts on 11 October 1937 and the building was officially opened on 15 April 1939 by the then Minister of Education, Advocate HA Fagan. Inspired by his impressions during a trip to the Middle East and Egypt, Gerard Moerdijk drew up plans, which he himself described as 'Persian with Afrikaans motifs'. Many criticised it as a forerunner for Moerdijk's Voortrekker Monument. The building served as a library until 1975.

OLD NATIVE RECEPTION DEPOT (PROES STREET)

Built in the 1920s by the Public Works Department of the Union Government, this building was intended to house black labourers who sought employment on the mines of the Witwatersrand, and to provide them with washing, cooking and sanitary facilities. These reception depots ultimately proved a financial burden on the state.

OLD NEDERLANDSCHE BANK (CHURCH SQUARE)
In 1888 the Nederlandsche Bank and Credit Corporation was established in the Netherlands, and a branch was opened to accommodate the interests of Dutch people in South Africa. The first building was erected on the northwest corner of Church and Andries Streets, but after a few years a new building was built on the southwest corner of Church Square. The new building was designed by the architect Willem de Zwaan and is built of redbrick and sandstone, and shows a definite Netherlands style. It was put into use on 2 December 1897. In 1903 the name was changed to Netherlands Bank and Credit Association of South Africa (today Nedbank).

OLD NZASM GOODS OFFICES (RAILWAY STREET)
The Nederlandsche Zuid-Afrikaansche Spoorweg-Maatschappij probably erected this building in 1896. It is the largest and best remaining example of the NZASM buildings in Pretoria.

OLD PRETORIA IRON MINES LIMITED (ISCOR)
The site includes the boiler and blower house of the blast furnace and adjacent chimney. This simple brick building and chimney form part of the iron installation of Cornelis Delfos' Pretoria Iron Mines Limited. It was here in 1918 that cast iron from indigenous ore was produced on a large scale for the first time in South Africa. Delfos was the major driving force behind the establishment of Iscor in 1928, which later developed around this installation.

OLD SYNAGOGUE (PAUL KRUGER STREET)
Designed by Iber and Bearwood and built by the building contractor Krocket in 1897–1898, this is the only existing example in Gauteng of the Byzantine architectural style popularised in the Victorian era. When the new synagogue was built, this building stood vacant for about ten years. It served as an annex to the Supreme Court when the notorious Treason Trials started on 1 August 1958; a number of the hearings were held at the Old Synagogue. Nelson Mandela and the late Steve Biko were among the 156 accused. A number of the Rivonia Trials were also held here in which Bram Fischer played a prominent role.

ORIGINALSECTION OF THE NORTHERN TRANSVAAL HEADQUARTERS BUILDING (VOORTREKKERHOOGTE)
The historic machine building, Staatsartillerie, stables and the western section of the main building were built in the 1890s by the Zuid-Afrikaansche Republiek Government, and form an important historic and architectural element in Defence Headquarters.

PAUL KRUGER HOUSE (CHURCH STREET)
Paul Kruger lived here from 1883–1900 before going into exile in Europe, where he died in Switzerland in 1904. His wife continued to live here on account of her ill health until she died in July 1901. The house was then used by the British Military Police, and also served as a maternity home until 1932.

PIONEER OPEN-AIR MUSEUM (PRETORIA ROAD, SILVERTON)
This simple, picturesque, mud-walled thatched cottage, with dung and peach-pip floor, dates from 1848 and was built by the Transvaal pioneer, David Botha. Outbuildings with various interesting features include an outside oven for bread baking, a tanning pit, threshing floor, wagon shed, water furrow and water mill.

SECTION OF THE ROOIHUISKRAAL BATTLEFIELD (FARM BRAKFONTEIN)
This property forms part of the Rooihuiskraal Battlefield, where a battle took place between Boer and British forces on 12 February 1881, during the First War of Independence

(1880–1881). At the time of this war, Pretoria was besieged by Boer forces for 100 days and this battle was the last of several skirmishes that characterised the siege.

PRELLER HOUSE (PELINDABA)
Gustav Preller, a well-known protagonist of Afrikaans, historian and journalist, built and occupied this house from 1935 until his death in 1943. Many of his later historical works were completed in this house.

PRELLER RONDAVELS (PELINDABA)
This dwelling, consisting of three stone rondavels, was built by Gustav Preller in 1920 and was initially used as a weekend residence. Dr Preller also placed the rondavels at the disposal of Afrikaans writers and architects.

PRETORIA BOYS' HIGH SCHOOL (BROOKLYN)
The foundation stone of the main building was laid on 17 July 1908. The school was officially opened on 15 April 1909 by General JC Smuts, as Colonial Secretary of the Transvaal. These buildings are good examples of Edwardian architecture and form an important link with the early history of education in Pretoria.

PRETORIA HIGH SCHOOL FOR GIRLS – MAIN BUILDING (PARK STREET)
An outstanding example of a Milner School, the main building was erected in Edwardian style in 1915. Pretoria High School for Girls was established by Lord Milner in 1902 as part of his efforts to anglicise the Transvaal. Miss Edith Aitken, the first headmistress, was a pioneer who fought for higher education for women and was determined to bring together the various cultural groups, as reflected in the school charter she formulated. Having had relatively few headmistresses through the years, the school has been fortunate enough to benefit from great stability of leadership. Although the various headmistresses have made changes in keeping with the times, standards of excellence and caring have remained absolute.

PRETORIA NATIONAL BOTANIC GARDENS (CUSSONIA DRIVE, BRUMMERIA)
The Pretoria National Botanic Gardens was founded in 1946 and today contains one of the most important and comprehensive collections of indigenous flora in the country. The garden is divided into 11 sections representing the major vegetation types of South Africa, and a portion is devoted to preserving the natural flora of the Pretoria area in its virgin state.

SITE OF THE SAMMY MARKS HOUSE (SWARTKOPPIES)
The site includes the so-called Zwartkoppies Hall, cellar and outbuildings (now known as the Sammy Marks Museum), Gill's Cottage, Swallow Cottage, Farm Manager's House, Dairy Cottage, Pott's Cottage, a building with horse stables, coach house and loft, a double-storey building with cow shed and loft, a single-storey cow shed, two silos, a cattle dip and a section of the old water canal and dams.

Sammy Marks arrived in South Africa in 1869, and was nominated a senator in the first Union Parliament (1910–1920). His home at Zwartkoppies was familiar to celebrities visiting South Africa and was renowned as one of the first modern dairy farms in the country. Prior to his death, he had prohibited the alienation of the property for four generations.

SITE WITH THREE HISTORIC WOOD-AND-IRON HOUSES (3, 4 AND 5 JACOBUS NAUDÉ STREET, VOORTREKKERHOOGTE)
These three identical corrugated-iron houses, which date from the early days of Roberts Heights (now Voortrekkerhoogte), create a charming street scene that give an impression of how Roberts Heights must have looked. The

houses were originally built as accommodation for junior officers and chaplains. They are characterised by long verandahs, decorative woodwork and large front gardens.

SKANSKOP FORT (FARM GROENKLOOF)

This fort is one of three built around Pretoria after the Jameson Raid. Designed by the French Military Engineer Leon Grunberg, it was erected by local representatives of Krupp. The fort was handed over to the government on 6 April 1897.

SOUTH AFRICAN AIR FORCE OFFICERS' CLUB BUILDING (VOORTREKKERHOOGTE)

This building was designed by Sir Herbert Baker and completed in 1903 as the official residence of the Commander-in-Chief of the British Forces in South Africa. Its first occupant was General (later Sir) Neville Lyttleton, whose successors, Sir Henry Hildyard and Lord Methuen, probably also lived in the house. From 1921 to 1932 the building was used by the South African Air Force as its headquarters.

SPRINGBOK PARK (HATFIELD)

Springbok Park, formerly known as Grosvenor Square, was conceived in 1905 with the township planning of Hatfield, but the development of the park did not commence until the 1930s. Since then it has been planted with indigenous flora only and has developed into one of Pretoria's most attractive and established parks.

STEYNBERG ESTATE (WONDERBOOM)

The estate was purchased in 1938 by the portrait painter and sculptor, Coert Steynberg. JS Cleland was responsible for the design of the bachelor's quarters and a studio, which was later developed into a fully fledged stone and unplastered brick house. A large statue of Louis Botha was sculpted in the studio.

THE GREEN MAGAZINE BUILDING (NO 619) (91 AMMUNITION DEPOT)

After the Jameson Raid in December 1895, the government of the Zuid-Afrikaansche Republiek realised that Pretoria needed protection against similar attacks. Fort Klapperkop, Fort Skanskop and the Artillery Camp (presently Defence Headquarters), as well as the Green Magazine, were strategically erected around Pretoria. Two German engineers, Von Dewitz and Werner, were responsible for the design and construction of these buildings, which were completed in 1898.

'DIE KRAAL' (BRUMMERIA)

In 1939 Jacob Hendrik Pierneef, the well-known South African painter, designed and subsequently constructed the building complex known as Die Kraal. The remains of an old Bantu kraal were found by Pierneef on the site and this served as inspiration for the design of the buildings in the local idiom.

TRANSVAAL MUSEUM (PAUL KRUGER STREET)

The history of the Transvaal Museum dates back to the founding of the Staatsmuseum of the Zuid-Afrikaansche Republiek in 1893, which was then housed in a room in the Raadsaal on Church Square. The present museum was designed in grand neoclassical style by JS Cleland, later Chief Architect of the Union of South Africa. At the time of the First World War in 1914 the building was occupied by a number of government departments as well as the museum itself.

UNION BUILDINGS (MEINTJIESKOP)

Designed by Sir Herbert Baker, the Union Buildings site includes the Delville Wood and World War II memorials, as well as the equestrian statue of General Louis Botha, the first Prime Minister of the Union, executed by Coert Steynberg and unveiled in 1946, together with statues of Jan Smuts and JMB Hertzog.

Because no building of this size had ever been erected in South Africa before, the contract was subdivided. The central block, including the colonnades, were awarded to Prentice & Mackie, while the east and west blocks went to Meischke. The overall length of the Union Buildings is 275m, the wings spanning 90m each, and the amphitheatre also 90m. Bronze vases in the amphitheatre are the work of Fanie Eloff and the gardens were designed by Sir Herbert Baker.

The cornerstone was laid on 26 November 1910 by the Duke of Connaught, on behalf of King George V, and the building was finished in 1913. It was intended that a member of the British royal family should perform the opening ceremony, but the outbreak of World War I made this impossible.

VOLKSTEM BUILDING (PRETORIUS STREET)

Die Volkstem was the first Dutch-Afrikaans daily newspaper to be printed north of the Orange River. At first a weekly, it appeared in Pretoria on 8 August 1973 but was later published on a bi-weekly basis under the name of *De Volkstem, Nieuws en Advertentieblad.*

During the first annexation of the Transvaal, the British administration prohibited publication of the paper from 1 to 23 October 1878, when the press was seized from 20 December 1880 to 2 April 1881. Because of the disastrous course of the war, publication of *De Volkstem* was suspended from June 1900 to March 1903. Its name was simplified to *De Volkstem* on 1 January 1905, and by 1 January 1927, the name had subtly changed to the Afrikaans version, *Die Volkstem*.

WIERDA BRIDGE (SIX MILE SPRUIT)

This bridge was completed in 1891 by Sytze Wierda, Director of Public Works of the Zuid-Afrikaansche Republiek.

WONDERBOOM NATURE RESERVE

The site includes a clump of trees known as the Wonderboom, as well as ruins of an Old Boer Fort and two historic caves. The Wonderboom Nature Reserve derives its name from a remarkable old fig tree, *Ficus pretorae*, belonging to the family *Moraceae*. This tree, the finest example of its species, at one time must have had a single trunk (whose age has been determined by radiocarbon dating to be about 900 years old). Its spreading branches touched the ground and took root. At such places new upright stems grew and they in turn also took root, so that, at present, the single tree has the appearance of a group of trees spreading over 50m, while the centre bole is over four metres in circumference and over 20m in height.

Even before the Anglo-Boer War (1899–1902), Fort Wonderboompoort was one of the first three forts erected on the outskirts of Pretoria to protect the capital at its northern entrance. About a mile to the northwest of the Acheulian hunters' camp is the Wonderboom, and a few hundred metres from this tree and in the 'poort' itself, is a small cave that was the first prehistoric site excavated in the Transvaal. During the 1890s, Thomas Leask, a pioneer anthropologist, excavated the cave and found Stone Age tools. Regrettably, the finds have been lost. A road cutting in the 'poort' exposed one of the largest accumulations of stone artefacts in Africa. Stone knives, heavy choppers, pear-shaped picks and axe-edged cleavers, axes and other tools lie in the places where they were left by Early Stone Age Man more than 50 000 years ago. No bones or organic materials of any kind were found.

RANDFONTEIN

This town was laid out on the farm Randfontein in 1890. It attained municipal status in 1929.

JONKER HOUSE (RIEBEECK LAKE)

The farm Randfontein was bought simultaneously with its neighbouring farm, Uitvalfontein, by Sir JB Robinson of Randfontein Estates Gold Mining Company, from Mathys Jonker. The development of this mine led directly to the establishment and development of the town of Randfontein in 1890. The 'Jonkershuis' and The Homestead, the original farmhouse that became the mine manager's house, are situated close to each other. Jonker House is an excellent example of an early three-roomed Transvaal farmhouse. Both the corrugated-iron roof and the verandah are typical. Particularly noteworthy are the thick stone walls.

OLD MINING COMMISSIONER'S POST AND TELEGRAPH OFFICE
(70 MARKET STREET, KOCKSOORD)

Designed by the chief architect of the Zuid-Afrikaansche Republiek, Wopkes Wierda, this building was in the Republican style, which Wierda developed and which deviated from the late-Victorian style of the British. The foundation stone of this, the first government building in Kocksoord, was laid on 5 March 1898 by General Kock. Hendrik Kock, the first Mining Commissioner appointed at Kocksoord, and his Chief Clerk, Frikkie Wolmarans, occupied this building until the outbreak of the Anglo-Boer War in 1899. During the war, the British occupied the building as a guard post. Thereafter, in 1903, it became a post office. By 1905 the building was being used for the newly founded English Medium Primary School. The latter moved to new premises in 1950 and the building once again reverted to a post office until 1971.

THE HOMESTEAD
(5 HOMESTEAD AVENUE, HOMELAKE)

The Randfontein Estates Gold Mining Company was founded in April 1889, and was responsible for the establishment and development of the town. The complex constituted a wood-and-iron office, single quarters, stables and the house itself. The Homestead was built between 1889–1890 for the then manager, Pope Yeatman, and has also housed JB Robinson and JWS Langerman. Additions were made in 1902 and a second storey added in 1937.

ROODEPOORT

The town originated on the farm Roodepoort as a gold mining camp in 1888. It attained municipal status in 1904.

MINESHAFTS OF FPT AND HW STRUBEN
(CONFIDENCE REEF, KLOOFENDAL)

FPT Struben discovered Confidence Reef on 18 September 1884, and it was there that he and his brother, HW Struben, mined the first payable gold on the Witwatersrand. The discovery of Confidence Reef caused prospectors to flock to the Witwatersrand, which, in turn, resulted in the discovery of the conglomerates of Main Reef in 1886.

OLD JAIL AND PRISON WARDER'S HOUSE
(SEVENTH AVENUE)

The design of this building was strongly influenced by the Glasgow Arts and Crafts Movement. The jail is a fine example of this style and is one of the few that have survived in South Africa.

OLD MUNICIPAL CHAMBERS (BERLANDIA STREET)

The old Municipal Chambers were designed by Charles Hosking and completed in 1906 as the first permanent office building for the Roodepoort-Maraisburg Municipality, and served this purpose until 1936. The western wing, added in 1918, was designed by the firm Baker & Fleming.

SPRINGS

Springs was first established as a coal-mining town in 1887, but later turned to mining gold. Its name probably comes from the many springs discovered in the area when it was first surveyed. It attained municipal status in 1912.

CENTRAL FIRE STATION
(BETWEEN WELGEDACHT AND BOKSBURG ROADS)
This fire station was erected in 1937–1938 and was taken into use on 13 July 1938. The foundation stone was laid by Councillor Sutter, a former Mayor of Springs, and opened by Councillor Redhill.

VEREENIGING

This town was established on the farms Klipplaatsdrift and Leeuwkuil with the discovery of coal in 1882, and was named after the company De Zuid Afrikaansche en Oranje Vrijstaatsche Kolen- en Mineralen-Myn Vereeniging. It attained municipal status in 1912.

BLOCKHOUSE (WITKOP)
This is part of the line of British blockhouses built during the Anglo-Boer War (1899–1902), which extended from Noupoort in the Cape to Pietersburg in the Northern Province, to protect the railway line.

DUNCANVILLE ARCHAEOLOGICAL SITE
(FARM KLIPPLAATSDRIFT)
This Stone Age site is situated on the wide alluvial terrace about 30m above the confluence of the Vaal and Klip rivers. It was discovered by Professor C van Riet Lowe, and the famous prehistorian, Henri Breuil, worked there. In 1960 it was excavated by Dr RJ Mason, who discovered 157 stone artefacts that might have been made by early Acheulian hunters.

KLIP RIVER QUARRY (FARM KLIPPLAATSDRIFT)
In 1920 road makers along the Vereeniging-Heidelberg road on the west bank of the Klip River opened a quarry containing implement-bearing gravels in an ancient bed of the Vaal River. The implements belong to the Stone Age and are representative of the Hand-axe or Chelles-Acheul culture, so-called after sites in France where similar implements were first discovered about 300 years ago. The 16 m terrace at Vereeniging is one of only two preserved sites of its kind. Its value as a place where a most important stage in the early evolution of prehistoric industry may be studied, is therefore unequalled. A comprehensive collection is housed at the University of the Witwatersrand.

ROCK ENGRAVINGS (REDAN)
These petroglyphs are a good example of the abstract art practiced during the Stone Age. The drawings probably had a ceremonial or mythological significance.

WESTONARIA

This town originated from the amalgamation in 1948 of the townships of Venterspost and Westonaria, proclaimed in 1937 and 1938 respectively. Initially known as Ventersport, it changed to Westonaria in 1952 after the township developers Western Areas Limited. The town attained municipal status in 1952.

PUMPHOUSE (ZUURBEKOM)
This pumphouse was erected in 1899 by the Johannesburg Water Works Estate and Exploration Company Limited. The Zuurbekom borehole has produced an exceptionally high yield of 27 million litres daily without fail since 1899. It lies near the source of the Klip River and was Johannesburg's first supply of fresh water.

KWAZULU-NATAL

Situated between the Drakensberg and the Indian Ocean, Natal was established as a republic by the Boers in 1838 and became a British Colony in 1843, joining the Union of South Africa in 1910. Previously a Bantustan under the old South African government, KwaZulu was incorporated into the province of KwaZulu-Natal in 1994 under the new South African government.

AHRENS

FORT AHRENS

These ruins are the remains of Fort Ahrens or Fort Perseverance, better known as Esikanesweni Laager. Fort Ahrens was erected in the 1860s and 1870s, not for military purposes, but as a refuge for the civilian population. Farmers of the neighbourhood did, in fact, avail themselves of it during the Zulu War (1878–1879) and the Bambatha Rebellion of 1906. Most similar refuges have been demolished, with the result that these ruins are virtually unique today, and provide a remarkable link with early Colonial Natal.

BABANANGA

NQENGELELE KA MVULANE (BUTHELEZI) MONUMENT

This monument was erected in memory of Nqengelele Buthelezi, senior counsellor to King Shaka Ka Senzangakhona.

BAYNESFIELD

BAYNES HOUSE (FARM NELS RUST)

Baynes House was built in the 1870s by R Lightfoot for J Baynes. It is a most imposing residence, built of Pietermaritzburg redbrick, with 'broekie lace' fascias. The rooms have high ceilings and are ornamented with beautifully fluted Roman columns, archways and bay windows. A high lookout tower tops the whole structure. Baynes, one of the Byrne Settlers of 1850, was a prominent agriculturist, a Member of Parliament and a philanthropist. He was particularly innovative in dairy farming.

FIRST CATTLE DIP CONSTRUCTED IN SOUTH AFRICA WITH PENS AT EACH END (FARM MEYERSHOEK)

This cattle dip was built in 1902 for Joseph Baynes and was the first erected in South Africa. Designed by civil engineer G Alexander, the dip has a curved corrugated-iron roof supported by gum poles. The site is of great significance in the development of stock farming in South Africa.

JOSEPH BAYNES MAUSOLEUM (FARM NELSRUST)

Set in an oval garden surrounded by a low stone wall, the Mausoleum was constructed in 1923 after the death of Joseph Baynes' second wife. The burial place of Baynes himself, it consists of a small chapel-like structure in Gothic-Revival style, with a corrugated-iron roof, copper guttering and bronze grilles.

OLD NELSRUST DAIRY (FARM NELS RUST)

At this dairy, built for Joseph Baynes in 1898, the commercial production of butter was pioneered in KwaZulu-Natal. As such it was also the first modern dairy in the country, and was designed in the Arts and Crafts style by

Kent & Price. It is built of local shale and has Pietermaritzburg redbrick quoining to the corners and windows. There is a wide and steeply pitched verandah, to keep the building and its perishable contents cool.

BERGVILLE

This town was laid out on the farm Klein Waterval in 1885 and was named in 1903. The name refers to the Drakensberg Mountains. Bergville attained municipal status in 1961.

BLOCKHOUSE (UPPER TUGELA)
This blockhouse was built during the latter part of the Anglo-Boer War (1899–1902) by British troops. It served as a link in the defence network of Natal against the incursions of Boer guerrilla fighters, and is the only known blockhouse of its kind in KwaZulu-Natal that has survived.

CAVE KNOWN AS MHLWAZINI (FARM SOLARCLIFFS)
Radiocarbon dating lends credence to the belief that this site was occupied between 2 700 and 2 000 years ago. A second period of occupation followed approximately 600 years ago and is possibly related to the arrival of the Bantu-speaking agriculturists.

Mhlwazini is one of the most important Holocene sites yet discovered in KwaZulu-Natal, and is noted both for the quantity and quality of artefacts preserved in this deposit. It has provided a significant contribution to the understanding of the period it represents.

RETIEF'S PASS
The first party of Voortrekkers to enter Natal, led by Piet Retief, set out from Blydevooruitzicht and commenced the descent of the Drakensberg along this pass on 14 November 1837 with 66 wagons. The party reached the foot of the mountain at Bethel on 18 November. Retief's Pass is therefore closely associated with the history of the Great Trek.

SITE KNOWN AS MGODUYANUKA
(FARM ZUURLAGER)
This site comprises a number of circular primary enclosures that vary between 5m and 20m in diameter and used to be livestock pens. In some cases secondary enclosures of similar or smaller sizes abut the primary structures. These groups are surrounded by the remains of the floors of a ring of huts.

Results from radiocarbon dating shows that Mgoduyanuka was built and occupied in the seventeenth and eighteenth centuries. Oral historical information suggests that the settlements were built by the Zizi people, who lived in the area until the Mfecane of the 1820s. The site has also furnished evidence of a fairly protracted period of Iron Age occupation.

Archaeologically, the Mgoduyanuka site has provided important and unusual examples of settlement patterns and Iron Age architecture, in the area known to archaeologists as the Natal Grasslands.

CAMPERDOWN

This small town was laid out on the farm Camperdown in 1865.

UMHLATAZANA ROCK SHELTER (FARM KIRKFALLS)
Deposits in the floor of this rock shelter built up to a depth of 2.5m as a result of human occupation for long periods over the past 100 000 years. It is the only known site in eastern South Africa with evidence that people were living in the region continuously between 45 000 and 12 000 years ago. It was during this time that the gradual transition from the Middle Stone Age to the Later Stone Age tradition took place.

COLENSO

The town was laid out in 1885 and was named after Bishop John William Colenso (1814–1883), first Anglican Bishop of Natal. Colenso attained municipal status in 1958.

BULWER BRIDGE AND TOLL HOUSE
The Bulwer Bridge is the oldest stone-and-steel structure in South Africa, while the Toll House is the oldest building in Colenso and the only surviving toll house in KwaZulu-Natal. Built in 1879, it is now the RE Stevenson Museum, named after the military historian.

COMPENSATION

In 1849 Edmund Morewood settled on a farm between the Tongati and Mhlali rivers and named it Compensation. After 1854, the sugar-planting project that he had initiated was abandoned.

MOREWOOD MEMORIAL GARDEN
(COMPENSATION FARM)
This Memorial Garden marks the site of the first sugar mill in KwaZulu-Natal, built by Edmund Morewood, a pioneer in sugar-cane cultivation and the first to produce sugar in Natal in 1851. The original pond from which water was drawn for sugar-making has been reconstructed, and there is a replica of the primitive mills used to crush the sugar in the earliest days.

DARGLE

Presumably named by Thomas Fannin, an Irishman who came to South Africa in 1847, Dargle's name was taken from a stream near Dublin, Ireland.

OWTHORNE HOUSE (DARGLE STATE FOREST)
This old farmhouse was built by William Charles Shaw on the original farm, Owthorne, in 1882. From 1879 to 1899 he farmed full-time at Owthorne, and in 1882 he erected his own sawmill just below the house. Since the 1950s, the property has served as accommodation for the overseer of the Dargle State Forest.

DINGAANSTAD

Dingaanstad is now a Dutch Reformed mission station; the first missionary was sent here in 1925.

DINGANES KRAAL, UMGUNGUNDLOVU
(BABANANGO DISTRICT)
uDingane (1788–1840), ruled the Zulus from 1828 until his death, and Umgungundlovu was his capital from 1829 until 1839.

The 'khanda' (head military kraal) was destroyed by fire on the orders of King Dingane when he decided to leave. However, on account of the site's excellent state of archaeological preservation, the museum (currently being developed) is primarily directed at the excavation, research and interpretation of the site as a typical example of a nineteenth century royal 'khanda', with emphasis on traditional Zulu social and political organisation, trade and technology. The research and interpretation of the historical events of the period include Zulu relations with the hunter-trader missionaries and Voortrekkers, and the resulting conflicts in this very sensitive period of the region's history.

In 1990, excavations revealed the floor of Dingane's great hut or 'ndlunkulu'. This was verified by features such as the size and number of supporting poles, which were described by early missionaries who had visited the site. Lumps of glass, remains of beads that were reported to have covered the poles and which melted in the heat of the fire that destroyed the hut when Dingane left, were found at the bases of the poles.

PIET RETIEF'S GRAVE (KWA MATIWANE)
The monument to Piet Retief and the 70 burghers who were killed here on Dingane's orders on 6 February 1838 stands on top of the hill. The graves lie at the foot of the hill. Kwa Matiwane means 'the place of uMatiwane', the son of Masumpa and Chief of the Ngwane tribe, who founded the Masopha tribe in Basutoland (Lesotho). On Dingane's orders, uMatiwane and his followers were killed here in 1829.

DUNDEE

This town was laid out in 1882 and named Dundee after the birthplace in Scotland of its founder, Thomas Paterson Smith. It attained municipal status in 1902.

APOSTOLIC FAITH MISSION (17 GRAY STREET)
The oldest church building in Dundee, this sandstone building was originally constructed as a Methodist church and was designed in Gothic-Revival style. Mrs J White laid the cornerstone on 26 November 1889 and the church was inaugurated in 1892.

BOSWELL'S STORE (74 GLADSTONE STREET)
This Victorian building, formerly known as the Masonic Hall, was built in 1898 as the Biggarsberg Unity Lodge. At the end of the Anglo-Boer War, the 1902 Treason Trials of the Natal rebels were held here It was purchased in 1935 by Ralph Boswell Robertson, MP, a wholesale and retail merchant.

CONISTON HOUSE (5 HARVEY PLACE)
A private residence, this late Victorian manor house was erected in 1906 for Mr Talbot, the first licensed chemist in northern KwaZulu-Natal. It is a good example of Natal Colonial building style and was built after the Anglo-Boer War, during a revival in the building industry in the area.

DUNDEE HIGH SCHOOL (TATHAM STREET)
The original section of the school complex was in use from 1907. The current staff room was built in 1934 as a school hall on the recommendation of the then Minister of Education, JH Hofmeyr.

JUDITH CHURCH
(FARM PADDAFONTEIN, DISTRICT)
This was the third church building of the Dutch Reformed denomination in Dundee since the town was established in 1882. With its straight end gables and neogothic windows and doors, this stone church was inaugurated in January 1885. It was named after Mrs Judith van Tonder, who donated 58 acres of land as a church farm.

OLD SOUTH AFRICAN POLICE STATION AND OLD COURT (GLADSTONE STREET)
Erected in 1887, the old Police Station was probably originally used as a church. It is an imposing sandstone building with a wide wooden verandah in traditional Natal style. The Court building is T-shaped and typical of the smaller government buildings at the end of the nineteenth century. The main entrance has a plastered gable in neoclassical tradition, which bears the monogram of Edward VII. The interior of the building is unchanged.

OLD SWEDISH CHURCH (ARGYLE STREET)
This church, designed by and built under the supervision of Reverend LT Nurenuis, was completed in 1898. The building is predominantly in the neogothic style, and has a particularly impressive clock tower.

PEARSON HOUSE (48 TATHAM STREET)
A typical Natal Colonial verandah house, Pearson House was erected c.1925 by Budge. Charles Pearson, the original owner, was a well-known and eminent trader in northern Natal.

RORKE'S DRIFT BATTLEFIELD (BUFFALO RIVER)
The Battle of Rorke's Drift was fought during the afternoon and night of 22 January 1879. A small British force of two officers and 110 men defended themselves bravely against repeated attacks by some 4 000 Zulus. Eleven Victoria Crosses were awarded as a result of the action.

RYLEY'S HOUSE AND OUTBUILDINGS
(70 KARL LANDMAN STREET)
Now known as Symonsdale, this Victorian building complex dates from 1902–1903 and is an excellent example of Natal Colonial architecture from that period. The house was built by Sir Edward Ryley, Minister of Agriculture in the Natal Parliament, on the site of the British camp and headquarters at the time of the Battle of Talana on 20 October 1899.

SITE OF TALANA BATTLEFIELD (FARM DUNDEE)
The Battle of Talana on 20 October 1899 was the first large battle of the Anglo-Boer War (1899–1902). From a military history perspective, it was also a most important battle. A cairn marks the spot where General Sir William Penn-Symons fell, mortally wounded, and there is also a small military cemetery. The remains of the two British forts, Boer and British gun emplacements and a Boer cannon road can still be seen on Talana Hill.

THE HOLLIES (29–31 UNION STREET)
The Hollies was built in 1886 for AA Smith, a local attorney and descendent of the town's founder, P Smith. It is a typical Natal verandah house, with a four-gabled cruciform roof and rounded columns supporting the verandah on three sides. The porch on the entrance side features wood figures.

THORNLEY HOMESTEAD (FARM TALANA HILL)
The Thornley farmstead was erected in about 1897 after Peter Smith, the founder of Dundee, purchased the farm for his youngest son. It was occupied by the Boers on 20 October 1899 during the Battle of Talana Hill, at which time the farmhouse and stables were used as a field hospital and a mortuary respectively.

DURBAN

Originally named Port Natal, the city was established on land ceded by the Zulu King Shaka, in 1828. It was named after Sir Benjamin D'Urban (1777–1849), Governor of the Cape from 1834 to 1838. The name was spelt Durban from about 1870. The city attained city status in 1935.

ATHERTON (295 FLORIDA ROAD)
This double-storey Victorian verandah home was designed by architect William Emery Robarts in 1903 for Mrs Joel, a member of the prominent Witwatersrand mining family. It was subsequently sold to the Boulle family, who retained ownership for 50 years. Atherton has been restored and is now a restaurant.

BEACHWOOD MANGROVES
(ENTRANCE UNDER ELLIS BROWN BRIDGE)
Mangrove swamps are one of the rarest and most scientifically interesting ecosystems, and occur in a highly specialised tidal environment. The Beachwood Mangroves are of significant botanical, educational and historical value as they are situated close to one of South Africa's cities with a variety of educational institutions.

BELLAIR RAILWAY STATION
(SARNIA ROAD, BELLAIR)
This mainly Victorian-style building was completed in 1900. It was built by the Natal Government Railways and replaced the original station of 1876–1878, which served the Durban-Pinetown railway line. The line was opened on 4 September 1878.

CAISTER LODGE (264 MUSGRAVE ROAD)
Currently a retirement complex, Caister Lodge is situated on the site where Sir Benjamin Wesley Greenacre, three times Mayor of Durban, built his house in about 1890. The present three-storey dwelling, in typical Berea style, was erected in 1923 by Walter Greenacre, son of Sir Benjamin, after the original building was destroyed by fire. The complex shows several signs of the Tudor-Revival style.

CITY HALL AND FRANCIS FAREWELL GARDENS (GARDINER STREET)
The City Hall, which is almost an exact replica of the Belfast City Hall in Northern Ireland, was built in 1910. This building also houses an art gallery, library and museum. Francis Farewell Gardens were named after Lieutenant F Farewell of the Royal Marines, who established the first white settlement at Port Natal. He was born at Wincanton, Somersetshire, in 1793, and served with the Royal Navy during the Napoleonic Wars. In 1822 he called at the Cape and set sail for Port Natal in 1824. He was killed in Pondoland in 1829 by Ngetho, the Qwabe Chief.

COLINTON (68 RIDGE ROAD)
This residence was built in 1898 by the architect William Street-Wilson for Sir David Hunter, General Manager of the Natal Government Railways from 1879 to 1906. It was named after his wife's birthplace, Mossy Hill, Colinton, near Edinburgh.

CONGELLA BATTLEFIELD (MAYDON WHARF)
The monument is dedicated to Dick van Rooyen, Abraham Greyling, Cornelius van Schalkwyk, Theunis Oosthuyzen and others who died at the Battle of Congella on 24 May 1842. The battle took place here, when a small Voortrekker military force warded off an attack by a British force of 139 soldiers under Captain TC Smith. Despite this battle the Voortrekkers continued to besiege the British fort.

COTTAM GROVE (303 AND 309 FLORIDA ROAD)
These two impressive Edwardian verandah houses were erected about 1903 on the instruction of mining magnate Sir Abe Bailey. After the Second World War the properties were joined and the houses fitted out as a hotel, known as the Dorchester. In 1972 the hotel's name was changed to Cottam Grove. Together with the adjoining manor house, Atherton, these houses form one of the most impressive groups of Edwardian villas in KwaZulu-Natal.

DOUBLE-STOREY VICTORIAN DWELLING (41 CEDAR ROAD)
With verandahs on two sides at both levels, this Victorian facebrick double-storey dates from the end of the nineteenth century. It belonged to the author and social anthropologist Mrs EL Roberts until her death in 1986.

DURBAN GIRLS' SECONDARY SCHOOL (88 CARLISLE ROAD)
This building complex, with diverse single-storey structures, was built in the 1920s. It was originally intended as a boys' school, but was occupied c.1930 by the High School for Indian Girls. The architecture is a variation on Indian traditional style, with gables in Edwardian idiom. Two verandahs extend to the pavement.

DURBAN LIGHT INFANTRY HEADQUARTERS (5 DLI AVENUE)
This site is intrinsically connected with the history and traditions of one of South Africa's most famous regiments. Architecturally, it is a significant building situated in an area where it is an important landmark. The double-storey regimental headquarters of the Edwardian period is of historical significance.

DUTCH REFORMED CHURCH (151 SMITH STREET)

Plans for this church, by the well-known church architects, Louw & Moerdijk, were approved in February 1923. The building is designed in the Cape Dutch-Revival style, with the main façade characterised by a large pedimented gable in which a prominent portico is set. The first church service was held on 2 February 1924.

ELEPHANT HOUSE (745 RIDGE ROAD)

Elephant House dates from about 1849 and is the most historic of the remaining Colonial period houses in Durban. It contributes greatly to the historic Ridge Road environment.

FAÇADES OF POINT ROAD RAILWAY STATION (POINT ROAD)

This Victorian railway station dates from the 1890s when the Natal Government Railways experienced a boom. The wrought-iron verandah and the brick-and-ochre work on the façade are of special interest.

FORMER WAR DEPARTMENT LORDS' GROUND BOUNDARY MARKER NO. 2 (OLD FORT ROAD)

This type of stone marker was once common in Durban and was used during the colonial era to demarcate property owned by the War Department. This beacon marked the corner of Lords' Ground, Durban's first cricket ground.

HOLLIS HOUSE AND PROPERTY (178 FLORIDA ROAD)

An Edwardian double-storey in Baroque-Revival style, the house was constructed by Jack Hollis, building contractor for the City Hall, Durban. The architect is thought to have been Stanley Hudson. Hollis was also the founder of Clairwood Race Course.

KING'S HOUSE (EASTBOURNE ROAD)

Erected in 1902, this building served as the seaside residence of the governors of Natal. The architects were Scott & Kirby, in association with the Colonial Engineer. After Union in 1910, it became the traditional Durban residence of the Governors-General of South Africa and later of the State Presidents. It now serves as a state guesthouse.

LILLIESHELL MANOR HOUSE (408 INNES ROAD)

This double-storey house was built for RH Tatham in 1896. Considerable changes were made in 1924 while the James family owned the property.

LITTLE CHELSEA (18 WINDERMERE ROAD)

Built for L Evans, this Victorian double-storey building, with cast-iron verandahs, was designed by architects Reid & Hurst in 1897.

LOCAL CULTURAL HISTORY MUSEUM (ALIWAL STREET)

Used to house the Local Cultural History Museum since 1965, this old courthouse was originally designed by the Colonial Engineer Peter Paterson. It opened on 24 May 1866 and is the oldest government building in Durban. The north wing was added in 1891 and the south wing in 1897. During the Zulu War of 1879, when Durban appeared to be in danger of attack, it was temporarily loop-holed. It was taken over by the Durban Corporation in 1910.

MONALTRIE (59 MUSGRAVE ROAD)

This Victorian villa was designed by the well-known architect William Street-Wilson in 1897, according to the free-Renaissance style. It also shows influences of Queen Anne style.

NARAINSAMY TEMPLE (984 INANDA ROAD, NEWLANDS)

Founded by one Narainsamy in 1896, the Temple is controlled by a family trust created by him. The designer and builder was Kristappa Reddy, whose main contribution to temple architecture was this building, with its finely decorated spire and prominent pyramid-shaped dome. It was built from 1906–1908. The chief deities of the Temple are Vishu, Siva, Ganesh, Soobramaniar and the Nauw Graha. Reddy (1863–1941) was a master builder indentured from North Arcot near Madras in South India.

NATAL HERBARIUM AND MEDLEY WOOD HOUSE (ST THOMAS ROAD)
The Natal Herbarium was designed by Walter Haygarth and built in 1902 for John Medley Wood (1827–1915), the founder. It is a neoclassical-style building with pedimented end gables and a verandah portico. It currently houses 75 000 specimens. Wood farmed at Tongaat and later moved to Inanda, where he started his collection of 50 000-plus specimens while studying the flora of Natal and Zululand. Medley Wood House, earlier used as the curator's residence, is a redbrick building dating from 1889. It has a complex roof and central bay window.

OLD FORT AND OLD CEMETERY (OLD FORT ROAD)
It was here that Captain T Charlton-Smith of the 27th Regiment (Royal Inniskilling Fusiliers) and a British military force situated their camp in 1842, and were besieged by the immigrant Boers under Commandant Andries Pretorius. To secure relief for the garrison, Dick King rode 965.61km to Grahamstown.

From 1842 to 1897 the fort was occupied by various regiments and detachments of the British army. In 1908 the British War Office leased it to the Durban Light Infantry and in due course this lease was continued by the Union Defence Department. It is currently maintained in conjunction with the Commission of the Royal Durban Light Infantry Comrades Association. The old barracks have been converted and presently house war pensioners.

The old cemetery contains the graves of British troops who lost their lives at the Battle of Congella against the Boers on 24 May 1845.

OLD LAW COURT (151 VICTORIA EMBANKMENT)
The original building, which stood on this site until 1910, was erected in 1861 as the Natal Government Hospital, for which it was used until 1879. From 1880 to 1894 it housed the Durban High School, and from 1895 to 1907 it accommodated a section of the Durban Boys' Model School. The court buildings, designed by the architect Stanley Hudson, were erected in 1911 and served as the Magistrates' and Regional Court until 1975 when they were renovated for the Supreme Court.

PORTVIEW (183 COWIE ROAD)
This double-storey Edwardian manor house was erected in 1905 by TBF Davis, a prominent resident of Durban and a founder of the University of Natal.

POST OFFICE (WEST STREET)
The old Durban Town Hall, at present the General Post Office, was designed in 1882 by Philip Dudgeon. The foundation stone was laid in 1883 and the building was opened in 1885. It is an outstanding example of neoclassical architecture, and plays an important role in the history of KwaZulu-Natal.

PROPERTY WITH GEOLOGICAL EXPOSURE (CORINTHIA STREET)
The glaciated pavement shows striations of Table Mountain sandstone at the base of the Dwyka pillite of the Karoo System, and is approximately 300 million years old.

PROPERTY WITH WILD FIG TREES (CNR WEST AND CHURCH STREETS)
This property forms an important part of the historic site of the first white settlement west of

Port Natal. The erf is one of the few open spaces in the Durban city centre and, with its indigenous trees, constitutes an important aesthetic element.

QUADRANT HOUSE (115 VICTORIA EMBANKMENT)
This building is aptly named, not only because of the site it occupies, which is a quadrant in shape, but also because of the quadrant – an instrument essential for navigation. In 1929, H Live commissioned architect Ritchie McKinley to design a building suitable for a naval training school. It was used as such until 1950.

QUEEN'S TAVERN (16 STAMFORD HILL ROAD)
The Queen's Tavern, which was built as a gentlemen's club in 1894, is one of Durban's few remaining links with the colonial past of KwaZulu-Natal. It is also the oldest licensed premises in the city. It served members of the Queen's Own Regiment, who were encamped nearby, and in whose honour the tavern was named. The Queen's was saved from demolition in 1983 when it was declared a national monument.

GA RICHES PRINTER BUILDING
(423 SMITH STREET)
The building was named after GA Riches, a town councillor from 1907 to 1935, and was the site of the School of Law, Howard College. It is an excellent example of the Classical-Revivalist style and forms an integral part of the architecture of Smith Street, one of the most historic streets in Durban.

RIVERSIDE SOOFIE MOSQUE AND MAUSOLEUM
(50 LOWER BRIDGE ROAD, NOW SOOFIE SAHEB DRIVE)
This mosque was erected by Hajee Soofie, who immigrated to South Africa in 1895. He was responsible for the construction of 11 other mosques, the establishment of 13 madressas and the laying out of a large number of cemeteries. Soofie died in 1911 and his body lies interred in the octagonal mausoleum, which he designed himself. He also established a madressa, orphanage, travellers' guesthouse and old age home here.

SASTRI COLLEGE (WINTERTON WALK)
The college was the first Indian High School and Teachers' Training College built in South Africa. In 1928 a double-storey complex, predominantly in the Berea style of the period, was designed by the architect Kallenbach and erected by Percy Osborn. The College opened early in 1929. The training section for teachers was transferred to the Springfield College in 1951.

SRI AMBIKA AMBALAVANAR TEMPLE COMPLEX
(890 BELLAIR ROAD, CATO MANOR)
The original Shree Ambalavanaar Alayam was the first public Hindu temple to be erected on the African continent. Built in 1875, it was damaged beyond repair during the floods of 1905. The present temple was designed by K Reddy and built by RK Pillay, and is known for its sculptures from India.

ST LOUIS ROMAN CATHOLIC CHURCH
(22 JACOBS ROAD, CLAIRWOOD)
On 10 February 1884 a plot in Clairwood was purchased by Bishop Jolivet for the erection of a mission church for 'Creoles'. A larger building was built in 1886 to accommodate Indian and coloured pupils, but the school was closed in 1889. After Bishop Delalle visited the grounds in February 1911, he recommended that a new church be erected. The present building was erected shortly after, and in 1932–1933 and 1944, extensive alterations and additions were effected. In September 1944 the completed church was ceremonially consecrated by Bishop Delalle. It is a massive sandstone structure with neogothic characteristics.

THE PASSIVE RESISTANCE SITE
(CNR UMBILO ROAD AND GALE STREET)

In 1946 the South African parliament passed the Asiatic Land tenure and Indian Representation Act, founded on separate residential areas for Indians, with some indirect representation in parliament. As a protest against this Act, the Natal Indian Congress, led by Dr Monty Naicker, with the support of the Transvaal Indian Congress under Dr Yusaf Dadoo, resolved to launch a second passive resistance campaign (the first was started by Mahatma Gandhi). They declared that many Indians were prepared to break the law and submit to arrest and punishment by occupying land denied them by the Act. They began camping on this site, an unused piece of ground, but disturbances arose through attacks on them by groups of white hooligans. This forced the police to intervene and almost 2 200 people were arrested, brought to trial and imprisoned.

TREVEAN HOUSE (258 WAKESLEIGH ROAD, HILLARY)

This imposing dwelling was designed and erected in 1882 by the well-known architects Robert Sellers Upton and Philip Dudgeon. The billiard room was added in 1898. Trevean House is probably the best example of a late Colonial-Victorian building in KwaZulu-Natal.

UNIVERSITY OF NATAL, HOWARD COLLEGE BUILDING AND MEMORIAL TOWER BUILDING
(KING GEORGE AVENUE)

Howard College was financed and built in 1931 by shipping magnate TB Davis in memory of his son Howard Davis, an engineering student who was killed in the First World War (1914–1918).

Financed from the University War Memorial Fund as a memorial to those who died during both world wars, the Memorial Tower's ground floor was completed in 1947. The Light of Remembrance, a nightly landmark, serves as a permanent reminder of this.

VICTORIAN DOUBLE-STOREY BUILDING
(73 MUSGRAVE ROAD)

This magnificent double-storey manor house, designed by the architect P Piekes and erected in 1904–1905, is an excellent example of a Natal verandah house erected at the beginning of the twentieth century. The fine detailing of the timber verandahs is noteworthy.

ELANDSLAAGTE

Elandslaagte developed from a railway siding between Ladysmith and Dundee. A geological survey undertaken in 1880 revealed that there were workable deposits of coal in this region of northern Natal, and Elandslaagte was one of the smaller towns that served the resulting mines.

ELANDSLAAGTE BATTLEFIELD
(FARM BRAAKFONTEIN)

The Battle of Elandslaagte on 21 October 1899 was the second action of the Anglo-Boer War (1899–1902). In this battle the Boers lost 60 men, while 140 were wounded and 200 were taken prisoner. The British casualties numbered 50 dead and 205 wounded.

MEMORIAL TO THE DUTCH CORPS
(FARM BRAAKFONTEIN)

This memorial, designed by G Moerdijk of Pretoria, was built by the firm Barker & Nel of Volksrust, and was erected by the citizens of the Netherlands in memory of members of the Dutch Corps who died during the Battle of Elandslaagte on 21 October 1899.

ESHOWE

Proclaimed a town in 1915, Eshowe became a borough in 1954. The name is taken from the Zulu language, and refers to the sound of the wind in the trees.

FORT ESHOWE/KWAMONDI AND NORWEGIAN CEMETERY

KwaMondi Mission Station, also known as Fort Eshowe, was occupied during the Anglo-Zulu War by British troops under Colonel CK Pearson. They were besieged here from 15 January 1879 to 4 April 1879.

KwaMondi was the mission station of the Norwegian missionary Reverend Ommund Oftebro, who was given the land by King Cetshwayo, making him the first white man in Eshowe. The Zulus could not pronounce Ommund, and so it became kwaMondi, 'the place of Ommund'.

The graves of Revered Oftebro and his wife can be seen in the cemetery.

FORT NONGQAYI

The fort was built by the British in 1883 to house the Zululand Native Police. The name 'nongqayi' means policemen, or mounted police. It now houses the Zululand Historical Museum.

HISTORICAL PORTIONS OF THE PRISON AND GOVERNMENT OFFICE

This historic building complex was erected in 1900 as a second-class prison. During 1901 it served as a transit camp for prisoners of war to Ceylon, and in 1906, during the Bambatha Rebellion, it was converted into a refuge for the inhabitants of Eshowe.

OLD RESIDENCY

Established as housing for the local Commissioner and Chief Magistrate, Sir Melmoth Osborne, this private residence was built in 1894 by Messrs Ogen and Schmidtman of the Department of Public Works. This was after the annexation of Zululand as part of Natal and the designation of Eshowe as the administrative seat of the Chief Commissioner and local Magistrate. After Union in 1910, the Residency housed various local magistrates, after which it was used for a while as a malaria research centre. It is a typical single-storey Natal house, with the original verandah intact. The house was slightly altered and special accommodation added prior to the visit by the British Royal family in 1947.

ESTCOURT

This town was laid out in 1848 and first named Bushman's River Post, or Bushman's Drift, after the Bushman's River. It was renamed Estcourt in 1863 after THSS Estcourt, a British MP who had sponsored many of the original settlers. It was proclaimed a town in 1905 and became a borough in 1914.

BARTLE HOUSE (ST GREGORY COLLEGE)

During the 1880s, two Dutton daughters established a school here known as Bartle House. While a war correspondent, Winston Churchill stayed here for a short time during the Anglo-Boer War. A double-storey, redbrick building with elements of rural Victorian style, Bartle House was an Anglican school for girls between 1904 and 1928. Since 1978, it has been occupied by the St Gregory College.

BLAAUWKRANTZ BATTLEFIELD

When the Voortrekkers entered Natal in November 1837 a large number camped in the Blaauwkrantz Valley. During the night of 16–17 February 1838, a Zulu impi, which had left Dingane's kraal shortly after the execution of Piet Retief, attacked these family groups, killing 61 men, 56 women and 155 children and a party of retainers. They also destroyed wagons and encampments and drove the cattle away. The grave of Gert Maritz can also be seen here. He died on 23 September 1838 near Loskop, and his remains were brought to Blaauwkrantz and buried here on 16 December 1895.

FORT DURNFORD (KEMPS ROAD)
This extensive fortification was designed by, and named after, Lieutenant-Colonel AW Durnford and was erected in 1874.

GREYSTONE FARM HOUSE (DISTRICT)
This impressive Victorian farmhouse, with its ornamental wood-decorated verandah was built in 1873 by Sir Frederick Moor, the last Prime Minister of the Colony of Natal. In 1968 the building was handed over to the Veld-and-Vlei Trust. It was in this vicinity (Vecht Laager) that the three-day encounter between the Voortrekkers and the Zulu impis took place following the 1838 Weenen massacres.

HATTINGSVLAKTE ROCK ENGRAVINGS
(FARM HATTINGSVLAKTE)
One of the most extensive rock engraving sites in KwaZulu-Natal, the engravings depict a variety of village layouts, which probably date from four Late Iron Age periods and show the evolution of local architecture from early times.

OLD AGRICULTURAL HALL (HARDING STREET)
An impressive sandstone building in neoclassical style designed by Kent & Price, the hall was officially opened in December 1901. It forms a unique civic complex together with the adjacent town hall.

SETTLER COTTAGE (87 LORNE STREET)
This thatched cottage probably dates from the 1870s, and is very closely connected with the early settlers in this area. According to legend it is the oldest existing house in Estcourt.

STONE WALL ALONG BOUNDARY OF GLENBELLO AND STOCKTON FARMS
(MISTY KOP TO HARRIS HILL)
This dolomite wall was presumably erected during the period 1870–1880 as a boundary wall between the farms Glenbello (formerly Tamboekieskraal) and Stockton (formerly Zuurbraak). The wall also played an important role during the Anglo-Boer War (1899–1902).

FORT MISTAKE

FORT MISTAKE (BIGGARSBERG PASS)
Built in the style of the Indian hill forts, this fort is architecturally unique in South Africa. It was an important element of the British fortifications that were erected between Ladysmith and Newcastle just before the First War of Independence in 1881. It is not surprising that the resemblance of this circular fort, loop-holed on three levels, closely resembles an Indian hill fort, when it is considered that both Colonel Wood and Major Dartnell were ex-Indian Army, and they were in charge of communications.

PRO NOBIS (FARM QUAGGASKIRK)
This dwelling, built of dressed stone, is an excellent example of a small Natal farmhouse in Victorian style. It was built in 1885 for Colonel JF Vanderleur de Carrey of the 98th South Staffordshire Regiment.

GLENCOE

The town was laid out in 1921 and was named after a valley in Scotland. It attained municipal status in 1934.

KAREL PIETER LANDMAN HOUSE
(UITHOEK FARM, DISTRICT)
Karel Landman originally came from Uitenhage in the Cape, and led a party of Voortrekkers to Natal. A Commandant at the Battle of Blood River, he later moved to the Waschbank area and probably built this house at Uithoek himself. Landman lived here from 1852 until his death in 1875. The house is typical of the dwellings built by the Voortrekkers at the time.

GREYTOWN

Laid out in 1850, the town was named after Sir George Grey, then Governor of the Cape Colony. It was proclaimed a township in 1896 and became a borough in 1915.

BALMORAL FARMHOUSE AND STABLES
(NEAR RIETVLEI)

The farmhouse was built in 1865 by Petrus Albertus Lyno Otto, who trekked from Caledon in the Cape in 1839. He was a land baron of great importance and influence in Natal, making a considerable contribution to agriculture. The farmhouse is typical of its period and possesses some outstanding features, such as thick shale walls, sneezewood floors and window surrounds, and yellowwood ceilings and windowsills. Of horticultural interest are the oak trees grown from acorns, and a vine brought from the Cape in 1839.

BIRTHPLACE OF GENERAL LOUIS BOTHA
(FARM HONINGFONTEIN)

This is the site of the house where Louis Botha, famous Boer General and the first Prime Minister of the Union of South Africa, was born on 27 September 1862.

GREYTOWN MUSEUM

This historic building was used as a dwelling from 1889 by JE Fannin, a prominent local figure of the time, and is a good example of a Natal-Victorian verandah house. In 1964 the Greytown Town Council opened a room to the public in the old Greytown Library, which housed a collection of photographs and other items of historical interest. The late Jean Tatham and Elsie Royden Turner took an active part in the project and this arrangement served for five years. In 1969 the Umvoti Museum Society was formed, and Ernest Dominy took over the work until 1972, when the Greytown Municipality acquired the present premises (the old Residency). Ernest Dominy became the first curator of this museum, a task he undertook until his death in March 1975.

GREYTOWN TOWN HALL (37 BELL STREET)

The cornerstone was laid on 23 June 1897 by the wife of WK Ente, Chairman of the first Town Board, but the building was only completed in 1903. The original plans were drawn up by architects Stott & Tomlinson, but as the Anglo-Boer War drained resources, only a section of the building, offices and tower were built. To celebrate the Jubilee of Queen Victoria a clock was bought from a church in Pietermaritzburg for the tower, but was later returned. It was subsequently decided to complete the building and W Street-Wilson was commissioned to redesign it. The Governor of Natal, Sir Henry McCallum, opened the Town Hall in 1904.

GROUTVILLE

This town was established as an American Missionary Society station in 1844 and was named after the missionary Reverend A Grout (1803–1894).

ALBERT LUTHULI HOUSE (CHARLOTTEDALE TOWNSHIP, LOWER TUGELA DISTRICT)

Chief Albert John Luthuli was born in Rhodesia (now Zimbabwe) in 1898, and died after being hit by a train near his home in Groutville in 1967. He became the President of the African National Congress in 1952, and was awarded the Nobel Peace Prize in 1961. He published his book, *Let My People Go,* in 1962.

HERMANNSBURG

The town was established on the farm Perseverance by the Hermannsburg Missionary Society in 1854, and was named after Hermannsburg in Germany.

LUTHERAN CHURCH
(FORMERLY PETER-PAUL KIRCHE)

The foundation stone of this neogothic Evangelical-Lutheran Peter-Paul Church was laid on 1 April 1868, and the building was consecrated on 23 February 1870. The church is closely associated with the history and founding of the Hermannsburg Missionary Society, and also with the colonisation of these and other parts of South Africa by German Settlers. On 5 May 1872, after a period of continuous rain, the tower collapsed. However, it was rebuilt in a modified fashion during September 1872.

MISSIONARIES HOUSE

Erected in German-Saxon style, this historic mission house was built to provide housing for the staff of the Hermannsburg Mission Station. It is probably the only German-Saxon house in South Africa, and was built by the first group of eight missionaries and eight colonists soon after their arrival in 1854. It consists of 16 bedrooms and eight living rooms, and was constructed of sun-dried bricks made on site. The building timber, of 'umdoni' and yellowwood, was cut into beams and boards by the men themselves.

At this centre of the Evangelical-Lutheran Mission, the first pupils were taught in 1856, and thus the German School of Hermannsburg was established.

HIMEVILLE

Himeville was proclaimed a township in 1905 and was named after Sir Albert Henry Hime (1842–1919), Prime Minister of Natal from 1899 to 1903.

HIMEVILLE FORT (ARBUCKLE STREET)

This loop-holed fort, the last structure of its kind erected in Natal, was built to provide protection for local farmers. In 1902 it was converted into a prison and a gaoler's house was added. It also served as a refuge during the Bambatha Rebellion of 1906.

OLD PRISON BUILDINGS (ARBUCKLE STREET)

Erected as a refuge during the Siege of Ladysmith in 1899, the prison building, with its loopholes, is presumably the last of its kind built by the Natal Colonial Government.

OLD RESIDENCY (ARBUCKLE STREET)

Built at the same time as the Himeville Fort in 1898, this building has been the home of the local Magistrate ever since. The single-storey, L-shaped house, with corrugated-iron roof, sandstone walls and a gable on the south of the main façade, features sash windows and four-panel doors. The front door is semiglazed with side lights, and the verandah is supported on timber posts with simple elongated brackets. The interior has random-width beech floors, and tongue-and-groove ceilings.

HOWICK

The town was established in 1850 on a section of James Archbell's farm. It was named after Viscount Howick (later Earl Grey), Secretary of State for the Colonies from 1846 to 1852. Proclaimed a township in 1916, Howick became a borough in 1961.

FAIRFELL HOMESTEAD (SHAFTON ROAD)

The house was built in 1872 by Sir George Sutton, who became the fifth Prime Minister of Natal in 1903. Wattle branches were first used for the fences and it was Sutton who noticed the liquid between the surface wood and the bark of the trees, and sent a sample of the bark to London for testing, leading to the discovery of the high tannic acid content of the bark. Sutton published the findings in 1889, and this was the start of wattle being used in the tanning industry. Later it was discovered that wattle also made excellent pulp for paper.

HOWICK FALLS

The falls are situated at the point where the Umgeni River cascades some 95m. They were named after Viscount Howick (Earl Grey). The first inhabitant of the nearby town of Howick was a hotelier, who operated a ferry. The best place to cross the Umgeni in the early days was just above the deep, fast-flowing river; many wagons were swept over the falls.

MUSEUM BUILDING (24 MORLING STREET)

This house, built during the late nineteenth century, is one of the oldest buildings in the Natal-Colonial style still existing in this area.

INANDA

The first settlers were a group of Methodists in 1850 under the patronage of the Earl of Verulam. Daniel Lindley established a mission station, which he named Inanda in 1858. The land was acquired by the American Board of Commissioners for Foreign Missions in 1859 and vested in the Natal Native Trust in 1904.

JOHN DUBE HOUSE (OHLANGE)

John Langalibalele Dube was born in 1871 in Inanda. In 1904 he founded the Zulu-language newspaper, *Ilanga Lase Natal*, later renamed *Ilanga* and still published today. In 1912 he became the first President of the African National Congress. He died in Durban in 1946.

OTTAWA HOUSE

This well-known and prominent mansion is linked to the growth of the South African sugar industry. Ottawa Sugar Estate was begun by Anthony Wilkinson, who came to Natal in 1856.

KEARSNEY

ISIVUNDU HOUSE (DISTRICT)

The building of this magnificent mansion began in 1901 and was completed in 1904. It was built as the Balcombe family home, and is one of the few remaining 'sugar palaces' in the province.

KEARSNEY CHAPEL (AT THE HOME OF THE LATE SIR LIEGE AND LADY MARY HULETT)

In 1870 the first wood-and-iron chapel was erected. It was enlarged in 1881 and a new chancel added. This chapel was in use until the present church was inaugurated in 1908. The chapel was designed by Stott of Stott & Kirby Architects, and built by Rorvik & Sons. They built around the old chapel, and when the new chapel was complete, the old chapel was dismantled and removed via the front door.

KOKSTAD

The town was founded in 1871 by the missionary William Dower. Named after Adam Kok III (1811–1875), the Griqua Chief who led his followers here from Philippolis in 1862, Kokstad attained municipal status in 1892.

KOKSTAD MUSEUM (104 MAIN STREET)

This building, with Victorian and Edwardian characteristics, dates from 1908. It was used as a public library until 1982.

VICTORIAN CAST-IRON BANDSTAND (MAIN STREET)

The ornamental bandstand dates from 1912. It was donated to the Town Council by engineers responsible for Kokstad's water scheme.

KWADUKUZA (FORMERLY STANGER)

This town was founded in 1873 on the site of Zulu King Shaka's kraal, Dukuza. Named after William Stanger (1811–1854), the first Surveyor-General of Natal, it attained municipal status in 1949, and was recently renamed kwaDukuza.

SHAKA MEMORIAL (COUPER STREET)
This memorial is dedicated to Tshaka ka Senzangakhona (c.1788–1828), the founder, king and ruler of the Zulu nation. It was erected by his descendant and heir Solomon ka Dinizulu and the Zulu nation in 1932. The town of kwaDukuza (previously Stanger) stands on the site of Shaka's kraal. It was here that he was assassinated by his two half-brothers, Dingane and Mhlangane. His body was wrapped in an ox hide and was buried in a grain pit, on which this memorial stands today.

SOUTH INDIAN SCHOOL (BALCOMBE STREET)
The original section was built in 1880 and served as the home of Mr Dukes. On 5 August 1895 he gave two rooms to be used as a school, of which he became the principal. Originally called the old Stanger European Government School, it is now the Stanger South Secondary School.

LADYSMITH

Ladysmith was founded in 1847 and proclaimed in 1850. Formerly known as Windsor and named after George Windsor, a trader, it was renamed after the wife of Sir Harry Smith, Governor of the Cape Colony (1847–1852). The town attained municipal status in 1899.

DUTCH REFORMED CHURCH
(103 MURCHISON STREET)
The present building is the third church on this site and was inaugurated on 10 August 1929. This octagonal church is an unusual example of the work of Gerard Moerdijk, and is built of rusticated sandstone, with a tiled roof. The well-integrated steeple with clock and weathervane, as well as a large rose window set in an oval voussoir, are particularly noteworthy.

HINDU THIRUKOOTAM AND SHRI GANASEE TEMPLE
(113 FORBES STREET)
This building is the oldest Hindu Temple in Ladysmith, and is the result of the amalgamation of the Hindu Thirukootam founded in 1910 by the Tamil inhabitants of Ladysmith, and the Shri Ganasee temple and hall erected in 1916.

KEERWEDER (25 KEATE STREET)
This gracious home is one of the finest examples of Victorian architecture remaining in Ladysmith. It was presented to Ds HF Schoon (1851–1930) on his retirement after many years of service in the Dutch Reformed Church.

NATAL GOVERNMENT RAILWAY BUILDING
(316 MURCHISON STREET)
The cornerstone of this double-storey Victorian sandstone building was laid on 25 September 1903 by Joseph Baynes. It was erected by the Natal Government Railways as a recreation centre for railway staff.

SOOFI MOSQUE AND PROPERTY
(41 MOSQUE SOOFIE ROAD)
Muslim traders arrived in Ladysmith in 1885. A wood-and-iron mosque was built in 1898 with funds donated from the community. The present mosque was completed in 1969, and is regarded as one of the most beautiful of its kind in southern Africa.

SPIOENKOP BATTLEFIELD (DISTRICT)
This battle of the Anglo-Boer War took place on 23–24 January 1900. Between 2 500 and 2 700 British soldiers and 58 Boers died during the encounter at Spioenkop.

THE RESIDENCY (11–13 WRIGHT ROAD)
This house is a prototype of what might be termed the 'Ladysmith vernacular', a type of residence that became popular around the turn of the nineteenth century.

TOWN HALL (MURCHISON STREET)
The Town Hall, the cornerstone of which was laid in August 1893, was designed and built by architects Walker & Singleton. Although badly damaged during the Siege of Ladysmith (1899-1900), it was was restored by Lucas in 1900.

WAGONHILL/PLATRAND BATTLEFIELD
During the Anglo-Boer War (1899–1902) this battle, on 6 January 1900, was an unsuccessful attempt by the Boers under Commandant Cornelius de Villiers, to attack the British defence line commanded by General Sir Ian Hamilton, and capture Ladysmith.

LIONS RIVER
This was one of the first districts in KwaZulu-Natal to be inhabited by whites. The original wagon road to the Transvaal ran up the Karkloof River Valley. The last lion in the district was shot in 1856.

OLD HOSTEL BUILDING (CEDARA AGRICULTURAL COLLEGE)
The foundation stone was laid on 28 April 1905 by Sir Henry McCallum, Governor of Natal. The builder was FW Lawrence and the architects Stott & Kirby. The restored building of the Natal Colonial Department of Agriculture and Mines was officially opened on 28 April 1993 by AT Meyer, Deputy Minister of Agriculture.

MATATIELE
Established in 1874, the town attained municipal status in 1904. The area is very swampy and home to many ducks and waterfowl, and the name comes from the Basuto word 'mada-I-yila', which means 'the ducks have flown'.

OLD POST OFFICE BUILDING, NOW MATATIELE MUSEUM (HIGH STREET)
The building was originally erected by John Hutt, for Messrs Barker and Heyns, to be used as a garage. In 1925 it was bought by the Dutch Reformed Church as a hall, and in 1968 it was sold to the Department of Postal Services, and used as a post office until 1984.

MOOI RIVER
Mooi River was proclaimed a township in 1921, and takes its name from the river along which it is situated. The town attained municipal status in 1959.

COMMANDANT'S HOUSE AND DOCTOR'S QUARTERS (WESTON AGRICULTURAL COLLEGE)
These two wood-and-iron houses were erected in 1900 and are relics of the British Military Remount Depot, which was established here shortly before the outbreak of the Anglo-Boer War in 1899.

HELEN BRIDGE (OVER THE MOOI RIVER)
The bridge was named after Helen Bisset, the second daughter of General John Jarvis Bisset, acting Governor of Natal at the time. It was the first bridge to span the Mooi River, at Mooi River Drift (later known as Weston), and was constructed to do away with long delays in wagon and carriage traffic going north when the river was in flood. The bridge was built in 1866 and was the first to charge a toll to defray building costs. Originally it was a single-span of 27.43m, but a central column was added in 1904, and the timber deck was replaced with steel and concrete.

MOUNT EDGECOMBE

This sugar-growing settlement was named after an estate in the west of England owned by the Earl of Mount Edgecombe.

GANESHA TEMPLE

This Hindu temple is the first building in South Africa designed by the well-known architect and builder, Kristappa Reddy. It was erected in 1899 and forms a unique part of South Africa's heritage.

Kristappa Reddy was indentured to Mount Edgecombe in 1898 at the age of 35, and the architecture and sculpture of the temple indicate that he was conversant with Silpa Sastras (a text that contains detailed rules for temple building). The Ganesha temple is dedicated to the god of wisdom, prudence, good luck and the dispeller and remover of all obstacles. It features a 'hundi' collection box, and it is common practice amongst devotees who pass the temple, to stop and place money into the 'hundi'.

MPENDLE

The town was established in 1894 and was named after a nearby hill. The name derives from the Zulu word 'impendle', meaning 'uncovered' or 'exposed'.

COLLINGHAM SHELTER

The Collingham Shelter contains a 50cm deep deposit, which accumulated during a 150-year period approximately 1 800 years ago. Subsequent occupations have resulted in thin deposits dating to around 1 300 and 700 years back. The site was excavated by A Mazel, and a part of the collapsed ceiling was removed to allow access to the deposit. Pieces of painted rock were found in the deposit and 19 different stratigraphic units were identified.

MTUNZINI

Named after the Zulu word meaning 'place of shade', Mtunzini was originally inhabited by John Robert Dunn (1833–1895) and his followers. Dunn was the white Zulu Chief who trekked to Zululand with his family's coloured maid, Catherine Pierce, as his common-law wife. He fought at the Battle of Ndondakusuka (1856). Adopting the Zulu custom of 'lobolo', he bought 49 Zulu wives and had 117 children. Cetshwayo granted him 400ha of land at Moyeni and 2 830ha at Mangete, where his descendants still live.

FORT TENEDOS (NORTH BANK, TUGELA RIVER)

Fort Tenedos was built at the time of the Anglo-Zulu War (1879) and named after the British warship of the same name. It housed the British forces involved in the first invasion of Zululand, and was intended to defend the area in the event of a Zulu attack.

RAFFIA PALMS

These palms, one of a species of 15 and the only true palm species indigenous to South Africa, have as their natural distribution, Kosi Bay, where they cover an area of 50ha. One theory as to how the palms ended up here, is that after CC Foxon, the Magistrate at Mtunzini from 1905 to 1921, saw the palms growing at Kosi Bay, he collected seeds and planted them on his return to Mtunzini.

Another theory is that the seeds were sent to Foxon by the Director of Prisons, who requested that he plant the seed as it was thought that this would reduce the cost of importing the fibre from West Africa via London. The fibre was to be used in the prison broom-making industry. An added advantage of this plantation of Raffia palms is the habitat it provides for the Palmnut Vulture, a very rare bird found, which is found in this area. Sighting of the first breeding was reported in 1953.

TUGELA BATTLEFIELD
(NORTH BANK, TUGELA RIVER)
A battle took place here on 17 April 1838. Voortrekkers and British traders from Port Natal, led by John Cane, Robert Biggar and John Stubbs, together with a handful of whites, coloureds and about 1 500 Africans fought against the Zulus.

NEWCASTLE

The town was laid out in 1864 and proclaimed a township in 1882. It was named after the Duke of Newcastle, Secretary of State for the Colonies in 1852 and 1859, and attained municipal status in 1891.

CARNEGIE LIBRARY (VOORTREKKER STREET)
The building was erected in 1915 in the Edwardian style and was designed by the architectural firm Chick & Bartholomew. This was the first Carnegie Library building to be erected in Natal.

FORT AMIEL (FORT STREET)
This structure was named after Major Amiel and was erected in about 1878. It was used by British soldiers during the Zulu Rebellion and the First War of Independence (1880–1881).

HILLDROP HOUSE (HILLDROP ROAD)
Erected by Sir Melmoth Osborne, resident Magistrate of Newcastle from 1868 to 1875, Sir Henry Ryder Haggard took occupation of this imposing building in January 1881. During his sojourn the Royal Commission, which drew up the terms of the Pretoria Convention and provided for the repossession of the Transvaal after the First War of Independence (1880–1881), held a meeting here. Present on this occasion were Sir Hercules Robinson, Sir Henry de Villiers, President Brand and Sir Evelyn Wood.

Sir Henry Ryder Haggard, an English author of romantic adventure stories and political books, was born at Bradenham, Norfolk, and died in London. Of his more than 60 adventure stories, his novel *Jess* was based on his experiences at Hilldrop. His best-known novel, *King Solomon's Mines*, was written in 1885.

HISTORIC BUFFALO RIVER BRIDGE
(BETWEEN NEWCASTLE AND UTRECHT)
This bridge was erected jointly by the Zuid-Afrikaansche Republiek and the Colony of Natal. It was officially opened on 1 October 1898 by JAR Johnstone, Minister of Agriculture for Natal, and SW Burger, member of the Executive Committee of the ZAR.

MAJUBA MOUNTAIN (DISTRICT)
The Battle of Majuba took place on 27 February 1881 during the First War of Independence. Ninety-two British troops under General Sir Pomeroy Colley were killed (including himself), and 134 injured when they were attacked by Boer forces under General Piet Joubert. A memorial to commemorate the Boer victory was unveiled on 8 March 1997.

OLD ARMOURY (SCOTT STREET)
The Old Armoury was presumably built in 1860 by military volunteers as an arsenal for the defence of the area around Newcastle. It was used as a mobilisation post during 1914–1918 and again in 1939.

O'NEILL'S COTTAGE (DISTRICT)
The Battle of Majuba, which took place on the 27 February 1881, was the culminating action of the First War of Independence (1880–1881), during which battles were fought between Transvaal burghers and British soldiers at Bronkhorstspruit on 20 December 1880, at Laing's Nek on 28 January 1881, and at Skuinshoogte (Ingogo) on 8 February 1881.

During the Battle of Majuba, the home of Eugene O'Neill was used as a makeshift hospital, and the chief terms to bring about an end to the war were negotiated here on 21 March 1881.

PAVILION
(ST DOMINIC'S ACADEMY, ST DOMINIC STREET)
St Dominic's Academy was founded in 1896. The Pavilion, a 30m wooden structure, was built in 1916 in Victorian style, and is one of the few remaining structures of its type in South Africa.

TOWN HALL (SCOTT STREET)
The Town Hall was designed by William Lucas and erected in 1898. It is the only colonial building remaining in Newcastle. With its stained glass windows and attractive clock tower, the restored sandstone hall is still in use.

During the Anglo-Boer War (1899–1902), the Boers occupied Newcastle and renamed it Viljoensdorp, after General Ben Viljoen. The inhabitants had evacuated the town, and the looted furniture was stacked in the Town Hall. Dynamite was also stored under the floor in one of the dressing rooms, but it is not known why the Boers did not blow up the Town Hall before they departed.

NEW GERMANY

Established in 1848, the town was originally named Neu-Deutschland (subsequently translated to the present name). It attained municipal status in 1960.

OLD GERMAN LUTHERAN CHURCH, INCLUDING FURNITURE AND ACCESSORIES
(SHEPSTONE ROAD)
The German Lutheran Church was erected in 1862 by the German immigrants who settled in New Germany under the Reverend Jonas Bergthiel. It is the oldest existing German church in KwaZulu-Natal, and the furniture and fittings are of exceptional cultural historic importance. The church was restored by Stellenbosch Farmers' Winery, and opened on 19 March 1976. Items of particular note include the altar, the pulpit, the baptismal font, a chandelier, the organ, altar rails, pews, a hymn board, altar candlesticks and the altar cloth.

NEW HANOVER

The town was founded in 1850 and was named after Hanover in Germany by the German Settlers.

HISTORIC LUTHERAN CHURCH
This cruciform church was erected in 1867 by German Settlers who moved to New Hanover from Bergthiel's New Germany settlement. The high steeple was added in 1885.

NOTTINGHAM ROAD

The town was founded in 1905 and was named after the Nottingham Regiment stationed here in the nineteenth century when trouble was expected from the Basuto.

ST JOHN'S GOWRIE PRESBYTERIAN CHURCH
Also known as the Upper Umgeni Presbyterian Church, this wood-and-iron church was erected in 1884–1885 on land donated by Byrne settler, John King. It was the first church to be built in the Upper Umgeni area.

NQUTU

The name is derived from Zulu 'inggutu', and means 'flat-topped vessel'. It described the hill after which it is named.

ISANDLWANA BATTLEFIELD (DISTRICT)
In the vicinity of the Isandlwana hill, a British force commanded by Lieutenant-Colonel

AW Durnford and Brevet-Lieutenant Colonel B Pulleine, was virtually annihilated on 22 January 1879 by a Zulu impi of between 20 000 and 25 000 men, under the command of Ntshingwayo ka Mahole Khoza. In this famous battle, 52 officers, 806 non-commissioned officers and men as well as 471 troops of colour and non-combatants on the British side lost their lives, while about 3 000 Zulus were killed. This battle led directly to the heroic defence of Rorke's Drift, which lies 16km to the west of the Isandlwana Battlefield.

PRINCE IMPERIAL MEMORIAL (NEAR NONDWENI)

This memorial marks the site where the Prince Imperial of France, son of Emperor Napoleon III and his wife, Empress Eugenia, died, and with it, the last hopes of the Bonaparte dynasty. His body lay in state in the old St Mary's Catholic Church in Pietermaritzburg before being taken to Durban and put aboard a Royal Navy ship. His remains were first buried at Chiselhurst, England, but were reinterred in the great Napoleonic mausoleum built in 1887 by Empress Eugenia at Farnborough Hill.

PADDOCK

PADDOCK RAILWAY STATION

This late Edwardian Railway Station and siding, together with the wood-and-iron buildings, water tank and platform, is an excellent example of the rural stations that were characteristic at the turn of the nineteenth century. The railway line from Port Shepstone through Izotsha, Bomela, Renken, Plains, Paddock and Harding, was constructed in 1911 to transport wattle from Harding to Port Shepstone.

PAULPIETERSBURG

Established in 1888, the town was originally named Paulpietersrust after President Paul

Kruger and General Piet Joubert. It then became Paulpietersdorp and finally changed to Paulpietersburg in 1896. The town attained municipal status in 1958.

HISTORICAL DROSTDY BUILDING

The Drostdy, erected in 1906, was the first British public building built in the area and represents the start of Colonial rule there.

KRUGER BRIDGE

This fine stone bridge was completed in 1898 on the instructions of the Government of the South African Republic.

LIBRARY BUILDING (KNOWN AS KRUGER CHURCH) (SMIT STREET)

The cornerstone of this impressive church was laid on 20 May 1899 by Ds PS Snyman. It was used as a storehouse by British soldiers during the Anglo-Boer War (1899–1902) and was only used as a church from 20 May 1904. According to legend, President Paul Kruger donated ten gold pounds towards the building fund. Due to poor membership, the church was disbanded in 1951 and was later used by the Evangelisch-Lutherische Gemeinde Paulpietersburg, who sold it to the municipality in 1969. The building has been restored and converted into a library.

PIETERMARITZBURG

The city was established in 1838 and was named after Piet Retief (1780–1838) and Gerhardus Marthinus Maritz (1798–1839), leaders of the Great Trek. It attained municipal status in 1855 and became the capital of Natal in 1857.

ALEXANDRA ROAD POLICE STATION (ALEXANDRA ROAD)

This building served as the Natal Mounted Police headquarters and was designed by the

Colonial Engineer Albert Hime, with the assistance of the Clerk of Works, A Singleton, in 1878. It was only completed in 1890 due to disruptions brought about by the Anglo-Zulu War, following which it housed the Natal Mounted Police (later the Natal Police in 1894). From 1921 to 1933 it served as headquarters of the South African Police.

BUTINE HOUSE (151 PIETERMARITZ STREET)
This magnificent double-storey manor house, with elaborate cast-iron verandahs, was built in the late nineteenth century and forms an integral part of the architectural character of Pietermaritz Street, which has remained predominantly Victorian.

CHRISTIAN SCIENCE CHURCH (LOOP STREET)
This imposing church building, with Gothic and Romanesque features, was originally built in 1903–1904 as a Congregational Church. It was designed by the architects Stott & Kirby.

CHURCH OF THE COVENANT/VOORTREKKER MUSEUM (CHURCH STREET)
This church was erected in fulfilment of the covenant made at the Waschbankspruit on 9 December 1838 by Sarel Cilliers, religious leader during the Great Trek. He made a promise to God, that if He would grant the Voortrekkers a victory over the Zulus, they would build a church in His honour, and commemorate the day of victory. After winning the Battle of Blood River on 16 December 1838, they started collecting funds for a church.

Building commenced early in 1840 and the church was inaugurated in 1841. The congregation was unable to afford a parsonage at that time, so they decided to use the building temporarily as a church, and once they could afford a proper church building, the old one would then be converted to a parsonage. The new Voortrekker Memorial Church was inaugurated in 1861 on the site where the memorial hall stands today, but the Church of the Vow was never to become a parsonage. It was sold to Vicar Brayhirst in 1863, and was subsequently used as a school, blacksmith shop, mineral-water factory, chemist and tearoom. In 1910 it was bought back and restored by the Church Council and was reopened as the Voortrekker Museum on 16 December 1912.

CHURCH OF THE VOW PULPIT, VOORTREKKER MUSEUM (CHURCH STREET)
The pulpit was made in 1841 and used by the Church of the Vow until 1861. It was then used in the Dutch Reformed church (Voortrekker Community, Pietermaritzburg) from 1861–1955.

CITY HALL (CHURCH STREET)
The City Hall stands on the site of the original Raadsaal of the Republic of Natal, which was completed in 1842 and served as a Supreme Court from 1846–1871. The first City Hall was designed by Street-Wilson and completed in 1893, but was destroyed by fire on 12 July 1898. The present city hall was built in 1900, and officially opened on 14 August 1901 by the Duke and Duchess of Cornwall and York, later to become King George V and Queen Mary. It is regarded as one of the best examples of its time.

CLARK HOUSE AND VICTORIA HALL (MARITZBURG COLLEGE)
These two buildings housed the original Pietermaritzburg High School. Clark House was built in 1887 and was designed by Philip Dudgeon. It was first known as the Main Building but was renamed after a headmaster, RD Clark. It has been described as 'the best example of collegiate Gothic in Natal'.

Victoria Hall was built in 1895 and was formally opened by the Natal Governor, Sir Walter Francis Hely-Hutchinson. It was used as a hospital during the Anglo-Boer War (1899–1902).

CONSERVATOIRE DE HAMMERSTEIN (141 ALEXANDRA ROAD)

Built in the late 1800s, this building was named after Oscar Hammerstein, a relative of a former owner of the house. This double-storey square facebrick house is a landmark and focal point of one of Pietermaritzburg's major suburban thoroughfares, and is one of the remaining elegant old homes in an area noted for the quality of its historic buildings.

DORCHESTER HOUSE (190 LOOP STREET)

The property on which Dorchester House was built during the first half of the 1830s was bought by J Ireland after its subdivision in 1892, and sold to F Shippey in 1894. Together with the adjoining house known as Norfolk Villa, it forms an impressive architectural unit. It is one of the finest examples of the late Victorian redbrick structures of Pietermaritzburg.

FORT NAPIER (HISTORICAL CORE) (NAPIERVILLE)

Fort Napier was named after General Sir George Napier, Governor of the Cape of Good Hope 1838-1844). It was founded by two companies of the 45th Regiment (1st Sherwood Foresters) on 31 August 1843, under the command of Major Smith. Imperial troops occupied the fort from 1843–1914.

OLD OFFICERS' MESS (FORT NAPIER)

The Officers' Mess, complete with clock tower, was erected 'temporarily' during the Anglo-Boer War (1899–1902) after being transported from India in 1899. A fine example of a wood-and-iron structure of the period, it now serves as a recreation hall.

ST GEORGE'S GARRISON CHURCH (FORT NAPIER)

This church was built in 1897 and was used as a military hospital during the Anglo-Boer War (1899–1902). The beautiful stained glass windows feature the Sheffield trademark, a daisy, and the carved choir stalls are the work of a British soldier who was stationed at Fort Napier. The Roberts Window bears the inscription: 'In sympathy with Field Marshall Lord Roberts and his wife Norah, on the death of Lieutenant Frederick Roberts, their only son, who was killed in the Battle of Colenso 15 December 1899. Was dedicated by the women of Pietermaritzburg.'

GIRLS' HIGH SCHOOL: MAIN BUILDING (1925), NORTH FLOOR (1927), GYMNASIUM (1934) AND NORMA BURNS HALL (1960), TOGETHER WITH THE FOUNTAIN AT THE ENTRANCE (186 ALEXANDRA ROAD)

This impressive group of neoclassical buildings forms the nucleus of the Girls' High School, which was opened on this site in the old manor house 'Morningside' on 4 August 1920. The latter, although altered, is still part of the school.

HISTORIC BUILDING (131 PIETERMARITZ STREET)

A fine late-Victorian redbrick residence, this house was built between 1893 and 1897 by GJ Cundell. It has a tiled roof with two unique stepped gables on the façade and three other gables on the main roof. Verandahs on both levels have typical wrought-iron work and timber balustrades.

HISTORIC COTTAGE (238 BOOM STREET)

This cottage is one of the oldest remaining unaltered houses in Pietermaritzburg, and appears on the town plan of 1876. It is of national and local architectural and historical importance, as it is the only surviving example of its kind. The single-storey cottage, with a saddle roof and three chimneys, is finished in Broseley tile on the street side and corrugated iron on the rear. Its walls are plastered clay brick. The front door and sash windows, as well as the verandah with its iron balustrades, are original.

ITALIAN PRISONER OF WAR CHURCH (EPWORTH ROAD)

This church was erected in 1944 by the Second World War Italian prisoners of Camp 4. It is situated on the outskirts of Pietermaritzburg and is still used by the Italian community. There were approximately 5 000 Italians detained here, and it was at the suggestion of Padré Conti that about 500 of them occupied themselves with the building of this little church. Construction commenced on 2 February 1943, and the stone used was carried by hand from a quarry some 2km away. In spite of this hardship, and with whatever tools they had at their disposal, the church was consecrated approximately one year later on 19 March 1944.

Over the years the church became derelict. In a ceremony held on 19 March 1995, the title deeds were handed over to a trust that had been formed by the Italian community to preserve this declared monument. A survivor of the camp, Salvatore Fadella, restored the church to its current state. In the grounds at the back of the church stands a stone lion, which was sculptured by the Italians and originally stood in the middle of the camp.

LOOP STREET POLICE STATION (CNR MURRAY LANE)

This Edwardian three-storey building was originally used as an engineering office by the Natal Government Railways. It was designed in 1901 by the architect EJ Wellman, who was assisted with the construction by GB Laffan. The building was completed in 1903 and used by the NGR until shortly before the outbreak of the First World War in 1914. A central pediment that rests on four heavy columns features the British royal coat of arms prominently on the front. The redbrick building now accommodates the local headquarters of the South African Police Services.

MACRORIE HOUSE MUSEUM (11 LOOP STREET)

Macrorie House was built in 1862 and was purchased in 1870 by Bishop WAK Macrorie. He lived here until his departure for England in 1892. Now a museum, the Victorian house is closely associated with the Anglican Church in South Africa. The appointment of Bishop Macrorie followed the rebellion of Bishop JW Colenso, when he openly challenged the Doctrine of Atonement and debunked the idea of eternal punishment.

This schism resulted in the establishment of two church factions: Colenso's Church of England in Natal (St Peter's) and the Episcopal Church of the Province in South Africa (St Saviour's). Colenso's position was taken over by Bishop Macrorie upon his arrival from England. Situated within the homestead is the Chapel of Bishop Macrorie.

MAIN POST OFFICE (LONGMARKET STREET)

The sandstone building was designed by William Lucas, predominantly in late Renaissance style, and built by the firm Williams & Bell. The cornerstone was laid on 14 February 1903. A window above the main entrance shows the pre-1908 Natal coat of arms, with wildebeest running from left to right.

MARIAN VILLA (282 ALEXANDRA ROAD)

Built in 1914 for Dr Conrad Akerman, this magnificent Edwardian homestead features high ceilings, an ornate exterior and mosaic verandahs. Dr Akerman lived here for only two years, when a personal tragedy caused him to sell the house to Clement Stott, the architect who designed it. Stott lived here for 10 years, after which it was occupied in 1928 by John Barker, a city councillor, and his family until 1962, when it was bought by the Dominican order. A chapel was included in the layout and it was converted into a convent. In 1980 Marian Villa became a home for the aged.

NATAL BOTANICAL GARDENS

These botanical gardens, the original section of which was established in 1870, comprise an exotic garden and an indigenous garden. The plane tree avenue of approximately 300m features 45 majestic plane trees planted by the curator, WE Marriott, on 8 May 1908, at the suggestion of Sir Matthew Nathan, last Governor of Natal. It is a world-renowned sight and stretches mainly through the exotic section. The indigenous garden was started in 1970 and contains natural KwaZulu-Natal vegetation.

NORFOLK VILLA (196 LOOP STREET)

In 1895 the Thresh family took transfer of this property and was probably responsible for the erection of Norfolk Villa. The double-storey building, which was also used as the residence of high-ranking Imperial military officers, is a prominent local landmark. It rates among the finest examples of late Victorian architecture in Pietermaritzburg.

OLD BOYS' MODEL SCHOOL (310 LOOP STREET)

This building is a good example of Victorian school architecture, and was designed by the Natal Colonial Engineer, Peter Paterson. It was erected in 1865 by Baverstock & Winter. The present Maritzburg College used the building from 1866 to 1888. In 1889 the Boys' Model School, which had been established in 1849, moved into the building and remained until 1978, when the school was changed to the Remedial Model Primary School.

OLD COLONIAL BUILDING (241 CHURCH STREET)

The Colonial Building was designed and built in 1898 by architect WH Powell in the late English Renaissance and Georgian-Revival styles.

OLD GOVERNMENT HOUSE (CHURCH STREET)

The front of this building was built of local grey shale stone in 1868 and was the residence of the Lieutenant-Governor of Natal, Benjamin Pine, who arrived in Natal in 1851. The Natal Government purchased the building from Benjamin Pine and established it as Government House from 1860–1910. After the rebellion of the Hlube tribe in 1873, it was here that Chief Langalibalele was tried and sentenced.

Empress Eugenie of France stayed here during her pilgrimage to Natal in 1880 to visit Prince Louis Napoleon's grave. The redbrick wing was built in three months in 1901 to provide accommodation for the Duke and Duchess of York (later King George V and Queen Mary). This historic building now forms part of the Natal College of Education complex.

OLD HARWARD BOYS' SCHOOL
(29 HAVELOCK ROAD)

Now the Pietermaritzburg Music School, the building originally housed the Harward Boys' School and later the College for Further Training. It was probably constructed in 1910, as this date has been inscribed on the main gable. It is a typical Edwardian school building with redbrick walls.

OLD LONGMARKET STREET GIRLS' SCHOOL
(LONGMARKET STREET)

This girls' school was erected between 1903 and 1911, and its architectural style is a fine and rare example of a Victorian school building. Of particular note are the different types of bricks used in this interesting example of Edwardian brickwork, especially along the Boshof Street façade.

OLD MAIN BUILDING
(UNIVERSITY OF NATAL, KING EDWARD AVENUE)

Also known as the Arts Block, this is the oldest building of the university, and the most architecturally impressive. The foundation stone was laid on 1 August 1910 by the Earl of Connaught and the building was opened in 1912.

OLD PARLIAMENT BUILDINGS
(237 LONGMARKET STREET)

The Legislative Council Building was erected to house the Legislative Council of the Colony of Natal, after the granting of Responsible Government on 1 May 1893. The foundation stone was laid on 12 September 1899 by the Honourable Sir Walter Hely-Hutchinson. Since 1910 various provincial departments have been housed in this building.

The Legislative Assembly Building was built to house the Legislative Council of the Colony of Natal. The foundation stone was laid on 21 June 1887 by Sir Arthur Havelock, Governor of Natal, in commemoration of Queen Victoria's 50th anniversary of accession to the throne. The building was opened in 1889.

OLD PENTRICH (UMSINDUZI) RAILWAY STATION
(WOODS ROAD)

A gabled Victorian brick building erected in 1906, this was the second of three station buildings at Pentrich. A section of the original platform has also survived. Part of the ground of 'Pentrich Grange' was sold to the Natal Government Railways in 1905. The owner, Robert Topham, emigrated from Pentrich Grange, Derbyshire, England in 1862.

OLD POLICE QUARTERS
(240 PIETERMARITZ STREET)

The old Police Quarters, a structure peculiar to the architecture of Pietermaritzburg, is an H-shaped building with a steep hipped roof of Broseley tiles and a high, plastered chimney.

OLD PRESBYTERIAN CHURCH (CHURCH STREET)

This church was erected between 1852 and 1854. The neogothic tower dates from 1874 and the church clock was installed in 1875. During the Zulu War in 1879 the church was converted into a fortified refuge, and was enlarged in 1883.

OLD ST MARY'S CHURCH
(CNR BURGER AND COMMERCIAL ROADS)

The original church for the African congregation was built in 1856, with most of the funds raised by Bishop Colenso from overseas. The church and ground upon which it stood was sold to erect the Natal Houses of Parliament, and St Mary's Church was demolished in 1887. When the new church was built, of dressed freestone and shale, the original plans were used by the contractor Jesse Smith and the carpenter Vinnecombe.

OLD SATYA VARDHAK SABHA CREMATORIUM AND WAITING ROOM (CREMORNE CEMETERY)

A Hindu cultural organisation, the Satya Vardhak Sabha, was established in 1928 in accordance with the Vedic doctrines of the Hindu faith, to promote the principles of hygiene and the philosophy of reincarnation. A crematorium was built that same year, KwaZulu-Natal's first, used by all faiths.

OLD SUPREME COURT (COLLEGE ROAD)

The history of the Old Supreme Court is inextricably linked to the legal system as it applied to black South Africans in the Colonial and Union periods. This court was part of a system of administration of customary law, which in the old province of Natal provided that crimes exclusively involving blacks be tried according to 'Native Law'. The building dates from about 1898, when the Native High Court was reconstituted after its abolition in 1895. It is a traditional Pietermaritzburg redbrick building, typical of official architecture in the late 1890s.

OLD UMGENI MAGISTRATE'S COURT
(244 PIETERMARITZ STREET)

Built by Major Durnford, Colonial Engineer in about 1877, the Old Umgeni Magistrate's Court is the oldest building on this site (together with the Old Colonial Building and Old Police Quarters).

OLD YMCA (195 LONGMARKET STREET)
The foundation stone was laid by Mrs John Smith, wife of the President of the Association, on 17 December 1880. The building was completed in 1881 and is a fine example of a double-storey verandah construction. A foundation stone was re-laid on Diamond Jubilee Day, 22 June 1897, by WE Bale Esq. The architect was LL Alexander, and the builder, JF Vinnicombe.

ORIGINAL ALLERTON STATE VETERINARY LABORATORY (438 TOWN BUSH VALLEY ROAD)
The original Allerton Laboratory was founded in 1897, and the first director was Lieutenant-Colonel Herbert Watkins-Pitchford. The laboratory consists of a double-storey brick building with a galvanised-iron roof. The ground floor was built approximately 1.5m below ground level, to keep the building cool. Pioneering medical and veterinary work in combating certain diseases and pests was conducted here.

ORIGINAL CELL BLOCK OF OLD PIETERMARITZBURG PRISON (2 BURGER STREET)
Built in 1862, the cell block replaced the Voortrekker Prison on the Market Square. It has been associated with several prominent Zulu prisoners, among them Nkosi Langalibalele Hlubi (1873) and King Dinizulu (1907–1909). The window above the front door was allegedly the spot from where public hangings took place; it is the only window in the complex that has bars that are hinged and padlocked.

OVERPARK HOUSE (122 LOOP STREET)
Overpark House dates from 1884 and is an excellent example of a Victorian verandah house in the Natal style. It features beautiful cast-iron trimmings and fireplaces. The house was built as a Presbyterian manse, and was first occupied by Reverend W Campbell. In 1897 it was bought by John Freeman, who undertook renovations and additions to the building and named it Overpark. Major restoration was effected by Mrs JR Long-Innes, who bought the house in 1980.

PUBLICITY HOUSE (63 COMMERCIAL ROAD)
This building, with its imposing entrance, was designed by JS Brunskill and was completed in 1884. It housed the Borough Police until 1933 and the South African Police until 1972, when it was acquired by the Publicity Association. Together with the City Hall and the Supreme Court, it forms an important historic and architectural group of buildings.

REID'S CABINET WORKS BUILDING (214 LONGMARKET STREET)
Reid's Cabinet Works, the oldest furniture-manufacturing company in Pietermaritzburg, was established by John Reid, who arrived in Pietermaritzburg in 1881, and started this business at the turn of the nineteenth century. It was the first triple-storey business house in Pietermaritzburg.

RUSSELL HIGH SCHOOL BUILDING COMPLEX (CHAPEL STREET)
In 1941 this school, which was founded in 1879, was renamed Russell High School, in honour of Robert Russell, Superintendent of Education from 1873 to 1903. The late nineteenth-century building complex forms a unique historic and architectural group and is closely associated with the development of education in KwaZulu-Natal.

SAN SOUCI HOUSE (65 TRELAWNEY ROAD)
San Souci, formerly known as Harwin House, was designed by the German architect Albert Halder, and was erected in 1883. This Victorian manor house, as well as its beautiful landscaped garden, reflects the affluence of its original owner.

SCOTTSVILLE PRIMARY SCHOOL (KING EDWARD AVENUE)
The redbrick school building, opened in 1915, was the last in Pietermaritzburg to be designed in typical Collegiate style. It is probably the only remaining roof of flat, red, clay tiles in the city.

TATHAM ART GALLERY (COMMERCIAL ROAD)
This former Supreme Court is an impressive facebrick building in Renaissance pavilion style. It is an integral part of the historic civic and government precinct in the city centre, and was designed in 1864 by Peter Paterson, who assumed office as Colonial Engineer in 1860.

TOWN HILL HOSPITAL (HOWICK ROAD)
Comprising the old Victorian and old North Park buildings, these two double-storey buildings form an integral part of the Town Hill Hospital, one of the oldest in Pietermaritzburg. The complex was designed by A Singleton, who designed the original Victorian asylum in 1876. The North Park Building is the former home of Sir Walter Hardinge, Chief Justice of Natal, and was built in the 1890s.

UMGENI WATER BOARD BUILDING (LONGMARKET STREET)
This double-storey building, with its wood and cast-iron decorated verandah, dates from the 1890s. It forms an integral part of the façade of Longmarket Street.

VOORTREKKER HOUSE (333 BOOM STREET)
Probably erected in 1846 by the Voortrekker Petrus Gehardus Pretorius, this double-storey building is a good example of Voortrekker architecture and is the one of the oldest buildings in Pietermaritzburg.

VOORTREKKER ROAD (WORLD'S VIEW ROAD)
The area is approximately 18.,29m wide and 182.88m long, and runs in a southeasterly direction from the tarred turning circle at the end of World's View Road to the edge of the nearby pine forest plantation. It encompasses a portion of the old Voortrekker Road, with the Town Hill Trig Beacon just within the northeast boundary. Here one can see a mosaic inlay showing the Voortrekker Road, from the direction of Blaukrantz and Bushman's River, up Allermans Drift and over the Umgeni River. It skirts past Howick to pass Cedara and The Knoll and then branches into two. The first route travels through World's View, Boesmansrand, into Pietermaritzburg and down to Port Natal, while the second route follows past Welverdient, Plessislaer, and Pietermaritzburg, and continues on to Port Natal.

This road was used by the Voortrekkers and later by other pioneers and transport riders. It is still visible, although corroded over the years, and winds down the hill into Pietermaritzburg through the plantations, then joins into Voortrekker Road alongside the Wykeham Collegiate.

WAYLAND HOUSE (149 PIETERMARITZ STREET)
This impressive double-storey Victorian manor house dates from the 1890s and forms an integral part of the historic façade of Pietermaritz Street, one of the oldest streets in Pietermaritzburg.

WELVERDIENT (CHURCH STREET)
This house is the oldest double-storey dwelling erected outside the Cape Colony. It was built in about 1840 by the Voortrekker leader, General Andries Pretorius, who also constructed the historic mill and the water furrow on the original site in Edendale. The property, originally known as Welverdient, was sold to the Reverend James Allison on 30 July 1851 and became part of a flourishing mission station known as Edendale. The house has been reconstructed at the Church of the Vow in Church Street.

PINETOWN

The town was laid out on the farm Salt River Poort in 1848, and was named after Sir Benjamin Pine (1809–1901), Lieutenant-Governor of Natal from 1849–1856, and Governor from 1873–1875. It was proclaimed a township in 1942 and attained municipal status in 1948.

INDIGO VATS (PARADISE VALLEY)

These vats were constructed by two Dutch immigrants, Colenbrander and Van Prehn, and were used between 1854 and 1856 for the manufacture of indigo dye.

REMAINS OF UMBILO WATERWORKS AND PORTION OF PARADISE VALLEY RESERVE (PARADISE VALLEY)

The Durban Corporation constructed the waterworks on the Umbilo River in 1884. Designed by the then Borough Engineer, FJE Barnes, the waterworks consisted of a storage dam, settling pond, sand filters, clear well and a circular reservoir. Water was first supplied to Durban on 21 July 1887.

PORT SHEPSTONE

The town was laid out in 1867 and was named after Sir Theophilus Shepstone (1817–1893), Secretary for Native Affairs (1856–1876) and Administrator of Zululand from 1884. Port Shepsone attained municipal status in 1934.

KNEISEL'S CASTLE (24 REYNOLDS STREET)

This magnificent late nineteenth-century residence, with its distinctive German Colonial features, was erected by Charles Frederick Kneisel, a settler from Mainz, Germany, shortly after his arrival in Natal in 1882. He also erected the Royal Hotel and the well-known market buildings in Port Shepstone.

OLD POLICE STATION BUILDING (ALSO KNOWN AS THE OLD FORT)

Built in 1897 by the Department of Public Works of the Natal Colonial Government for the Natal Police, it was used by them until the formation of the Union (1910), and since then it has been used by various departments of the South African Police.

PORT SHEPSTONE LIGHTHOUSE AND THE ORIGINAL LIGHTHOUSE KEEPER'S HOUSE

Port Shepstone's first lighthouse, a green candle-powered masthead lantern mounted on a platform on the southern bluff, was installed in 1895, and served both as a navigational and signal light until the present lighthouse was erected in 1906. This unusual cast-iron structure is one of the two oldest functioning lighthouses on the KwaZulu-Natal coastline.

RICHMOND

The town was established in 1850 and was first named Beaulieu. It was then renamed after the Earl of Richmond, father-in-law of Sir Peregrine Maitland, who was Governor of the Cape from 1844–1847.

BLARNEY SETTLER COTTAGE (FARM DUNBAR ESTATE)

Fred (the son of a Byrne settler) and Sophia (Opie) McLeod built Blarney Cottage in 1878–1879. This delightful cottage is still in near perfect condition. A shed dates from the same period.

CARNARVON MASONIC LODGE (57 RUSSELL STREET)

This rectangular brick building, with Victorian embellishments, was erected in 1883 to accommodate the local Freemasons Lodge. This lodge was established in 1876 and named after the fourth Earl of Carnarvon.

LYNMOUTH GLACIAL PAVEMENT (FARM HOPEWELL, DISTRICT)

Of notable geological significance, the Lynmouth glacial pavement site exhibits good evidence of glacial activity and a prolonged period of glacial deposition of the Dwyka formation over a period of 40 to 60 million years, beginning approximately 300 million years ago. In the Natal Midlands, one large ice sheet moved over the Natal Group sandstone bedrock, leaving behind polished surfaces (glacial pavements) and telltale scratches (striations) of debris carried by the glacier.

RICHMOND AND BYRNE DISTRICT MUSEUM (46 VICTORIA STREET)

The Byrne Settlers, founders of Richmond in 1850, were Presbyterians of Scottish origin. This museum is appropriately accommodated in the old Presbyterian manse, built in 1882. It is an A-shaped villa, with a lean-to structure at the rear and a corrugated-iron roof with a verandah. It was built of shale, a style that was unique to the settlers of the Richmond district.

ST LUCIA

The name dates from the era of Portuguese exploration, when navigators discovered it in 1507.

GREATER ST LUCIA WETLANDS PARK/RESERVE

St Lucia was declared a World Heritage Site by the United Nations Environmental, Social and Cultural Organisation (UNESCO) in December 1999. Since 1895, the St Lucia Game Reserve has been expanded considerably and is one of the oldest parks in Africa. It also has the largest estuarine lake in Africa, which extends along a massive stretch of coastline from Mapelane to Kosi Bay. The largest concentrations of hippo, crocodile and bird life on the continent are to be found here.

TONGAAT

This small town was proclaimed in 1945 and was named after the Tongati River.

JAGANNATHU PURI TEMPLE (WADD STREET)

This richly ornamented temple was constructed by Pandit Shiskishan Maharaj (1871–1949), a Hindu priest who immigrated to South Africa in 1895, originally as an indentured labourer. The temple, which is the only replica of the ancient original temple located in Puri, Orissa, is surrounded by a moat and is dedicated to the warlike god, Jagannathi.

TUGELA RIVER MOUTH

The name Tugela derives from a Zulu word meaning 'the startling one'. The Tugela River is the third most important river in South Africa after the Vaal and Orange rivers.

FORT PEARSON (HAROLD JOHNSON NATURE RESERVE) (SOUTH BANK)

Early in November 1878 two companies of the Buffs built and garrisoned this fort, which was a stout earthen redoubt set on a high knoll overlooking the drift. The fort was named after Colonel CK Pearson, Commander of the British during the first invasion of Zululand. During 1879 the fort was garrisoned by various units until it was abandoned at the end of September 1879.

ULTIMATUM TREE (SOUTH BANK)

It was under the shade of this fig tree, on 11 December 1878, that the High Commissioner's ultimatum, which was to be passed on to Cetshwayo, was read to three principal chiefs headed by Uvumandaba, 11 subordinate chiefs and about 40 of Cetshwayo's followers. The British delegation included JW Shepstone (Secretary for Native Affairs), who read the document, C Brownlee (Commissioner for

Native Affairs, Cape), HF Fynn (Magistrate) and Colonel Forester Walker. The 4 000-word document was drawn up by Sir Bartle Frere.

TWEEDIE

TWEEDIE HALL (FARM TWEEDIE HALL)

This double-storey manor house was designed by William Street-Wilson, a prominent Victorian and Edwardian architect. James Morton Snr, grandfather of the present owner, bought the farm in 1868 and named it after Tweedie Hall in Lancashire, England. The house was completed in 1893. Wire fencing and a silo were used on this progressive farm for the first time in KwaZulu-Natal.

TWEEDIE RESEARCH STATION

The historic core of this farmhouse was erected c.1868 by G Ross, who purchased the farm in 1867. In 1873, the farm passed to Dr Peter Sutherland, a noted physician, botanist, geologist and surveyor, who also became Surveyor General of Natal from 1854 to 1887. After the formation of the Union of South Africa in 1910, the farmhouse was enlarged in the verandah style of the time. After it was bought by Sappi (Pty) Ltd in 1972, the house was enlarged and restored. It is used as a research station for the pulp and paper industry.

ULUNDI

Ulundi was established on the site of the Royal Zulu Kraal where the Zulus were finally defeated by the British on 4 July 1879.

GRAVE AND MONUMENT OF KING DINGANE KA SENZANGAKHONA

The grave and monument are in memory of King Dingane ka Senzangakhona who was assassinated in 1840 and who lies buried here.

NODWENGU

The site of Nodwengu was the kraal of King Mpande Zulu, who reigned over the Zulu kingdom from 1840 to 1872. His grave is within the precincts of this complex. King Mpande was the son of King Senzangakhona, who was also the father of King Shaka and King Dingane.

The Nodwengu Museum built on this site was officially opened on 20 August 1983 by his descendant, heir and successor and the reigning monarch, His Majesty King Zwelethini Mbongi Goodwill ka Bhekuzulu. Another descendent of King Mpande is his great, great grandson, Minister Prince Dr Mangosuthu Gatsha Buthelezi.

ONDINI

Ondini was the last royal residence of King Cetshwayo, and was built on this site after his return from exile in January 1883. It was overrun and burnt to the ground by the British after the Battle of Ulundi on 4 July 1879.

The royal section of King Cetshwayo's kraal has been extensively excavated by archaeologists and meticulously reconstructed. There is a site museum, which interprets life in the royal kraal during Cetshwayo's reign. Ondini also houses the KwaZulu Cultural Museum, with exhibits of the history and arts of the Zulu people.

ULUNDI BATTLEFIELD SQUARE AND CEMETERY

On this site a British force, commanded by Lord Chelmsford and consisting of 4 165 Europeans and 1 152 Bantu, successfully fought against Cetshwayo and his army, a Zulu impi of approximately 20 000. Interesting from a military history standpoint, Chelmsford's force advanced in a hollow, oblong formation, with the cavalry inside and Gatling guns in front. Concentrated fire broke successive waves of assault in this final battle of the Anglo-Zulu War on 4 July 1879.

UMZINTO

Umzinto was proclaimed a township in 1950 and its name in Zulu means 'kraal of achievement'.

GREEN POINT LIGHT HOUSE
(BETWEEN UMKOMAAS AND SCOTTBOROUGH)

The so-called Aliwal Shoal is one of the greatest dangers to ships using the Durban harbour, and many ships have been wrecked here over the years. In 1889 wooden beams were erected at Mahlongwa Head at the northern end and at Scottburgh at the southern point of the shoal. At the turn of the nineteenth century these two beacons were moved, one to Port Shepstone and the other to Green Point.

In 1905 a new cast-iron lighthouse was erected at Green Point. This structure is at present one of the two oldest functioning lighthouses on the KwaZulu-Natal coast. It also has the distinction of being the first lighthouse in South Africa to be fully automated, on 18 November 1961.

UNDERBERG

Underberg lies at the foot of the Drakensberg. It was one of the last districts to be settled, with the first farms established in 1886.

MPONGWENI CAVE (COBHAM STATE FOREST, UMZIMKULU WILDERNESS AREA)

This cave contains a large number of prehistoric rock paintings and is of considerable historical and scientific importance.

UTRECHT

First known as Schoonstroom after the farm on which it was laid out in 1855, the area was renamed Utrecht after the city in the Netherlands in 1856. It became a township in 1904 and a municipality in 1920.

BLOOD RIVER BATTLEFIELD (UTRECHT DISTRICT)

It was on this site that a group of Voortrekkers, under the command of Andries Pretorius, succeeded in resisting the onslaught of the far superior Zulu forces on 16 December 1838. It is the most famous battle site in South Africa. For many years the site was the property of the Dutch Reformed Church of Utrecht, as it was situated within the geographic boundaries of the congregation. It was later transferred to the Transvaal Nederduitsche Hervormde Kerk.

DIRK UYS HOUSE (61 CHURCH STREET)

This is one of the oldest buildings north of the Tugela River and dates back to 1856. It was the home of 'swart Dirk' Uys, who was the first commandant of Utrecht after the district became part of the Zuid-Afrikaansche Republiek. The façade work was completed by Senator Jacobus Johannes Uys. It was here that Prince Imperial Louis Napoleon visited Sannie, the daughter of 'swart Dirk'.

DUTCH REFORMED CHURCH (50 CHURCH STREET)

The foundation stone of this magnificent building was laid on the 23 October 1891 by Commandant General Piet Joubert of the Zuid-Afrikaansche Republiek. The inauguration of the building followed on 21 April 1893. The induction service was conducted by Reverend Dr Andrew Murray, Moderator of the Church of the Cape Colony, and the elder brother of Mrs Neethling, wife of Reverend Neethling.

GEORGE SHAW HOUSE (67 CHURCH STREET)

This house, with its late Victorian features, was built in 1905 by George Shaw, Postmaster of Utrecht (1893–1897) and later a businessman.

MAGISTRATE'S COURT (57 VOOR STREET)

This building was erected between 1894 and 1899 by the government of the Zuid-Afrikaansche Republiek.

OLD DUTCH REFORMED CHURCH PARSONAGE
(CHURCH STREET)
The parsonage was officially taken into use on 12 October 1888. The Reverend HL Neethling, his wife and two daughters were the first occupants. The sandstone house, with a corrugated-iron roof and a front gable on which the date 1887 appears, is the oldest parsonage in KwaZulu-Natal.

OLD REPUBLICAN POWDER MAGAZINE
(PRESIDENT STREET)
This powder magazine was erected in 1893 and is one of three similar structures built by the Zuid-Afrikaansche Republiek, the other two being in Heidelberg and Lydenburg.

PIETER LAFRAS UYS MONUMENT
(CHURCH STREET)
Pieter Lafras Uys was an early settler and one-time landdrost of the district. He fought alongside the British in the Anglo-Zulu War (1879) and was the Commandant of some 40 men, including his four sons. He was killed at Hlobane on 28 March 1879 while courageously going to the aid of his eldest son.

ROTHMAN HOUSE (65 CHURCH STREET)
This dwelling was erected in 1909 by JJ Rothman, a prominent businessman from Utrecht. It is a good example of a Natal Colonial house in the late Victorian style.

TOWN HALL (44 VOOR STREET)
The Town Hall dates from 1913 and is a brown-stone building of considerable character. It forms an integral part of the historic core of Utrecht.

VALLEY OF A THOUSAND HILLS

The region covers parts of Camperdown, Ndwedwe, New Hanover, Pietermaritzburg and Pinetown districts. The valley and its many hills were formed through erosion by the Umgeni River and its tributaries.

CYCADS (SITUATED AT MONTESEEL)
This cluster of three female cycads (*Encephalartos natalensis*) was visited in 1940 by Sir Arthur Hill, head of Kew Gardens, who estimated that the rootstocks were at least 2 000 years old.

VRYHEID

The town, which was established in 1884 as the capital of the New Republic, attained municipal status in 1912. Its name means 'freedom' in Afrikaans.

BOSHOF HOUSE (219 EAST STREET)
This elegant dwelling is based on the Edwardian building style and was erected in 1905. It is situated on a section of an erf granted in 1895.

CARNEGIE LIBRARY (LANDDROST STREET)
An imposing Edwardian building, the library was erected in 1908 with funds granted by the Carnegie Trust. The land on which it stands was a gift from the Vryheid Town Council.

DWELLING HOUSE (58 PRESIDENT STREET)
This imposing dwelling was erected in 1920 and is an excellent example of the Tudor-Revival style.

FORMER NEW REPUBLIC FORT
The fort was added to the New Republic Raadsaal in 1887 and was built of whinstone, a particularly hard stone that cannot be dressed. The building, with four cells, was the prison, and was also used as a post office and a police station. One of the cells houses an exhibition of firearms that were used in several wars.

FORMER NEW REPUBLIC RAADSAAL
(LANDDROST STREET)
Together with the former New Republic Fort, this property forms Nieuwe Republiek Museum. It was erected as the Council Chamber and Government Office of the Raadsaal in 1885.

KAMBULA BATTLEFIELD (DISTRICT)
During the Battle of Kambula on 29 March 1879, a British force of approximately 2 000 men under the command of Colonel Evelyn Wood (later Field Marshall Sir Evelyn Wood, VC, CB) successfully defended themselves against a Zulu impi of 20 000 men under Mnyamana Buthelezi. About 2 000 Zulus perished here.

MAGISTRATE'S OFFICE BUILDING (CHURCH STREET)
The cornerstone of the magistrate's office was laid on 14 November 1930 and additions were made in 1935–1936. This building has importance in the context of the historic street block that includes the Old Raadsaal.

NEDERDUITSE GEREFORMEERDE KERK
(131 HIGH STREET)
Built at a cost of R26 000, the Nederduitse Gereformeerde church was consecrated on 12 October 1894. The building was constructed from local stone and is predominantly in neogothic style. The cornerstone was laid in 1891 and therein is contained copies of important documents, together with a history of the district.

NORTH GUN POINT AND SOUTH GUN POINT
(LANCASTER HILL BATTLEFIELD)
These two fortifications were erected by British forces during the Anglo-Boer War on 18 September 1900 on Lancaster Hill to strengthen their position there. This led to the eventual retreat of the Boer forces on 12 December 1900.

OLD BANTU ADMINISTRATION BUILDING
(LANDDROST STREET)
This rectangular building dates from about 1930 and forms, particularly from an architectural point of view, an integral part of the historic core of Vryheid.

ORIGINAL SANDSTONE SCHOOL BUILDING
(VRYHEID HIGH SCHOOL, CHURCH STREET)
Shortly before the Natal Colony accepted responsibility for education in the recently annexed district of Vryheid on 3 February 1903, plans for the first official local school were drawn up and it was opened on 5 February 1906. Now enclosed by the new school buildings, the original school building is regarded as exceptional because it is built of dressed sandstone, while most other buildings of the same era in KwaZulu-Natal are brick buildings.

POLICE STATION (LANDDROST STREET)
This sandstone building with its Victorian verandah dates from the end of the nineteenth century, and forms an essential part of the historic and architectural character of Landdrost Street.

VICTORAN DWELLNG (95 PRESIDENT STREET)
It is presumed that this Victorian sandstone house was erected shortly after the plot concerned was allocated in 1886. The house has two prominent bay windows on either side of the façade.

WEENEN

The town was laid out in 1838 and takes its name from the Dutch word 'weenen' which means weeping. The name refers to the massacre by the Zulus of 182 Voortrekkers in the area in 1838 after the execution of Piet Retief and his party by Dingane.

COOLAMGAUSE BUILDING AND ABDOOLGAFOOR
GOOLAMSAHIB ARABIAN MERCHANT BUILDING
(RETIEF STREET)
These predominantly Edwardian shops date from the beginning of the twentieth century and form an impressive architectural entity.

WESTVILLE

This town developed from a settlement of German immigrants in 1848 and was named after Martin West, the first Lieutenant-Governor of Natal in 1845. It attained municipal status in 1956.

BERGTHIEL HOUSE LOCAL HISTORY MUSEUM
(16 QUEENS AVENUE)
Bergthiel House, the core of which dates from 1847, forms the nucleus of the Westville residential area. It was built by Jonas Bergthiel, an industrialist and Member of the Legislative Council from 1857–1866, as the centre for the administration of the well-known New Germany settlement. The Westville Municipality purchased the building in 1983, and the museum was officially opened on 29 September 1990 by the Administrator of the Federal Republic of Germany, Dr Immo Stabreit.

WINTERTON

The town was laid out in 1905 and was originally named Springfield. It was renamed in 1910 in honour of the Secretary for Agriculture in Natal, HD Winter.

RUINS OF MARIANNE CHURCH AND
SURROUNDING BANK (FARM DOVETON)
These ruins are all that remain of the second Dutch Reformed Church in KwaZulu-Natal, which was in use from 1852–1874. It was named after the wife of the then Minister of Pietermaritzburg, Dr Faure.

MPUMALANGA

Formerly known as the Eastern Transvaal, Mpumalanga is the second smallest province of South Africa. It has a colourful and rich history, fanned by the discovery of gold and other minerals, as well as the presence of big game hunters in the area now covered by the Kruger National Park.

AMSTERDAM

This Scottish settlement was established by Alexander McCorkingdale in 1866. Formerly named Roburnia, the town's name was changed to Amsterdam in 1882 in gratitude for Dutch sympathy towards the Transvaal Republic during the First War of Independence (1880–1881). Municipal status was attained in 1881.

OLD GAOL
The original section of this well-preserved stone building was commissioned by the Government of the South African Republic and completed in 1890, only nine years after Amsterdam had been proclaimed a township. Two rooms were added in 1899.

BARBERTON

The town was established in 1884 and was named after Graham Hoare Barber (1835–1888), who discovered a gold-bearing reef here earlier that same year. Barberton attained municipal status in 1904.

BELHAVEN HOUSE MUSEUM (LEE ROAD)
Now a museum, this Victorian house was erected in 1904 for Robert Nisbet, a wealthy businessman. From 1914 to 1978, it belonged to the Duncan family. In 1982 it was restored by the Transvaal Provincial Administration.

18 BOWNESS STREET
This well-preserved house and outbuildings of wood and iron were erected by JS Stopforth in the 1880s. Because the building complex has remained unaltered, it provides an important cultural history link with the old Barberton.

E.T.C. BUILDING (PILGRIM STREET)
Completed for Sammy Marks early in 1887, this office building dates from Barberton's boom period. It is thought to be the oldest existing multi-storey building in the old Transvaal.

GLOBE TAVERN (PILGRIM STREET)
This former tavern was opened in 1887, two and a half years after Barberton was founded. It is typical of the wood-and-iron buildings that characterised the gold fields of the Eastern Transvaal during the last quarter of the nineteenth century.

HISTORIC GUARD HOUSE (LEE ROAD)
This wood- and corrugated-iron guard house was erected by the British in 1901 to protect the concentration camp, the camp hospital and the town during the Anglo-Boer War (1899–1902).

MASONIC LODGE
LODGE OF ST JOHN IN THE SOUTH)
(24 JUDGE STREET)
A single-storey building designed in neogothic style, the building was erected in 1884 as

the Union Church. In 1887 the Jubilee Memorial Lodge, under the Grand Lodge East of the Netherlands, was inaugurated, after which, on 27 December 1887, the Lodge of St John in the South was consecrated under the Grand Lodge of Scotland. In 1888, the two lodges purchased the building from the Union Church.

OLD NZASM STATION BUILDING (ELANDSHOEK)
According to old photographs, the old Elandshoek station building was built of wood and corrugated iron. It was considered that this structure should be replaced by a more permanent building, and 1897 can be assumed to be the date that the present building was completed. Elandshoek Station is a very good example of the typical station buildings built by the Nederlandsche Zuid-Afrikaansche Spoorweg-Maatschappij for the Lowveld station crossings. Since 1897 the station has served the railway uninterruptedly.

OLD STOCK EXCHANGE (PILGRIM STREET)
This was the second stock exchange building in Barberton, built by De Kaap Goldfields Stock Exchange Limited and opened on 13 April 1887.

PROPERTY AND BUILDING (24 KELLAR ROAD)
Built by Samuel Todd in 1887, this single-storey Victorian-style wood-and-iron house has two bedrooms, a verandah and porch, and an outside kitchen. Todd played an important role in the history of Barberton as he was the first person to import lychees into South Africa and to grow fruit in the Lowveld.

SITE OF AEROPLANE ACCIDENT
(NEAR MBUZINI SETTLEMENT)
This is the site of the air crash in which President Samora Machel was killed in October 1986. He was the first president of the independent Mozambique.

BELFAST

The town was established on the farm Tweefontein in 1890, and was named after the birthplace in Ireland of the father of the farm's owner. Belfast attained municipal status in 1966.

COVENANT MONUMENT (STEYNSPLAATS FARM)
Erected to commemorate the vow taken in 1838 by Voortrekker leader Andries Pretorius and his men shortly before the Battle of Blood River, this obelisk was erected in 1886. It is the oldest monument of its kind in the old Transvaal area.

HISTORIC NAVAL GUN BARREL
(BELFAST HIGH SCHOOL, DUGGEN STREET)
This 60mm-calibre cast-iron naval gun barrel bears the inscription 'G.B. (or CB) 1803'. Weighing 115kg, it is 880mm long, has a front diameter of 110mm, a rear diameter of 180mm and rests on a wrought-iron base. During the British occupation of Port Natal in 1824, led by Captain TC Smith, and the subsequent skirmish with a Voortrekker commando under General AWJ Pretorius, the gun barrel was captured from the British. It was one of the first enemy objects to be captured by the Voortrekkers.

SITE WITH PREHISTORIC STONE RUINS OF BANTU KRAALS (BLAAUWBOSCHKRAAL FARM, DISTRICT)
These unique stone kraals were probably built by members of the Hamitic Bantu culture in prehistoric times. The method of construction used is similar to that used at the Zimbabwe ruins in Zimbabwe.

BETHAL

This town was established on a section of the farm Blesbokspruit in 1880, and was named after the wives, Eliza(beth) and (Al)ida, of the farm's original owners. It attained municipal status in 1921.

OLD MAGISTRATES' BUILDING (MARKET STREET)
This building was designed in 1893 by the Zuid-Afrikaansche Republiek architect, Wierda. A second phase, in 1910, was designed by the architect P Eagle of the Public Works Department of the Transvaal.

OLD NEDERDUITSE HERFORMDE CHURCH
(72 VERMOETEN STREET)
The present congregation of Bethal originally resorted under the Heidelberg congregation as part of the ward of Blesbokspruit, until a separate congregation was founded in 1891. The original Hervormde church building was designed by Gerard Moerdijk, and the cornerstone was laid by the reverend LE Brand on 23 January 1926. Consecration took place in December 1926. Until a new church was built in 1965, this stone building served as a place of worship.

ERMELO

The town was laid out on the farm Nooitgedacht in 1879, and was named after Ermelo in the Netherlands. In 1901 Ermelo was razed to the ground by British forces, but was rebuilt after 1903.

STONE HUT VILLAGE (TAFELKOP, DISTRICT)
Approximately 90 hemispheric stone huts make up this settlement, described as the largest and best preserved of its kind. Although the date of its erection is unknown, it was probably earlier than the nineteenth century. Also unknown is the tribe responsible for the settlement, but it was probably one of the Khatla groups, such as Kholokoe, Phuting or Tlokoa.

EVANDER

Established in 1955 by the Union Corporation Limited to provide suitable accommodation for the employees of three gold mines (Winkelhaak, Bracken and Leslie), Evander was named after Evelyn Anderson, widow of the then Managing Director of the company.

BOREHOLE UC65 (WINKELHAAK FARM)
In 1951, borehole UC65 was the first prospecting hole to penetrate the auriferous Kimberley Reef in the vicinity of the present Evander. This event led to the development of an important new South African gold field, the Evander Gold Field.

GRASKOP

This small town was originally a gold mining camp, laid out on the farm of Abel Erasmus, Native Commissioner of the Transvaal Republic in 1880-1881. Named after a gold mining settlement, the area also has manganese, asbestos and phosphate mines.

NATURAL ROCK BRIDGE (GOEDEHOOP FARM)
This natural sandstone bridge over the Vaal River is approximately 22m long, five to eight metres wide and four metres high. Large natural rock bridges are rare landforms and this bridge can justly be regarded as one of South Africa's geomorphological gems.

KOMATIPOORT

The town is named after the Komati River and the gorge (Afrikaans 'poort') that cuts through the Lebombo Mountains. Komati is a word of Swazi origin ,and means 'river of cows' (hippos).

HISTORIC NZASM RAILWAY BRIDGE
(OVER THE KOMATI RIVER)
The British firm Clarke & Wirth, and the Dutch firm Van Hattum & Kie, were responsible for the

construction of this bridge in 1890. Natural stone for the abutments and piers was shipped from Belgium to Delagoa Bay, and transported to the site by rail.

LYDENBURG

Established on the farm Rietspruit in 1850, this town attained municipal status in 1927. Lydenburg means 'town of suffering', and recalls the tribulations of the Voortrekkers.

DUTCH REFORMED CHURCH (CHURCH STREET)
Built in neogothic style and a replica of the Mother Church in Stellenbosch, this church was consecrated in 1894. It has a beautiful Dopper-kiaat pulpit. With the adjoining historic school and the first church opposite, they form an important historic and architectural group.

FIRST CHURCH AND SCHOOL (CHURCH STREET)
The earlier of the two churches, called the Voortrekker Church, was built in 1852 and also served as the first school. It is the oldest Dutch Reformed Church building north of the Orange River, and the oldest school building in the former Transvaal. Now restored as a museum, it was used as a school for 30 years and thereafter as the church hall.

GEOLOGICAL EXPOSURE (DWARSRIVIER)
The Dwars River occurrence (unique chromite bands in anorthosite) will long invite controversy and be a scientific museum piece for those entrusted with the exploitation and exploration of the chromite deposits in the Bushveld Igneous Complex. The Chrome ores of Zimbabwe in the Great Dyke originated in a similar fashion.

OLD BRIDGE OVER SPEKBOOM RIVER
(BETWEEN LYDENBURG AND OHRIGSTAD)
The foundations of this bridge were laid in 1894, and it was completed on 21 June 1897 as part of the former South African Republic's extensive bridge-building program of that period. During the Anglo-Boer War (1899–1902) the bridge was partially destroyed, but it was rebuilt with stone shortly after the war.

POWDER MAGAZINE (VILJOEN STREET)
This historic magazine was built during the years 1879–1880 by the 94th Regiment under the Command of Lieutenant-Colonel PO Anstrutter, following the Sekhukhune War.

SITE WHERE MERENSKY REEF WAS DISCOVERED (MAANDAGSHOEK FARM)
Hans Merensky (1871–1952), geologist and farmer, discovered a platinum reef 48km long in 1924, that was later named after him. After this and other discoveries, he became a wealthy man and willed his money for the establishment of a trust fund for the continuation of his work in the interests of South Africa.

Z.A.R. POST BOX (KANTOOR STREET)
This historic post box, bearing the inscription 'Pletterij den Haag 1893', is one of the earliest examples of the pillar post boxes ordered from the Netherlands by the Postmaster General of the South African Republic. Manufactured in 1893, it dates from the same period as the nearby Dutch Reformed Church building.

MIDDELBURG

Established on the farm Sterkfontein in 1866 and initially named Nazareth, Middelburg was given its present name in 1874. The reason for the name change is uncertain. It attained municipal status in 1903.

DE RUST FARMSTEAD (BOSCHHOEK FARM)
This imposing late Victorian farmhouse was erected by FJ Bezuidenhout shortly after the

Anglo-Boer War. Designed by MCA Meischke and constructed by J Joubert, De Rust is one of the most complete farmsteads that have survived in the area of the old Transvaal.

CYCAD *ENCEPHALARTOS MIDDELBURGENSIS* (BANKFONTEIN FARM)
There is general agreement that cycads, as we know them, evolved in the period of the coal measures estimated at about 50 million years ago, when dinosaurs roamed the land. The *Encephalartos Kaffirbread* tree (broodboom, Kafferbrood, Hottentotsbrood, Boesmansbrood) is the only genus in the family *Zamiaeae* in Africa. Of the 36 species of *Encephalartos* in Africa, over two-thirds occur in southern Africa, the main area of distribution being the Zoutpansberg and Waterberg of Mpumalanga.

DUTCH REFORMED MEMORIAL CHURCH (SOUTH STREET)
This little church was erected shortly after the Anglo-Boer War (1899–1902), commemorating the 1 400 women and children who died in the local concentration camp.

FORT MERENSKY (BOTHSABELO)
Originally called Fort Wilhelm, it was built by the missionary Alexander Merensky and his followers at the mission station that he established there in 1865.

OLD NZASM STATION BUILDING (CLEWER STATION, SCHOONGEZICHT FARM)
This railway station is an important feature of the railway line from Pretoria to Delagoa Bay, constructed between 1890 and 1894 by the Nederlandsche Zuid-Afrikaansche Spoorweg-Maatschappij. Probably built in 1894, it was the only refreshment post on the route. The stepped gables are noteworthy and are a reminder of the Dutch contribution to the Oosterlyn (Eastern Line), as it was known.

MEIJER BRIDGE (OVER KLEIN OLIFANTS RIVER)
Meijer Bridge is one of the fine stone bridges built by the Zuid-Afrikaansche Republiek. It was constructed in 1896 by an Italian contractor, Celso Giri.

WITKERK (JOUBERT STREET)
This imposing neogothic church was completed in 1890 and is one of the oldest existing Nederduitse Gereformeerde church buildings in the old Transvaal. It is also the only church north of the Vaal River designed by the well-known church architect, CO Hager.

NELSPRUIT

Laid out on the farm Cascades, this town was named after the three Nel brothers who grazed their cattle here every winter. It was proclaimed in 1905 and attained municipal status in 1940.

LIME KILNS (NGODWANA, GROOTGELUK FARM)
These kilns were erected at the turn of the nineteenth century to slake the very pure limestone derived from the nearby mine. At one stage they supplied the whole Barberton district with lime and played an important role in the reclamation of gold in that area.

OLD SCHOOL (ANDERSON STREET)
This building was inaugurated on 22 May 1917 and was the first school building to be erected in Nelspruit. It occupies an important place in the history of the town's development.

OHRIGSTAD

Originally laid out in 1845, this town was named Andries-Ohrigstad after the Voortrekker Andries Hendrik Potgieter, and Georgius Gerardus Ohrig (1802–1852), a merchant from Amsterdam and a friend of the Voortrekkers. Abandoned on account of deaths caused by malaria in 1848–1849, the present town was re-established in 1923.

REMAINS OF VOORTREKKER FORT
The site features the remains of the fort built before 1847 by the Voortrekkers to protect themselves and their families against possible attacks from local tribes.

PILGRIM'S REST

The town was laid out on the farm Ponies Krantz in 1870 as a gold-diggers' camp after the discovery of alluvial gold by Alex Patterson. The whole town has been restored and preserved as a 'living' museum.

BERLIN WATERFALLS (BERLYN FARM)
These attractive waterfalls, which have a drop of 45m, as well as the surroundings, form an integral part of the natural beauty of the Mpumalanga escarpment.

HORSESHOE WATERFALL (SABIESHOEK)
This waterfall, the basin into which it gradually cascades and the surrounding cliffs covered in indigenous plants, form an essential part of the natural beauty of the area.

LONE CREEK WATERFALLS (CEYLON FARM) AND MAC-MAC WATERFALLS (GEELHOUTBOOM FARM)
These attractive waterfalls, which drop 68m in a single cascade and 65m in two uninterrupted cascades respectively, and the indigenous forests in the kloofs below, are all part of the natural beauty of the Mpumalanga escarpment.

PILGRIM'S REST TOWN
Purchased as a 'living' museum, the Transvaal Provincial Administration in 1974 restored the town and all the original buildings from 1880–1915 to their original state.

ROOSENEKAL

The area was named after Field-Cornet Stephanus Johannes Roos of the Potchefstroom Commando, a hero of Majuba, and Commandant Frederik Senekal of the Rustenburg Commando, both of whom died during the war against the Mapoch tribe in 1882–1883. A village arose from the 'Mapochs gronden' holdings, allocated to volunteers who had participated in the Mapoch War. Surveyed by GR von Weilligh and divided into 150 erven, the area was proclaimed a village on 13 January 1886. During the Anglo-Boer War, Rosenekal and 20 other villages were destroyed.

MAPOCHS CAVES
This area contains valuable ethnological relics, and features prominently in the war against Njabel in 1882–1883.

SABIE

Founded by the hunter HT Glynn in 1880, this town developed on the farm Grootfontein as a gold-diggers' camp. It was named after the river Sabie.

HUNTINGTON HOUSE AND STABLES
Huntington House was built on the farm Grootfontein in 1896 for HT Glynn, the founder of Sabie, making it the oldest house in the town. The Glynns lived there until 1928, playing an important role in mining and agricultural activities, and contributing to the development of the town.

VOLKSRUST

The town of Volksrust was laid out on the farms Boschpad Drift, Rooibult/Llanwarne, Verkyk and Zandfontein in 1888. Named by Dorothea de Jager, daughter of Dirk Uys ('swart Dirk'), probably in longing for people to live in peace after the Battle of Majuba. Volksrust attained municipal status in 1904.

GRAVEYARD AND TOMB OF GENERAL PIET JOUBERT (RUSTFONTEIN FARM)

General Piet Joubert (1831–1900), one-time Commandant-General of the Zuid-Afrikaansche Republiek, as well as his wife are buried in this graveyard, in an architecturally impressive mausoleum.

OLD NZASM STATION BUILDING AND ZAR CUSTOMS BUILDING (SAREL CILLIERS STREET)

Even before the Oosterlyn (Eastern line) was completed in 1894, it became clear that Pretoria and Johannesburg also needed a connecting railway line to the Suidoosterlyn in Natal. In August 1895, the line from Volksrust to Standerton was opened amid much celebration.

Comprising a large station building, locomotive shed, goods and customs shed, loading and receiving shed and houses for staff, the Volksrust station was built by the Natal Government Railways according to NZASM specifications. It was called an Island Station, in other words, the railway lines run on either side of the platform.

RUINS OF CONVENTION BRIDGE

It was here, in a railway coach in the middle of the bridge, that President Paul Kruger and Sir Henry Loch, British High Commissioner, signed the Swaziland Convention in November 1894. Although the convention permitted the Transvaal Republic to negotiate with the Swazis to obtain powers of administration without incorporation, the Swazis refused to agree, and in 1894 a further convention dispensed with the agreement. In February 1895 a Resident Special Commissioner arrived from the Transvaal to administer the territory.

WAKKERSTROOM

Wakkerstroom was laid out on the farm Gryshoek in 1859. It was originally named Marthinus-Wesselstroom after Marthinus Wessel Pretorius, the first president of the Transvaal Republic. The town then became known as Wesselstroom, and later changed to Wakkerstroom.

OLD APOSTOLIC CHURCH OF SOUTH AFRICA (CHURCH STREET)

This well-preserved former Anglican Church, previously known as St Mark's, was consecrated on 6 April 1890 by the Bishop of Pretoria, the Right Reverend HB Bousfield. Built of laterite, the building has a fine stained glass window, installed in about 1959.

OLD MAGISTRATES' OFFICE (ENGELBRECHT STREET)

This single-storey sandstone building was constructed in 1898 by GA Ramplen for the Department of Publieke Werken of the Zuid-Afrikaansche Republiek.

OLD ROAD BRIDGE (ACROSS MARTHINUS-WESSELSTROOM)

This bridge was designed by the Zuid-Afrikaansche Republiek's Department of Public Works and was erected by A Klute. It was completed in 1893 and was one of the last steel bridges commissioned by the ZAR. On 24 May 1904, Father David Bryant baptised the first black Zionist in South Africa in the Marthinus-Wesselstroom next to this bridge.

WATERVAL BOVEN

Originally established on the farm Doornhoek as a railway supply depot in 1895, the town derives its name from the fact that it is situated above the waterfall in the Elands River.

NEDERLANDSE ZUID-AFRIKAANSCHE SPOORWEG-MAATSCHAPPIJ TUNNEL
The tunnel was part of the NZASM railway line built from 1891 to 1895 between Pretoria and Lourenço Marques (Maputo) in Mozambique. In view of the gradient, it was fitted with a rack-railway, which remained in service until 1908.

WATERVAL ONDER

This area originally bore the Dutch name of Waterval Beneden (beneath the waterfall), but was later adapted to Afrikaans (under the waterfall).

BRIDGE OF FIVE ARCHES (DOORNHOEK)
A particularly fine stone structure, this bridge was originally built for the NZASM railway line between Pretoria and Lourenço Marques (now Maputo) in Mozambique.

KRUGERHOF
President SJP Kruger lived in this house from 30 June to 28 August 1900, during which time the affairs of the state of the South African Republic were conducted here.

NORTHERN PROVINCE

Encompassing a large part of the old northern Transvaal, Northern Province is characterised by bushveld, rich grasslands and hills. Much of the province's history centres on its share of the Kruger National Park and some gold fields. The area is, however, rich in archaeological sites.

DUIWELSKLOOF
The railway halt at this spot was originally named Modjadje in 1914, after the chieftainess whose settlement is nearby. One theory on the name is that early transport riders experienced trouble in accessing the kloof in the rainy season with their heavy-laden wagons, and named it 'Devil's Gorge'.

CYCADS (MODJADJE/MODJADJI LOCATION)
'Modjadje-Lobedu Rain Queen' is an honorary title of the queen of the Lobeda, a tribe near Duiwelskloof in the Letaba area. Called the Rain Goddess and Transformer of the Clouds Khifidola-maru-a-Daja, she is the central figure of two popular books, *She,* by Sir Rider Haggard (1887), and *The Bush Speaks,* by BH Dicke (1936). *Cycad Encephalartos transverosus* is the Modjadje cycad, which occurs on the 'sacred mountain', the home of Modjadje.

KOPPIE KGOPOLWE
The koppie and its surroundings are rich in Iron Age archaeological remains and are of particular significance to the tribes in this vicinity.

LOUIS TRICHARDT
Laid out on the farms Bergvliet and Rietvlei in 1899 and named after the Voortrekker leader Louis Trichardt (1783–1838), this town attained municipal status in 1934.

ELIM HOSPITAL COMPLEX (DISTRICT)
The mission of the Swiss Missionary Society (Mission Romande) was founded in 1883 by Ernest Creaux. The site incorporates the main building complex of the Elim Hospital, including the 1912 addition, the doctor's house, and the old Indian ward.

FORT HENDRINA
This movable iron fort dates from the nineteenth century and is the only known example of its kind in the old Transvaal region. Fort Hendrina was moved to a different site and was used by the police force, at which time it was named Fort Schutte. When the fort was occupied by the British forces during the Anglo-Boer War (1899–1902), it was once again renamed Fort Edward.

STONEHENGE (FARM BERGVLIET)
This farmhouse was erected for RH Stevens in about 1906, and is allegedly the oldest dwelling in the vicinity of Louis Trichardt.

MESSINA
Messina was founded on the farm Berkenrode in 1904. The name comes from the Bavenda word 'musina', which means 'spoiler', and refers to the copper that spoilt the iron mined in this area by the early Bantu tribes.

ARCHAEOLOGICAL SITE (FARM GREEFSWALD)
Known as K2, this site was originally occupied around 950 AD. It contains a wealth of cultural material representing a major economic and political transitory phase in southern Africa, during the settlement of agriculturists and pastoralists in an area previously inhabited mainly by hunter-gatherers. Furthermore, the K2 people were involved in the development of trade with the peoples of central southern Africa and the traders of the Indian Ocean.

BAOBAB TREES (VOGELENZANG, MESSINA, SINGELE, BERKENRODE, PRINZENHAGE, STOCKFORD AND TOYNTON FARMS)
These baobab (*Adansonia digitata*) or cream of tartar trees grow to a height of 12–18m and have massive swollen boles (24–27m) that terminate in a number of branches so small as to appear quite absurd in comparison. The pure white gardenia-like flowers are 12–15cm across and the fruit is about 22cm long, and 1m in diameter.

MAPUNGUBWE ARCHAEOLOGICAL SITE (GREEFSWALD FARM, DISTRICT)
This site, which consists of Mapungubwe Hill and the adjacent Southern Terrace, was inhabited in 950 AD. By about 1050 AD people of the so-called Mapungubwe culture started settling here, and the occupation continued until shortly after 1200 AD. The Mapungubwe archaeological site represents the continuation of a major economic and political transition phase in the history of southern Africa.

The Mapungubwe people traded with the east coast of Africa and a sociopolitical ruling class developed on Greefswald, which, up to then, had been unknown in the southern African pattern of life. The site has yielded more golden artefacts than any other archaeological site in southern Africa.

VERDUN RUINS (FARM VERDUN, DISTRICT)
One of the most southerly examples of the Zimbabwe culture discovered to date, the Verdun ruins indicate a curved corridor leading to the main enclosure on a high precipice. The main interest in them lies in the link between the Bavenda and Zimbabwe cultures.

NYLSTROOM

Laid out on the farm Rietvlei in 1866, this town was named after a nearby river and attained municipal status in 1959.

STRIJDOM HOUSE
Advocate JG Strijdom, Prime Minister of South Africa from 1954 to 1958, lived in this neo-Cape Dutch house. The design was done by Gerard Moerdijk.

WATERBERG REFORMED CHURCH
The historic Waterberg Reformed church was built in 1889 and was taken into use on 23 November that same year. President Paul Kruger of the Zuid-Afrikaansche Republiek was present at this occasion. During the Anglo-Boer War (1899–1902), a wing was added to the northern side of the building, which transformed it into a cruciform church.

PHALABORWA

Phalaborwa was founded on the farm Laaste No 198, by the Phosphate Development Corporation in 1951.
The current town is situated on an old mining centre where centuries ago local tribes mined iron and copper.

IRON AGE SITE (FARM SCHIETTOCHT)
The claims area contains a remarkably well-preserved smelting oven used in the Phalaborwa area in the old Transvaal's Iron Age.

PIETERSBURG

This town was established in 1884 on the farm Sterkloop and was named after Commandant-General Piet Joubert (1831–1900), acting State President of the Zuid-Afrikaansche Republiek. This capital town of the Northern Province attained municipal status in 1903.

FIRST DUTCH REFORMED CHURCH BUILDING (TOWN SQUARE)
The Nederduitse Gereformeerde congregation Zoutpansberg was established in September 1872 at Renosterpoort by the well-known Missionary Stephanus Hofmeyr, with the Reverend PJJ Boshoff, who in 1899 entered service as the first minister.

Boshoff immediately began with construction and by 18 October that year, a 400-seat church was consecrated. The building served as such until 1917, when the entrance and tower were demolished. Thereafter, it was used as a shop and storage area. In 1981 the Pietersburg City Council decided to restore the building, re-erecting the tower and entrance. The building now houses the Hugh Eksteen Museum.

FIRST GOLD-CRUSHING SITE (FARM EERSTELING)
Gold was discovered at Eersteling in 1871 and was first crushed by hand. The original gold-crushing plant came into being when the technique was improved by using a boulder. The plant remained in operation until 1874. On the site, a granite stone (now in the Transvaal Museum, Pretoria) was used as a millstone to crush the ore.

FIRST GOLD POWER-PLANT SITE (EERSTELING)
Edward Button imported the first stamp battery and steam engine from England in 1872. All that is left of this gold power plant is the chimney, which was built of Aberdeen granite.

OLD BRITISH FORT (MARABASTAD, NOW KNOWN AS EERSTEGOUD)
During the First War of Independence (1880–1881), the British built this fort. (Other British forts in the Transvaal were at Potchefstroom, Rustenburg, Pretoria, Lydenburg, Wakkerstroom and Standerton.) This fort was besieged for 105 days by Boer forces and, of the 140 British soldiers garrisoned there, five were killed and one wounded. Only one Boer was killed during the siege.

RHEINGOLD BUILDING (MARKET STREET)
This Victorian building was erected in about 1910 as a shop by H Möschke. The richly decorated and prominently situated Rheingold building is presently the only one of its kind in the centre of Pietersburg, and houses the Pietersburg Museum.

POTGIETERSRUS

This town, first named Vredenburg, was established in 1852 but was renamed Pietpotgietersrust in 1858 after Pieter Johannes, the son of Voortrekker leader Andries Hendrik Potgieter. By 1870 the town was abandoned on account of fever in the area and hostility from the local inhabitants. It was re-established in 1890, and by 1939 the name was shortened to Potgietersrus. Municipal status was granted in 1935.

GROUP OF *ACACIA ALBIDA* OR *FAIDHERBIA ALBIDA* (RIETFONTEIN MOKENG, DISTRICT)
This group of Apiesdorings or Ana Trees is unusual in that this species seldom appears in this area, usually only flourishing further north.

MAKAPAN CAVES (FARM MAKAPANSGAT)
Makapan, an Ndebele chief, fled here with his followers after killing a party of Boer men, women and children in 1854 at Moorddrift. After

a 25-day siege they were wiped out by a punitive expedition. Fossil remains of Australopithecus have also been found here.

MOORDDRIFT MONUMENT (DISTRICT)
In 1854 chiefs Makapan and Mapela killed 28 men, women and children at Makapans kraal, Mapelas kraal and at Moorddrift.

OLD STONE SCHOOL BUILDINGS AND OUTBUILDINGS (97 VOORTREKKER STREET)
Now a museum, this old Edwardian stone school building was erected in 1916. In 1918 it was used temporarily as a hospital during the Spanish influenza epidemic, and was used as a primary school until 1964.

PALAEONTOLOGICAL SITE (FARM MAKAPANSGAT)
The Limeworks Cave, rich in fossilised bones, has yielded remains of the ape-man Australopithecus. These caves were formed in pre-Cambrian dolomite limestone, belonging to the Dolomite Series of the Transvaal System.

SCHOEMANSDAL

Founded as Zoutpansbergdorp or Oude Dorp by Commandant-General AH Potgieter in 1848, this town was renamed Schoemansdal in 1855 by Stephanus Schoeman. On 18 July 1867 it was evacuated and burnt down on account of an uprising by the Bavenda tribe.

VOORTREKKER SITE
The remains of AH Potgieter are interred here, the site of the evacuation and destruction of Schoemansdal in 1867.

WARMBATHS

Laid out on the farms Het Bad, Noodshulp, Roodepoort and Turfbult in 1882, the town was proclaimed Hartingsburg, but it was renamed Warmbaths in 1920 after the hot springs in the area. Warmbaths became a municipality in 1932.

BLOCKHOUSE (FARM HET BAD)
After the surrender of Pretoria in the Anglo-Boer War (1899–1902), Republican forces adopted guerrilla tactics. As a counter measure, the British forces erected a system of blockhouses to divide the combat areas into sectors. This blockhouse was part of the most important line of blockhouses from Noupoort to Pietersburg.

ZOUTPANSBERG (ENVIRONS)

DZATA RUINS (NTLEGLE VALLEY)
The Bavenda are thought to have emigrated north to an area in Zimbabwe, named Dzata. Towards the end of the seventeenth century, they moved to the Zoutpansberg, also naming their new settlement Dzata. Within the dry stone walling is a recessed stone seat typical of modern Venda practice. This settlement was built by the Venda chief, Dambanyika, after crossing the Limpopo River, which forms the border between South Africa and Zimbabwe. After the chief was entombed in a collapsed cave, his followers moved a settlement further away, hence the Dzata I and Dzata II sites.

MACHEMMA RUINS (FARM SOLVENT)
These ruins are linked to the Zimbabwe culture and are of great importance. The settlement on the top of the koppie was the chief's stronghold.

REPTILE FOOTPRINTS (FARM PONT DRIFT)
These fossilised reptile footprints in sandstone were made when a dune from earlier times was later covered by Basalt flows. The animals of the vicinity presumably fled to the dune as a large number of fossilised prints of various animals are found against a steep slope.

NORTH WEST PROVINCE

This area comprises the former Western Transvaal, part of the former Northern Cape and most of the former Republic of Bophuthatswana. As part of the old Transvaal, it was colonised by the Boers after the Great Trek of 1836, became a British Colony in 1902, and joined the Union of South Africa in 1910.

BROEDERSTROOM

Situated south of the Hartbeespoort Dam, this town is said to have been named after two brothers of General Andries Pretorius, namely HPN and HA Pretorius, who lived there. The name derives from the Dutch world 'broeder', which means brother.

ARCHAEOLOGICAL SITE
(FARM HARTBEESPOORT, DISTRICT)
Carbon datings indicate that this Iron Age site dates from about 480 AD, which makes it one of the earliest known dwelling places of food producers south of the Limpopo River. A large number of hut floors, iron-smelting furnaces and artefacts have been exposed here, as well as the remains of several individuals.

DELAREYVILLE

This town was laid out in 1914 and declared a border industry area in 1968. It was named after General Jacobus Hercules (Koos) de la Rey (1847–1914).

DUTCH REFORMED CHURCH (DELAREY STREET)
Before the founding of Delareyville, church services were held in farm schools. The first congregation was formed in 1912 in a cart shed at Barberspan and the town was originally named Salt Waters, the name of the farm on which it was founded. The government later changed the name to Delareyville in honour of Koos de la Rey. In 1913 Reverend CGR du Toit was appointed as minister, even though there was no church at this stage, and one was only built in 1936–1937. The church was designed by the architect Gerard Moerdijk. The original tiled roof was replaced with corrugated iron after it was damaged in a hailstorm. A carpet covers the parquet floors.

KLERKSDORP

Although the area was settled by 1837, the town was only named in 1853, after its first Landdrost, Jacob de Clercq (popularly 'de Klerk') (1791–1888). The town attained municipal status in 1903.

DUTCH REFORMED MOTHER CHURCH
(ANDERSON STREET)
In 1866, the Dutch Reformed Church established the Hartbeesfontein congregation to serve the inhabitants of the former Western Transvaal, including Klerksdorp. The architect was JE Vixseboxse, who had previously worked under Sytze Wierda on the official buildings in the Zuid-Afrikaansche Republiek. The contractor was PJ Kruger.

The church was built in neogothic style on the plan of a Roman cross. Its foundation stone was laid by the Vice President of the Zuid-Afrikaansche Republiek, PJ Joubert, and the building was inaugurated in October 1898 by Professor PJ de Vos. Galleries were added in 1918 and an organ installed in 1927.

FOUNTAIN VILLA
(21 HENDRIK POTGIETER STREET)

Although records for this property in the Deeds Office date back to 1892, it is known that the structures here date back to an earlier period. Being among the first 12 stands measured in Klerksdorp, the ground was purchased in 1905 by Johannes Petrus Mazureik from Dolf Carlin, who in turn approached Hancock, the Town Engineer, to build him a house. Designed by Hancock, this double-storey house in late Victorian style, with verandahs, balconies, cast-iron handrails and steel ceilings, as well as delicate brickwork and inlaid woodwork fireplaces, is exceptional.

HISTORIC CORRUGATED-IRON HOUSES
(13, 15 CONVENT AVENUE)

In 1837, before Potchefstroom was proclaimed, 12 Voortrekker families settled on the banks of the Schoonspruit, where CM du Plooy, the original owner of the farm Elandsheuwel, lived. This section was later called Old Town, but after gold was discovered by AP Roos on the farm Rietkuil, New Town was re-established on the other side of the Schoonspruit, and water canals were dug on the western bank for farming purposes.

Thomas Leask settled in Klerksdorp in 1871 and purchased the ground from Andries le Grange. After subdivision he sold the ground to Edgar Chittenden in April 1990, and it is here that the two houses were built. Both have more rooms than the average miner's house, and it is probable, therefore, that they were built for people of a higher cultural background or a higher income group. There are also more decorations, such as ornamental woodwork on the bargeboard and decorations on the verandahs. The houses do not have sliding windows, as expected, but more elegant hinged windows and brick interior walls. They are the only wood-and-iron houses that remain in Klerksdorp.

RAILWAY STATION BUILDING AND FLAG ROOM
(DELVER STREET)

The old Klerksdorp Railway Station building was completed in 1897 by the Nederlandse Zuid-Afrikaansche Spoorweg Maatskappij, and is one of only a few elegant station buildings erected by the NZASM. For about nine years the Klerksdorp Station remained the western terminus of the so-called South Western Line and, as such, it maintained an important place in the Transvaal Railway network. The old flag room was erected in the same style as that of the station building.

ROCK ENGRAVINGS
(FARM BOSWORTH, PREVIOUSLY KNOWN AS DOORNHOEK 24, DISTRICT)

Although their origins are unknown, these prehistoric engravings are thought to date from the Later Stone Age.

This archaeological site is celebrated for the large number of dolerite stones found there, which exhibit outstanding rock engravings. These depict a wide variety of the erstwhile fauna of the Transvaal, human figures and artistic renderings of animals such as rhinoceros in vivid action. Because many of the engravings and surrounding rocks have been defaced, some have been removed to the Zoological Gardens in Johannesburg for improved preservation.

LICHTENBURG

Lichtenburg was founded in 1866, but only proclaimed in 1873. It attained municipal status in 1904.

HISTORIC CATTLE DIP
(FARM UITGEVONDEN, ELANDSPUTTE)
In December 1924, during the construction of this cattle dip, JA Voorendyk discovered a diamond. This led to further discoveries of diamonds on Elandsputte (a section of Uitgevonden) and eventually to the spectacular diamond rushes on Elandsputte in 1926 and Grasfontein in 1927. In 1927, diamond production on the Lichtenburg diggings reached its peak (2 100 861 carats), it nearly resulted in the collapse of the South African diamond market.

STONE CHURCH, LICHTENBERG
NG CONGREGATION (GERRIT MARITZ STREET)
The cornerstone of this stone church was laid on 14 June 1890. In 1928, under the direction of Gerard Moerdijk, the building was substantially enlarged and the striking portico and spire were added. During the Anglo-Boer War (1899–1902) the building was used by the British as a fort. On 20 September 1914 General JH de la Rey was buried from this stone church (klipkerk).

MAFIKENG
Originally known as Mafeking, this town was established in 1885 by Sir Charles Warren. Its name Mafeking is said to be derived from a Tswana word meaning 'place of rocks'. The town attained municipal status in 1896.

CANNON KOPJE FORT
The site features the remains of the British fort built by Sir Charles Warren in 1884, which was used during the Siege of Mafeking.

FORT ELOFF (OLD IMPERIAL RESERVE)
This imposing stone fortification was erected in about 1880 by Sir Charles Warren and played an important role in the Anglo-Boer War (1899–1902).

MARICO (DISTRICT)
The Voortrekkers settled in this region as early as 1845, and on 31 October 1871, the Transvaal Volksraad proclaimed it a separate district, with Zeerust as the principal town.

WATER MILL (FARM NAAUWPOORT)
This cast-iron water wheel and mill is one of only a few water mills in the area of the old Transvaal to be preserved *in situ*. It was probably built sometime between 1900 and 1910, and is representative of the last type of mill in South Africa that operated with millstones.

POTCHEFSTROOM
Formerly known as Mooirivierdorp, Potchefspruit and finally Potchefstroom, this town was founded in 1838 by the Voortrekker leader Andries Hendrik Potgieter, and became the first municipality in the former Transvaal. The present name appeared on a document for the first time on 16 October 1840.

ADMINISTRATION BUILDING AND SELBOURNE HALL
(POTCHEFSTROOM COLLEGE OF AGRICULTURE)
Both the administration building, which was the first building of the Potchefstroom College of Agriculture to be erected and which was occupied in 1907, and the Selbourne Hall in which the Afrikaner Cattle Breeder Society was established in 1912, are closely associated with the history of agriculture in South Africa.

ANDREW CARNEGIE LIBRARY AND TOWNHOUSE
(POTGIETER STREET)
The Carnegie Library is a single-storey building just north of the town hall, and was completed in 1911. The building was the work of the architects NT Cowin and EM Powers. Consideration was given to building the library

sympathetically in style with that of the town hall as the latter is considered to be the architectural highlight of Potchefstroom. Even the portal is identical to that of the town hall.

DUTCH REFORMED CHURCH (CHURCH STREET)

This fine church is the second church building of the Voortrekker Congregation of the Transvaal of the Dutch Reformed (Nederduitse Hervormde) Church. It was taken into use on 24 February 1866.

GOETZ-FLEISCHAK HOUSE (GOUWS STREET)

This restored homestead was erected for AM Goetz, resident magistrate of Potchefstroom, between 1860 and 1863. Apart from the restored outbuildings on the property, it is the only Karoo-style house in Potchefstroom that has maintained its original appearance. The house, therefore, forms an important cultural and historical link with the old Potchefstroom.

HEIMAT BUILDING AND MAIN BUILDING (POTCHEFSTROOM UNIVERSITY)

Both these buildings represent important milestones in the history of the development of the Potchefstroom Universiteit vir Kristelike Hoër Onderwys. The neo-Cape Dutch building known as Heimat, designed by Gerard Moerdijk and completed as a students' hostel in 1927, was the first permanent building to be erected on the university campus. The main building, designed by the firm Louw & Louw, was inaugurated in 1931 and was the first and most important permanent academic building on the campus.

HISTORIC DWELLINGS (72–76 LOMBARD STREET)

During the years directly after the Anglo-Boer War (1899–1902) there was a revival in building activity. The history of these houses is linked with the history of Potchefstroom. The original owner of stand 75 was Christoffel Lombard, after which it was transferred to Carl Olen in 1907 (72 Lombard Street). Olen arrived from Sweden at the age of 17 in 1863, and started working for Charles Reid. By 1874 he was the owner of 25 ox-wagons and transported goods between Durban and Potchefstroom. He was also a pioneer in the milling industry of the Zuid-Afrikaansche Republiek.

In 1907, 76 Lombard Street was transferred to Helen Harriet Gaisford, wife of architect and lawyer John Gaisford. All three houses (72, 74 and 76) were built by him. John Gaisford was also among the first motorcar owners in Potchefstroom. In 1920, Stand 75 (74 Lombard Street) was subdivided and Israel Solomon took transfer of a section of it. These houses date back to the late-Victorian/early Edwardian era and were probably built in 1900. Two of the houses (74 and 76) are almost identical. Of particular interest is the cast-iron lattice work on the roof ridges and both houses have gables.

HISTORIC GEREFORMEERDE CHURCH BUILDING (MOLEN STREET)

In 1905 the Theological School of the Gereformeerde Church was transferred from Burgersdorp to Potchefstroom. This complex of four buildings was erected from 1905–1907 to accommodate the Theological School and its subsections, as well as a professor and students. Dr JD du Toit (Totius) occupied the professor's residence for 13 years and several of his volumes of verse originated here. He also worked on the Bible translation and a rhymed version of the Psalms. Furthermore, the University of Potchefstroom and the Hoër Skool Gymnasium developed from the Theological School and its Preparatory School respectively.

HOUSE OF PRESIDENT MW PRETORIUS AND OUTBUILDINGS (VAN DER HOFF AVENUE)

Marthinus Wessel Pretorius served as Commandant-General of Rustenburg and

Potchefstroom (1853–1857), State President of the Zuid-Afrikaansche Republiek (1857–1860 and 1864–1871), State President of the Republic of the Orange Free State (1860–1863) and member of the Triumvirate during the First War of Independence (1880–1881). He had this house built for himself in 1868, and lived here until he sold it in 1894.

KRUGERSKRAAL HOMESTEAD AND PROPERTY (TYGERFONTEIN, DISTRICT)
During the period 1920–1950, the Reverend JD du Toit (Totius), the well-known Afrikaans theologian lived here at various times, and it is here that he worked on the Afrikaans translation of the Bible and the majority of his rhymed versions of the Book of Psalms.

NORTHERN WING OF THE NUTRITION AND FAMILY ECOLOGY BUILDING (POTCHEFSTROOM UNIVERSITY FOR CHRISTIAN HIGHER EDUCATION)
This building was originally used as a physics and biochemistry laboratory. On 4 February 1935, the tender for the erection of two buildings (a Laboratory for the Natural Sciences and a Women's Lodgings) was awarded to Sterrenberg & Lutz, who completed the contract on 20 November 1935. The laboratory was the first permanent building erected on the campus of the Potchefstroom University for Christian Higher Education.

OAK AVENUE
An oak avenue of approximately 6.84km was planted about 1910. It lends both dignity and aesthetic character to the streets along which it is situated:
+ From the entrance to the dam recreation resort via Calderbank Lane, Thom Street, Van Riebeeck Street to Retief Street
+ Retief Street to Kruger Street
+ Kruger Street to Wolmarans Street
+ Wolmarans Street to Kock Street
+ Kock Street to Botha Street
+ From Botha Street to the entrance of the Agricultural Research Institute.

OLD BERLIN MISSION COMPLEX (DU PLOOY STREET)
Pastor CW Moschütz of the Berlin Missionary Society arrived in Potchefstroom from Makapaanspoort on 28 March 1872 to establish a mission station. He built himself a parsonage, of which he took occupation on 21 August 1872. He also opened a school that began with 20 pupils. The foundation stone of the school building and the wagon house were laid on Ascension Day in 1875. Due to Moschütz's ill health, Pastor Köhler arrived on 5 October 1874 to assist him, but Moschütz died the same day. The old Berlin Mission Complex is the only church building in Potchefstroom that still forms part of a historic complex. The architecture of the church itself is Gothic Renaissance, while the school building is in nineteenth-century Karoo style.

OLD DUTCH REFORMED CHURCH BUILDING (MAURY AVENUE)
One of the first churches built by the Dutch Reformed Church in South Africa, this church was designed by the Reverend D Postma in 1865 and was inaugurated on 12 January 1867. The General Synod held its annual meeting here in 1869 and took the decision to establish the Church's own theological seminary. A simple elongated structure under a thatched roof, the church has triangular gables at both ends. In 1922 the old building was made available to the Physics Department of the then Potchefstroom University College.

OLD FORT AND CEMETERY
Major RWC Winsloe of the 2nd Battery, Royal Scots Fusiliers and the 213 officers, non-commissioned officers and men under his

command were besieged in the fort by the Boers from 16 December 1880 until 21 March 1881. British losses were 25 killed, 54 wounded, and six due to illness.

OLD MAGISTRATE'S COURT (GREYLING STREET)

Initially housing the offices of the magistrate, police, clerical staff and post office, this building's cornerstone was laid on 6 July 1895. Architecturally the building differs from most other buildings of the ZAR era in that its mansard roof shows obvious French influence.

OLD POLICE STATION (GREYLING STREET)

Built in 1939, the old police station was designed in neo-Georgian style with symmetrical façade, sliding windows and an arched entrance with rustic finish.

OLD POST OFFICE (GREYLING STREET)

This double-storey redbrick building in neogothic style was constructed in 1909. On either side of the arched entrance is a bay window, of the sliding frame type. The old post office, police station and magistrate's court form the largest section of the western façade of the Hervormde Church Square.

OLD POWDER MAGAZINE (WOLMARANS STREET)

The powder magazine was erected between 1841 and 1863 and is one of the oldest existing buildings in Potchefstroom. This stone building played an important role from the time of its construction, especially during the First War of Independence (1880–1881).

ST MARY'S ANGLICAN CHURCH (AUTO LANE)

A visit by the first Bishop of the Orange Free State, Bishop Twells, resident in Bloemfontein in February 1862, led to the establishment of the first Anglican church in Potchefstroom. It was early in 1865 that Reverend W Richardson arrived to begin work on the first church north of the Vaal River. The foundation stone was laid by President Marthinus Wessel Pretorius on 25 March 1867. After the First War of Independence (1880–1881), a chancel was added in memory of Reverend Richardson and the men who fell in the siege.

After the first church was demolished, the present St Mary's was completed in 1891. It was designed by John George Crone and built by Augustus Falconer. The foundation stone was laid on 25 March 1890. In August, when the walls were almost complete, the chancel arch collapsed, leading to the resignation of Crone together with some members of the building committee. John Gaisford, an architect connected with the church for over 40 years, came to the rescue. An opening service was held on 14 June 1891 without a ceiling and without the interior walls being plastered. Both ceiling and walls were completed in 1897. With the arrival of Reverend A Devonshire in 1911 and his motivation, a war memorial plaque was erected in the church after the First World War. The memorial hall was formally opened by HRH Prince Arthur of Connaught, Governor General of the Union of South Africa.

SUPERINTENDENT'S RESIDENCE
(WITRAND CARE AND REHABILITATION CENTRE)

This house was erected after the Anglo-Boer War (1899–1902) as the official residence of the Officer Commanding the British Garrison at Potchefstroom, and formed part of the military cantonments there. It is an important link with Potchefstroom's military past and serves as an example of the type of accommodation erected for senior officers at that time.

TOWN HALL (POTGIETER STREET)

Built to a design of William Black and William Fagg of Cape Town, and constructed by George F Warren of Potchefstroom under the supervision of WH Coultas, the Clerk of Works, the Town

Hall is a double-storey structure with a façade divided into two by an imposing 26.52m clock tower. The large copper clock was custom built, and bears the lettering 'Potchefstroom anno 1909, B Eysbouts, Austin Nederland'. The building was opened on 10 March 1909, with General Smuts as the guest of honour.

VOORTREKKER FORT (ALLEGED) (FARM ELANDSFONTEIN)
According to tradition, this stone fort was built by the Voortrekkers under the leadership of Andries Hendrik Potgieter. It was presumably erected in 1842 to serve as a shelter for women and children in case the men had to leave for Port Natal to assist the Voortrekkers there against a British invasion.

WD PRETORIUS HOUSE AND OUTBUILDINGS (CHURCH STREET)
This building was erected in about 1853 by CJ Uys and is probably the oldest existing dwelling in Potchefstroom, with its outbuildings dating from 1863. WD Pretorius enlarged the eastern side and provided a new main entrance in 1888. The complex was restored to its original 1888 appearance in 1984 by Bruinette, Kruger, Stoffberg Incorporated.

RUSTENBURG

This town was founded on the farms Kafferskraal and Witpensfontein in 1850, and proclaimed in 1851. It attained municipal status in 1918.

BARN AND FOUR HOUSES (BOEKENHOUTFONTEIN)
From 1862–1903 the farm was the property of State President SJP Kruger. The house, dating from 1841, is the oldest in the province. The other houses date from 1863, from the 1870s (the Kruger Homestead), and from 1892 (built for Kruger's son Pieter).

DUTCH REFORMED CHURCH (PLEIN STREET)
Construction of this neogothic church building started in 1898, but due to the outbreak of the Anglo-Boer War (1899–1902), the finishing touches could only be done in 1903. During the war the building was used by the British as a hospital. In 1974 it was tastefully restored and the interior is particularly impressive.

KROONDAL LIBRARY BUILDING (KROONDAL, DISTRICT)
This plain little building, now housing a library, was completed early in 1898 as the first permanent school building at Kroondal. Together with the nearby old Lutheran Church it forms the historic core of Kroondal.

OLD ANGLICAN CHURCH (VAN STADEN STREET)
This church, originally built in 1871, was reconstructed on its present site in 1967 as a result of the efforts of John Pilkington-Richardson, and is one of the oldest Anglican churches in the North West Province.

OLD LUTHERAN CHURCH (KROONDAL, DISTRICT)
Since 1889, Kroondal has been the centre of the Hermannsberg Missionary Society's activities in South Africa, and construction on this quaint eclectic church started in 1895. It was the first church building at Kroondal, and was inaugurated on 24 June 1896. In 1919 a vestry was added, but since then the building has remained unchanged.

SCHOCH HOUSE (BOSCHDAL)
Built for the well-known William Robinson in neoclassical style before 1874, this is the oldest existing dwelling in the immediate vicinity of Rustenburg. It was acquired by August Schoch in 1874, who developed it into a valuable estate. After the Anglo-Boer War (1899–1902), Boschdal was used as a centre for the repatriation of Boer families.

SYRINGA TREE MONUMENT (CHURCH STREET)
A granite replica of the stump of the syringa tree marks the site where it was decided to form the Reformed Church (Gereformeerde Kerk) on 10 February 1859.

VRYBURG

This town was founded as the capital of the Republic of Stellaland in 1883, and its name is derived from the republicans who called themselves 'vryburgers' (free burghers). It attained municipal status in 1896.

OLD POLICE STATION (9 VRY STREET)
This stone-structured police station was built by Lewis & Becket in 1886 and was completed the following year. Used as a police station until 1890, when it was considered to be 'too far from the town', it is the oldest remaining building in Vryburg. The building was subsequently converted to a house by MC Genis, who bought it on 29 September 1890.

The old police station is a simple cottage design and still has the original floor plan, with the exception of an additional room at the rear, which was built at a later date.

ST STEPHEN'S ANGLICAN CHURCH
(MCKENZIE STREET)
St Stephen's Anglican church was erected after church officials had negotiated for an independent parish and separated from the Kimberley congregation. The tiled-roofed, stone building has a rectangular plan, while a semicircular baptistry and apse were added in 1919 and 1930, respectively.

During the Anglo-Boer War (1899–1902), the service register frequently recorded the attendance of soldiers and the burial register recorded the names of a number of British soldiers who died in Vryburg.

TIGERKLOOF INSTITUTE BUILDING COMPLEX
(FARM WATERLOO, DISTRICT)
This was once the main centre for higher education of the Tswana people of the Northern Cape, Bechuanaland (Botswana) and scholars from as far afield as Matabeleland. The Institute was founded in 1904 by the London Missionary Society, and WC Willoughby was the first principal. The Tierkloof Institute eventually comprised nine departments, a high school, a teachers' training centre, a Bible school (for training ministers and evangelists), a training school and industrial school (for woodwork, building, leatherwork, dressmaking and domestic science).

In 1956 the Institute was taken over by the then Department of Native Affairs. With the uprising of 1960, some of the buildings were burnt down and the institute was closed and a new training centre built in Mafikeng. The state advertised for the site to be demolished but it was taken over by the Reverend Keyter of the Dutch Reformed Church Vryburg East, who formed the youth association, Deo Gloria, which has restored the church building, dining room and some of the other buildings.

Imported from England, the first wood-and-iron building was erected on 26 March 1904. Other buildings constructed that year, or shortly thereafter, that still exist, include the stables, an asbestos hut, a wooden building (1904), a carpenters' workshop and machine room. The cornerstone of the school building was laid on 19 September 1905, and classrooms were built as follows: first (1906), second and third (1907), and fourth (1909). The school complex was completed in 1911. The dining room (1910) has a clock tower with a clock donated by Headman Khama, father of Sir Seretse. Living quarters were built in 1910, the principal's residence in 1908, and the principal's office in 1911. The Arthington Memorial Church was mainly the handiwork of scholars of Tierkloof.

The cornerstone was laid on 29 September 1925 by Reverend JE Jennings and the building was officially opened by Talbot Wilson, chairman of Arthington Trustees, in 1933. It is built of stone with a pitched corrugated-iron roof, stained glass windows, a concrete floor, a wooden ceiling and a stone altar.

WOLMARANSSTAD

This town was laid out in 1888 on the farms Rooderand and Vlakfontein, and was proclaimed in 1891. It was named after Jacobus MA Wolmarans, a member of the Executive Council.

RUINS OF REVEREND BROADBENT'S HOUSE (LEEUWFONTEIN)

Samuel Broadbent and Thomas Hodgson were missionaries of the Wesleyan Mission Society who settled under the Barolong Chief Captain Sefunêlô in Makwasse in 1823. This was the first mission station in the former Transvaal. In 1823 Broadbent built a house of mud, wood and grass, which was totally destroyed after his departure. In 1826 Thomas Hodgson and James Archibell built a stone house, the ruins of which are all that remain. When the Municipality of Wolmaransstad requested the Historical Monuments Commission in 1936 to fence off the ruins, they contended that the ruins were of the Broadbent house, and that the first white child born in the former Transvaal, Lewis Broadbent, was born there.

ZEERUST

This town was laid out on the farm Hazenjacht in 1867 and proclaimed in 1880. It was originally named Coetzee-Rust, but was later abbreviated to the present name of Zeerust. The town attained municipal status in 1936.

ST JOHN THE BAPTIST CHURCH

According to Canon Noel Roberts in his history of Marico, 'Lest we forget', this church was built in 1873. In 1892 the thatched roof was replaced with corrugated-iron and an altar made of English oak was added in 1915, with the panelwork around the altar completed after the Second World War. St John the Baptist church was the third Anglican Church to be built in the former Transvaal. The first was St Mary's in Potchefstroom and the second, St Alban in Pretoria (not to be confused with the present cathedral). The ground on which the church stands was donated in 1886 by Diederik Jacob Coetzee, the founder of Zeerust. The church bell has an interesting history; the Reformed church in Jacobsdal ordered two bells from Holland and donated one to St John the Baptist church.

EXPLANATORY NOTES

- The term 'Dutch Reformed Church' is often a generic English equivalent that could apply to any of the three branches of the Afrikaans 'reform' churches in South Africa, although in most instances it refers to the 'Nederduitse Gereformeerde Kerk'. Both terms are found in this book because both terms appear in the original declarations published in the *Government Gazette*. The English translation of the 'Gereformeerde Kerk in Suid-Afrika' is the 'Reformed Church in South Africa'. The same applies to 'Mother Church' and 'Moeder Kerk'.
- Ds: this is an abbreviation for 'Dominee', a minister in the Dutch Reformed Church.
- The 'Church of the Covenant' and 'Church of the Vow' refer to the same building. Different declarations have used both terms, possibly resulting from an official change to the name of the event, a vow taken by Voortrekker leaders, Andries Pretorius and Sarel Cilliers on the eve of the Battle of Blood River (16 December 1838).
- Note the difference in the sense of the 'Dutch Reformed Church' and the 'Dutch Reformed church'. The former applies to the entire denomination and the latter to a specific building of the denomination.
- A 'stoep' is a South Africanism for a verandah.
- There might sometimes appear to be discrepancies in the spelling of town or farm names e.g. 'Mooi Meisjes Fontein' and Mooimeisiefontein. This is often a result of the modernisation of an original Dutch name to its Afrikaans equivalent.
- An erf is a plot/stand.